# WITH ——— ARROW, SWORD, AND SPEAR

# WITH

# ARROW, SWORD, AND SPEAR

## ALFRED S. BRADFORD
### Illustrated by Pamela M. Bradford

FALL RIVER PRESS

© 2001 by Alfred S. Bradford

This 2007 edition published by Fall River Press,
by arrangement with Greenwood Publishing Group, Inc.

Fall River Press
122 Fifth Avenue
New York, NY 10011

ISBN: 978-0-7607-9257-5

Printed and bound in the United States of America

3  5  7  9  10  8  6  4  2

To My Daughter, Elizabeth

I hope that this book is the closest she ever comes to war.

# CONTENTS

Illustrations and Maps                                              ix
Preface                                                            xiii
Introduction                                                        xv

PART I. THE ANCIENT EAST                                            1
   1. Civilized War                                  3
   2. The Egyptians                                   9
   3. The Chariot People                             13
   4. The Egyptian Empire                            21
   5. Balance of Power                               29
   6. The Hebrews                                    33
   7. The Assyrians                                  41
   8. The Medes and Chaldaeans                       47
   9. The Persians                                   53

PART II. THE GREEKS                                                61
   10. The Greek Way of War                          63
   11. "Go Tell the Spartans"                        69
   12. The Peloponnesian (Archidamian) War           79
   13. The Peloponnesian (Decelean) War              87
   14. The Demise of Hoplite Warfare                 95
   15. Philip and the Macedonians                   101
   16. Alexander the Great                          109
   17. Into India and Beyond                        117

PART III. THE EAST                                                123
   18. India: Chandragupta                          125
   19. China: Spring and Autumn                     129
   20. China: The Warring States                    137

21. China: The Former Han                                          143
22. China: The Later Han                                            153
23. The Parthians                                                   159

PART IV. THE ROMAN REPUBLIC                                         165
24. The Development of the Roman System                             167
25. Hannibal                                                        177
26. The Conquest of the Mediterranean                               191
27. The Breakdown of the Roman System                               199
28. Julius Caesar                                                   209

PART V. THE ROMAN EMPIRE                                            221
29. The Creation of the Empire                                      223
30. The Army of Trajan                                              231
31. The Ascendancy of the Army                                      239
32. The Awful Third Century                                         245
33. Reform and Revolution                                           253
34. The Fall of Rome                                                263

Afterword                                                           273
Sources                                                             283
Index                                                               303

# ILLUSTRATIONS AND MAPS

## ILLUSTRATIONS

### By Pamela M. Bradford

(A. S. Bradford drew 1, 2, 4, 6, 20, 24, 26, 28b, 30, 31, 33, 39, 40, 41, 45, and 62.)

Cover Image: Assyrians Assault a Town
Frontispiece (A Scene from the Siphnian Treasury, Delphi)

| | |
|---|---|
| 1. Timeline for this Book | xiv |
| 2. "Homeric Melee," Attic Figural Krater, 760-750 B.C. | xvii |
| 3. The Palette of Narmer | xix |
| 4. The Stele of Rimush | xix |
| 5. Mycenaean soldiers | 1 |
| 6. Sumerian soldier from the "Standard of Ur" | 2 |
| 7. Sargon of Agade | 2 |
| 8. The Stele of Vultures | 8 |
| 9. Narmer the Unifier | 12 |
| 10. The Egyptian King in a Chariot | 20 |
| 11. Thutmose III | 27 |
| 12. Seqenenre | 28 |
| 13. The Sea-Peoples | 28 |
| 14. The Battle of Qadesh (A Shardana Mercenary Kills a Hittite) | 32 |
| 15. Ashurnasirpal | 40 |
| 16. Assyrians in Chariot | 40 |
| 17. Assyrian Cavalry Pursuing Camel Riders | 45 |
| 18. Assyrian Cavalryman | 52 |
| 19. The Hoplite | 61 |

20. The Panoply (diagram of the equipment)                            62
21. The Phalanx (from the Chigi vase)                                 62
22. The Grieving Hoplite (from a grave stele)                         78
23. The Trireme: a Reconstruction and a Relief                        85
24. Trireme Tactics (diagram)                                         86
25. The Spartan Soldier                                               94
26. Diagram of the Battle of Leuctra                                  99
27. A Macedonian Soldier with a Sarissa                               100
28a. Alexander the Great   b. Alexander in Action                     108
29. Persian against Greek (carved gem and seal)                       115
30. Diagrams of Alexander's Major Battles                             116
31. Depictions of Combat                                              123
32. The First Emperor                                                 124
33. Siege Warfare (Bronzes from the Warring States Period)            136
34. Chinese Soldier and Horse                                         142
35. A Chinese Chariot                                                 152
36. A Parthian Horse Archer                                           163
37. An Italian Hoplite: a. Palestrina ivory plaque, 300-250;          165
    b. Bronze, Fifth Century
38. One of Pyrrhus's Elephants (Campanian Painted Dish)               175
39. Diagram of the Battle of Zama                                     189
40. The Development of the Roman Legion                               190
41. Diagram of the Battle of Cynoscephalae                            197
42. Second Century Soldier (Ahenobarbus Relief)                       198
43. Attacking Legionnaire (Mainz Relief, I A.D.)                      198
44. Julius Caesar                                                     220
45. The Siege                                                         221

SCENES FROM THE COLUMN OF TRAJAN (46-57)

46. Crossing the Danube                                               232
47. Building a Camp                                                   233
48. Building a Road                                                   233
49. Battle of the Iron Gates                                          234
50. Driving the Dacians                                               234
51. Repelling an Attack                                               235
52. Cavalry Battle                                                    235
53. A "Tortoise"                                                      236
54. A Skirmish                                                        236
55. Assault on Sarmizegethusa                                         237
56. The Last Battle                                                   237
57. Portrait of Trajan and a Detail from the Column                   238

58. Two Soldiers in Scale Armor (III A.D., Dura-Europas)              244
59. A Roman Soldier (from a tombstone, c. 214 A.D.)                   262
60. Constantine's Troops (312 A.D.)                                   262

61. Hadrian's Wall                                                          282
62. Graffiti from the Notebook of Charles Edson                             299

**MAPS** (All maps were prepared by A. S. Bradford)

1. Areas and Empires Discussed in this Book                               xviii
2. The Ancient Near East and Sumer and Akkad                                  2
3. The Nile Valley                                                           12
4. Expansion of the Chariot People                                           20
5. Egyptian Empire with an Inset of the Iron Age Invasions                   27
6. Kingdom of David                                                          39
7. The Assyrian Empire                                                       40
8. The Fall of Assyria                                                       46
9. The Persian Empire                                                        52
10. Sequence Maps of the Greek World                                         60
11. Overview of the Persian Wars                                             68
12. Overview of the Peloponnesian War                                        78
13. Macedonia and Philip                                                    100
14. The Empire of Alexander the Great                                       108
15. Sequence Maps of Asia                                                   122
16. The Warring States                                                      124
17. Han China and the Silk Road                                             158
18. Maps Illustrating the Expansion of the Roman Republic                   164
19. The First Punic War                                                     166
20. The Second Punic War and Hannibal's Victories                           176
21. Caesar's Gaul                                                           208
22. Caesar's Civil War Campaigns (Detail Map of Ilerda)                     220
23. Sequence Maps of the Roman Empire                                       222
24. Fall of the Roman Empire                                                272

# PREFACE

This survey of ancient warfare gives an account of warfare from the first civilizations (roughly 3000 BC) to the fall of the Roman Empire in the West and the later Han in China. This account follows most closely those ancient sources which show personal knowledge of warfare, emphasizes significant changes in technology, tactics, and organization, and analyzes the campaigns of the foremost military leaders of the ancient world.

Throughout this work I have attempted to be consistent with the spelling of names, but, in addition to the difficulties of transcribing foreign names and of shifting conventions, the different civilizations depicted here used different names for the same places and peoples. I have tried to employ one name only for one place or one people. For example, for the Chinese Hsiung-nu, who appear to be the Roman Huns, I write "Huns (Hsiung-nu)" or simply "Huns."

The notes are arranged by "Part" and "Chapter" at the end of the book in the section "Sources." The notes are divided into "General Works," which provide a background to the whole chapter or part, and "Notes to the Chapter." The chapter notes are organized by page number.

## 1. Timeline for this Book

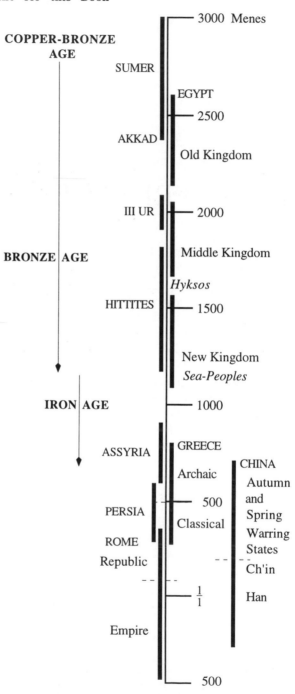

**COPPER-BRONZE AGE**

SUMER

EGYPT

AKKAD

**BRONZE AGE**

III UR

HITTITES

**IRON AGE**

ASSYRIA

PERSIA

ROME
Republic

Empire

3000 Menes

2500

Old Kingdom

2000

Middle Kingdom

*Hyksos*

1500

New Kingdom
*Sea-Peoples*

1000

GREECE
Archaic

500

Classical

$\frac{1}{1}$

500

CHINA
Autumn
and
Spring
Warring
States

Ch'in

Han

# INTRODUCTION

The first literary work about war in the Western world is Homer's *Iliad*. The *Iliad* is a powerful story, told with vivid language, about heroism and fear, duty and honor, sorrow and loss; it has appealed to generation after generation, from the audience of its own day down to the present day; it is the only literary work surviving from the ancient world that takes us inside the hearts of the combatants as they struggle in hand-to-hand combat.

The *Iliad* (composed about 800 B.C.) relates an incident from the tenth year of the Trojan War (which, if it occurred at all, occurred about 1200 B.C.). The war was caused by the kidnapping of the Greek queen, Helen, by Paris, a Trojan prince. Helen's husband, Menelaus, and his brother, Agamemnon, collected an enormous force to seek revenge. No Greek army (so Homer thought) could take a fortified city by siege; rather it would have to deny the Trojans free use of their own land, harry them continually until they abandoned Troy and conceded their land to the Greeks, or, short of that, negotiated some end to the war: to give up Helen and all her possessions, to pay an indemnity (perhaps half the wealth of the city), or to agree to a duel between the aggrieved parties, Menelaus, the injured husband, and Paris, the offending kidnapper. Homer's war did end when the heroes used a subterfuge—the Trojan horse—to get within the walls of Troy.

The Greeks of Homer's time had just emerged from the tribal stage, they had the slenderest of resources at their command, they did not build, nor need to build, massive fortifications, they did not obey any central authority and they did not have an extensive bureaucracy, but rather they lived in societies ruled by the heads of aristocratic families alternately cooperating and competing. We characterize these societies, their armed forces, and the wars they fight, as "primitive" (defined by studies of primitive societies and primitive warfare of our own time).

Primitive "armies"—as in the *Iliad*—are organized by familial relationships and do not fight in formation. Primitive wars—as in the *Iliad*—are caused by wife stealing or cattle rustling; they are circumscribed by ritual, though the ritual may vary—a limit to the fighting in space and time (one day on an appointed field perhaps), verbal intimidation, boasting and war cries, and the trading of lineages; the confrontation proceeds with increments of violence, threats, the brandishing of arms, the throwing of stones and spears, or the shooting of arrows; if this phase of the confrontation (when quick feet are a warrior's best friend) does not satisfy honor, then the next phase proceeds to actual duels of individual champions, man to man. If a champion is wounded or killed, the duel may become a melee, as both sides contend for control of the fallen. In general, the warriors have modest war aims—to force the other side to run away—and they rarely pursue, or attempt to annihilate, a fleeing enemy. Thus in the *Iliad*, as the warriors work themselves up with boasts and war cries to an exchange of missiles and then to a melee, so the goddess of battle-lust, Eris, grows on the field until her head touches the sky.

Warfare in the *Iliad* is characterized by ritual, by individual prowess, and by the duel. Hector, the Trojan prince, challenges the Greeks to appoint a champion to meet him in single combat (but when he sees his opponent, the gigantic and muscular Ajax, he would rather withdraw his challenge—discretion is not shameful when it is Zeus who "makes a mighty man a coward"). Hector, however, tells Ajax that he is not intimidated by his boasts. "Ajax, don't try to frighten me as though I were a little boy or a woman who knows nothing of war. I know how to fight and kill an armed man."

Ajax wounds Hector and would have finished him off, if night had not ended the combat; with the night the two heroes exchange gifts and return to their own lines.

Sometimes when two champions exchange words, they don't fight at all: Glaucus and Diomedes met and they were eager to fight each other, but when Glaucus named his father and his grandfather, Diomedes fixed his spear in the fruitful earth and he said, "You and I have a family connection. My grandfather feasted your grandfather for twenty days and they swore eternal friendship. Let us avoid the spears of each other even in the melee."

In the most famous duel of the *Iliad* Menelaus and Paris fight to assign blame, bring retribution, and end the war.

"The two heroes took their stance opposite each other on the appointed ground and they shook their spears at each other, each man in the grip of rage. And then Paris threw his spear and he struck Menelaus right on his evenly–balanced shield, but the spear did not penetrate the bronze; the point twisted on the powerful shield. And now Menelaus, in his turn, hefted his bronze spear and prayed to Father Zeus, 'Zeus up above, grant to me to be avenged on the one who wronged me earlier, noble Paris, and let him be tamed under my hands so that generations of men still to come will shudder at the thought of breaking the bonds of hospitality.'

"He threw the spear that casts a long shadow and he struck the son of Priam on his well–balanced shield and the powerful spear pierced the shield and broke through the intricately decorated breast plate, and the spear ripped through the tunic on his side but he dodged and avoided black destruction. Then Menelaus drew his silver studded sword, raised it, and struck Paris on the point of his helmet, but the sword shattered and fell from his hand, broken into three or four pieces. Menelaus leaped on him and seized the horse–hair crest of the helmet and he knocked him down and dragged him towards the well–greaved Achaeans—and the embroidered strap under Paris' delicate throat was strangling him—and he was dragging him and about to win great glory, but the daughter of Zeus, Aphrodite, had been keeping close watch, and she broke the strap, and Menelaus held an empty helmet in his mighty hand."

A duel may lead to a melee. The general melee (the least common type of fighting) pits side against side in hand-to-hand combat, perhaps over the body of a slain hero, and the melee continues until one side breaks and runs. Then the best warriors are the fastest runners—who can catch and kill or cripple the fleeing enemy—it is no accident that the greatest warrior of the *Iliad* is Achilles the *swift–footed.*

## 2. Homeric Melee

In one melee Diomedes, on foot, is attacked by two men in a chariot. Diomedes throws his spear and kills one of the men, the other jumps from the chariot and runs away; the Trojans flee. Greek heroes run them down and kill them, but then a Trojan archer hits Diomedes in the shoulder and Diomedes retreats to his chariot where his driver pulls out the arrow. The goddess Athena breathes new life into Diomedes and he runs amok in a melee of foot and chariot. The Trojans almost break but the war god Ares rallies them and Diomedes is forced to retreat—"We cannot fight the gods!"—until Athena helps him wound Ares and drive him from the field.

The life of the aristocrat as portrayed by Homer was a round of feasting, athletic competition, hunting, and fighting. (Diomedes' object was to win glory, but in the pursuit of glory, he, and the other Greek aristocrats, did very well in the collection of booty.) The aristocrat found justification for his position in society in his descent from the gods, from his duty to the society, and from his general physical superiority. Sarpedon, the son of Zeus, says to his friend Glaucus,

"My friend, we are honored as though we were gods. Why? Is it not because we are the first to risk our lives in battle against the enemy? Do not our soldiers in their armor say, 'Not without glory are the kings who hold our land, for they have the courage kings should have and they fight in the front ranks of the battle line.' But if we could run from this battle and live forever without sorrow or death, I would not fight in the front rank nor would I lead you into the man-destroying battle. As it is, ten thousand kinds of death are waiting to ambush us mortal men, we cannot escape, so let us go, and give glory to someone else, or win it for ourselves."

Primitive though Homer's war might have been in organization, tactics, and equipment, ninety generations of soldiers have recognized their own thoughts and feelings in the thoughts and feelings of the heroes of the *Iliad*.

## Map 1: Areas and Empires Discussed in this Book

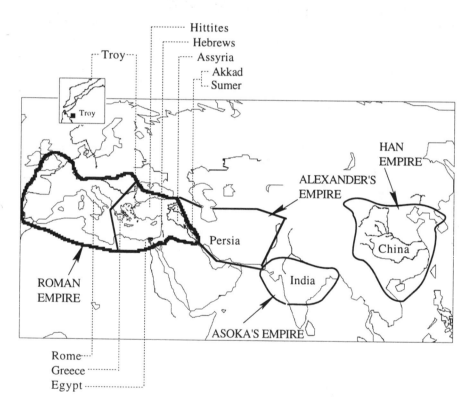

## 3. The Palette of Narmer

This palette depicts the king in the process of uniting Upper and Lower Egypt. The king wields the favorite weapon of the kings, the war mace. Seizing the enemy by the hair of his head appears in depictions of war from Greece to China.

## 4. The Stele of Rimush

This Stele depicts the three principal weapons of antiquity. Notice how the spear is held, not where we would expect the balance to be, but at the end.

# Part One
# The Ancient East

The great powers of the ancient Near East have certain characteristics in common: they all had organized armies which fought in formation in distinct units, they all had organized supply systems, both to maintain the army while it was not on campaign and to support the army in the field, they all distinguished themselves by the gods they worshipped, so that Egyptians could be thought of as the people who worshipped pharoah, the Assyrians as the people who worshipped Ashur, and so on; they all had a chain of command in peace and war. On the other hand, none of them assimilated the defeated peoples, so that each power's empire remained subservient only so long as the imperial power maintained its power. The most successful ancient power in the near east (in terms of centuries of stability) was the Old Kingdom of Egypt. It was stable and secure because the people were united behind the god-king, because the general condition of Egypt was prosperity, and because the borders were secured by Egyptian power and geography.

## 5. Mycenaean Soldiers

## Map 2: The Ancient Near East and Sumer and Akkad

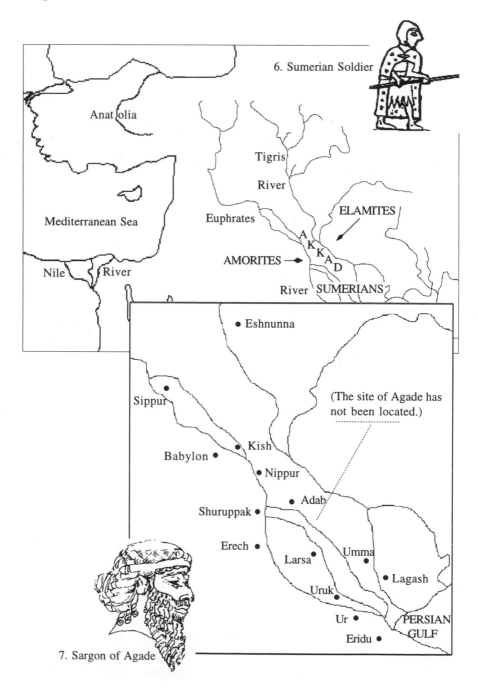

6. Sumerian Soldier

Anatolia

Tigris
River

Euphrates

ELAMITES

A K K A D

AMORITES →

Mediterranean Sea

Nile River

River  SUMERIANS

• Eshnunna

Sippur •

(The site of Agade has not been located.)

Babylon •   • Kish

• Nippur

• Adab

Shuruppak •

Erech •          Umma
         Larsa •

         Uruk •        • Lagash

              Ur •    PERSIAN
         Eridu •       GULF

7. Sargon of Agade

# 1

# Civilized War

## The Conquering Invaders Triumph and Then Turn Against Each Other

By the time the *Iliad* was written, the civilizations of the Near East had been waging organized warfare for more than two thousand years. The first literate civilizations and the first organized armies appear almost simultaneously in the river valleys of the Tigris and Euphrates and in the valley of the Nile. The civilized people of the Tigris and Euphrates, the Sumerians, had invaded southern Mesopotamia from the Persian Gulf sometime around 3100 B.C. and so completely subjugated the inhabitants, the Subarians, that the word, *Subarian*, came to mean "slave" in the Sumerian language. The conquerors had a common language and culture, they had reason to cooperate—to maintain the irrigation system and so ensure their own livelihood and to defend themselves from external enemies—but, nonetheless, they divided themselves into separate, independent walled cities that controlled territories of some 1,800 square miles.

Their religion supported their divisiveness. Men, their priests told them, were of a troublesome nature, because they had been created from the mingled blood of gods and monsters slain in a titanic battle; these troublesome men had been parcelled out into newly created cities, each city had been assigned to a god, and in the cities men had built their god a home, a temple where they were to fulfil their purpose by serving their god; when men proved too unruly to serve the gods well, the gods brought "kingship down from heaven." Thus, the Sumerians believed, they themselves and their city owed total loyalty to their own god, all property belonged to their god, their god's power depended upon how much territory the city controlled, their human ruler (the *ensi*—chosen by the army from a hereditary and divinely-approved list) was the representative of the god and his job was to ensure that the god was satisfied.

The most famous ensi, Gilgamesh, was transformed with the passage of time from the flesh and blood ensi of Uruk to a hero of myth and legend; in the *Epic of Gilgamesh* he is the son of a goddess and a mortal, he himself is mortal, but he has the ambition of a god. When he went out to fight against the cities of

Kish and Ur, he armed himself with a sword, a bow and arrow, and his 180 pound cast axe, "hero's strength." The ambitions of Gilgamesh and his eagerness to satisfy his god were not good news for the people of Uruk; they prayed to the gods to send Gilgamesh a worthy rival who would keep him occupied so they could live their lives in peace.

Gilgamesh and the other ensi's could field armies of from 5,000–10,000 men (mostly drawn from the farm—as a rule of thumb in ancient societies five people had to work the land to feed six). The men fought in a phalanx, shoulder to shoulder, protecting the line with their shields and themselves with helmet and a metal-studded cape. They used copper weapons, spear and axe. (The phalanx did not use the bow and arrow.) Phalanx tried to break phalanx by shoving, jabbing with the spear, and hacking with the axe. The ensi's also employed carts pulled by four onagers (wild donkeys). Each cart had a shield in front, a driver, and a warrior armed with spears. The carts may have shaken the opposing phalanx by their noise and their appearance, or by the threat of outflanking the enemy, or they may have been used to ride down those who fled.

At first the Sumerian armies dominated Mesopotamia. Their neighbors' ill-disciplined, stone-armed, slow-moving forces had no chance against the Sumerian phalanx, but all too soon those neighbors began to adopt copper weapons and semi-organized tactics. Their neighbors to the west, the Amorites, nomads of the desert, infiltrated Mesopotamia (even before our written records begin); some of them adopted the agricultural life of the Sumerians and Sumerian civilization and military practices. These Amorites were known as the Akkadians. The neighbors to the east, who dwelled in the mountains, were the Gutians and the Elamites. The Gutians and, to a lesser extent, the Elamites considered Sumer and Akkad a treasurehouse to be raided. Consequently, they were a threat to all Sumerians (and Akkadians) and the Sumerians needed to—but seldom did—cooperate against them. The Sumerians were so convinced of their superiority over their neighbors that the leaders of each city ignored their dangerous neighbors and strove for domination over the other leaders. Some of them did subdue other cities—and then they took to themselves the name *lugal* ("big man")—but none of them was powerful enough to unite the whole of Sumer, and their short-sighted ambitions undermined the strength of Sumer.

The history of two cities, Lagash and Umma, illustrates the Sumerian problem. Lagash and Umma had been founded to protect Sumer from Elam, but they fell into a dispute about a district which lay between them. Their overlord, the king of Kish, awarded the district to Lagash and delineated the boundary by digging a ditch along the boundary and by placing a boundary stone (with his decision inscribed upon it) next to the ditch, but the two cities, which should have used their resources against Elam, instead wasted them in a century-long (2550-2450) struggle for the possession of the district.

First, the ensi of Umma pretended to accept the decision of his overlord, but when he observed that the ensi of Lagash had turned his attention to the sea and foreign expeditions, the ensi of Umma overturned the boundary stone and occupied the district. He fought off the first attempt by the ensi of Lagash to recover the land, he defeated the ensi's son—the son was killed in the fighting—but the successive ensi's of Umma were defeated by the grandson (by name Eannatum), ensi of Lagash. Eannatum knew that he could not expect Umma to accept this defeat unless he offered a compromise: he established Lagash's possession of the district by fixing the boundary . . . again . . . with a ditch, a boundary stone, and a temple, but he allowed the citizens of Umma to cultivate the district upon payment of rent.

Eannatum was a "great man," and like so many "great men" in history he continued from one conquest to another; he defeated a coalition of Elam, Umma, and the southern cities, but while he was campaigning against them, Kish and a coalition of northern cities invaded the territory of Lagash. He returned, routed them, and took the title "king of Kish," but his two great victories did not end the war—he had to defeat Elam again and then Kish again and then again Elam and Kish. In the end Eannatum, himself, was defeated and killed.

When his brother became the ensi of Lagash, the ensi of Umma repudiated the agreement on the disputed district, seized it, drained the boundary ditch, overthrew the stone marker, and razed the temple. He allied himself with the northern "foreigners" and he fought a great battle against Lagash in the disputed district. The ensi of Umma was killed in the fighting and Umma was defeated. The ensi of Lagash erected a monument (the "stele of vultures") to celebrate the victory, but a kinsman of the slain ensi collected an army, made himself the ensi of Umma, seized the district, and invaded the territory of Lagash.

By now the two sides were so exhausted that they agreed to accept arbitration: Lagash received the land and was made responsible for the upkeep; Umma was excused from paying all the accrued back rent. Neither Umma nor Lagash nor the neighboring cities that had been drawn into the war had gained anything from the fighting, and they had introduced the neighboring state, Elam, into their conflict. In the end, the Akkadians, a Semitic–speaking people living in Mesopotamia on equal terms with the Sumerians, united behind a champion, Sargon "the Great." Sargon spoke Akkadian (a Semitic language), and he was considered an outsider by the Sumerians (though culturally he was almost indistinguishable from them). Sargon's account of himself draws on the mystery and magic found in Sumerian literature—

I never knew my father. My mother bore me in secret on the banks of the Euphrates. She placed me in a wicker basket and sealed the cover with tar. She threw the basket into the river, but I did not sink and the river brought me to Akki, a water carrier. Akki adopted me and raised me. He made me his gardener and the goddess Ishtar gave me her favor.

As Sargon was rising from gardener to royal cupbearer, the Sumerian ruler Lugalzaggisi (the ensi of Umma) attacked and sacked the city of Lagash; he conquered Uruk and he claimed sovereignty over the "four quarters"—Sumer itself and the lands on the borders of Sumer. He defeated Sargon's king and killed him, but Sargon escaped and founded a new city, Agade, where he attracted a population of Amorites from the desert and Akkadians from within Mesopotamia. Agade became a powerful city that split Mesopotamia in two, Sumer and the Semitic-speaking Akkad, but Lugalzaggisi did not realize that Sargon was dangerous . . . until too late.

Sargon set out to defeat Lugalzaggisi, get revenge for the death of his king, and conquer Sumer; his strategy is clear, though the details of his campaigns are lost: he surprised his enemies, maneuvered against them, massed his troops at one point while his enemies were divided, took the offensive when his enemy was unprepared, and always had a clear, obtainable objective. Sargon attacked Uruk, while Lugalzaggesi was campaigning elsewhere, fought a battle against fifty ensis allied to Lugalzaggisi, defeated them, and broke through the city wall before Lugalzaggisi could return. When Lugalzaggisi rushed to the defense of his city, Sargon defeated him, captured him, put him in stocks, and exhibited him around Sumer. Next Sargon took Nippur, the religious center of Sumer, and then he attacked and carried the principal cities, Ur, Lagash, and Umma. He proclaimed, "I washed my spears in the southern sea."

Sargon's whole reign was spent in defending his empire from the mountain people who raided Mesopotamia and from rebellions: he had to mollify people who spoke different languages and lived in different cultures. At first, he tried not to offend the Sumerians—when he needed land, he purchased it—but in the end, in the face of continued rebellion, he took stronger action: he levelled city walls and eliminated centers of resistance, he garrisoned Sumer with Akkadian governors and Akkadian troops, and when still he had not pacified Sumer, he confiscated tracts of land, expelled the Sumerians, and resettled the land with Akkadians. Sargon had tried to treat the Sumerians fairly, but his concept of fairness was radically different from theirs—he believed that men appointed their rulers and men owned the land; Sumerians believed that the gods appointed rulers and the gods owned the land and, therefore, as they saw it, Sargon not only had no right to dismiss Sumerian rulers or to dispose of their land, but he was committing sacrilege when he did it.

Sargon discovered another limit to his conquests: although he led his armies to the shores of the Mediterranean Sea, when he tried to march them north into Anatolia, they mutinied and he was forced to turn back. Sargon, like every ruler, depended upon the will of his army, and he accepted the limits of what it would allow him to do in order to preserve its loyalty. Because of the army's loyalty Sargon was able to pass his empire on peacefully to his son Rimush. Rimush, however, had to suppress a Sumerian revolt and nine years after his accession he was assassinated. When his brother, the second son of Sargon, succeeded him, he, too, had to suppress a Sumerian revolt, and he, too, was assassinated. He was succeeded by his son, Naram-Sin.

Naram-Sin had to suppress a revolt by the Sumerians, the revolt spread to the whole empire, and the perilous situation encouraged the Gutians to invade Mesopotamia. Naram-Sin repulsed the Gutians, defeated the rebels, took the title "king of the four-quarters" (that is, king of the whole world), and announced to his subjects that he was a god. If the Mesopotamians, and particularly the Sumerians, had accepted his claim (a not impossible claim given that they believed that gods can grow old and die), then (in logic) they would have been compelled to accept his right to confiscate land and depose rulers. He failed, however, to convince them and never reconciled the Sumerians to Akkadian rule.

Towards the end of Naram-Sin's thirty-seven-year reign he again had to stop a Gutian invasion, but this time he was unable to expel them from his empire. He died, and his son inherited the continuing war against the Gutians and, to compound his troubles, a new Sumerian revolt. The Sumerians regained their freedom, the empire crumbled, and the Akkadian was driven back to the confines of his home city, Agade. The Sumerians rejoiced in their freedom, but not for long, because they quarreled with each other, they overlooked the threat of the Gutians, and the Gutians invaded, conquered Sumeria, and held it for a hundred years. The empire of Sargon and his heirs was gone, but it left a legacy—all subsequent rulers in Mesopotamia dreamed of re-creating Sargon's empire.

In the midst of the twenty-second century a Sumerian hero, the king of Uruk, drove the Gutians out of Mesopotamia and convinced the Sumerians—with the help of his victory—to put aside their differences and unite behind him. When he died in an accidental drowning, his successor, Ur-nammu, took control of Sumer in one campaign, subjugated Akkad, took the title "king of Sumer and Akkad" and characterized himself as "the son of a god." With the powers this divine status gave him (the right to control the land and appoint the ensi's), Ur-nammu dedicated himself to the restoration of a ravaged and depressed land: he encouraged the reconstruction of temples, city walls, roads, harbors, and, most important of all, the irrigation system. Sumer became prosperous once more.

Ur-Nammu established a century-long dynasty (the Third Dynasty of Ur) that passed on through his son to his grandson and his great-grandson. The son led a series of campaigns in the mountains and as far away as Assyria; for the Assyrian campaign he had four hundred miles of roads and relay stations built from Ur so he could march to his area of operations in twenty days. The grandson continued the campaigns against the mountain tribes, but the great-grandson was thrown on the defensive, he faced Elamite raids to the east, and he tried to stem the invasions of the Amorites from the desert in the west by building walls along the western border.

The last in the line of Sumerian kings, the successor of the great-grandson, had to contend with increasing instability, invasions from all sides, and the breakdown of cooperation within Sumeria. Roads were cut, trade disrupted, famine spread and with it inflation, and the cities began to look out for themselves. One of the king's governors maintained his own troops and ships and finally declared his independence. A coalition of Subarians (in the north), Gutians, and Elamites ravaged Sumeria, destroyed Ur, and led the last king off as a prisoner (about 1950 B.C.).

The Sumerians dominated Mesopotamia because of superior technology and superior organization, but they fell to fighting among themselves, and they could not prevent their neighbors from adopting Sumerian technology and military organization. Mesopotamians suffered from a lack of geographical, social, political, and religious unity.

The next chapter describes a culture united behind a single ruler.

## 8. The Stele of Vultures

# 2

# The Egyptians

## *Geography and Religion Unite and Protect a People*

In contrast to the Sumerians, the Egyptians occupied their homeland, the valley of the Nile, peacefully by infiltration; once in the valley of the Nile they coalesced first into separate kingdoms and then they were united in one kingdom under a ruler they considered god-on-earth. The world, they believed, had been made and organized just for themselves. They not only thought that the other inhabitants of the world were scarcely human—a thought not by any means confined to Egyptians—but that the rest of the world itself was chaotic and perverse. Their river, the Nile, was perfectly ordered—its current carried boats downstream, the wind blew them back upstream—and the Nile's regular flooding renewed the fields and made farming so easy that in the Delta men had "only to throw out seeds to reap a crop." The sea to the north and the deserts west and east isolated the Egyptians from the rest of mankind, except for merchants, some infiltrators, and the occasional raid. Another kingdom, Nubia, did lie to the south, but the stretch of Nile that separated the two kingdoms was difficult to traverse and, in the end, the Egyptians proved to be much more dangerous to the Nubians than the Nubians were to the Egyptians. In short, the Nile ensured its people peace and prosperity . . . so long as they remained united.

The first settlement of the Nile Valley, the events that led to the formation of kingship, to the consolidation of the two kingdoms of Upper (Southern) and Lower (Northern) Egypt, to the growth of the powers of the kings of Upper Egypt and their determination to unite Egypt, all these events occurred before any records were made. The first extant records show "Scorpion," the king of Upper Egypt, digging an irrigation canal and promoting agriculture, defending his realm from foreign incursion and expanding his rule into the Delta; in the representation he is not only the central figure, or the most important figure, he is the *only* important figure. Scorpion's successor on the throne of Upper Egypt, King Narmer, completed the unification of the Upper and Lower kingdoms, consolidated the symbols of the rulers of both kingdoms, and adopted the title, which all later kings used, "king of Upper and Lower Egypt." The *palette of*

*Narmer* portrays events from this unification, a super-human figure, armed with a war mace, defeating his enemies.

Narmer pushed his campaign into the Northwest Delta and perhaps into Libya. In scenes of siege warfare his companion gods appear in their earthly forms—a scorpion, falcon, and lion—and they hack through the enemy's walls. In Egypt, as in Mesopotamia, the divine and the mundane were intertwined, but in Egypt the king not only had the gods' active help in carrying out their will, but he was, himself, a god—the "good god." When the king took the field, so did the god. The very definition of an Egyptian—as opposed to the other inhabitants of the world—was a person who believed that his king was the "good god" who interceded for him with the pantheon of the "great gods" and to whom he owed allegiance and service. Egyptians believed, as did the Sumerians, that their god owned the land, but the Egyptian god was manifest and needed no ensi to interpret his will.

Narmer's successors continued to consolidate the union of Upper and Lower Egypt, they conducted campaigns in the south against Nubia, and they campaigned in the Sinai and in the northwest against the Libyans. Their objectives were twofold, to ensure the security of Egyptian borders and to control the sources of copper and turquoise. They left no written accounts of these wars of early Egypt, but in their monuments they portrayed themselves as they wanted their subjects to see them—the king smiting a kneeling Asiatic, the king with his foot upon a Nubian, the king proclaiming "40,000 of the Northerners" slain. He did have an extensive hierarchy of officials—civil and sacred—and he ruled Egypt rather as an emperor, with the Nile valley and the Delta divided into sacred precincts and civil districts, each with its own governor who was responsible to the royal staff and ultimately to the king.

The kings of the Old Kingdom (2686–2181 B.C.) are best known for their pyramids. They had no regular army or navy, no professional officers, and when they needed soldiers or sailors, they drafted them (and commandeered ships). They built fortifications at Elephantine (the boundary between Egypt and Nubia at the first cataract), they led or sent expeditions into Nubia to control the burgeoning trade, they expanded trade up the eastern coast of the Mediterranean and to Crete, and twice they transported troops by ship to invade Palestine. Under the constant threat of Egyptian raids (the kings' objective was not to conquer Palestine but to dominate it), the scattered villages of Palestine became towns fortified with stone walls. On the kings' monuments Egyptians with bows and daggers fight hand to hand with bearded foreigners, they take a Canaanite town, and they use Nubian mercenaries. Always the kings are portrayed as the principal warriors, their preferred weapon is the mace, and their enemies fall prostrate on the ground before them.

The last great king of the Old Kingdom (c. 2350) was Pepy II, who became king at the age of six and died at the age of one hundred. He administered his kingdom through his right hand man, the vizier, who in turn administered it through the forty-two nomarchs (the leaders of the districts—nomes—of Egypt).

When Pepy II died, the nomarchs (who had become wealthy and powerful men) fought for their own independence and the subjugation of their neighboring nomarchs. The system by which Egypt had been ruled for 650 years broke down and as Egyptian influence waned in Palestine, Palestine was overrun by the Amorites (who also invaded Mesopotamia), cities were abandoned, the countryside ravaged, and "Asiatics" infiltrated from Palestine into the eastern Delta.

In Egypt the eventual victor (after about fifty years) among the nomarchs, the ruler of Thebes, founded the Middle Kingdom (c. 2050–1786). The Theban kings solved one of the two biggest problems of government—how to ensure an orderly succession of power—by appointing and promoting their successors while they themselves were still alive and vigorous. The kings kept a standing army and called upon the nomarchs to bring other troops if required (levying about one in 100 men for the army). They divided their forces between a general of Upper and a general of Lower Egypt. The kings of the Middle Kingdom pursued an aggressive strategy in Palestine and Syria intended to deter attack on Egypt, but their strategy provoked a counterattack, the Delta fell to the invaders, and the unified kingdom of Egypt was torn apart.

The Sumerians and the Egyptians shared common problems—defense against invasion and the maintenance of a vast system of irrigation; these problems required a united society. The Egyptians maintained their unity by subservience to a god-king, one symbol of one land and one people. The Sumerians tried the same solution during the Third Dynasty of Ur, but under pressure from outside their tendency to disunity reappeared. The Egyptians made their system work because they were isolated and they shared the same belief—that they were ruled by a god on earth. The Sumerian military advantage over the Egyptians—the phalanx, the cart, body armor, shields, unit discipline—is less significant than the disadvantage of their geography and their culture of division.

Societies that are not homogeneous or geographically isolated must meet a military challenge generation after generation, must maintain stability in government and yet be able to adapt to changing circumstances, must quash dissent within the society, but must maintain the loyalty of all strata of society. History shows us many Sumerias and few Egypts.

**Map 3: The Nile Valley**

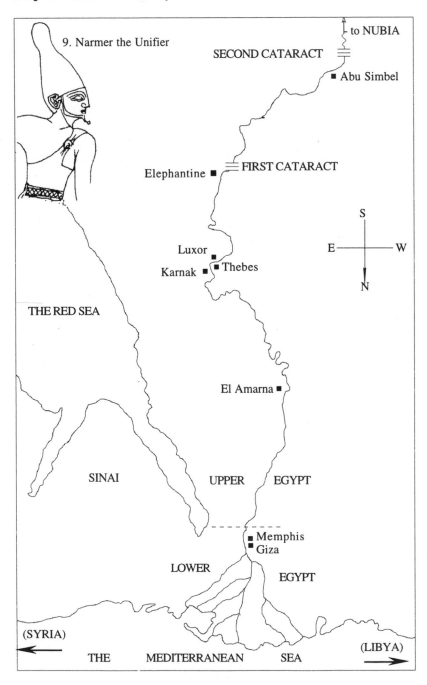

9. Narmer the Unifier

SECOND CATARACT

to NUBIA

■ Abu Simbel

Elephantine ■ ≡ FIRST CATARACT

S

E ———— W

N

Luxor
■
Karnak ■ ■ Thebes

THE RED SEA

El Amarna ■

SINAI

UPPER    EGYPT

■ Memphis
■ Giza

LOWER

EGYPT

(SYRIA)

(LIBYA)

THE    MEDITERRANEAN    SEA

# 3

# The Chariot People

## *Technology Transforms Warfare and the World*

At the beginning of the second millennium the Near East was divided between a number of minor powers—"No king is powerful all by himself, a dozen obey the man of Larsa, another dozen the king of Eshnunna, the same the king of Qatna, twenty obey the king of Yamkhad, and ten or fifteen kings obey Hammurabi, the Babylonian." Into this world of minor powers broke one of the most massive invasions of all time, an invasion of a number of tribes who had in common their mastery of a new technology, the chariot, and the languages they spoke, all descended from one mother tongue, which we call Indo-European. These Indo-European tribes invaded Mesopotamia, Greece, Europe, Anatolia, the Iranian plateau, India, and the borderlands of China.

### THE CHARIOT

The Indo-European tribes had trained teams of horses, developed a lightweight chariot, and combined the chariot with their expertise in the use of the composite bow to produce a highly mobile platform from which they could deliver accurate, rapid fire. Their massed chariots overwhelmed native people from western Europe to the borders of China. One tribe (from the group of Indo-Europeans known as Indo-Iranians) invaded northern Mesopotamia, joined one of the native peoples there, the Hurrians, and formed the kingdom of Mitanni; another tribe invaded southern Mesopotamia and Elam, where they formed a part of the new Kassite kingdom; and a third tribe divided into the Aryans and the Iranians: the Iranians occupied the Iranian plateau, the Aryans invaded India and destroyed the thousand–year–old Harappan civilization. Another tribe, the "Argives," invaded and conquered Greece.

The Indo-Iranians were the first to develop the light, two-wheeled, spoked horse-drawn chariot. (The chariot builders were so esteemed that they were believed to have been the inventors of fire.) Aryan words for the chariot and parts of the chariot became current in every language of the Near East and beyond. The word for chariot—*ratha*—is found in the Latin *rota*. Aryan horse-training manuals were used by the Hittites and Indo-European chariot men were the premiere mercenaries of the Near East.

The chariots were light and fragile. Weight, and therefore strength, was sacrificed to speed; chariots were easily tipped over, splintered by arrows, and broken. On-the-spot repairs could be made with cord (but the cord was especially vulnerable to enemy arrows). The chariot's axle was about four feet, four inches, the wheel about three feet in diameter, the pole seven feet, ten inches long. The box was made of leather on a light wood frame. Under it was a wooden axle fastened to the middle of the box by leather straps. The wheels were fitted to the projecting ends of the axle with lynch pins. The outer rim of the wheel was covered with metal. The wheel was spoked (probably six spokes). The pole angled up. The yoke was fixed to the pole with leather straps and the yoke went over the backs of the horses and attached to their necks.

Originally the chariots were drawn by two horses, later four. Some horses were armored with chain mail or leather robes or wooden breastplates. The perfect horse was lean but strong, docile to command, fast and deep-winded, with wide nostrils, swelling cheeks, no ill markings, and fearless in the din of battle. White horses and the "horse of the north and northwest" were so prized that they were given pet names—they knew their drivers and, if the drivers were killed, their horses wept for them, as the horses of Achilles "withdrew from the battle and began to weep. The hot tears flowed down their eyelashes to the ground because of their longing for their driver; their flowing manes were fouled in the dust because they hung their heads down in their yoke-collars."

The chariot was manned by a driver and a noble warrior. The driver was of good birth (nobles might drive for their friends). The driver stood on the right. He had the duty to direct the chariot to the enemy's weakest point, to estimate his animals' strength and his warrior's and to withdraw if need be. He could drive straight and fast and he could wheel and make circles. He was the enemy's primary target, unprotected as he was. To the driver's left was the warrior, sitting on a little seat or standing. He wore some armor—certainly a helmet, breastplate, arm protector—and he had within reach a bow and arrow, spear, sword, dagger, and mace. His chariot was so filled with weapons that it was like a fortified town.

The premier weapon was the compound bow and arrows tipped with metal or horn—"The bow strikes fear, the bow wins the battle, the bow breaks the enemy and sweeps the battlefield clean." The bow was drawn to the ear—"As the bowstring is drawn tight, she whispers with a woman's voice, she presses close to the archer's ear, as though she would speak to him, and she holds her love, friend arrow, in a tight embrace." The mark of a great warrior was his ability to fire many arrows quickly and accurately. (Carts, which were probably part of the organization of the chariot arm, resupplied the warriors with arrows.) When a warrior died, he was laid out with the bow in his right hand.

Arrows were made from reed or cane, some as long as the chariot's axle, tied with sinew, feathered, and engraved with the archer's name or the king's name.

Some were poisoned, some were particularly short to use in close quarters, some—by the sixth century B.C.—were all of iron and rubbed with oil for use against elephants, some had knife-shaped or crescent-shaped heads (which could decapitate an enemy), some had flat-tipped heads, and some carried fire.

The warriors also employed lances and javelins, some with barbed points, for throwing and, perhaps, for stabbing, and swords, the shaft-headed axe, the war mace, and slings. They tried to terrorize the enemy with the noise of war drums (smeared with blood), conches, and bells, and once, at least, an army burned rotten hemp to discomfit the enemy ranks.

## THE HITTITES

The first of the Indo-European invaders were the Hittites. They entered the mountainous area cradled by the Halys River in central Anatolia, they used the mountains to protect themselves from their enemies, they consolidated and then they spilled out and conquered the rest of Anatolia. The Hittites believed that war was the only honorable calling for a gentleman. Their king was, first and foremost, their war leader; he was elected by the men under arms meeting in assembly. The assembly had, in theory, the power to depose the king and, in practice, did conduct trials of the nobility at the discretion of the king. The king used a council of elder nobles to advise him and to act as ambassadors, judges, and generals, but the king was an absolute monarch, the supreme war leader, and the indisputable religious leader; he was considered to be under the gods' protection—a kind of superhuman being—and at his death (his people believed) he joined the gods and became a god himself.

The kings kept a register of their deeds, begun by the first great king (about 1700). A typical entry (for king Mursilish) reads like this—"When Mursilish was king among the Hittites he assembled all his relatives and his army and by the might of his arm he conquered the enemy. He extended the borders of the Hittites down to the sea. He marched on Aleppo and he destroyed Aleppo. He brought prisoners and their property back to his royal city. He marched on Babylon and he destroyed Babylon, he attacked the Hurrians, and he brought Babylonian prisoners and their property back to his royal city."

## THE ARYANS

The Aryans lived by a warrior's code of honor. The Aryan king, as the invader and the foremost warrior, took possession of all the booty, the cattle and the horses, the crops, the orchards, and the water; he organized the folk and led them to victory by his example, he was the protector of his people, and he distributed the profits of war. In peacetime the king prepared for war and after the winter rains led his people on raids.

"A prince knows nothing better than combat. Warriors are happy when there is war. If you refuse to go to war, you are dishonored. Everyone everywhere will speak of your loss of honor. Dishonor for a prince is worse than death. The noble chariot men will say, 'He ran away from battle.' They will have contempt for you. What greater pain is there than this? Is it not better to die in battle?"

The Aryans organized their army by tribe, clan, and family in units of 180 (three times 60) and 21 (three times seven). The military formed a separate class, led by the nobility. The leaders of each chariot division had a pennant, or some personal symbol, and bells on the rim of their chariot. The chariots did not rush into battle, each individually, but they organized to give each other protection, with the least experienced ready to learn from the example of the more experienced. Chariots lead the charge and guard the rear.

Drums announced the beginning of battle. The warriors called on their gods for help—"burn up the enemy, kill them with the arrow, let not one be left alive. Indira, be unconquered. Be king over the other kings. Kill with your flaming arrow, kill those who do not worship you." The horses laugh in the midst of battle. Their forefeet trample the enemy. No one can stop the chariot warrior, as he slaughters the enemy, unless he meets another chariot. When the battle was won the charioteers claimed the bulk of the booty. Skilled workers recovered the smashed chariots and scavenged the wreckage of two to build one new chariot.

These were the people who invaded the Iranian plateau and the region of Afghanistan–India. The Iranian branch occupied the Oxus Valley, separated into independent tribes, and spread to the borders of south Russia and, by the middle of the second millennium, to the borders of China and the Shang kingdom (1600–1028 B.C.).

## CHARIOTS IN CHINA

The Shang adopted the chariot from their Indo-European neighbors. The Shang, however, manned their chariots with three men—the noble warrior, his driver, and a servant (who replenished the warrior's arrows and other weapons). The chariot warriors formed into a separate and privileged class in Shang China. Horses were rare enough and expensive enough that few could afford them, or even acquire them, and the class that could afford them remained small and, because of its exclusive control of the chariot, it remained dominant.

The Shang state was centered in northern Honan (north of the Yellow River). The king lived in a palace in a town protected by a mud brick wall. The Shang were continually at war with their neighbors. The king was the head of a bureaucracy and he led an army divided into units of 100, three of which—the right, the left, the center—formed a "division." The king called upon the nobility (the chariot warriors) who ruled some thirty principalities and who owed him military service. His authority was supported by Shang religion. He was worshipped as a god after his death. As always through Chinese history the Shang faced the problem of nomadic incursions and the Shang dynasty came to an end when the king was engaged in a long war on the frontier and was overwhelmed by rebellions in his rear.

## CHARIOTS IN INDIA

The Aryans (the word means "noblest") crossed the head waters of the Indus River to the Ganges, they moved far enough north to know the Himalayas, and, later, they traced the Indus to the sea. They followed their god Indira—*surely those who sacrifice to the gods will defeat those who do not*—and, they believed, just as they fought their human, non-Aryan enemies, their gods fought the native, non-Aryan, gods. The Aryans had to conquer a land with numerous fortified towns, some 460 by 215 yards with a complex gate system, guardrooms, and a rampart of mud or mud brick raising the citadel above the flood plain, forty feet wide, thirty-five feet high, inclined inward with towers. The Aryans destroyed dams and unloosed the waters to undermine the mud brick forts, they reduced the towns by siege or by assault, they breached walls with battering rams, and they set the towns aflame with fire arrows.

As the Aryans expanded across the rivers and defeated their enemies, the Dasyus (a word that evolved from meaning "foe" to meaning "devil"), they took their women captive and enslaved them, and they developed a caste system with themselves at the top. By the time of the Rig-Veda the Aryans were well enough established to be fighting each other and using the Dasyus as allies. By the sixth century B.C. they were building massive forts of stone surrounded by moats and living in cities (which had developed around these forts) As they struggled with each other to control the land their ancestors had conquered and to assert their overlordship, they found themselves threatened with siege, and, in preparation, they gathered supplies, drove the frivolous—dancers, clowns, and singers—out of town, forbade drunkenness, destroyed bridges, confiscated boats, dug trenches and lined them with pungi stakes. They forbade anyone to enter or leave town without the password.

The biggest battle of the Rig-Veda period was the Battle of the Ten Kings at the waters of the Parushni. Hymns celebrate the victory of the Aryan king Sudas who fought ten allied tribes and defeated them. After this battle he crushed an alliance of three tribes at the Jumna, he divided up the lands among his nobles, and he ruled at the head of the caste of the nobility over the third caste, the people. (The second caste was the priesthood.)

The chariot remained a symbol of rule throughout ancient Indian warfare though, as a weapon, it was superseded by cavalry and elephants.

An Indian epic looks back a thousand years (or more) to the days following the Aryan conquest of northern India when the most powerful Aryan kingdom (Kurus) faced a challenge from a new kingdom (the Pandavas). This paraphrased description is as close as we can come to an eyewitness account of chariot warfare.

### The Battle Between the Kurus and the Pandavas

The bloodthirsty Kurus did not care whether they lived or died. They raised their standards and charged the Pandavas. The two sides shot arrows at each other, and the arrows struck men on both sides, but the men did not retreat. Chariot shaft struck chariot shaft and broke, and yoke spike struck yoke spike and shattered. Some warriors formed teams to fight against the teams of warriors on the other side. Men hungered to take the lives of men and their chariots were so tightly packed in places that they could not move. The twang of bowstrings and their striking against the leather wrist guards of the warriors was awful to hear, but none retreated. Our mighty chariot warriors shot so many arrows—long, snakelike arrows—that they hid the sun. They shot flaming arrows, too. And then these mighty chariot warriors, enraged by the wounds they had suffered, threw challenges at one another.

The Bull–of–Battle with his bodyguard of five mighty chariot men penetrated the Pandava host, and his standard, the palmyra, could be seen pressing forward through the ranks of the enemy. He used arrows with broad heads, he shot them straight and true, and he decapitated his enemies and he shattered the yokes of their chariots and their standards; he seemed to be dancing on his chariot as it ran along. Then a foeman in his anger, Hero, charged with his chariot and his yoke of excellent tawny horses towards the Bull–of–Battle's chariot. His standard was chased with pure gold and it resembled a spreading tree, and he hit the Bull and his bodyguard, one with one arrow, another with five, and yet another with nine arrows, and he drew his bow as far as it could be drawn and he shot one arrow that cut off his enemy's standard. And he fired one broad-headed shaft, perfectly straight, and he decapitated a chariot driver. And with another keen-edged arrow he severed the gold-decked bow of another chariot warrior. And that mighty chariot man hit all of them with many sharp-pointed shafts, in his anger, and he seemed to dance on his chariot. And the gods, who witnessed his lightness of hand, were pleased.

## CHARIOTS IN GREECE

The Indo-European chariot people who invaded Greece seem to have come by sea, first to attack Thessaly, the largest, most fertile plain in Greece and from there, overland or by sea, they invaded and conquered, in different waves, the plains of Boeotia, the best horse country in Attica, Marathon, Kirrha, Eleusis, Argos, and Pylos (and other places around Pylos), and from there they moved down into the Eurotas Valley. A century later they took to the sea again, invaded Crete, and conquered the Minoan civilization there.

They were led by kings who commanded a chariot nobility. Some of the nobility were heavily armored. They fought from chariots; they had a driver and they used a bow and arrow. They conquered the local inhabitants, they built huge fortresses (heavily influenced by Hittite types), and they exploited the conquered. These early kings, and nobles, were enormously wealthy, with trading (and plundering) connections throughout the Near East—ostrich eggs from Nubia transhipped through Egypt, from Mesopotamia lapis lazuli, from Crete faience and alabaster, from Syria raw ivory, from Anatolia (the Hittites) silver, from the Baltic amber and gold. They had trading connections with the Hittites and the

Kassites and many others, but they were most heavily influenced by a considerable civilization already established in Crete and the southern Aegean.

Later Greeks attributed this civilization to the powerful ruler of the sea, Minos (and which we, therefore, call the Minoan civilization, 2000–1400 B.C.). The kings and the nobility lived in sprawling (labyrinthine) palaces without fortifications. Their art is remarkably free of combat; rather it depicts sport—boxing and bull vaulting—and scenes from the sea, sea creatures and ships. The Minoans sailed between Crete and Greece, the Near East, and Egypt. Within Crete the palaces cooperated, outside Crete the Minoan ships controlled piracy and dominated the Aegean, and the Minoans grew wealthy on trade.

We can detect a pattern behind Minoan prosperity: as their resources increased, the kings used the resources to build and maintain ships, the ships, by war and trade, brought more resources, the kings and nobility increased the fleet of ships enough to gain supremacy in the Aegean and to eliminate any rivals. The result (though not necessarily inevitable) was an internally prosperous and stable society free of threat of invasion and unconcerned with war. By contrast, when the Mycenaeans had conquered all the places worth conquering, they did what all conquerors seem to do: they turned against each other—or so their massive fortifications would indicate—and tried to dominate and unify the rest.

By the thirteenth century, the Mycenaeans were organized into classes under a supreme ruler (the *wanax*) and subordinate rulers. The wanax maintained the *heqetai* (the "followers"—who may have comprised his chariot force), raised and supported district by district. The chariot warriors wore protective armor, all bronze or linen tunics of several layers reinforced with bronze. When these warriors died, they were buried with their most treasured possessions, arms, daggers, and swords (of bronze). Their chariots were stored, and inventoried, in the palaces, from wheels to "heels" (steps for the rear of the chariot). Whole frames were also stored. One tablet at Knossus lists 246 chariot frames. Some tablets list the name of a man, followed by the sign for body armor (a suit for the driver and a suit for the warrior), a complete chariot, and a pair of horses. A series of almost 100 tablets survives, perhaps the record of a unit of 100 chariots, but not every tablet records a complete chariot team, so if this is a unit of 100, it is lacking equipment, men, and horses. Swords, axes, lances, and arrows are also inventoried.

By the end of the thirteenth century the Mycenaeans were under attack from the sea. In the district of Pylos, some tablets record that bronze (a scarce resource) was stripped from temples to make arms. Five tablets describe conditions just before the sack of the palace—800 men are detached to be "watchers of the coast" (800 men scattered over ninety miles). Some of the heqetai were with them, apparently as commanders of troops, concentrated in the most likely areas of attack. One tablet written in haste lists dedications to the gods and suggests human sacrifice.

Their imminent destruction was upon them.

## Map 4: Expansion of the Chariot People

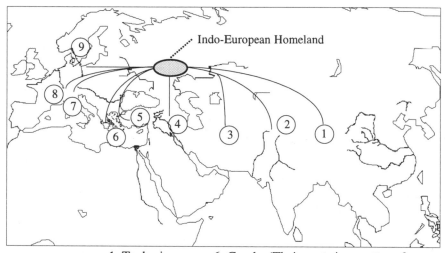

Indo-European Homeland

1. Tocharians
2. Aryans
3. Iranians
4. Mitanni
5. Hittites
6. Greeks (Their route is a matter of controversy.)
7. Latins
8. Celts
9. Germans

## 10. The Egyptian King in a Chariot

# 4

# The Egyptian Empire

## *The Defeated Avenge Their Defeat and Conquer the World*

The movement of the Indo-European tribes set the whole of the Near East in motion and drove the Amorites from Mesopotamia. The Amorites were joined by other peoples, Indo-European mercenaries hired both to fight and to train their employers in the use of the chariot, the composite bow, bronze armor, and bronze-edged weapons, and by Hebrews (a people then new in the records of the Near East); together these peoples (called Hyksos—"bandits"—by the Egyptians) invaded Egypt, conquered the Egyptian Delta (Lower Egypt), and forced the rest of Egypt into vassalage to them. They adopted Egyptian customs, language, and dress, except that they retained their personal names and the worship of their own gods. They ruled Egypt for 200 years (the Second Intermediate Period, 1786–1575) and for most of that time they maintained their exclusive control of horse and chariot.

The Egyptians became well acquainted with horses and chariots—from the wrong end!—but not until the time of Seqenenre, king of Thebes, did they acquire horses and chariots enough—and the expertise—to challenge the Hyksos.

"Once upon a time the whole land of Egypt was in misery and no king ruled the whole land, but the Hyksos king, Apopi, was in Avaris and he collected tribute from all of Egypt. He collected tribute from Lower Egypt and he collected tribute from Upper Egypt. King Apopi worshipped his foreign god and built temples to him and made offerings and with his councilors prayed to him every day, just as though they were worshipping Ra, and allowed no other god to be worshipped.

"In the city of Thebes, however, was king Seqenenre, and king Seqenenre worshipped no god except Ra and he was beloved by Ra and king Apopi was angry with his vassal Seqenenre because Seqenenre worshipped Ra and so he sent a messenger to Seqenenre and the messenger said to him,

"'King Apopi says to you, 'Leave the hippopotamus pool that is in the city center, for my sleep is disturbed by the noise of the hunt.'"

(Hunting hippopotamus was the exclusive prerogative of the king of Egypt.)

The story breaks off with the words, "King Seqenenre burst into tears and he called all his nobles and the captains of his army and he told them of the message and they were at a loss for words," but we know that Seqenenre did revolt and we know what happened to him, because his body was preserved by the dry sands of the desert and we can see the savage wound dealt to his skull by a battle axe (see p. 28). Despite his death, however, the battle must at least have been a draw, because Seqenenre's successor, Kamose, attacked one of the vassal cities of the Hyksos (and founded the New Kingdom).

"I obeyed the commands of Ra and I broke down the walls, I slew the people, and I forced the queen to come down to the river. My soldiers were like lions and they rejoiced as they divided up the property and they carried off slaves and cattle and milk, fat, and honey."

With this success there came a new aggressive spirit. The Egyptians now knew that they could fight the Hyksos and win; as so often in history, the victors had taught the vanquished how to fight. In the process of three generations of war, the Egyptians developed a professional military class. Kamose's successor, Ahmose, attacked the Hyksos capital and drove the Hyksos from Egypt. One of Ahmose's ship captains left this account (paraphrased):

"My father was an officer of the king Seqenenre. While I was a young man, I took his place as an officer under king Ahmose in the ship called *Offering*. After I took a wife, I was transferred to the fleet of Lower Egypt. I marched behind the King's chariot. His Majesty, himself, witnessed my courage at the siege of the city of Avaris.

"I joined the ship *Shining-in-Memphis*. In the canal near Avaris I fought hand to hand with the enemy and I cut off a hand as a trophy. The Royal Herald was informed and the king gave me the medal of valor. Again I fought hand to hand and I took a hand. His Majesty gave me a second medal of valor.

"When his Majesty fought in Upper Egypt against the rebels, I went into the water and I took a prisoner of war. I made him march ahead of me on the road past the rebel town. The Royal Herald was informed and the king presented me with double gold. In the fighting when the king took Avaris, I captured one man and three women and the king gave them to me to be my slaves.

"The king campaigned in southern Judah and besieged Sharuhen for three years before he took it. I captured two women and took one hand. The king awarded me gold for bravery and the prisoners as slaves."

The kings drove the Hyksos from Egypt and they created a security zone in Asia that evolved into an empire and brought them into contact with the other major powers of the Near East. King Thutmose I (c. 1511) led the Egyptian army into Mesopotamia "to enslave the dirty ones, the foreigners hated by the god" who lived by the Euphrates River, "that backwards river which flows downstream when it flows upstream," (that is, it flowed opposite to the direction the Nile flowed). The Egyptians believed that their own ways and the ways of their land were "right" and all others were "wrong," and, of course, the "right" should rule the "wrong."

The kings had to take their army out every year to punish those who had rebelled and to intimidate those who had not. They trained their heirs to shoot the bow and work the chariot, to become the foremost warrior of Egypt, to command the army, and the professional officer corps. During campaigning season the kings were absent from Egypt and they depended upon their queens (who had the authority to rule but who could not supplant the king) to supervise the vizier and break him if he appeared to be a threat to the king. This system worked as long as the king was strong enough to check the power of vizier, queen, and priest.

As the Egyptians advanced into the Near East, they also invaded and conquered the northern parts of Nubia; they imposed their own system upon the Nubians, administered conquered Nubia just as any nome of Egypt was administered, and Egyptianized the Nubians. On the other hand, the Egyptians did not have the resources—nor the Asians the inclination—to extend the borders of Egypt into Asia. Rather the pharaohs left the rulers of the conquered area in place as vassals of the pharaoh. They required these rulers to take an oath of loyalty to the pharaoh, to renew the oath regularly, and swear it anew at any change in rulers, Egyptian or foreign. In the presence of the pharaoh these vassal rulers expressed their obedience by groveling on their bellies before the king.

The vassals owed Egypt a yearly tribute, support for the Egyptian troops quartered on them, the upkeep of the realm, and the requisition of workers if need be. The pharaoh ruled his vassals through an "Overseer of the Northern Lands" and a bureau charged with the correspondence to and from the foreign lands. He turned the empire into a kind of extended family: he added the daughters of the "allied" kings to his harem (as "wives"), but in return he was expected to pay a bride-price worthy of his own dignity. Thence forward these rulers were "brothers" and "inlaws." The rulers' sons might be held in Egypt in the "pages' castle," where they were taught Egyptian language and manners. When the father died (or was deposed), the son, now thoroughly Egyptian, would return to his kingdom to succeed his father. Protocol demanded frequent formal letters to inform the pharaoh of significant news on a regular basis. The omission of "best wishes" could signal trouble in the relationship. Envoys went back and forth and gifts were exchanged. The foreign kings preferred gold, but sometimes they received a visit from an Egyptian god (that is, a statue).

Thus the pharaoh had several ways to determine whether his vassal was disloyal: if the pharaoh did not receive the tribute on time, or he did not receive the required correspondence, or some of the courtesies were omitted, or he heard of suspicious behavior, reported by his garrison, then the pharaoh had the implied threat that if the vassal did not satisfy him, he could send the vassal's son to replace him, or, of course, he could bring his army. The pharaoh claimed as his empire an area larger than he had in reality conquered: many places avoided conquest by acceding to his request for tribute (the tribute most prized, and most necessary to the army before Thutmose II, was horse and chariot); others, named as vassals, were protected by their obscurity or inaccessibility.

Thutmose I was a strong king. Thutmose II maintained the empire, but upon his death he left behind a tangled situation. He had been married to his half-sister Hatshepsut, but he named the son of a harem girl to be his successor (Thutmose III). Hatshepsut became queen-regent and married Thutmose III off to her own daughter. The ambitious Hatshepsut intended to rule Egypt in her own name, but as a queen she was forbidden the throne, so in 1503 she had herself proclaimed *king*. (In some portraits she is shown bearded.) She could rule Egypt, but she had not spent her childhood training in the use of the chariot and the bow, and she could not command the army; for seventeen years the army was idle. Not everyone thought idleness was bad or that the profession of soldier was good.

"You think the soldier is better off than the scribe?

"Listen then. A boy is recruited and brought to the barracks. During training he is beaten on his back, punched in the eye and knocked flat. He is beaten like a rug. He is black and blue from the beatings. He is ordered to Syria, to march over the mountains carrying his rations on his back like a donkey and his back is bent like a donkey. He has to drink foul water. He falls out at day's end and has guard duty all night. When at last he faces the enemy, he is as weak as a trapped bird.

"If somehow he survives, he has to be brought back to Egypt on the back of a donkey. His clothes are stolen. His servant runs away. He takes to his bed, as used up as rotten wood.

"That is the life of a soldier."

During the reign of Hatshepsut the small kingdom of Qadesh expanded its domain to include most of the Eastern Mediterranean seaboard. In 1482 the "Asiatics" rebelled. Hatshepsut was forced to send out the army and let her co-ruler, Thutmose III, command it. (We never hear of Hatshepsut again.) Thutmose was king for thirty-two years after her death; in that time he expanded the Egyptian empire to its greatest extent.

Thutmose III's first task was to recover the seaboard lands from the king of Qadesh (who was front man for the king of Mitanni). Thutmose was informed that the king of Qadesh had mobilized his allies ("300 princes"), his chariot forces ("hundreds of thousands"), and his infantry ("millions") and Thutmose ordered his own army to mobilize (a process requiring two and a half months). The king drafted one-tenth of the manpower of Egypt and organized them into divisions of 5,000 men with twenty companies in each division and five platoons in each company. His army could march at a rate of about fifteen miles a day. A journal (now lost) of the campaign against Qadesh was kept and a summary (extant) was inscribed on a temple wall. Place after place fell to the king; detachments were left to mop up the few places that resisted.

Joppa was one of the major cities that continued to resist, and Thutmose left a general named Thuti to besiege Joppa. Thuti invited the leader of Joppa to a conference and got him drunk. The drunken Joppan asked if he could see the famous war-mace of King Thutmose (the mace called "Beautiful"); General Thuti took it in his hand, stood in front of the leader of Joppa, and said, "Look at me,

Prince of Joppa. Here is the war-mace of King Thutmose, the lion of courage and the son of war—his father Amun has given him the strength to slay his enemies."

General Thuti struck the leader of Joppa, knocked him down, and had him tied up. Then he had 500 sacks brought and he ordered 200 soldiers to get in 200 sacks and he filled the other sacks with weapons and chains and fetters and thongs and he had them sealed up. Five hundred soldiers disguised as porters carried them slung on poles and the general ordered them, "When you have entered the city, release your comrades, seize all the people in the city, and bind them."

Thuti sent a messenger to the charioteer of the leader of Joppa, (who was waiting outside) and he told him, "Your master orders you to go and say to his wife, 'Thuti is coming over to us with sacks of tribute,'" and the messenger led the soldiers into the city and they released their comrades and they seized the people of the city, man and woman, old and young, and they bound them.

That night Thuti sent a message to King Thutmose, which said, "Good news. Amun, your father, has delivered the prince of Joppa and all his people and his city to you. Send men to take the captives away and fill the house of your father Amun, king of gods, with male and female slaves. They are cast beneath your feet for ever and ever."

Before he crossed the Carmel range, word came to Thutmose that the enemy army had mustered at Megiddo. The king called a staff meeting to determine which of three routes they should take: the staff proposed that the army should advance by the eastern, and easiest, route around the Carmel range. The problem with that route was that the enemy also knew that it was the easiest. The staff rejected the middle route since it ran through a narrow pass where the army would have to march in single file. Thutmose said to them, "Take not the counsel of your fears," and chose the bold course.

The army climbed towards the pass for two days and traversed the pass on the third day; it needed seven hours to clear the pass, but Thutmose caught his enemies completely by surprise. The enemy rushed to cover Megiddo while Thutmose had his army encamp before the city and the enemy.

The order was given to sharpen weapons, to post guards, and to be ready to fight "the wretched foreigners." In the morning the enemy took one look at the Egyptian army, drawn up for battle, and broke in flight; the kings of Qadesh and Megiddo fled, too, but the gates of Megiddo were closed, and they had to be hoisted up over the walls by their clothes.

Thutmose ordered a pursuit to the city, but his troops' discipline broke down at the opportunity to plunder the enemy camp. The result was that only eighty-three enemy were killed and about 300 taken prisoner. Thutmose had to put Megiddo under siege. The Egyptians dug a moat around the city while Thutmose made a nearby fortress his headquarters. The siege lasted seven months. While the siege continued, the king and his subordinate commanders conducted raids throughout the homelands of the princes allied with Megiddo. When he took

Megiddo, he broke organized resistance in the Near East. Thutmose replaced some of the rulers and sent others back to their cities. He captured 2,000 horses.

Through the next decade Thutmose reduced the cities still holding out, curbed the ambitions of Qadesh, and prepared the way for a campaign against Mitanni, the power, so it seemed, behind the rebellion of Qadesh. Thutmose crossed the Euphrates at Carchemish and proceeded down stream. On his eighth campaign Thutmose III gave a kind of press interview.

"No one in that land of Mitanni dared face me. Its cowardly master had run away. I seized his cities and his towns and set them on fire. My Majestic Self turned those cities into ruins which will never be rebuilt. I plundered the people and took them as slaves. I destroyed their stores of food and cut down their crops. I even cut down all their fruit trees and their land is now dust blown by the wind. My Majestic Self destroyed that whole land. That land is now ashes and dust and will never support crops again."

(The scribe interjected in the account, "What a king! He crossed the Euphrates after the aggressor and he pursued that dirty wretch throughout all the lands of the Mitanni. Indeed we may boast of his prowess in battle.")

The neighbors of Mitanni, the rulers of the Babylonians, the Assyrians, and the Hittites, sent their congratulations to Thutmose. Thutmose continued to campaign in northern Syria and to wrest the lands from the control of Mitanni. (The successors of Thutmose III continued desultory campaigning in Syria until the major powers finally reached an accord defining each other's area of interest.)

Thutmose III established the permanent empire. As empires go, perhaps, the subjects were not too bad off. They had to support small garrisons of five to twenty-five men and pay a yearly tribute. Every year Thutmose went forth on a triumphal tour to collect tribute, punish rebels, add new territory, and display the power of Egypt to his subjects. The Egyptians had come to love war for war's sake, which is called *militarism*, and to love the implements of war:

"Take care of the horses bound for Syria, the pair of horses and their stable hands and grooms. The horses are full of grain and rubbed down twice and their coats are sleek. The chariots are of berri-wood and full of weapons. Eighty arrows are in the quiver. There are lances, the sword, the knife, the whip, the chariot mace, the staff, the spear of the land of the Hittites, their points are of bronze of six-fold alloy. The breastplates lie beside them."

War can also be profitable. A scribe has left us a record of one campaign's tribute paid to Thutmose III:

"I followed my master into upper Syria and I inventoried the take: silver, gold, lapis lazuli, various gems, chariots, and horses without number, and herds and flocks in their multitudes. I acquainted the chiefs of Syria with their compulsory yearly labor. I assessed the levy of the chiefs of the land of Nubia in electrum."

Egypt was a power known, and conciliated, in the whole of the Eastern Mediterranean. Wealth poured in to the king and his court and to the nobility and to the priesthood. Gradually, the different parts of society sorted themselves out, and the classes crystallized into a kind of caste system. The son of a soldier became a soldier, a farmer's son was a farmer, a scribe's son a scribe, and so on. So long as the king commanded the army's respect and loyalty, Egypt thrived.

## Map 5: Egyptian Empire with an Inset of the Iron Age Invasions

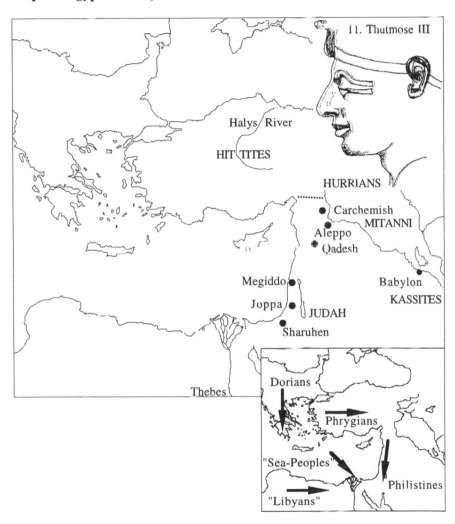

## 12. Seqenenre

## 13. The Sea-Peoples

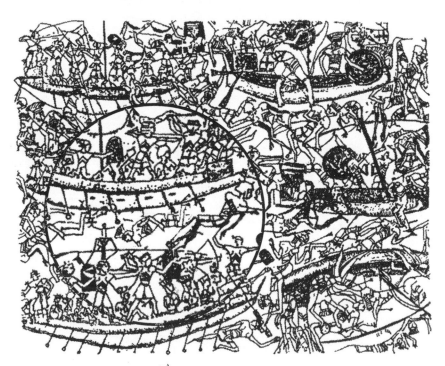

 Shardana mercenary

 One of the "Sea-Peoples"

Egyptian

# 5

# Balance of Power
## *Divided Leadership Allows New Enemies to Form*

No living Egyptian could remember a time when the Egyptians had not been supreme in the Near East, and no one could imagine a time when Egypt would no longer be supreme. The Egyptians had enemies: states and peoples who wanted their independence or feared that they might be the next target of Egyptian aggression or were lured by the thought of all that wealth in Egypt, but even the Egyptians' potential rival, the Hittites, although they were growing more powerful, were no match for the Egyptians so long as the Egyptians were well led. Then Amunhotep IV (1379–1362) became king of Egypt.

Amunhotep was a strange man, completely self-centered and focussed on his own concerns to the exclusion of the outside world. He was physically unable to drive a chariot and shoot the bow, and he was a fanatic. He changed his name to Akhnaten, he worshipped Aten (the disk of the sun) and only Aten– the other gods might exist, but they were unimportant; and the only war he cared about was his revolution (the Amarna Revolution) inside Egypt, to force the priesthood to reject Amun and accept Aten.

Under his indifference the empire fell away and the Hittites moved into the power vacuum. Finally, in 1351, concerned officials forced a compromise on the king—his queen (Nefertiti) was expelled from the court and Akhnaten accepted a co-regent, Tutankhaten. Soon Akhnaten disappeared, the city (Amarna) he had built as the center of his revolution was destroyed, and his name was excised from all records. The priests of Amun took control again, Tutankhaten changed his name to Tutankhamen in 1347, but belief in a god-king died with Akhnaten, and so did the empire.

None of the powers then in the Near East—the Hittites, the Kassites (Babylonians), Mitanni, or the strongest of them all, the Egyptians—could remain powerful without calling upon the resources of the others. The Egyptians, despite a breeding program of their own, had to import horses, and the complete panoply of chariot, horse, and personal weapons drew from all the powers, but one region was essential: no state could become preeminent unless it controlled Syria and the Mediterranean coast. Hence the great powers contended continually to control that area and to protect their trading rights.

At the time Akhnaten became king of Egypt, Shuppiluliumash became king of the Hittites. He became king of a nation in crisis; a civil war had left his capital city burned and in ruins and he was under attack by a coalition of half a dozen neighboring countries. For twenty years he fought in the north, to secure his northern border, and in the south, to control Syria.

The main arm of the Hittite army, as with all Near Eastern armies of this period, was the chariot corps. Each chariot had a crew of three men clothed in leather garments that reached to mid-calf and a helmet. One man drove, the second wielded the offensive weapons (the lance and the bow), and the third provided protection with a shield. The infantry, which seemed to play a subordinate role, wore high-crowned helmets, no body armor (if their artwork depicts them accurately), a battle axe, sword, and one-handed shield. The troops—because of the geography and climate of Anatolia—would be mustered in the spring and used in the summer.

The soldiers swore an oath to the king and to the royal family; to ensure their oath, they underwent a magical ritual, in one part of which a blind woman and a deaf man were brought before the army and the army was told, "Look upon this blind woman and deaf man. Whoever violates his oath to king or queen, let his oaths take him—let them strike him blind, let them make him deaf. He will be as blind as this blind woman. He will be as deaf as this deaf man. May his oaths destroy him—himself, his wife, his children, and all his kinfolk."

Should they ever be defeated, "they perform a ritual behind the river, as follows: they divide in half a man, a goat, a puppy, and a little pig; they place half to the right and half to the left, and in front they make a gate of wood and in front of the gate they light fires to the right and to the left, and the troops walk on the path between and when they come to the river they sprinkle water over them."

Shuppiluliumash's first great triumph was diplomatic: he convinced the king of Kizzuwatna, the buffer state between the Hittites and Mitanni, and a state offering access to Syria, to support the Hittites. The king of Mitanni accused him of sharp practice. He replied, "When a people under my control deserted to the Mitanni and I wrote to the Mitanni king and said, 'Return my subjects,' the king replied, 'No. Originally these people had settled in our country. Yes, they did flee later to the land of the Hittites, but now they have come back. The cattle have chosen their barn.'

"The king would not return my subjects and I wrote, 'What would you think if some people seceded from you and came over to me?' and the king replied, 'Exactly the same.' So now the people of Kizzuwatna have chosen their barn and they are Hittite cattle. The land of Kizzuwatna rejoices in its liberation."

While Shuppiluliumash held his own on the battlefields of Syria, he outmaneuvered the king of Mitanni off the battlefield. He contracted a marriage alliance with the king of the Kassites (in Babylonia) to make a royal Kassite princess his wife and queen, and he took advantage of the indifference of the Egyptian king, Akhnaten, to isolate the kingdom of Mitanni. Then Shuppiluliumash crossed the Euphrates, sacked the capital of the Mitanni, and forced the king of Mitanni to flee. He recrossed the Euphrates and made a show of force in Syria. Most of the Syrian cities previously subject to Mitanni came over to him and many of the Egyptian possessions as well. The rulers loyal to the Egyptians beseeched King Akhnaten for help; they received no reply. The kingdom of Mitanni broke up. Shuppiluliumash now had no equal in the Near East.

When Akhnaten died, and then Tutankhamen, the Egyptian royal family was thrown into turmoil; a princess wrote to Shuppiluliumash and asked him to send a son to marry her and become king of the Egyptians. Shuppiluliumash was so taken aback by the request that he called a council to advise him and he sent an envoy to investigate whether the princess was sincere. At last, Shuppiluliumash was convinced and he did send a son, but Shuppiluliumash had lost the moment, his son was murdered, and the Hittites lost whatever chance they might have had to found a new dynasty in Egypt.

At the height of his power, his troops brought a plague back from campaign; Shuppiluliumash caught it and died. (Plague in similar circumstances killed the Athenian democratic leader Pericles and the Roman emperor Lucius Verus.) Shuppiluliumash's successor had as great a task as Shuppiluliumash had had; he faced a two-front war, one to the west, where he fought for ten years, and one in Syria, where his generals fought. He used a combination of diplomacy (divide and conquer), fortification (in the west), and offensive war to extend the Hittite sphere of influence from Anatolia to the Euphrates and Syria.

As the new king of the Hittites fought against his enemies, a new dynasty (the Nineteenth Dynasty) in Egypt attempted to recover all that Akhnaten had lost. These kings had to settle threats from Nubia, Libya, and the sea (from which pirates raided the coast of Egypt), before they could concentrate on the greater threat of the Hittites. The Egyptian king Ramses II and the Hittite king Muwatallish met in a battle that was supposed to decide who would control Syria—the battle of Qadesh (around 1300 B.C.).

As Ramses neared Qadesh, he was informed by two Hittite "deserters" that Muwatallish and the Hittite army were far to the north. Ramses believed the deserters and continued to advance in column, himself first with the Amon unit (chariots), followed by the Ra (archers), Ptah (spearmen), and Sutekh (axmen)—each division was named for an Egyptian god; as the Amon division crossed a northern tributary of the Orontes, Muwatallish advanced from his position of concealment on the eastern bank of the Orontes, crossed the Orontes, attacked the Egyptian army (which was still marching in column), and routed the Ra (archer) division. After routing the Ra division, the Hittite army turned north, crossed the tributary after the head of the Egyptian column, and forced it into flight. Ramses rallied the broken division and reformed it (single–handed, according to his own account). The Amon division then held out until the Ptah division arrived on the field of battle and forced the Hittites to retire.

Both sides had been roughly handled, but both sides claimed victory. The Hittite king asked for an armistice the next day—as was always the case in chariot warfare, the chariots needed to be repaired and refitted—but in the end the Egyptians retired. Finally the Egyptians and Hittites agreed to a line of separation that would define their spheres of influence in Syria. The line slightly favored the Hittites. The Hittites then controlled the most powerful empire in the Near East. They did not know it, but their kingdom had less than a century to live.

In 1232 B.C. "Northerners from all lands" attacked Egypt from the west by land and from the north by sea. The Egyptian king repelled the attack (and took prisoners into his service as mercenaries), but a generation later Ramses III had to repel a larger invasion, part from the sea, part from the land to the east. (These invaders were called the "Sea Peoples.") Ramses had a temple monument built and on it had inscribed an account of the campaign (1191 B.C.)—"The foreign countries in their islands made a conspiracy. No land could stand before their arms, not the Hittites, Cilicia, Carchemish, Arzawa, and Alashiya, but, one by one, they were cut off. The Sea Peoples camped in Amurru. They ravaged its people, and they made its land look as though people had never lived there. They were coming, setting the country on fire, coming forward toward Egypt. Their confederation was the Philistines, Tjekker, Sheklesh, Denyen, and Weshesh lands united."

The scenes cut into the temple walls show a massive sea battle involving Egyptians fighting with bow and arrow and foreigners of different sorts fighting with sword and spear. Ship rams ship and the enemy's ships have overturned. The Egyptians preserved their kingdom, but they lost their empire and they were not strong enough to recover it.

These invasions fundamentally changed the world of the Eastern Mediterranean. They divided Greece into a land of many small centers of no particular wealth and few resources, they broke the Hittites, and they allowed new kingdoms to emerge on the eastern Mediterranean seaboard: the Phoenicians, the Philistines, and the Hebrews (who formed a locally powerful kingdom under David and Solomon).

## 14. The Battle of Qadesh (a Shardana mercenary kills a Hittite)

# 6

# The Hebrews

## *God Leads a People in War*

When the Israelites looked back on their past, as recorded in the Old Testament, they believed that they were looking upon a record of the will of God manifest in every victory and every defeat. While the Old Testament seldom offers enough description of battles to reconstruct them, it does show us what one particular ancient Near Eastern people believed was the relationship between themselves and their God. Three episodes, the episodes of Joshua, Gideon, and David, illustrate this relationship especially well, and, in particular, in war.

### JOSHUA

The conquest of Israel is attributed to Joshua and his successors. Joshua was an experienced man of war. He reconnoitred the land across the Jordan River and when he discovered a weak spot—the morale of the people in Jericho was low—he ordered his people, divided by tribe, to follow behind the Ark of the Covenant; under the command of God he crossed the Jordan and and he was able to seize Jericho when God caused the walls of the city to fall. Joshua ordered all the gold and silver within the city to be consecrated to God, and, after they had consecrated the spoils, they burned the city to the ground.

Joshua sent his men from Jericho to reconnoitre Ai, and when they returned to Joshua, they told him, "Only two or three thousand men are necessary, for there are few men in Ai."

But the 3,000 Israelites broke and ran from the men of Ai and Joshua tore his clothes, fell on his face to the earth before the Ark of the Lord, and he and the elders of Israel threw dust on their heads and they lay there until evening.

"Alas, O Lord God," said Joshua, "why did You ever bring this people across the Jordan, only to deliver us into the power of the Amorites? I wish that we had been content to remain on the other side of the Jordan! O Lord, what can I say after Israel has turned his back on his enemies? When the Canaanites and all the inhabitants of the land hear of it, they will surround us, and wipe us off the face of the earth; and what will You do then for Your great name?"

"Rise!" God said to Joshua. "What use is it to fall on your face? Israel has sinned; you have violated the covenant with me, which I enjoined on you; you have taken some of the consecrated things; you have stolen them, lied about them, and put them among your own things, and thus you Israelites cannot stand up against your enemies, but you turn your backs on your enemies for you have become polluted yourselves. I will not be with you anymore, unless you get rid of the polluted things. Rise, consecrate the people, and say, 'Consecrate yourselves for tomorrow; for thus says the God of Israel: polluted things are among you, O Israel; you cannot stand up against your enemies until you remove the pollution from your midst. In the morning then, you shall present yourselves by tribes; and the tribe which the Lord indicates shall come forward by clans; and the clan which the Lord indicates shall come forward by families; and the family which the Lord indicates shall come forward by individuals. Then he that is indicated as having the polluted things shall be burned, together with all that belong to him; because he violated the covenant of the Lord, and because he committed an infamous act in Israel.'"

So Joshua discovered the culprit and he sent messengers, who ran to the tent, and found the cloak hidden in his tent, with the money underneath it. They took the things from the tent and brought them to Joshua and all the Israelites; and they laid them before the Lord. Then Joshua, accompanied by all Israel, took Achan, the descendant of Zerah, and the silver, the cloak, the bar of gold, his sons, his daughters, his oxen, his asses, his sheep, his household, and all that belonged to him, and all Israel stoned them and they burned them all up.

Then the Lord relented from his fierce anger and the Lord said to Joshua, "Do not be afraid or dismayed; take all the warriors with you and march against Ai. I will deliver the king into your power, together with his people, his city, and his land. You shall do to Ai and its king as you did to Jericho and its king, except that you may take its spoil and cattle as your booty. Set an ambush for the city west of it."

Joshua picked out 30,000 of the most courageous warriors, and sent them off by night, and he commanded them, "You are to lie in ambush against the city, to the west of it; do not go very far from the city, but all of you be ready. I and all the troops with me will draw near to the city, and then, when they come out against us, we shall flee from them as we did the first time, and they will come out after us, until we draw them away from the city; for they will say, 'They are fleeing from us as they did the first time.' Thus we shall flee from them, and then you must rise from your ambush, and take possession of the city. The Lord your God will deliver it into your power. As soon as you have seized the city, set the city on fire, doing as the Lord directed. Now I have given you your commands."

Then Joshua sent them off, and they went to the place of ambush west of Ai while Joshua himself spent that night with the people. Next morning Joshua rose early and mustered the people, and with the elders of Israel marched at the head of the people to Ai. Then all the people, that is, the warriors that were with him, marched up until they came near it. Arriving in front of the city, they encamped north of Ai. As soon as the king of Ai became aware of the army of

Joshua, he hurried out with all his people to meet Israel in battle, without knowing that there was an ambush for him west of the city. Joshua and all Israel pretended to be beaten by them and fled in the direction of the desert. Then all the people that were in the city were called out to pursue them; and in pursuing Joshua, they were drawn away from the city. Not a man was left in Ai or Bethel that did not go out in pursuit of Israel; they left the city unguarded and pursued Israel. Then the Lord said to Joshua, "Stretch out the javelin that is in your hand toward Ai; for I will deliver it into your power."

So Joshua stretched out the javelin that was in his hand toward the city; whereupon the men in ambush rose quickly from their position and they ran and they entered the city and captured it and they set it on fire. When the men of Ai looked back, they saw the smoke of the city rising to the heavens. They had no chance to flee this way or that; for when Joshua and the main body of Israel saw that the men in ambush had captured the city, and that smoke was rising from the city, they turned back and attacked the men of Ai. Then the others came out of the city against them, and thus they were caught between two bodies of Israelites. They slew them until not one remained or escaped. The king of Ai they took alive and brought him to Joshua.

When Israel had finished slaying all the inhabitants of Ai in the open desert where they had pursued them, and all of them had fallen by the sword until they were at an end, all Israel turned back to Ai, and put it to the sword. The total number of those that fell that day, including men and women, was twelve thousand, namely, all the people of Ai.

Joshua defeated thirty-one kings and established the homeland of the Israelites.

## GIDEON

In the period of the Judges the army of Israel was drawn from the separate tribes and was largely infantry—which fact required them to use terrain to protect themselves from the Canaanite chariots. Sometimes Israel defeated its neighbors, sometimes it was defeated by them. They raided each other, ambushed each other, and used various stratagems, like the one Gideon used to defeat the forces of Midian.

Now the Midianites, Amalekites, and all the Kedemites were lying along the valley like locusts, and their camels were innumerable, being like the sands on the seashore. Gideon infiltrated the outposts of the warriors that were in the camp and he heard a man telling his comrade a dream.

"I dreamed," he said, "that a crust of barley bread came tumbling into the camp of Midian, and coming to a tent, struck it so that it fell, and turned it upside down, so that the tent lay flat."

"That," his comrade responded, "is nothing other than the sword of Gideon, the son of Joash, an Israelite. God is delivering Midian and all the camp into his power."

As soon as Gideon heard the telling of the dream and its interpretation, he bowed in reverence; and returning to the camp of Israel, he said, "Up! for the Lord is delivering the camp of Midian into your power."

Then he divided his 300 men into three companies, put trumpets into the hands of all of them, and empty pitchers, with torches inside the pitchers.

"Watch me," he said to them, "and do what I do; when I blow the trumpet, you also must blow your trumpets all around the camp, and say, 'For the Lord and for Gideon!'"

When Gideon and the hundred men that accompanied him reached the outskirts of the enemy camp at the beginning of the middle watch, just when the guards had been posted, they blew their trumpets, and smashed the pitchers that were in their hands; whereupon the three companies blew their trumpets and shattered their pitchers, holding the torches in their left hands and the trumpets in their right to blow them, and they cried, "For the Lord and for Gideon!" Then all the camp cried out and fled and the camp fled as far as Bethshittah in the direction of Zererah, as far as the edge of Abel–meholah, near Tabbath. Israelites were mustered from Naphtali, Asher, and all Manasseh to pursue Midian; and Gideon sent messengers all through the highlands of Ephraim, saying, "Come down against Midian, and seize the streams against them as far as Bethbarah, and also the Jordan."

When Gideon reached the Jordan, and crossed it, with the 300 men who accompanied him, they became exhausted in their pursuit. So he said to the men of Succoth, "Pray give some loaves of bread to my followers because they are exhausted in my pursuit of Zebah and Zalmunna, the kings of Midian."

But the officials of Succoth said, "Are the persons of Zebah and Zalmunna already in your hands that we should give bread to your host?"

"Then," said Gideon, "when the Lord delivers Zebah and Zalmunna into my hands, I will trample your bodies among desert thorns and briers!"

From there he went up to Penuel, and spoke similarly to them; but the men of Penuel answered him as the men of Succoth had. So he said also to the men of Penuel, "When I come back in triumph, I will tear down this tower."

Now Zebah and Zalmunna were at Karkor, and their army with them, about 15,000 men, all that remained of the Kedemite army, since the fallen numbered 120,000 swordsmen. Gideon went up the caravan route, east of Nobah and Jogbehah, and attacked the camp as it lay off its guard. Zebah and Zalmunna fled, but he pursued them and captured Midian's two kings, Zebah and Zalmunna, and struck panic into the whole army. Then Gideon, the son of Joash, returned from the battle at the slope of Heres. He captured a youth belonging to Succoth, and questioned him, so that he wrote down for him a list of the seventy-seven officials and elders of Succoth. Coming to the men of Succoth, he said, "Here are Zebah and Zalmunna, concerning whom you taunted me, saying, 'Are the persons of Zebah and Zalmunna already in your hands that we should give bread to your exhausted men?'" Then he took the elders of the city along with desert thorns and briers, and he trampled the men of Succoth into them. Also the tower of Penuel he tore down, and slew the men of the city. Then he said to Zebah and Zalmunna, "Where are the men whom you slew at Tabor?"

"They were like yourself," said they, "just like the sons of a king in stature."

"They were my brothers," said he, "the sons of my mother. As the Lord lives, if you had let them live, I would not be slaying you."

Then the Israelites said to Gideon, "Rule over us, you, then your son, and then your grandson; for you have saved us from the power of Midian."

But Gideon said to them, "I will not rule over you, nor shall my son rule over you, since the Lord rules over you."

Thus were the Midianites brought into subjection to the Israelites, so that they never raised their heads again; and the land enjoyed security for forty years, during the lifetime of Gideon.

## DAVID

The greatest of the wars in the Trans-Jordan region was the war between the Israelites and the Philistines. The Philistines had "three thousand chariots and six thousand horsemen, and people as numerous as the sand by the side of the sea; and they came up, and encamped in Michmash, on the east side of Bethaven. The people hid themselves in caves, in thickets, in rocky crags, in caverns, and in pits. They crossed the fords of the Jordan to the land of Gad and Gilead, but Saul was still in Gilgal, and all the people were ready to desert him."

Saul and the men of Israel were gathered together and encamped in the valley of Elah; and they drew up in line of battle facing the Philistines. The Philistines were stationed on the mountain on one side, and the Israelites were stationed on the mountain on the other side, and the valley was between them. Then there came out a champion from the camp of the Philistines, named Goliath of Gath, whose height was nine feet. He had a helmet of bronze upon his head and he was clad with a coat of mail of bronze scales, whose weight was about 164 pounds. He had greaves of bronze upon his legs and a javelin of bronze across his shoulders. The shaft of his spear was like a weaver's beam, and the head of his iron spear weighed twenty pounds; and his shield bearer went before him. He stood and shouted to the battle line of Israel and said to them, "Why have you come out to draw up the line of battle? Am I not a Philistine and you the servants of Saul? Choose for yourselves a man and let him come down to me. If he is able to fight with me and can kill me, then we will be your servants; but if I overcome him and kill him, then you shall be our servants and serve us. I challenge the ranks of Israel this day," said the Philistine, "give me a man that we may fight together."

When Saul and all Israel heard the words of the Philistine, they were terrified and panic-stricken. Now in the camp of Saul was the son of Jesse, David, who had come to the camp to bring food for his three older brothers and the men of Israel said to him, "Have you seen this man who came up? Surely he comes to taunt Israel."

Then David asked the men standing by him, "What shall be done for the man who overcomes that Philistine and takes away the reproach of Israel? For who is this uncircumcised Philistine, that he should taunt the battlelines of the living God?"

The people replied to him, "Whoever overcomes him, the king will make very rich and will give him his daughter and make his father's house free of taxes in Israel. Thus shall it be done for the man who overcomes him."

When Saul heard the words which David spoke, he ordered that David be brought before him, and David said to Saul, "Let not my Lord's courage fail him; your servant will go and fight with this Philistine."

"You are not able to go against this Philistine to fight with him," said Saul to David, "for you are but a youth and he has been a warrior all his life."

But David said to Saul, "Your servant has been a shepherd with his father's flock; and when a lion or a bear would come and take a sheep out of the flock, I would go out after him and attack him and deliver it from his mouth; and if he rose up against me, I would seize him by his beard and wound him and kill him. Your servant has slain both lion and bear; and this uncircumcised Philistine shall be as one of them, since he has taunted the battlelines of the living God. The Lord who delivered me from the paw of the lion, and from the paw of the bear, will deliver me from the hand of this Philistine," said David.

So Saul said to David, "Go, and may the Lord be with you."

Saul clothed David with his garments and put a helmet of bronze on his head and equipped him with a coat of mail. He also girded David with his sword over his outer garments; and David struggled to move, for he was not used to them.

"I cannot go to battle in these, for I am not used to them," said David to Saul. So David put them off him. But he took his stick in his hand, and chose five smooth stones out of the brook and put them in his bag, and with his sling in his hand he advanced toward the Philistine. The Philistine approached David cautiously, having the bearer of his shield directly in front of him, but when the Philistine saw David, he scorned him; for David was youthful and ruddy, and of attractive appearance.

"Am I a dog that you come to me with sticks?" said the Philistine to David. The Philistine also cursed David by his gods; and the Philistine said to David, "Come to me and I will give your flesh to the birds of the air and to the beasts of the field."

Then David said to the Philistine, "You come to me with a sword and a spear and a javelin, but I come to you in the name of the Lord of hosts, the God of the battlelines of Israel whom you have taunted. This day the Lord will deliver you into my hand, that I may slay you and sever your head from your body; and I will this day give your dead body and the dead of the camp of the Philistines to the birds of the air and to the wild beasts of the earth, that all the earth may know that there is a God in Israel, and that all this assembly may know that not with sword and spear does the Lord deliver, for the battle is the Lord's and he will give you into our hands."

Now when the Philistine arose and came and drew near to meet David, David also hastened and ran toward the line to meet the Philistine. David put his hand in his bag and took from it a stone and slung it and it struck the Philistine on his forehead; and the stone sank into his forehead, so that he fell on his face to the earth. So David overpowered the Philistine with a sling and a stone, and he struck the Philistine, and slew him, although there was no sword in David's hand. Then David ran and stood over the Philistine, and took his sword, and drew it out of its sheath, and slew him, and cut off his head with it Now when the Philistines saw that their champion was dead, they fled; and the men of Israel and Judah arose and raised a shout and pursued the Philistines to the entrance to Gath and the gates of Ekron, so that the wounded of the Philistines fell down all the way from Shaaraim to Gath and Ekron. When the Israelites returned from pursuing the Philistines, they plundered their camp, but David took the head of the Philistine and brought it to Jerusalem; and he put his armor in his tent.

After David took Jerusalem, he made it the center from which he conducted his wars against the Philistines, the Edomites, the Ammonites, and the Moabites, the neighbors of Judah and Israel. After he had subdued them, he secured an advance base to the north at Succoth and attacked and defeated the Aramaeans. The history of his reign is a history of almost continuous warfare, which in the end led to a unified kingdom stretching from the Euphrates to the Egyptian border.

David's army had a core of veterans, a levy of Israel, and foreign mercenaries. Behind his army was a militia divided into twelve divisions (of 24,000 each), drawn from all the tribes; each division had to serve for one month on a regular rotation. His son Solomon introduced the chariot to the Israeli army and made it the principal force of his army, a force of perhaps 1,400 chariots and 4,000 horses. Thus he created a professional standing army. After Solomon's death the unified kingdom split into two, the kingdoms of Israel and Judah.

## Map 6: Kingdom of David

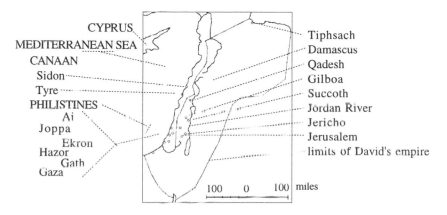

# Map 7: Assyrian Empire

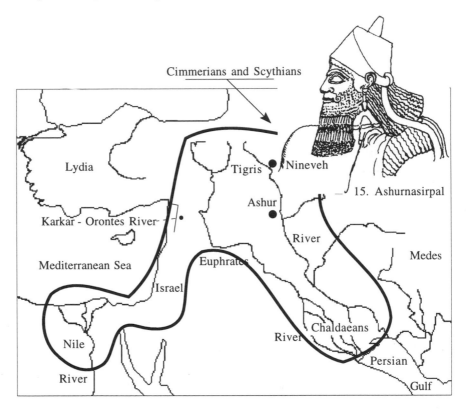

Cimmerians and Scythians

Lydia

Tigris  Nineveh

15. Ashurnasirpal

Ashur

Karkar - Orontes River

River

Mediterranean Sea

Medes

Euphrates

Israel

Chaldaeans

Nile

River

Persian

River

Gulf

## 16. Assyrians in Chariot

# 7

# The Assyrians

## *The Ultimate Army, The Ultimate Terror*

The Assyrian king, like other Mesopotamian kings, was expected to glorify the god of the Assyrians—Ashur—by conquering for him as much territory as he could and by bringing back to his temple (and his kingdom) as much loot as he could. In the 300 years of the ninth, eighth, and seventh centuries, the Assyrian kings could pride themselves on how much they had pleased Ashur—they were the supreme power of the Near East.

The Assyrians rose to power because others had fallen. So long as Egypt, the Hittites, the Kassites, Mitanni, were strong, they were weak, a march state (that is, a state, like Macedonia, which lies along the lines of communication between major powers) constantly embroiled in others' wars. At the beginning of the ninth century, as their neighbors grew weaker, they were able to close off the mountain passes that led into their heartland, their agricultural center, and they began to prosper; as they grew stronger they turned from defense to attack.

Each spring after the crops were in the ground, the kings called up the army. They patrolled the borders of the kingdom and raided those who in the past had raided them. They forced their neighbors to submit and to swear an oath by Ashur and the other Assyrian gods, to submit to the Assyrians, to obey, and to pay tribute. Those who forswore their oath brought down the wrath of Ashur himself and the Assyrian army. Those who refused to swear were defeated and plundered. These first wars combined elements of self-defense, crusade, and brigandry, but by the middle of the ninth century the Assyrians had become the preeminent power in the Near East and their goals shifted from self-defense to aggrandizement: they considered the world their private hunting ground and they transformed their annual campaigns into an immensely profitable enterprise.

The Assyrian king Ashurnasirpal in one campaign in one small district acquired 40 chariots with men and horses, 460 horses broken to the yoke, 120 pounds of silver, 120 pounds of gold, 6,000 pounds of lead, 6,000 pounds of copper, 18,000 pounds of iron, 1,000 vessels of copper, 2,000 pans of copper, assorted bowls and cauldrons of copper, 1,000 brightly colored garments of wool and linen, assorted wooden tables and couches made of ivory and overlaid with gold from the ruler's palace, 2,000 head of cattle, 5,000 sheep, 15,000 slaves, assorted daughters of noblemen with dowries, and the ruler's sister. The ruler's successor was required to pay an annual tribute of 1,000 sheep, 2,000 bushels of grain, 2 pounds of gold, and 26 pounds of silver. In the same campaign Ashurnasirpal attacked five countries and nine major cities and wrote of one typical campaign against a city of "rebels," "Ashur spread terror among them. The leaders and prominent men of the city came to the king before the siege operations even began and begged for their lives. They threw themselves at my feet and said, 'Do what you will with us, kill us or let us live, whatever you want.'

"I took the city by assault and I skinned alive all the leaders of the rebels and I built a pillar which I covered with their skin. Some of them I walled up, some I impaled on the pillar, and others I tied to stakes around the pillar. Some royal officers had rebelled and I dismembered them.

"I burned many captives alive and many I took alive. I cut off their noses, their ears, and their fingers; I put out their eyes. I made one heap of the living and another of heads, and I hung their heads from tree branches around the city. I burned the young men and women alive.

"I bricked up twenty men in a wall of the palace alive. All the other survivors I left to die of thirst in the desert."

Ashurnasirpal was a "good" Assyrian king. As well as a conqueror, he was a hunter, a scholar (his specialty was botany), and a builder. In 879 B.C. he celebrated the dedication of the palace he built in Nimrud by a feast lasting ten days and serving 69,574 guests.

The Assyrian king, Shalmaneser III, reigned for thirty-five years (858–824). During his thirty-five years, he conducted thirty-one campaigns. In one campaign he attempted to subdue the Medes and the Persians, but he only succeeded in forcing the two tribes into cooperation with each other. In another campaign he put Babylon under his "protection" and he advanced into Syria, where at the battle of Karkar (853 B.C.) he defeated a combined army of Israelites, Aramaeans, and Phoenicians with a force of 3,900 chariots, 1,000 cavalry, 50,000 infantry, and 1,000 camels.

Shalmaneser III said of the battle of Karkar, "I killed 14,000 enemy soldiers with the sword. The battlefield was so small that their bodies did not have room to fall and the whole of the countryside became their cemetery. Their bodies made a bridge over the Orontes River."

His success created two problems. First, the Assyrians had campaigned farther and farther afield—Shalmaneser received tribute from places as far away as Phoenicia, Palestine, and Samaria (the capital of the Israelites)—until they ran up against the kingdoms of Media, Elam, and Egypt. They had not worked out a system to supply and move their army (which could march twenty miles a day), to defend their conquests from the major powers, and to ensure the flow of annual tribute. Secondly, the king's success had profited only the king (and Ashur), and the nobles wanted their share and more independence. Civil disturbances between the court and the nobles broke out in the reign of the boy-king, Adad-nirari III (810–783), whose regent was his mother, Sammuramat. During her regency—and the period of civil unrest—the Medes and Persians consolidated their hold on the Iranian plateau.

Tiglath-pileser III (king from 744–727) put an end to the civil disturbances—"I smashed my enemies like pots"—and he reorganized the kingdom, the army, and the empire. He divided the empire into provinces, each with a governor or an overseer. The governor was required to maintain "store–cities" (where the Assyrian king could marshall and supply his forces), he was required to ensure the collection of tribute, and he was required to keep the king informed on the state of his province by a constant interchange of messages. The army provided the administration and maintained communications between the "provinces" and the king.

The Assyrians ruled by terror, they created a legacy of hatred, they ravaged the Near East, and they gave nothing in return, not their language nor their culture, not peace, only a kind of terrorized security (which may have benefited some Aramaean merchants and the Phoenicians), but hated as they were, still no one could match the Assyrian army. The Assyrian army was the largest in the Near East; perhaps, if fully mobilized, it could muster as many as 200,000 Assyrians, and, after Tiglath-pileser instituted the practice of drafting from the provinces, the Assyrians could call upon a total of 1,000,000 men; Tiglath-pileser assigned the provincial levies to areas far from home, so that one province would keep another province in line and thus solve the basic problem of empire, how the lesser number (of Assyrians) could rule the greater number (of subjects). He also used mass transportation as a means to break his subjects' will—in two years (742–741) he transported 30,000 Syrians to the Zagros mountains and 18,000 Aramaeans from the Tigris to Syria. In another year he transported 154,000 people. The Assyrian kings also hired mercenaries, replaced the annual call up of militia with a standing army, and organized their kingdom to ensure a sufficient agricultural base to support the elite units—the chariot corps and the light and heavy cavalry—on a permanent basis.

The army was organized into "army groups" of 20,000 men, "armies" of 10,000 (which would have their own standards and names), "divisions" of 1,000, "battalions" of 200, "companies" of 100, "platoons" of 50, and "squads" of 10 men. Chariot units were organized around a basic unit of 50. The first Assyrian chariots were pulled by teams of two horses, had a crew of two men, and had tire rims of iron with studs for better traction, but in time the chariots became heavier as more armor and a third man were added.

The Assyrians were the first to organize regular cavalry units. Their cavalry and their chariots formed the heart of the Assyrian army and required a reliable and steady supply of horses. A bureaucracy was created to keep track of the number, condition, and location of horses. The supply of horses was one of the chief responsibilities of the governors and one of the objectives of Assyrian aggression—they made regular raids into Media to rustle horses.

The principal personal weapon was the bow. The archer was protected by a shield-bearing companion. In siege warfare the archers tried to clear the walls of the city while other soldiers built a ramp up to the city, positioned battering rams, undermined the walls, or tried to surmount the walls by an assault with siege ladders. The siege of a large city could last as long as a year, but once the Assyrians arrived, only the luckiest of chances could save the victim.

In the reign of Sargon II, 721–705, the kingdom of Elam won a victory over the Assyrians at Babylon. The Egyptians, who, as the Assyrians came closer to their borders, had become more afraid of them, tried to create a coalition against them before it was too late. The Israelites thought they saw their chance of independence in the defeat of Sargon and the support of Egypt and they refused to pay the required tribute to the Assyrian king. The Israelite prophets predicted doom for their own people, "They shall fall by the sword, their infants shall be dashed in pieces, and their pregnant women ripped open."

Sure enough the Assyrians laid siege to Samaria about 722 and took it. The Assyrian king, Sargon II, wrote in his annals of that year that he took 27,290 slaves and that he resettled Israel with Mesopotamians. He transported ten tribes of Israelites to other parts of his empire—the ten tribes of Israel disappear from history—and two tribes were left in the kingdom of Judah, the tribes of Judah and Benjamin. Under Sargon's successor the Egyptian king convinced the king of Judah, Hezekiah, to rebel. The Assyrian king, Sennacherib, came with his army and he sent a message to Hezekiah.

"Tell Hezekiah this: The great king, the king of Assyria, says to him, 'What trust is this you have? Do you believe that you can rely upon a spoken word to give you strength in war? Who is this in whom you have reposed so much trust that you would rebel against me? You have reposed your trust in this broken reed, Egypt, which pierces the hand that rests upon it. This is what the pharaoh, king of Egypt, is to those who trust him.'"

Sennacherib reported in his annals that "Hezekiah the Judean did not submit. I took forty-six of his fortified cities, forts, and an uncountable number of villages by assault and siege. I transported 200,150 people. Hezekiah himself I shut up in Jerusalem, his capital, like a bird in a cage."

Jerusalem itself was saved: "That night the angel of the Lord struck down 185,000 in the Assyrian camp. And when scouts went out early in the morning, the Assyrians were all dead. And Sennacherib, king of Assyria, departed, and went to dwell at Nineveh."

Nonetheless, the kingdom of Judah became a vassal of Assyria.

Sennacherib (704–681), by and large, delegated the campaigning to his generals. His successor, Esarhaddon (680–669), conquered Egypt; the conquest was a logical reponse to Egyptian meddling in Palestine and Syria, but the attempt to hold Egypt against constant rebellion drained the manpower of the empire, and then, at the worst possible time, the Scythians and Cimmerians (wild, nomadic horsemen of the steppes) swept down through the empire on a massive raid in search of booty. The Assyrians were thrown into confusion, they could not stop the raid, and they lost their reputation for invincibility; worst, they had to divert their forces away from their vassal states on the Iranian plateau, the Medes and Persians, and the Medes and the Persians now became independent. The independence of the Medes and Persians cut off the Assyrians' best source of horses.

Ashurbanipal (668–627) was the last great king of the Assyrians. He was beset with constant rebellions, first, in Egypt (in reponse to which he sacked Thebes), then in Phoenicia, and again in Egypt where the new vassal king, Psammetichus I, heeded an oracle that "bronze men would come from the sea" to aid Egypt, enlisted Ionian and Carian mercenaries wearing bronze armor, and rebelled. Psammetichus was joined in the rebellion by Ashurbanipal's brother, Shamash-shum-ukin, the viceroy of Babylon.

For three years Ashurbanipal fought a coalition of Phoenicians, Philistines, Judaeans, Arabs, Chaldaeans (Babylonians), Elamites, Lydians, and Egyptians. In the end, he forced Shamash-shum-ukin to immolate himself, he pursued the Arabs into the desert "where dwells thirst that dries the throat and no birds fly in the sky," he chained a rebel by his jaw to the city gate, he ravaged the country of Elam (which had been the last check on the expansion of the Medes and Persians), he enslaved the Phoenicians (they lost their markets, and control of the sea, to the independent Ionian Greeks), and he defeated the Egyptians. Ashurbanipal was triumphant, a great king, a king who had been taught "the secrets of reading and writing, the signs of heaven and earth. I studied the sky with the oil divination masters; I worked out the intricate and obscure problems of division and multiplication. I have mastered the obscure scripts of Sumer and Akkad and I have read with pleasure the tablets written before the flood.

"Every day I mounted my horse and I loved to ride. I would ride up to my hunting lodge. I drew the bow, I fired the arrow. I threw heavy lances as though they were javelins. I took the post of driver in the chariot and I made the chariot go. I practiced with the light shield and the heavy shield of a heavy-armed archer.

"At the same time I learned courtesy and the ways of a king. I stood by my father and I gave orders to the nobles."

Ashurbanipal was a great king. He could not know that he would be Assyria's last great king.

## 17. Assyrian Cavalry Pursuing Camel Riders

## Map 8: The Fall of Assyria

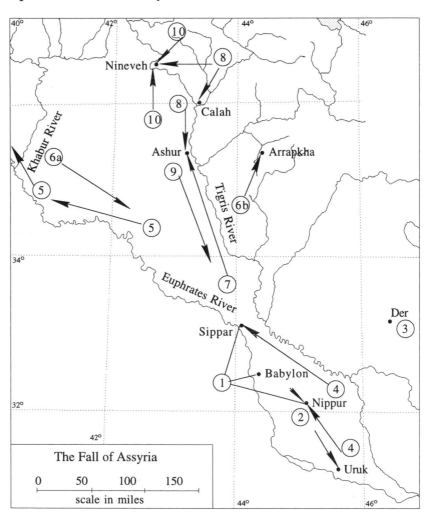

The Fall of Assyria

0    50    100    150

scale in miles

# 8

# The Medes and Chaldaeans
## *The Ultimate Result of Terror*

Ashurbanipal had been an effective king, but apparently towards the end of his life (627) he lost his grip.

"Why have sickness, ill-health, misery and misfortune befallen me? Hatreds in the land and dissension in my family remain with me. Disturbing scandals continually oppress me. Misery of mind and of flesh bear me down. I spend my days crying out, 'Oh!' and 'Alas!'"

The end of the empire was just thirty years away.

Ashurbanipal was survived by an older son who expected to be king and a younger son, still a boy, whom the chief eunuch (for his own reasons) put on the throne. To the Assyrians, as to most of those who hold power, the world appeared immutable—the Assyrians had ruled past living memory under the overlordship of the god Ashur and they expected that they would continue to rule. So long as they believed in Ashur and destiny rather than in the primacy of human decision and action they were vulnerable. They made themselves particularly vulnerable because they took sides in the dynastic dispute between the older and the younger son. East and west their provinces and vassals broke away, Phoenicia, Judah, Babylon, and Elam.

Meanwhile, the Medes recovered from twin disasters—in 653 Phraortes, king of the Medes, had attacked Assyria and had been defeated and killed, and then the Scythians overran Media and the kingdom fragmented. The new king of the Medes, Cyaxares (as we know him from the Greek form of his name, Uvarkhshatra) reunified his kingdom.

In 627, the year Ashurbanipal died, the Chaldaeans (a desert people), led by their ruler, Nabopolassar, fought a battle throughout one whole day with the Assyrians in the city of Babylon and then fought a second battle that established Nabopolassar's claim to be king of Babylonia (626).

The Chaldaean king and the Median king eventually joined together to destroy Assyria. Their war, the war that brought Assyria down, has to rank as one of the greatest and most significant wars in human history, ten years long, marked by strategic reach and great battles, the coordination of allies ill-known to each other at the beginning of the war, brilliant direction, balanced victories and defeats, and yet known to us only in the barest outline, this war which wiped Assyria off the face of the earth.

First (1—*the numbers refer to the map*) Nabopolassar was recognized as king in Sippar, Babylon, and Nippur. Then (2) the Assyrians' counterattack took Nippur and held it until 616. Nabopolassar retreated to Uruk (which had a sizeable pro-Assyrian contingent), fought a battle there, and held on to that city. The Assyrian army encamped near Babylon and the Assyrian king had free access to Babylon. As the Assyrians were campaigning against Nabopolassar (3) there was a rebellion at Der. The young king led the army himself against (apparently) the chief eunuch who had put him on the throne. The eunuch's rebellion was put down. At the end of the rebellion another son of Ashurbanipal fought his way to the throne "against the enemies of Assyria."

By 623 (4) the older son of Ashurbanipal had been proclaimed king of Assyria. Nabopolassar and the Assyrians fought over Uruk (and control of the lands south of Babylonia) and Nippur, both cities coming under siege. By 620 Nabopolassar had gained control of Sippar (the entry into Babylonia). Nabopolassar besieged Nippur (620–617). The siege produced starvation and inflation. People sold their children to acquire food. Uruk changed hands several times. In 616 Nabopolassar (5) began an assault on Assyria itself (to relieve Assyrian pressure on southern Babylonia). He campaigned up the Euphrates River and defeated an Assyrian army at Gablini and continued as far as the river Balikh. This relieved pressure on Babylonia and allowed Uruk to be secured, but the Egyptians (6) now considered Nabopolassar to be a greater threat than the Assyrian king and they joined in an alliance with the Assyrians. An allied Egyptian–Assyrian army pursued the retreating Babylonians, attempted to cut them off at Gablini, failed, and fought a battle later in the year at Arrapcha (Kirkuk). The Babylonians won again and Nabopolassar secured the whole of Babylonia. (Meanwhile the Medes had supplanted Elam and gained exclusive control of the Iranian plateau.)

In 615 Nabopolassar (7) made an assault on Ashur itself. He failed to capture it and retreated down the Tigris River to the fort Tikrit. As Tikrit gave access to Ashur, the two armies struggled for control of it for ten days, and in the end Nabopolassar held on to the fort. In 614 the Medes (8) attacked Nineveh and Calah and captured the town of Tarbisu (just north of Nineveh). The Medes took and sacked Ashur—"The Mede made an attack upon the town and he destroyed the city wall. He inflicted a terrible massacre upon the greater part of the people, plundering the city and carrying off prisoners." Nabopolassar arrived just too late to join in the battle, but over the ruins of Ashur ("turned into a garbage dump") Nabopolassar and Cyaxares made an alliance, and the son of Nabopolassar, Nebuchadrezzar, married the daughter of Cyaxares, Amytis.

In 613, despite the reverses of 614, the Assyrians (9) remained confident of ultimate victory. They assigned Scythian allies to hold the Medes in check while the king in person led an invasion of Babylonia. In 612 the Medes, the Babylonians, and the erstwhile Assyrian allies, the Scythians, attacked Nineveh

(10). After three months the allies broke through the walls (perhaps by destroying the dams which diverted the River Khosr around the walls through moats) and sacked the city. "They made a strong attack against the city and in the month of July the city was captured. On that day the Assyrian king was killed."

The fortified city Calah was easily taken as the Assyrians had dismantled its fortifications for repair and had not finished the repairs by the time of the final assault in 612.

The allies hunted down refugees. Their aim was to exterminate the Assyrian people. No one missed the Assyrians much and throughout the Near Ancient people rejoiced. Nahum records:

"Woe to the city, bloody throughout, full of lies and booty. The crack of the whip and the noise of the rumbling wheel, and the galloping horse and the jolting chariot; the charging horseman and the flashing sword, and the glittering spear and a multitude slain, and a mass of bodies, and no end to the corpses. They stumble over the corpses.

"Your shepherds slumber, O King of Assyria; your nobles sleep. Your people are scattered upon the hilltops, with none to gather them. There is no healing for your wound. Your hurt is incurable. Everyone who shall hear the news about you, will clap his hands over you, for against whom has not your malice continually gone forth?"

The Assyrians dominated the Near East for almost 300 years. As long as they had stability in the rule and a professional citizen core to their army, they were invincible. Nonetheless, the underlying philosophy of the Assyrians, their exclusivity, the requirements of their god Ashur, the use of terror—which works only so long as the subjects have no alternative—and demands without benefits, made everyone an enemy of the Assyrians.

The victors in the war cooperated after the war: the Medes had no interest in taking over the empire of the Assyrians, and they guaranteed the Chaldaeans a secure eastern border and a free hand to reestablish the Assyrian Empire under Chaldaean rule. The Chaldaeans had only one rival: the Egyptians. The Egyptians took advantage of the defeat of Assyria to invade Judah—they fought a battle with the Judaeans, defeated them, and killed their king—and then they advanced to the north and tried to prevent the Chaldaeans from crossing the Euphrates.

Nabopolassar took his son Nebuchadrezzar ("May the god let him succeed me") as equal partner. Nabopolassar administered Babylon and Nebuchadrezzar led the army into Syria to fight the Egyptians; he met them at the Battle of Karkemish in 605 B.C. The Egyptians had hired Greek mercenaries, but they were not enough to defeat the Chaldaeans. (Greek and Carian mercenaries fought both for the Egyptians and for the Chaldaeans—perhaps even against the Assyrians and certainly in the later wars—"you are home safe, my brother, from a land at the ends of the earth and you have your sword, its hilt of gold and ivory, and with that sword you did a mighty deed: you killed a fighting man but three inches short of a hundred inches tall.") Nebuchadrezzar cut off the Egyptian line of retreat, forced them to battle, and did not allow "one of them to escape to his own land." At the moment of victory, however, he heard that his father had died; Nebuchadrezzar rode to Babylon. where within two weeks he was firmly established on the throne.

The Chaldaeans and the Egyptians fought a series of campaigns for the control of the eastern seaboard. In 601 B.C. they fought a full-scale battle on the borders of Egypt which led to massive destruction on both sides. The Chaldaeans had to use the next year to rebuild their forces. Jehoiakim, the king of Judah, believed that the Egyptians had won the battle and in the winter of 598–597 refused to pay tribute to the Chaldaeans. On the sixteenth of March 597 Nebuchadrezzar captured Jerusalem. He had 3,000 Jews deported to Mesopotamia in an attempt to break the will of the Judaeans. The next king of Judah, Zedekiah, was caught in an impossible situation between Egypt and Babylon; each power demanded his fealty, or punishment would follow. Zedekiah had to choose and he chose the wrong side. In 587 he rebelled from the Chaldaeans, Nebuchadrezzar took Jerusalem, and Zedekiah was captured.

"So they took the king and brought him up to the king of Babylon and they gave judgement upon him and they slew the sons of Zedekiah before his eyes and put out the eyes of Zedekiah and bound him with fetters of brass and carried him off to Babylon."

Nebuchadrezzar's personal account says: "I uprooted the enemy everywhere and made that country happy. I brought all the refugees back to their villages. I gave the whole of Lebanon peace and security."

While the Chaldaeans had been strengthening their hold on the Fertile Crescent, the Medes, under their king Cyaxares, had been expanding north into Anatolia. There they encountered the kingdom of Lydia and the king of Lydia, Alyattes. Alyattes had already brought the Greeks of Asia Minor under his control, and he used them extensively as advisers and in his army as soldiers and engineers.

The Lydian and Median army faced each other, ready for battle, on 28 May 585 (the first exactly dated event in Western history). Before the two sides could actually engage in battle, there was an eclipse of the sun. (The eclipse is famous also because it marks the beginning of Western science—Thales, a man of mixed Greek and Carian descent from the city of Miletus, had travelled through the Near East, to Egypt, and perhaps to Babylon, and he had studied their astronomical records. He was able to predict the eclipse and thereby prove that eclipses were regular heavenly events, not a supernatural warning of disaster.) The eclipse convinced both sides to submit to the arbitration of the Chaldaean king, Nebuchadrezzar. Nebuchadrezzar established the Halys River as the boundary between the two powers.

In 562 Nebuchadrezzar died. He had done his duty as king of the Chaldaeans. He had brought the former empire of the Assyrians under Chaldaean control and enlarged it. He had ensured a stable succession—his son succeeded without turmoil—but he had a son who was not competent to be king. Within two years the son was assassinated and different factions fought for the throne, until in 556 Nabonidus became king.

Nabonidus (556–539) had a special reverence for the goddess his mother worshipped, the goddess of the moon, Sin, and his greatest ambition was to repair a shrine of Sin under Median control. To repair the shrine would require war against the Medes and Persians; they called him "insane, an enemy of Marduk, and a coward." He conducted several successful campaigns in Syria and then for reasons that are obscure he withdrew himself from Babylon in a self-imposed exile of ten years. During this period Cyrus became king of the Persians and the Medes, secured most of the Iranian plateau, subjugated Elam, defeated Lydia, and finally in 529 seized Babylon in a campaign so quick and so smooth that the chronicles (the daily record of events) were not interrupted, and some of the inhabitants did not find out for three days that the city had changed masters.

## Map 9: The Persian Empire

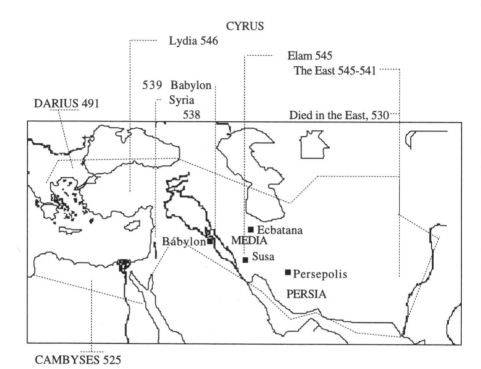

CYRUS

Lydia 546

Elam 545

The East 545-541

539  Babylon

Syria

538

DARIUS 491

Died in the East, 530

■ Ecbatana

Babylon ■  MEDIA

■ Susa

■ Persepolis

PERSIA

CAMBYSES 525

## 18. Assyrian Cavalryman

# 9

# The Persians
## *Justice and Genius Triumphant*

Cyrus, the man who became king and created the Persian empire, told a story of his rise to power that is reminiscent of the story told by Sargon the Akkadian. Astyages, king of the Medes (585–550), dreamed one night that his daughter flooded the world with her urine. The king married her off to a Persian noble to get rid of her. (Medes and Persians were closely related. They spoke the same language. Persians were members of court, they ruled their own country, they intermarried with the Medes at the highest levels, and they were intimates of the king, but the royal family was Median.) In the first year of her marriage the king dreamed that a vine sprang from her womb and encircled the world, and so he brought his daughter to the palace and gave her newborn son to his vizier, Harpagus, to kill. Harpagus was afraid that someday the king would regret this decision and punish the agent, so he gave the child to a herdsman. The herdsman's wife had just had a stillborn baby, she substituted her dead son for the baby prince, and she raised the boy as her own. When the boy was ten, he was playing a game called "king" with some young aristocrats; one of the young aristocrats refused to obey orders and Cyrus beat him up. King Astyages summoned Cyrus to court to be punished, but instead he recognized Cyrus as his grandson. The king soon learned the truth, but he told Harpagus that, in fact, he was grateful because the crime had weighed on his conscience and to show his gratitude he invited Harpagus to a feast. After Harpagus had eaten, Astyages gave him a basket with the leftovers—the head, hands, and feet of his son.

Whatever the truth of the story may be, Cyrus was raised at the court and when he came of age he was sent to rule Persia (559 B.C.). Once in Persia he used his personal clan, the Achaemenids, to unite the Persians against Astyages. Cyrus found an ally in Nabonidus, the king of Babylon, who had had a dream in which the great god of the Babylonians, Marduk, said to him, "The gods will cause Cyrus, the Median king's little slave, to advance against him with his little army. He will subdue the Medes."

Astyages sent Harpagus with an army to put down the Persian insurrection, but Harpagus brought his army over to Cyrus. When Astyages led a second army himself against the Persians, his army mutinied, seized the king, and handed him over to Cyrus. Cyrus became king of the Medes and the Persians and Media became the first province (satrapy) of Persia.

The army Cyrus commanded depended on its foot soldiers formed in a double line of archer and lancer (or swordsman): the archer would fix his leather-and-osier shield in the ground in front of him and shoot arrows at the enemy, while the lancer offered protection should the enemy get too close. The *Iliad* describes just such a duo—"Teucer, having strung his recurved bow, stood behind the shield of Ajax. While Ajax shifted his shield around, Teucer would choose a target, aim his bow and fire at some one in the host. Then as that one fell, breathing out his life, Teucer would dash back again, like a child running to its mother, and Ajax would protect him with the flashing shield."

The Persian army was organized (like the Assyria army) into "regiments" of 1,000 men further divided into hundreds and tens. The ten would form in file, its leader armed with a lance, the rest, depending on tactical circumstances with bows or swords or both. The shields could be put in front as a sort of wall behind which all could fire their arrows. A second-in-command would close the file.

Ten regiments made a division of 10,000. The "Immortal" division was the king's personal unit and within the unit one regiment of 1,000 was formed from the nobility and was the king's personal guard. Cyrus drew his cavalry from the Medes, then famous for their horses as well as their horsemen, but he was determined to create a Persian cavalry as good as the Median. To that end the Persians changed their national dress to trousers and short shirt and Cyrus changed the whole ethos of the nobility: they were to ride everywhere and to be ashamed to be seen walking.

Cyrus, by virtue of past Median actions, now claimed Assyria, but for a time he had to put the claim in abeyance, because Croesus, the king of Lydia, took advantage of the Median civil war to cross the Halys River and seize part of the Median empire. Croesus had already formed alliances with the Egyptians, with the king of Babylon (behind Cyrus's back), and with the Spartans on the Greek mainland, and he believed that he had won the support of Apollo and the oracle at Delphi. He had a first-rate army composed of Ionian heavy infantry and Lydian cavalry, which was easily the equal of the Persian cavalry. For his part Cyrus tried to induce the Ionians to revolt, but he persuaded the citizens of only one city, Miletus.

In 547 Cyrus made a circuit through the Zagros mountains, Assyria, and North Syria, to test the forces of Lydia. He found that they were strong enough to prevent his breaking into Lydia by force and so, as winter approached, he withdrew. Croesus dismissed his levies and his allies until the spring campaigning season. Cyrus waited until the allies had departed and then launched a swift attack. He caught the Lydians by surprise. Croesus brought up the Lydian cavalry, but Cyrus sent a camel corps against them, and the Lydian horses were thrown into disarray by the sight and smell of the camels. The Lydians dismounted and fought on foot but they were forced back into their capital city. Croesus sent out a call for help to all his allies, but before they could respond, Cyrus's troops scaled the walls and took the city.

Cyrus appointed a Lydian as civil administrator of the conquered country—Cyrus established Persian policy, to build an accord within the empire by using local leaders wherever possible—but the Lydian used his treasury to hire mercenaries from Ionia, and with the mercenaries he attacked the Persian satrap. Cyrus sent an army and published an order that any man taken armed would be sold into slavery. The Lydian army melted away, the rebellion was put down, and the Persians began the subjugation of Ionia, the major source of the mercenaries. The conquered Greek cities were placed under tyrants, then the usual form of Greek government and one which made sense to the Persians. From the Persian point of view, the subjugation was quickly accomplished through a combination of bribery and force. The matter was not important enough for Cyrus to conduct operations in person.

Babylonia was quite another matter. Inflation was out of control, large numbers of citizens were being drafted, graft was widespread, and the irrigation system broke down and caused a famine, while Nabonidus, the king, was involved in some sort of religious reform. A large number of Babylonians saw Cyrus as their only hope. Cyrus's entree into Babylon came through Elam. The Persians respected the Elamites, from whom they had learned of Mesopotamian culture and civilization, and the Persians and the Elamites were much alike. The Babylonian governor of Elam brought Elam over to Cyrus and Cyrus made Elam a dependency of Persia.

Elamite troops attacked Erech in south Mesopotamia and continued to harass Babylon for six years, while Cyrus was subduing the tribes on the eastern borders of the empire, until he had fixed his eastern border on the Jaxartes River and Bactria. Once he had subdued the eastern tribes, he was free to turn on Babylon. In the campaigning season of 540–539 Cyrus launched his attack on Babylonia. The enemy army tried to prevent his crossing a tributary of the Tigris. A Greek engineer had the Persian army dig 360 channels, so that the river was spread out and could be forded. The same engineer had the army divert a river from a city Cyrus wanted to take; the diversion left an easy access to the city.

In 539 Cyrus surprised Babylon and entered it so swiftly that the Babylonian king reentered his city without realizing that it was in Persian hands. Cyrus declared himself king of Babylon, king of Sumer and Akkad, and king of the four quarters, traditional titles harkening back 2,000 years to the days of Sargon the Akkadian, the first world conqueror. He proclaimed that he was the prince of peace. Marduk favored him, gave him victory, and he would restore Marduk and all the other gods. Nabonidus was lampooned—he was insane, stupid, destructive; Nabonidus had mocked Cyrus because he was illiterate, but God sent Cyrus a clear sign.

Cyrus was a good king, and he and the Persians gave the Near East good government, perhaps the best it has ever had. He appointed native satraps, where possible, and he fostered repairs of temples, public buildings, and irrigation systems. Cyrus issued an order that all transported people were to be allowed to return home. In the Old Testament he is a hero.

"Cyrus, king of Persia, says this: The God of the heavens has given me all the kingdoms of the earth, and he has enjoined me to build him a temple in Jerusalem. Whoever there is in Babylon of his people, if he desires to go, his God be with him; let him go to Jerusalem, and there build a temple for the God of Israel, since he is the God who is in Jerusalem. Whoever resides in any place as an alien, let the authorities in that place aid him on his way with money and supplies and pack animals, as well as with voluntary offerings for the temple of God in Jerusalem."

All of Palestine and Syria, including the Phoenicians, pledged their allegiance to Cyrus. The Phoenicians brought him a trustworthy war fleet equal to the Greeks and he formed that whole area along with Babylon into one satrapy named "Across the River [Euphrates]." Cyrus patterned the organization of his empire after the Chaldaean empire (which had been patterned after the Assyrian empire), but he formed provinces (satrapies) much larger than the Assyrian provinces had been and he allowed the governor (satrap) considerably more power. The satrap was a "protector of the kingdom," a kind of monarch surrounded by his own court and administration. He was the commander of the levies of troops in his own satrapy, the supreme judicial authority, and he could pass on the satrapy to his son. Cyrus tried to control the satraps through frequent orders and communications. In time the satrapy system became a threat to the crown, and the king appointed the satrap's secretary, chief financial official, and general in charge of the Persian troops. These men were under the king's direct orders and they reported directly to the king. In addition the "king's eye," a spy or inspector general, inspected the satrap once a year.

After cuneiform signs had been developed for the Persian language, all inscriptions and all documents were written in Persian, Elamite and Akkadian, though Aramaic was the official language. The Persians were aware that they were taking over areas with 2,500 years of history behind them. The people were tired of war and conquest; they had seen everything and they were not impressed by anything. The Persian conquest made so little difference in the Babylonian's daily life that within twelve days of the conquest, Babylonian documents were being dated by the regnal year of Cyrus. Business went on as usual, the banking firms that had been wealthy and successful before the conquest were still wealthy and successful afterwards.

After Cyrus had consolidated his empire, he began preparations to invade Egypt (which had been allied to Lydia), but before he could launch the invasion, he had to complete the subjugation of the border tribes in the east. The campaign was important enough to require the presence of Cyrus himself—perhaps his greatest accomplishment was the unification of the Iranian plateau under one (Persian) king—but in one of a series of battles fought against a tribe kin to the Scythians and ruled by a queen, Cyrus was killed.

His epitaph read: "Here I lie, Cyrus, king of kings."

Cambyses (530–522) was the eldest son of Cyrus and the officially recognized heir to the throne. Cyrus had appointed him his personal representative in charge of Babylon, where he kept the old administrative staff in power, and, when he went east to campaign, he appointed him regent of the kingdom. Cambyses succeeded his father and followed Elamite custom and married his sisters, to keep the blood lines in the family. He had to deal with some unrest within the empire, which he put down, he continued Cyrus's campaigns on the borders, and then he turned his attention to Egypt.

Egypt was the last rival to the power of the Persian empire. The Egyptians had aided the enemies of Persia. They had been allies of the Assyrians and later they had helped the Lydians. Now Cambyses sent a demand to the Egyptian king, Amasis, that he must provide a daughter for Cambyses's harem. Whatever else the Egyptian might have felt about this, he could not do it without acknowledging that he was the vassal of Cambyses, and so he refused.

Amasis was confident that he could defend his kingdom: he had a large contingent of Greek mercenaries and he could depend upon the difficult terrain of the approaches to Egypt; unfortunately, he had also rammed through a program to reduce the power of the priests and they were ready to welcome the Persians. Amasis died before the invasion; his son, Psammetichus III, was left to defend Egypt. He decided to meet the Persians at the Egyptian border (rather than defending the line of the Nile). He had no allies—the Phoenicians remained loyal to the Persians, the Greek islands stayed neutral, the admiral of the Egyptian navy refused to bring the fleet to an engagement, and the commander of the Greek mercenaries deserted to Cambyses. Just about everyone thought that the Persians would win.

Psammetichus's Greek mercenaries proved their loyalty to the king and each other by slitting the throats of their ex-commander's sons over a bowl, mixing the blood with water and wine, and drinking it. The battle was hard fought, no quarter was given by Greek to Greek, and the Persians were victorious. In 525 Memphis was taken and Psammetichus was captured. Cambyses allowed him to live, and if Psammetichus had accepted the situation and had proved his loyalty, eventually he might have been made satrap of Egypt, but the Egyptians hungered even more fiercely than the Greeks for independence.

Cambyses gathered an army to conquer Ethiopia, but he was forced to retreat and he had to hold the border at Elephantine. He established, or reinforced, a Jewish military colony there: the mercenaries had been Egyptianized—they worshipped many gods, one of whom was Yahu. Cambyses, legend had it, was tipped over the edge by his failure in Ethiopia. He went mad, he tried to destroy the gods of Egypt, and he attacked the sacred bull, Apis. Far from madness his attack on the priesthood may simply have reflected his belief that Egyptian resistance was rooted in their religion and that the resistance came from the priesthood, which, consequently, he tried unsuccessfully to limit.

He died in 522, perhaps murdered, and he was followed to the throne by a usurper, Darius, later called Darius the Great. Darius was a follower of the

religion of Zarathustra, who had been born about the middle of the sixth century
in the province where Darius's father was satrap. The sixth century was a time of
religious ferment, as it was a time of political ferment. Zarathustra (or Zoroaster)
asked questions about the origin and the purpose of man. He sought for order in
chaos, and he found the answer in an analogy with the ox. As the ox serves man,
so man serves Ahura-Mazdah. Each seeks a wise master, one who will use the
creature gently and will allow the creature to fulfill its purpose. The arch-enemy
is the Lie and the daevas (other gods). When a man dies, he will come to the
edge of a chasm, and he will start across on a broad way; if he has been a
follower of the truth, he will have the same broad way all the way across, but if
he has lived the Lie, the way will narrow until he is balanced on the edge of a
sword.

Darius worshipped Ahura-Mazdah and he never mentions any other god by
name. He was a monotheist and he attributed his reign to Ahura-Mazdah, his
personal god. "To me," he says, "Ahura-Mazdah was a friend." He attributes to
him all his abilities, riding, shooting, controlling his emotions, and following
the truth. He condemns his opponents, and all evil men, as followers of the Lie,
and chief among the followers of the Lie was the person he overthrew, Bardiya.

Darius's view was almost the view of an ensi, that he had a responsibility to
God to administer the kingdom by God's will, that he was a caretaker, enjoined
by the ethical code of God to create peace and harmony, not to be a proselytizer,
certainly not a crusader for his religion. As king of many diverse peoples and
religions he could not allow any rivalry between Ahura-Mazdah and other gods.
So Darius wrote: "When Ahura-Mazdah saw that this earth was in turmoil, he
bestowed it on me. He made me king. I am king. By the will of Ahura-Mazdah I
restored the earth to its proper state. Much that was evil, I made good. The
satrapies were in chaos, one man killed another. By the will of Ahura-Mazdah I
caused men to refrain from killing. They fear my law so much that the strong
will not harm the weak."

Darius wrote a letter to one of his satraps on behalf of a Greek temple.

"King of Kings, Darius son of Hydaspes, says this to his slave Gadatas: I
have learned that you have not been obedient to all of our ordinances. In that you
have labored in my land, the part across the Euphrates, to plant and cultivate the
land of Asia Minor, I praise your initiative and, because of this, great favor for
you will lie in the house of the king. But, in that you have counted my behest
on behalf of the gods as nothing, if you do not change your ways, I will have
you experience the temper of a king who has been wronged, for you made the
gardeners of the temple of Apollo pay a tax and ordered them to till sacred land,
you, who are ignorant of the attitude of my ancestors towards God."

Technically, however, the follower of Ahura-Mazdah, should never follow
the Lie, but should fight the daevas wherever they may be found. Xerxes, the son
of Darius, went farther than his father: "Within the satrapies there were places
where previously the daevas had been worshipped. By the will of Ahura-Mazdah I
uprooted that cult of the daevas."

Persian rule was mild, based as it was on local custom and justice. The Persians had many times the resources of the Assyrians, they allowed people to maintain their sense of national identity, and they admitted non-Persians into the Persian administration. The Persian kings, if they had looked to the past, no matter how distant, might have concluded that the twin necessities of warfare, organization and command, could be accomplished only by a king, that only a king could raise an army, train it, feed it, move it, and bring it prepared to a battlefield to meet the enemy, that all the mighty nations of the past had been ruled by kings, Thutmose III, Sargon the Great, Shuppiluliumash, David, Tiglath-pileser, and that the Persians themselves had become great only when they evolved from tribal judges to absolute monarchs. Nations that were divided against themselves, like the Sumerians and the Greeks, dissipated their resources fighting amongst themselves. Only a nation ruled by an absolute monarch could marshall the resources to succeed in war.

## Map 10: Sequence Maps of the Greek World

THE ARCHAIC AGE (800-479)

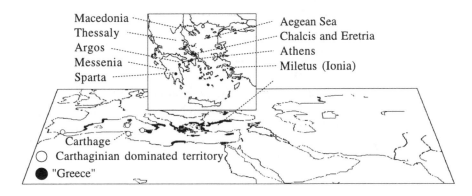

Macedonia
Thessaly
Argos
Messenia
Sparta

Aegean Sea
Chalcis and Eretria
Athens
Miletus (Ionia)

Carthage
○ Carthaginian dominated territory
● "Greece"

THE CLASSICAL AGE (478-323)

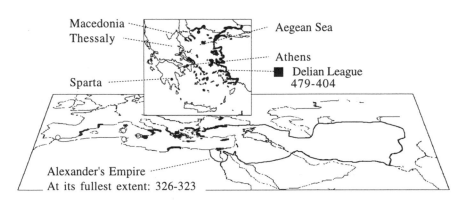

Macedonia
Thessaly

Aegean Sea

Athens
■ Delian League
479-404

Sparta

Alexander's Empire
At its fullest extent: 326-323

THE HELLENISTIC AGE (322-146)

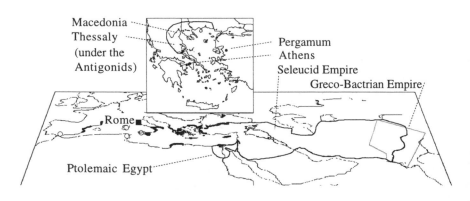

Macedonia
Thessaly
(under the
Antigonids)

Pergamum
Athens
Seleucid Empire
Greco-Bactrian Empire

Rome ■

Ptolemaic Egypt

# Part Two
# The Greeks

A new economic class develops into the dominant unit in the armed forces. This class compels a limited democracy—and in Athens where the oarsmen are dominant, a radical democracy—and assumes the normal role of the aristocracy in war. Even when Greek democracy falls to Macedonian monarchy, the heavy Greek phalanx remains the basic element of battle.

## 19. The Hoplite

## 20. The Panoply

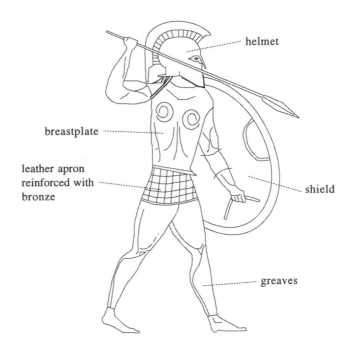

helmet

breastplate

leather apron
reinforced with
bronze

shield

greaves

## 21. The Phalanx

# 10

# The Greek Way of War
## *Warrior Class, Ruling Class*

After massive raids and invasions destroyed Mycenaean civilization, the survivors and the invaders broke into small groups separated from each other by the mountains of Greece. They farmed, or grazed, the plains and sought refuge from pirates, or their own neighbors, on the natural citadels of which Greece abounds. Here and there, their leaders, men who claimed direct descent from the gods, organized themselves and their followers around these places of refuge: they built shrines to their gods on these natural citadels (*polis* in Greek), they met there to settle disputes and to conduct business, and they were the first to risk their lives in the defense of their crops and their flocks. When they fought, they fought in the way of the heroes of the *Iliad*, as individual champions, privately trained, armed, and armored, but, unlike the heroes of the *Iliad*, they learned to cooperate with each other and to accept that they were part of a larger entity, the polis.

They cooperated because their cooperation made the polis a powerful instrument through which they could protect their own interests and dominate their neighbors—as Argos dominated the Argolid, Athens Attica, and Sparta Laconia. Greece soon became a land of separate, independent polises; as their populations grew, the Greeks reacted, as so many other peoples in similar situations had reacted, by ordering their surplus population to find new homes. The movement of Greeks that followed (Greek colonization), with its hundreds of separate military expeditions spread over the eighth and seventh centuries, forms one of history's most massive coordinated undertakings; it consumed greater resources—with greater returns—than any of the wars Greeks fought among themselves and, perhaps, greater than any single war fought in the ancient world.

Each polis— or sometimes a few cooperating polises—dispatched its own expedition. Each expedition was an independent military operation under the sole command of a man—the founder—who was "to ring the town about with a wall and have the houses built, to make shrines for the gods, and divide up the farmland into lots." The polises chose the sites they would colonize under the direction (as they believed) of Apollo of Delphi and under his direction they settled colonies from the coasts of the Black Sea south to North Africa and west to Italy, Sicily, and on to the coasts of Spain.

They sought places such as Odysseus described, "an island, wooded, with innumerable wild goats, where there were no shepherds or farmers and the land had never known the plow. It would bear crops in season and it had fruitful, well–watered meadows by the grey sea, just right for growing vines. There was rich soil for plowing and every season men could reap a harvest. A good harbor made anchor stones and ropes to tie down the stern unnecessary. You could beach your ships and relax until the longings of the sea life and fair winds beckoned you out again. By the harbor was a spring with fresh, cool water."

The colonies were politically independent but culturally, socially, and spiritually linked to the mother city. They shared the same calendar, festivals, and institutions. They sent envoys to the most important festivals of the year, and, in some cases, they sent yearly offerings. In turn, they could call upon their mother city for help, but they seldom had to, because, by and large, Greek settlement was welcomed and the settlers did not have to fight to establish or maintain themselves. A king in Spain offered land to Greek settlers, the Etruscans admired and bought Greek pottery and adopted the Greek alphabet, Scythians in the region of the Black Sea learned the Greek language, married Greek wives, and adopted Greek names.

Usually the Greeks did not have to fight, although they were prepared to do so, because they came by sea and did not have to force their way through populated territory, and because they settled on land the indigenous population did not use. Sometimes, however, a colony did provoke its neighbors. The Phocaean colony at Alalia committed such blatant acts of piracy "that the Carthaginians and Etruscans each provided sixty ships to a united fleet and fought the Phocaeans (with sixty ships) in the Sardinian sea. The Phocaeans won the victory, but it was no victory at all, because they only had twenty ships survive the battle and these ships, their rams bent, were useless, so the Phocaeans gathered their women and children and all their possessions and abandoned Alalia."

Many of the colonies were joint foundations of Chalcis and Eretria, neighboring polises on the island of Euboea and the two leading seapowers; their cooperation ended when Eretria grew prosperous and so aroused the envy of the Chalcidians that they ordered the Eretrians to abandon their city and settle away from the plain (the Lelantine Plain) shared by the two cities. The aristocrats of both sides agreed not to use long range weapons against each other and so they fought hand to hand, with spears and swords, in the plain. Soon, as each side appealed to its allies, the war spread throughout the whole of the Greek world and to the colonies that had been founded jointly by Chalcis and Eretria. In the end Eretria lost its island empire, and both cities lost their trading center on the eastern seaboard of the Mediterranean.

Under cover of the Lelantine War the Spartans invaded Messenia (their neighbor to the west). The Messenians had not yet combined into a single polis; they lived in seven separate towns and, although they occupied one of the largest and most fertile plains in Greece, they had little or no iron and scant bronze. The Spartans "swore an oath that neither the length of the war, if it wasn't decided in a short time, nor any reverses, if there were any, would turn them away before they had conquered with the spear and possessed the Messenian land."

The Spartans started the war with a surprise attack on Ampheia (Ampheia is a Messenian city on the border with Sparta), and they caught the city with its gates open. For the next four years the Spartans raided Messenia, drove off livestock, and harvested and removed the crops, but they destroyed nothing that they expected would be useful to them one day. Finally, after four years the Messenians decided to leave all their villages in the plain and settle on Mount Ithome. After twenty years of war the Messenian aristocrats "left the rich land and fled from the massive peaks of Ithome. The Messenians were forced to take an oath that they would never rebel from the Spartans nor work any new change; second, that they would bring to Sparta half of everything their fields produced. And it was ordered that at the deaths of kings and other men in official positions, that both men and women from Messenia should come in black clothing, and a penalty was laid upon those who disobeyed."

The Spartans now had to control a large subject population—the helots—and they also had inveterate enemies in the exiled Messenian aristocrats who settled throughout the Peloponnesus and passed on their enmity to their sons and grandsons. The Lelantine War and the conquest of Messenia were a prelude to the great struggle between Sparta and Argos for the control of the Peloponnesus.

In the beginning of the seventh century, the last king of the royal Argive line, King Pheidon, invented a new way of fighting—the *hoplite phalanx*. With a general rise in prosperity and the introduction of coined money throughout the Greek world a new prosperous, nonaristocratic class formed. Pheidon called on this new class of prosperous men to arm themselves as *hoplites*. The hoplite takes his title from his equipment (the *hopla*, the "stuff")—helmet, breastplate, greaves, a thrusting spear, and most important, the shield (the *hoplon*). The circular shield (weighing between twelve and fifteen pounds) covered its bearer from chin to knee. The panoply ("all the stuff") weighed fifty to sixty pounds (on a man 5'2" to 5'4"). A man so accoutered was like a one-man tank; Pheidon's innovation, however, was not the armored man, but the forming of armored men into the *phalanx*.

In this formation (perhaps necessitated by a lack of training in individual combat) each man crowded in next to the man to his right so that his right side would be protected by that man's shield. Every man in formation was completely protected except the rightmost man. He was the guide and he usually guided the formation to the right to avoid being flanked by the enemy formation. As long as the phalanx did not break, the soldiers were relatively well protected. When the old aristocracy fighting in the old way met "men who stand their ground the aristocrats are not up to it. Since they are not in formation they are not ashamed to give ground; retreat and attack are both equally honorable to them and their manhood is never tested (for each individual always has a good excuse for saving himself)."

Pheidon used the phalanx to defeat the Spartans at the battle of Hysiae in 668 B.C. and, thereafter, to make Argos the dominant power in the northeast Peloponnesus. As with many reformers, however, Pheidon failed to anticipate the consequences of his creation—the men in the phalanx, the hoplites, demanded political rights. With an ironical twist familiar to all who study history, Pheidon ended his life trying to prevent the hoplite class from overthrowing his friends (the Bacchiad aristocracy) in Corinth. Within as little as a decade other leaders had emulated him, organized the hoplite class, formed them into a phalanx, and stopped Argive expansion.

The Spartans, too, after their defeat by Pheidon's hoplites, trained hoplites and created a phalanx, but their defeat was a signal to the Messenian exiles to lead a "rebellion" in Messenia. The ensuing war lasted for twenty years and required every man the Spartans could muster into their (new) phalanx. The fighting was desperate, as exhortations of that time to the Spartans show—"Spartans, show no fear of a multitude of men. Do not flinch. Let every man hold his shield straight forward and make life his enemy and the black spirits of death as desired as the rays of the sun . . . . Close with the enemy. Set foot by foot, shield on shield, helmet on helmet. Fight hand to hand with your long spear."

In the end the Spartans put down the Messenian revolt, forced all Messenian refugees to leave the Peloponnesus, and transformed their own society into a mixture of aristocratic prerogatives and hoplite rights. "I don't care," wrote a Spartan leader of that time, "how fast a man can run in a race or how good he is at wrestling, even if he's as tall and strong as a cyclops or faster than the wind. I don't care if he's handsome or rich or a mighty king. I don't care if he is a persuasive speaker or famous in any way, if he has not been brave in war, if he has not endured the sight of wounds and corpses, if he has not stood close and struck at the enemy. This is prowess. This is the noblest honor man can win."

The Spartans created a new citizen class, a large body of men—the hoplites—permanently under arms and supported by helot labor. They called themselves the "Equals" and each of them was given an allotted portion of land for their support. They lived in a military camp and their only business was soldiering. They were led by their two kings and a council of twenty-eight aristocrats (above the age of sixty), but they had the right to meet in assembly at stated times and to vote.

From the age of six boys were trained for the phalanx. They lived in a barracks and were commanded by older boys. Until they were ten they underwent mild physical training, music (heavily concentrated on patriotic songs), reading, and writing. The boy of 10 to 13 began competitive exercises in music, dancing, and athletics. After the thirteenth year, the boys cut their hair, went barefoot, were given one garment to last the rest of their training; they played and exercised naked.

At eighteen the boy passed out of boyhood training and entered a provisional period in which he supervised other boys or joined the *krypteia*, the secret police of Sparta (used against the Messenian helots). Any helot found out and about at night the boys killed; they killed any helot who seemed especially big and healthy or who exhibited leadership qualities. (There was no blood guilt in killing them, because the Spartans declared war on the helots every year.)

From the age of twenty–one to thirty, the Spartan men lived in barracks. They were Sparta's ready reaction force. From the age thirty to sixty the Spartan was expected to maintain a household. All citizens ate dinner (pork blood soup) in common messes, fifteen to a table. Each member of the mess had to provide a stated amount of supplies from his land, or he was ineligible for the mess. Anyone who was not a member of the mess, was not a citizen. At the age of sixty the citizen was released from military service.

As the duty of the men was to fight, and if necessary die, in battle, so the duty of women was to produce sons to fight in battle. As the noblest sacrifice of the man was death in battle, so the noblest sacrifice of the woman was death in childbirth.

The Spartans became the premier hoplite power in Greece, but every polis developed a hoplite phalanx. Often the aristocratic leadership tried to use the hoplite phalanx in war and to ignore the hoplites in peace, but the hoplites had the power to demand political concessions and to receive them, or break the state. Some aristocratic governments found an acceptable compromise—as the Spartans had instituted a hoplite assembly that met regularly—but in those polises where the aristocrats would not compromise, the hoplites found a champion (usually from a collateral branch of the aristocracy) and used force to put him in power. Such a man was called a *tyrant*. (The tyrant was a ruler outside the law who held his position through force, though many tyrants were popular.) The tyrants curtailed the power of the aristocracy and gave the hoplite class a share in the state. Tyranny, or the fear of tyranny, led to a broadening of the ruling class. In the end most polises in Greece became hoplite democracies.

A third effect of the hoplite revolution was the creation of a kind of man who could say, "I earn my bread with my spear and with my spear the Thracian wine and on my spear I lean to drink." Archilochus (whose name means Leader of a Battalion) was born on the island of Paros towards the beginning of the seventh century. He was the son of a noble father and a slave mother and he received the traditional aristocratic education of arms, athletics, and music, but he was left on his own to earn his living. He tried his luck in Thasos. The Thasians had a treaty with the Thracians to mine gold, but the Thasians attempted to cheat the Thracians, the Thracians caught them, and Archilochus had a bad experience: "Some Thracian is bragging that he has my shield, which against my will I had to leave in a wood, so that I could escape the thrust of death. Well, let that shield go. I will find another one just as good."

When Archilochus became "unpopular in Thasos," he returned home to Paros and finally died at the age of fifty fighting in a battle as a citizen soldier.

Archilochus was the first soldier ever (whose works survive) to write of his own feelings and experiences.

The hoplite reform transformed Greek social and political life. The hoplite class assumed the outlook of the aristocratic class—the ethics of war, the definition of a good citizen. As men met in the wrestling ground and exercised there for beauty, sport, and war, they formed a bond with each other and a way of life—the only way of life—that enabled them to remain physically conditioned for that one campaign and that one battle, twenty minutes to live or die.

## Map 11: Overview of the Persian Wars

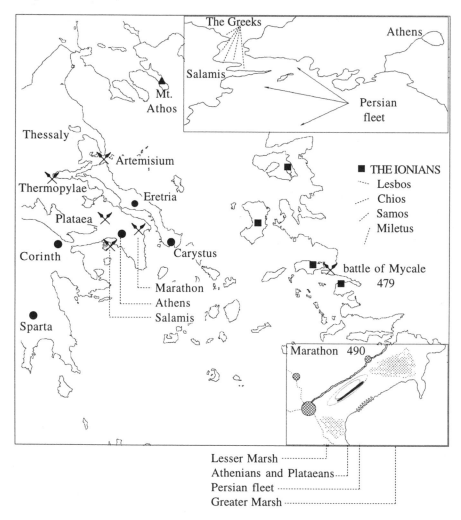

Lesser Marsh
Athenians and Plataeans
Persian fleet
Greater Marsh

# 11

# "Go Tell the Spartans"

## *A Common Objective Compels Unity of Command*

By the middle of the sixth century the Spartans had the largest and the best army in Greece, they were total masters of Messenia and Laconia, they had tried and failed to conquer the whole of the Peloponnesus, and, instead, they had adopted a policy to expel tyrants, to support the development of hoplite democracies, and to dominate the Peloponnesus through a network of alliances, which they called "the Spartans and their allies," but we call "the Peloponnesian League." In 546 the Argives challenged the right of the Spartans to lead the Peloponnesus and the Spartans and the Argives fought a battle. Both sides suffered high casualties, but the Spartans won. In the same year the Spartans' ally, King Croesus of Lydia, was defeated by Cyrus and the Spartans sent an embassy to warn Cyrus that Sparta would not tolerate Persian influence in Ionia.

"Who are these Spartans?" Cyrus asked. He believed that the Greek polises were merchant states like the Phoenician cities, and, as such, negligible, and he had contempt for a government without a single absolute ruler, and then, too, the Spartans had been allies of his enemies. Cyrus united the whole of the Asian Near East from the coast of Asia Minor to the Indus River (where in 530 B.C. he died fighting). His son Cambyses (530–522) conquered Egypt. Cambyses's successor, Darius (522–486 B.C.), transformed the valley of the Indus into the twentieth satrapy, one so wealthy that it paid a third of all tribute gathered from the Asian provinces, and he invaded Scythia (today the Crimea). He intended to put an end, once and for all, to Scythian incursions into his empire. He planned to sweep the Scythians all the way from the Danube River in the west to his blocking forces in the east, trap them between the two forces, and annihilate them.

Darius employed a Greek engineer to build a permanent bridge over the Bosporos and a bridge of boats that could be transported up the Danube to a suitable crossing point. He ordered his Ionian subjects (under the command of their tyrants) to guard the bridge while he invaded the Scythian homeland. Darius soon faced the classic dilemma of a conventional army fighting a highly mobile force with no fixed place it had to defend. He could not compel the Scythians to stand and fight, he could not prevent their destroying the supplies he needed to support his army, and he had to decide when he could no longer advance without endangering his chances of withdrawing. Rumors of disaster reached the Ionian Greeks defending the bridgehead and an Athenian named Miltiades—he was the master of the Chersonese—advised the Ionians to destroy the bridge and maroon Darius. Darius was saved by a tyrant who pointed out that if Darius fell, all the tyrants would fall with him.

When Darius returned, he expelled Miltiades from the Chersonese and he let his suspicion of the tyrants show. The tyrants decided to act against him before he could act against them; the tyrants laid down their tyrannies, installed free institutions, formed a League of Ionians, and met in a common council to discuss rebellion from Persia. They sent an envoy to Sparta to try to enlist the support of King Cleomenes, but when the envoy let slip how large the Persian empire really was, Cleomenes ordered him out of Sparta and out of the Peloponnesus. The envoy travelled to Athens and convinced the Athenian assembly to send aid, and he also persuaded the Euboean city of Eretria to help. The Athenians sent twenty ships, the Eretrians five, and together with the Ionians they attacked Sardis, the capital of Lydia, shut the Persian commander up in the citadel, and burned the town. The Athenians and Eretrians then returned home, where they remained, while the Persians converged on the Ionians by land and sea. The Ionian "attack of sheep upon wolves" seemed to be doomed to a quick end, but then the Ionians defeated the Persians at sea (498 B.C.) and the Carians (Ionian allies) annihilated a Persian army on land (497 B.C.).

These two victories paralyzed the Persians and gave the Ionians three years in which to prepare for the inevitable attack, but the Ionians bickered among themselves, couldn't agree on a coherent strategy, and failed to win strong allies. The four great Ionian naval powers, Chios, Lesbos, Samos, and Miletus, fought the Persians with a fleet of 300 ships at the Battle of Lade in 494 B.C.; the Chians distinguished themselves by their bravery, but the Samians deserted the fleet, the Lesbians followed them, and the Ionian cause was lost. The Persians reduced Ionia city by city, transported the population of Miletus to Mesopotamia, and hunted everywhere (except in Samos) for traitors to Persia. Darius, however, was less interested in revenge than in stability and he appointed Mardonius, his son-in-law, to investigate the Ionians' grievances. Mardonius replaced the tyrannies with democracies, established courts to settle claims, and redistributed the tax burden. All in all, the Persians did not treat Ionia badly, but they relegated Ionia to a backwater of the empire.

Most Greeks now believed that the might of Persia was invincible, but two men, Cleomenes, the Spartan king, and Miltiades, the Athenian, saw rather that the disunity of the Ionians had cost them the war, and each man, in his own way, set out to prepare for the war with Persia. Cleomenes took steps to ensure the primacy of Sparta in Greece and the unity of Greeks under the leadership of Sparta. His first step was to deny the Persians any possible base in southern Greece. In 494 he invaded the Argolid and (at the battle of Sepeia) he routed the army of Argos. The fleeing soldiers sought refuge in a sacred wood. Cleomenes set the woods on fire and immolated the Argives. When he suspected that some of the leaders of the Aeginetans might favor the Persians, he arrested them and handed them over to the Athenians.

Darius sent heralds throughout Greece to demand "earth and water," that is, submission to the Persians, and the moment of decision had come. Miltiades (one of the ten "generals") barely convinced the Athenians to reject the Persian demands and to seek an alliance with the Spartans. The Spartans told the Persian ambassadors to find their own earth and water and threw them down a well. They agreed to an alliance with the Athenians and, under the leadership of Cleomenes, they created a new, more unified Peloponnesian League, which formed the basis for the alliance against Persia. If, in the end, many of the states in the alliance preferred not to send troops to fight the Persians, at least none actively aided the enemy.

In 491 Darius sent Mardonius to subjugate Thrace and Macedonia as preparation for an invasion of Greece. Mardonius lost part of his fleet in a storm off Mt. Athos and was so badly wounded by a Thracian raiding party that he was put out of action for the year 490. Darius, then, appointed his nephew, the Persian Artaphernes, and a Mede named Datis to command a large naval expedition (with transport for their cavalry), to cross the Aegean, and to attack Athens and Eretria. By the end of the summer they had captured Carystus, the harbor on the southern tip of the island of Euboea; from this harbor they were poised to attack either Athens or Eretria. The Eretrians hoped their walls and their 3,000 hoplites and 600 cavalry could delay the Persians long enough for the Athenians to come to their aid, but the Athenians, faced with the Persian threat at Carystus, did not dare send any of their troops to Eretria. The Persians quickly concluded their siege of Eretria.

An Athenian endurance runner travelled the 150 miles to Sparta in forty-eight hours with the message: "Spartans, the Athenians need you!" and the Spartans replied that their law forbade them to venture out until the moon was full (12 September 490), but as soon as the moon was full, they would come with their army. (The Athenians at that time and historians ever since have believed that the Spartans used their law to conceal their indecision in this moment of crisis.)

The Athenians heard that the Persians had landed their army at Marathon under the guidance of the exiled Athenian tyrant, Hippias. (Marathon was a good place for cavalry and a place with personal significance for Hippias.) The Athenians mobilized their army of 10,000 hoplites; they were joined by their neighbors, the Plataeans, with 1,000 hoplites. The force was commanded by the Athenian polemarch (commander-in-chief) and the ten generals (one of whom was Miltiades). The Athenians arrived too late to prevent the landing, too late even to contain the Persians, if the Persians had pushed inland immediately, but the Persians' horses were seasick and the Persians gave them time to recover. This delay allowed the Athenians to take up a position along a ridge guarded on its flanks by two marshes; there they blocked the Persian force and the two sides waited.

The Persians hoped that the Athenians would welcome Hippias back, and the Athenians hoped that the Persians would be unable to supply themselves for long and would withdraw or that the Spartans would arrive before the battle. After eight days (when the Spartan army had begun its march to Athens) the Persians decided to withdraw—they couldn't hope to carry the Athenian position on the ridge with their cavalry and light infantry, and they had to act quickly before the Spartans arrived, but they had placed themselves in a vulnerable position because they had to load the horses first with the infantry as a screen and so denude themselves of their best arm, the cavalry.

Five Athenian generals were content to let the Persians sail away, but Miltiades convinced four generals and the polemarch to give the order for the Athenians and Plataeans to form their phalanx and charge. The phalanx split as the wings converged on the ships and the Athenian and Plataean soldiers tried to prevent the ships escaping. The brother of the great Athenian playwright Aeschylus caught hold of the stern of a ship; a Persian chopped his hands off. When the Persian fleet put to sea, the Athenians hunted down the abandoned Persian infantry and killed them all (6,400 Persians—the polemarch had vowed to pay the gods for every dead Persian, so the Athenians were careful to count each corpse; 196 Athenians were killed). The Persian fleet withdrew back across the Aegean Sea. The Athenians had met the Persians, they had beaten them, and they had done it without the Spartans. (Two thousand Spartans arrived on the day after the battle.) The Athenians thought Marathon was the greatest battle ever fought.

The battle of Marathon established that Persian light infantry was no match for the Greek hoplite, that the Athenians would fight, and that the Spartans would come to their aid (even if they were dilatory). On the other hand, Marathon had revealed Athenian naval weakness, and many Athenians still believed that Athens was no match for the Persian empire. The Athenians had found a leader, Miltiades, but Miltiades did not live long to enjoy the fruits of his victory, and his supporters turned to an Athenian named Themistocles to continue the anti-Persian policy. Feelings ran hot in Athens and in the midst of the debate, the Athenians found themselves in a war with Aegina (487–481), and the Athenians were embarrassed to find that Aegina ("the eyesore of the Aegean") had a navy superior to their own. When in 483 a large new vein of silver was discovered at the Athenian mines at Laurium, Themistocles proposed that the silver be used to build and man a fleet of 200 triremes; the objectives of the proposed fleet were, first, to defeat Aegina, second, to control the Aegean and defend Athens from the Persians, and third (though unstated), to provide employment to oarsmen and construction crews. Themistocles' proposal was carried, the Athenians built a fleet of 200 modern triremes, and their new fleet overwhelmed Aegina.

The Athenians and the other Greeks were lucky: Darius had died in 486, before he could avenge Marathon, and his son Xerxes (about thirty-two years old) had to put down an Egyptian revolt before he could avenge his father's defeat. His closest adviser and strongest advocate for invasion was his uncle, Mardonius. (Other Persians believed that there were already too many Greek scribes, engineers, advisers, traders, soldiers, and sea captains in the empire.)

Xerxes prepared for the expedition with all the care possible. He had a canal dug through the peninsula of Mt. Athos, he built roads and bridged rivers and the Hellespont, he ensured that his navy was outfitted with the latest ship, the trireme, and he sent advance forces, army and navy, to occupy Thrace and Macedonia. While the Persian king prepared his invasion, the Spartans and Athenians established a congress at Corinth, where questions of strategy and command could be settled. They called themselves "the Greeks," a title that implied that any Greek helping the Persians was a traitor. (We call the alliance "the League of Corinth" or the "Hellenic League.") The "Greeks" sent envoys all over the Greek world, but in the end the "Greeks" comprised the Spartans and their allies and the Athenians and their allies under the supreme command of the Spartan kings; Themistocles was second in command of the naval forces.

The "Greeks" decided to exploit the mountain ranges, rough sea, and the lack of provisions, to force the Persians to fight on Greek terms. The Spartans wanted to fortify the Isthmus, Athens wanted Attica defended, and, after a half-hearted attempt to defend the Vale of Tempe near Mt. Olympus, they decided to make their stand by land at Thermopylae and by sea at Artemisium. Most Greeks believed that the Persians would win and most Greeks either joined the Persians (that is, *medized*) or remained neutral. Even the oracle at Delphi told the Athenian envoys, "Why sit there? Run, run as far as you can," and only slightly ameliorated its pronouncement when the envoys begged for a helping word: "a wooden wall alone will remain unsacked . . . . O divine Salamis, you shall destroy the children of women."

Themistocles convinced the Athenians that the second pronouncement was good news, because the oracle would not have described Salamis as "divine," but as "baleful" or "fatal" or "cruel," if the Greeks were going to lose, and the "unsacked" wooden wall was the Athenian fleet. They voted to man their fleet and to move the whole population from Athens, part to Salamis and part to Troezen (in the Peloponnesus). They sent a large part of their fleet to Artemisium, to fight the Persian fleet there, while the Spartans and their allies guarded the pass at Thermopylae—this is an exceptionally narrow pass leading from Thessaly into Greece. The Spartans were to delay the Persians until the two fleets had fought. (The Persians employed the Ionian and Phoenician fleets.)

The commander-in-chief was the Spartan king, Leonidas. Leonidas brought to Thermopylae 300 chosen Spartans (each of whom left behind a son to replace him, should he be killed), 2,800 hoplites from the Peloponnesus, and several thousand more troops recruited from the districts around Thermopylae. The Greek fleet at Artemisium numbered 271 ships: the Athenians had provided 127 ships (half their fleet, some manned by the Plataeans), the Corinthians provided forty ships. The Persians set sail against Artemisium in a storm and lost many ships, but the survivors caught the Greeks by surprise and captured three ships. They selected one prisoner, the handsomest of the Greeks, and cut his throat as a sacrifice.

Meanwhile, the Persian army reached the pass at Thermopylae and Xerxes sent a scout on horseback to see how many Greeks there were and what they were doing. The scout came back and told the king that he had seen the Spartans exercising and arranging their hair. Xerxes laughed and called upon Damaratus, an exiled king of Sparta and adviser to Xerxes, to explain what the Spartans were doing. Damaratus told him, "These men are preparing to fight us for the passageway. For their custom is, when they are going to risk their lives, they fix their hair."

Xerxes did not believe a word he said, and he waited four days for the Greeks to run away. On the fifth day, he ordered the Medes to advance on the Greeks and take them alive, while he watched. Many of the Medes fell, others took their place, and they fought until Xerxes ordered them to withdraw and ordered his Immortals to take their place, but the Immortals could not accomplish any more than the Medes, both because of the restricted pass and because of the quality of the Spartans. The Spartans would seem to run away without order or discipline, and the Persians would shout in triumph and chase them, but then the Spartans would halt, about-face, and cut down their disorganized pursuers. Day after day Xerxes sent his troops into battle, day after day the Greeks took turns defending the pass, and Xerxes could not force his way through.

While the struggle went on at Thermopylae, the two navies engaged in a full-scale battle at Artemisium. The fight lasted all day and ended in a standoff, except that the Greeks had the advantage of the prevailing current, which brought them the wreckage from the battle, where they could salvage what they could and destroy the rest. Half the Greek fleet was damaged and needed to refit, so they decided to retreat to their second line of defense and sent liaison officers to tell Leonidas that they were going to withdraw and that he need not defend the pass any more.

The Persian king, meanwhile, had learned of a pass around Thermopylae from a medizing Greek, and he sent a force to flank the Spartans. Leonidas was warned of the movement in plenty of time to withdraw, he had no tactical reason to remain—and he did send his Peloponnesian allies home—but he decided to remain with the Spartans and to keep the Thebans (who would either die now with him or live to fight for the Persians). Leonidas may have remained to fulfil the Delphic prophecy that either Sparta would be sacked by the barbarians or the city would lose a king.

The last battle was fierce. The Greeks knew they were going to fight to the death and they fought as hard as they could; their spears were broken and they fought with the fragments, they used their swords, and when those broke, rocks and their teeth. Leonidas was killed and the Persians rushed forward to claim his body; Greeks and Persians pushed back and forth over the body four times until the Greeks pulled the king's body back with them to a hill in the narrowest part of the pass and there they stood (except for the Thebans alone, who withdrew and surrendered) until the Persians overwhelmed them. All the Spartans with Leonidas were killed and many noble Persians, among them, two sons of Darius. Eventually the Greeks were buried in the place where they fell and this epitaph was written for the Spartans:

Go tell the Spartans, you who pass us by,
That here obedient to their laws we lie.

The victorious Persians marched down, occupied, and sacked Athens. Xerxes opened secret negotiations to persuade the Athenians to betray their allies (as Samos had in the Ionian revolt) in exchange for favorable terms; the Athenians refused, even though their commander, Themistocles, had to threaten to lead the Athenians to the west out of the war and found a new city, before the Spartans would agree to keep the fleet at Salamis and fight there. Themistocles did not trust their resolve, he could see no sign that the Persians intended to initiate a battle, particularly in the narrows between Salamis and the mainland, where the Greek triremes, which were stouter if less maneuverable, would have the advantage, and so he sent Xerxes a secret message with just enough of the truth—the Greeks were divided, and some of them wanted to withdraw from Salamis—that Xerxes believed the rest, that some would withdraw behind the island that very night while the others were in disarray and unready for battle. Xerxes was ready to believe that Themistocles, or any Greek leader, would betray the other Greeks, and he ordered part of his fleet to sail around the island to block any escape and ordered the rest to attack at dawn. The Athenian tragedian Aeschylus (who participated in the battle) wrote an account of the battle as he imagined the Persians saw it.

"Our crews ate their dinner and got themselves in order; the rowers bound a thong around each oar, and, when the sunlight faded, every man was at his oar, every man at arms, and man encouraged man and rowed the triremes to their appointed stations. All night the captains kept their crews awake, but the Greeks did not set sail secretly, and, when the dazzling chariot of the sun began to cross the sky, a song–like, happy tumult sounded from the Greeks, and echoed from the island rocks. We were afraid, for we had not expected this, and they, as though they never intended to flee, chanted a solemn paean, and rushed to battle. At once we heard the sound of oars striking the water and soon we saw them all. First the right wing and next the whole fleet advancing and we heard a great concerted cry,

"'Greek sons, advance. Free your fathers' land, free your children, your wives, the sanctuaries of your paternal gods, the grave sites of your ancestors. Now the struggle is joined. All is at stake.'

"A Greek ship began the charge and sheared off the entire stern of a Phoenician vessel. Each captain drove his ship straight against some other ship. Triremes struck their bronze beaks together. At first the stream of Persian arms held its own, but when the mass of our ships had been crowded in the narrows and none could render another aid and each smashed its bronze beak against another of its own line and shattered their whole array of oars, then the Greek triremes recognized their chance, hemmed us in and battered us on every side.

"The hulls of our vessels rolled over and the sea was hidden from our sight, so thick were the wrecks and slaughtered men. The shores and reefs were covered with our dead and the foe kept striking and hacking our men in the water with broken oars and fragments of wrecked ships. Groans and shrieks together filled the open sea until night hid the scene."

Themistocles' strategy and his stratagem at Salamis had won a stunning victory; if, however, the battle had gone the other way and the Persians had won, not a Greek ship would have escaped, and Themistocles still would have been the hero of the hour, but in that case Xerxes' hero.

The Persian fleet retreated to the Hellespont and the Athenians were let loose in the Aegean, Xerxes left Mardonius in command and returned to Asia. Mardonius withdrew into winter quarters and began a new effort to detach Athens from the league. The Athenians wanted their city back, they wanted the Spartans to fight the Persians, but the Spartans seemed reluctant, and so the Athenians let the Spartans learn of the offer Mardonius had made to them, in effect, to make them the satrap of a Greek province. The Spartans, in the end, decided that they could not afford to defend the Isthmus of Corinth (their favored strategy) if they lost Athenian support. The Spartans mustered an army of 30,000 hoplites (10,000 from Laconia), and they also took 35,000 helots as light-armed troops. The army was commanded by Pausanias, the nephew of Leonidas and regent to the new king (the infant son of Leonidas). As the Greek army advanced Mardonius evacuated Attica and retired to the vicinity of Plataea.

The Greeks, after some initial skirmishes, moved across the plain of Plataea and occupied a ridge south of, and running parallel to, the Asopus River; the Persians pitched their camp on the north bank. Neither side could easily cross the river and attack the other and the soothsayers—both sides used Greek soothsayers—predicted that an attack would be disastrous. Nonetheless, after ten days of inaction, Mardonius sent his cavalry across the Asopus to harass the Greeks (who did not know how to defend against horse archers), and the cavalry fouled the spring from which the whole Greek army drew its water.

Pausanias and his staff decided to withdraw at night back across the plain to the line of foothills, where they could protect themselves from the Persian cavalry and secure their supply line, but when the appointed hour came, most of the Greeks in the center took off at a run—they were convinced that the order to retreat was an admission of defeat and they intended to take refuge in the city of Plataea and, from there, to flee back to their homes—and one of the Spartan unit commanders refused to retreat at all. The Athenians decided not to move until the Spartans did, and Pausanias spent most of the night arguing with his unit commander. At last he decided to leave the unit behind and he set out. The Athenians began their movement directly across the plain while the Spartans marched by the foothills of Cithaeron to protect themselves from the Persian cavalry. In the midst of the movement Pausanias received a runner from the unit left behind asking him to wait. He paused for the unit to catch up and the sun rose.

The Persian scouts had already reported to Mardonius that the ridge was deserted and Mardonius was convinced that the Greeks were in flight and that he had to catch them before they could escape. He ordered his army out, each unit to advance as soon as it could, and thus his fastest units caught up with the Spartans first and attacked them. (The Theban phalanx, and the other medizing Greeks, crossed directly over the ridge, down into the plain, and there forced the Athenians to fight.)

Pausanias ordered his soothsayer to perform a sacrifice, as they were going to engage with Mardonius and his army, and the soothsayer said the signs were not favorable. Pausanias ordered the soothsayer to perform another sacrifice, and he ordered his men to protect themselves with their shields but not to charge. Meanwhile the Persians were massing in front of the Spartans (who they thought were so scared that they would not even fight back), they fixed their shields in the ground, shot arrows at the Spartans, and wounded many of them. By massing, however, they lost their power to maneuver, and when, at last, the soothsayer announced that the signs were favorable and the Spartans charged, the Persians had no choice but to fight at close quarters. The Persians dropped their bows and fought hand to hand at the hedge formed by their wickerwork shields. The Spartans broke the line of shields down and the two armies fought, again hand to hand. The Persians grabbed hold of the Spartans' spears and tried to wrench them from their grasp; they were no less courageous than the Spartans, but they were unarmored, inexperienced in this kind of fighting, and were not as skillful as the Spartans. Mardonius himself was there on a white horse and had around him his guard of the thousand bravest Persians. All around him the fighting was the fiercest and the Persians were holding their own, until a Spartan aristocrat struck Mardonius and killed him, and the Spartans killed Mardonius's elite guard, and the rest of the Persian army turned and fled. Ninety-one Spartans died in the battle and, in their victorious battle against the Thebans, fifty-two Athenians.

The victorious Greeks decided to pursue the Persians, destroy the bridge at the Hellespont, and free all of Ionia. At the battle of Mykale they again defeated the Persian fleet, landed, attacked, killed both Persian commanders, and annihilated the Persian army. The battle of Mykale began the second Ionian revolt. The Greeks enrolled the rebels— Samos, Chios, Lesbos, and the other islanders—as members of the League of Corinth and then the League navy set out to the Hellespont. The Greeks of the Aegean and Ionian Coast were freed.

# Map 12: Overview of the Peloponnesian War

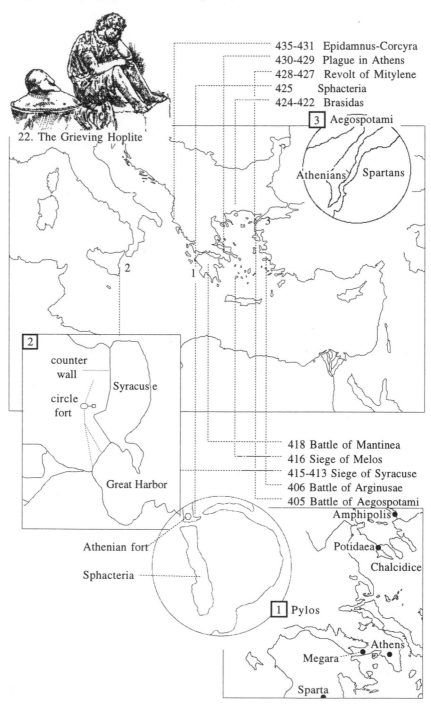

22. The Grieving Hoplite

435-431  Epidamnus-Corcyra
430-429  Plague in Athens
428-427  Revolt of Mitylene
425      Sphacteria
424-422  Brasidas

3  Aegospotami

Athenians  Spartans

2
counter wall
circle fort
Syracuse

Great Harbor

Athenian fort
Sphacteria

418 Battle of Mantinea
416 Siege of Melos
415-413 Siege of Syracuse
406 Battle of Arginusae
405 Battle of Aegospotami

Amphipolis
Potidaea
Chalcidice

1  Pylos

Megara  Athens

Sparta

# 12

# The Peloponnesian (Archidamian) War

## When the Common Danger Is Removed

The Spartans and Athenians together had defeated the greatest military power in the world at that time, but half a century later the Spartans and the Athenians fought such a war against each other that, in the words of one Greek writer, they "murdered Greece." The Athenians blamed the Spartans. First, Pausanias (they claimed) let the victory go to his head, he began to treat his allies as though they were helots, and he conspired with the Persians. The Athenians were asked by the allies to assume command of the fleet and they did. (The Spartans got rid of Pausanias.) Second, the Spartans tried (in vain) to prevent the Athenians from rebuilding their city walls. Third, in 465, when the Spartans suffered a devastating earthquake—only one building was left standing in Sparta—and the Messenian helots revolted and the Spartans appealed to Athens for help, the Spartans dismissed the army the Athenians sent and all but accused the Athenians of intending to help the helots; the Athenians immediately set about forming an anti-Spartan alliance of Argos, the Thessalians, and themselves.

The Athenians, for their part, were far from blameless. They used their command of the allied fleet to transform what was supposed to be a naval alliance (the Delian league) into an Athenian empire. Athenians determined the amount of money, ships, and crews each member owed and they punished the recalcitrant. (The first payment of the members was 460 talents: 460 talents would commission and crew forty-six triremes and keep them at sea for the eight-month sailing season.) Under the leadership of Pericles the Athenians became the masters of the Aegean Sea. Pericles recognized the power that command of the sea gave Athens, but he also recognized that Athens itself was vulnerable to siege, and, therefore, he had walls (the "long walls") constructed that connected the city of Athens to the Piraeus (its port) and made Athens an island on the mainland.

The Athenians not only had the largest fleet in the Aegean, but they had also developed several battle tactics so sophisticated and so demanding that other navies could not perform them. The Athenians would row as fast as they could at their enemies and then at the last moment veer just enough to glide down the side of the enemy ship; the Athenian oarsmen would pull their oars in, the enemy, caught by surprise, would not, and their oarsmen would be battered, the oars broken, and the ship helpless. Or the Athenians would dash through the enemy line and turn, before the enemy could, and take them in the rear. Or they would circle the enemy, until they could catch an enemy ship with its side to them, and then they would ram it and roll it over.

The Athenians were conscious that they had a new source of power, the democratic navy—Democracy, one Athenian wrote, while despised by all the right people, because it gives control to the wrong people, nonetheless is justified because the people man the fleet and the fleet has brought Athens its power. The Athenians have a hoplite force (composed of the right people) which, while not as good as the Spartan hoplite force, still is better than any force its subjects can muster and so is sufficient to control them. Moreover, their subjects are divided by the sea and cannot combine against the Athenians (the way the allies of the Spartans could combine against Sparta). A naval power can ravage the land of a stronger power: they can find a weakly defended place to land, catch the enemy completely by surprise, plunder and burn, and if the enemy forces approach, reembark and sail away. They can undertake distant expeditions. Ground forces have to move at the speed of the infantry, they have to arrange for supplies along the way, and they have to fight their way through hostile territory. A naval power can carry its own provisions and it can travel without hindrance wherever the sea reaches.

Pericles attempted to annihilate all naval opposition, to create a land alliance equal to Sparta's, and to free Egypt from Persia. The Egyptian expedition was a disaster, the land alliance was defeated by the Spartans, and the Athenians were unable to gain supremacy at sea. Pericles had to recognize the limits of Athenian power, to seek limited objectives, and to reformulate Athenian strategy. In 448 the Persian king issued a decree ending the Persian wars, and two years later the Athenians and the Spartans agreed on a thirty-year truce. The Athenians gave up all their mainland possessions except Naupactus, they agreed (as did the Spartans) to respect the independence of Delphi, and they agreed not to commit aggression against Sparta or Sparta's allies, as the Spartans agreed to respect theirs. All parties not included in the truce, except for Argos, were free to join either side and to be included in all the conditions. Both sides guaranteed freedom of the seas for trade, and they agreed to submit their differences to arbitration.

Three events shattered the treaty and precipitated the great war between Athens and Sparta. Pericles, determined to demonstrate Athens's power, convinced the Athenians to pass a decree barring the Megarians from trade within the Athenian empire. This decree was, in fact, a blockade, since ships could hardly move without touching at a port within the empire. Secondly, the Athenians demanded that Potidaea (a city within their empire but a colony of Corinth) demolish the city wall next to the sea. When the Potidaeans refused, the

Athenians laid siege to the city. Third, the island of Corcyra, not included in the thirty-year truce, asked the Athenians for help against Corinth, and the Athenians agreed, because they hoped to use the siutation to facilitate the destruction of both the Corinthian and the Corcyraean fleets.

Late in 432 Sparta called a meeting of its allies. The allies asked the Spartans to declare war on Athens. Archidamus, the Spartan king, advised caution, but the Spartans, presented with the question *Have the Athenians broken the treaty?* voted *yes*. The Athenians had a large fleet, a reserve of 6,000 talents, an empire of perhaps 300 states that paid a tribute of 400 talents/year, and an income of 400 talents/year from Athens itself. They set aside 100 hulls and 1,000 talents to be used only if Athens was attacked by sea. The Spartans as leaders of the Peloponnesian League and allies of Thebes could muster a hoplite army of 50,000.

The Spartans expected to invade Attica, bring the Athenian army to battle, defeat it, negotiate the terms of peace, and go home the victors, but when they did invade Attica in May 431 under the command of Archidamus, Pericles refused to allow the indignant Athenians to give battle. Pericles' strategy was to attack the coasts, harass shipping, and wait out the Peloponnesians. The Spartans did not know how to respond to the Athenian strategy, but the Athenians did not appreciate how expensive the war would be and how difficult it would be to break the will of their enemy. The Spartans devastated Attica, the Athenians raided the Peloponnesian coasts and pressed the siege of Potidaea.

In 430, in the early summer after the Spartan army had been in Attica forty days, a plague broke out in Athens. The plague came to Athens by sea and was particularly devastating because Pericles' strategy required all Athenians in Attica to crowd into the city. The plague (430-429, 427-426) killed thousands, caused public order to break down and, in 429, killed Pericles. Without Pericles the war lost direction, but the siege of Potidaea continued—even though a quarter of the Athenian troops died of the plague—until the Potidaeans, driven to cannibalism, agreed to Athenian terms to leave their city with their lives and the clothes on their backs. The siege of Potidaea cost the Athenians 2,000 talents. The Spartans, in turn, put Plataea under siege. They constructed a double wall around the city, so that there could be no rescue, and spent two years in an effort that was all out of proportion to the strategic value of Plataea. In the end, they took Plataea and executed all the survivors.

At sea, the Athenians defeated the Peloponnesian fleets and proved themselves as superior to the Peloponnesians on the sea as the Spartans were on land. When (June 428) a member of the Athenian empire, Mytilene on the island of Lesbos, rebelled, the Athenians besieged Mytilene and compelled the Mytilenians to surrender. The Athenian assembly followed the advice of Cleon (a demagogue and Pericles' successor) and voted to execute every adult male in Mytilene and enslave the rest of the population as an example for the rest of their subjects. They dispatched a trireme with the orders, but after a night of reflection, they changed their minds and dispatched another trireme to rescind the first order. The oarsmen kept to their task all day and by their exertions managed to arrive just as the orders brought by the first trireme were about to be carried out. Still, 1,000 men were executed. The walls of the city were dismantled. All ships were confiscated. All their possessions on the Asian coast were forfeited and, except for the land of Athens's one ally, all land on the island was divided into 3,000 lots of which 300 lots were dedicated to the gods and the rest were distributed to Athenian settlers. The Lesbians had to work the land and pay 100 talents a year rent for it.

Every Greek city was divided into factions, one pro-Spartan, the other pro-Athenian, and many cities were fighting civil wars, though none more brutal than the civil war in Corcyra, the city that had provoked the war. The democrats murdered sixty oligarchs and fined the rest, the oligarchs armed their slaves, set parts of the town on fire, and fought the democrats in a battle ended only by the arrival of twenty Athenian ships and 500 Messenian hoplites. The Athenians kept the peace in Corcyra, but, later, when the Corcyraean fleet (their strongest arm) sailed out to meet a Peloponnesian fleet, the crews fought among themselves, two ships deserted, and thirteen were captured. Finally, the democrats set about murdering every last oligarch. Corcyra was in shambles. The widespread civil wars left all of Greece weaker, money became scarce, and the crops were left in the fields.

In 425 the Athenians raised the league tribute to 1,000 talents, they voted to send a fleet to Sicily, and with the fleet they sent their best general, Demosthenes, and a force of soldiers to use against the Peloponnesians, if he saw an opportunity on the way. The fleet had to put in at Pylos because of bad weather; Demosthenes recommended to the commander of the fleet that they build a fort there, but the commander refused. When the bad weather continued and the Athenian fleet could not sail, the sailors grew bored and built the fort on their own initiative; and when the weather cleared and the fleet continued on its way, Demosthenes remained behind with his detachment of troops and five ships.

The Spartans recalled their army from Attica and the Peloponnesian fleet from Corcyra. They failed to dislodge the Athenians with an assault by land and sea, and so they landed a detachment of 440 troops on Sphacteria (an island that partially closes off the harbor of Pylos) to take the Athenians from the rear. They presented Demosthenes with a chance for a brilliant coup. He sent ships to recall the Athenian fleet, and the Athenian fleet returned and caught the Spartans by surprise, put their fleet out of action, and marooned the Spartan soldiers on the island of Sphacteria.

The Spartan command panicked. They asked for an armistice, they sent envoys to Athens, and they offered the Athenians peace and an alliance if the Athenians would only return their men. The Spartans were prepared to betray their own allies and give the Athenians practically everything they were fighting for, but their offer was rejected—Cleon convinced the assembly that the Athenians could not trust the Spartans to keep their word and, anyway, if the

Spartans were so desperate for peace now, what would they be like when the Athenians actually captured the soldiers on Sphacteria? The Athenians had 14,000 troops and total control of the sea around Sphacteria, but they could not prevent rafts of food being floated over or helots swimming underwater to the island with leather bags filled with a mixture of poppy seed, linseed, and honey or helots crashing their boats—filled with provisions—on the island. Soon, the Athenians found themselves conducting an uncertain siege.

Cleon urged the assembly to send out someone who would do something. When his arch rival Nicias was chosen to go, Cleon said that if he himself had been chosen, he would have captured the Spartans in thirty days. Nicias offered to withdraw in his favor, Cleon tried to back out, but the assembly chanted "Sail! Sail!" and he had to go. By chance, when he got to Sphacteria, a fire broke out on the island and burned off all the cover. For the first time Demosthenes was able to estimate the number of Spartans on the island (more than he thought), to study their location, and to plan a campaign. Eight hundred Athenians landed at dawn, overran the first Spartan guard post, killed the thirty or so hoplites there, and secured the landing. Demosthenes then disembarked 800 archers, 800 peltasts, his Messenian troops, and all the Athenian soldiers except for the garrison of the fort at Pylos. His army seized the high ground around the Spartans.

The Athenian hoplites were reluctant to come to grips with the Spartans, but their light-armed troops kept up such a barrage of arrows, stones, and javelins that they forced the Spartans to pull back and encouraged the hoplites to be more aggressive. The Spartans could not see through the dust and ash swirling over the battlefield, they could not hear commands because the Athenians were shouting, and they were being hit from every side. After some had been killed and many wounded, they retreated to a fort on the upper end of the island and there, all day, they withstood the Athenians' attack until a band of archers led by a Messenian circled around the cliffs and got behind and above the Spartans. The Spartans had to abandon their position or be annihilated.

At this point Demosthenes and Cleon halted the Athenian attack and offered the Spartans a truce to discuss surrender. The Spartans conferred with heralds from the mainland, the heralds told them, "Do what you think best so long as it is not dishonorable," and the Spartans surrendered. Of the original 440, 292 surrendered, of whom 120 were full Spartan citizens. Their surrender sent shock waves through Greece. One of the Athenians said to a Spartan prisoner, "I guess the arrows killed all the brave ones." The Spartan replied, "That would be a valuable arrow indeed which could pick out just the brave."

The Athenians transported their prisoners to Athens, and they sent word to Sparta that the prisoners would die if there was another invasion of Attica. The Athenians placed a Messenian garrison at Pylos, helots deserted in droves, and Pylos became a running sore in the side of Sparta. The Athenians captured the island of Cythera, they almost took Megara, they raided the coasts with impunity, but they suffered losses, too—1,000 hoplites killed and 200 captured at Delium, their land ravaged, the plague. Many Athenians wanted peace, although the majority led by Cleon had rejected all Sparta's offers.

The Athenian intransigence drove the Spartans to adopt a desperate scheme proposed by one of their leading citizens and finest soldiers, Brasidas. They sent Brasidas with 700 helots (whom he was to train as hoplites) and enough money to hire 1,000 mercenaries to raise the cities of Chalcidice in revolt. Brasidas won over many of the cities in Chalcidice by the force of his personality and by his promise that the Spartans had no hidden agenda, no interest in ruling the Chalcidians, only in defeating Athens and freeing the Greeks. He declared that he would never deceive them, and they believed him. He persuaded the most important Athenian possession in the region, the city of Amphipolis, to come over to him. He took the city before the local Athenian commander could react (and that commander, the historian Thucydides, was driven into exile). The rest of the Chalcidians contrasted the moderation of Brasidas with the harsh and autocratic Athenian commanders and rushed to join the rebellion.

Brasidas changed the war totally. The Athenians—to prevent the loss of the major source of their ship-building timber and the loss of part of their (now) 2,000-talent/year tribute from their empire—accepted a one-year truce on the basis of the status quo to discuss a full treaty. The one-year truce was signed in March of 423. Two days after the signing, Brasidas accepted the surrender of Scione. (He was unaware of the truce.) The Athenians demanded that Scione be returned. Brasidas offered to submit the matter to arbitration. The Athenians sent an expedition with instructions to execute the entire citizenbody of Scione. Then Brasidas accepted the surrender of Mende, on the grounds that the Athenians had broken the truce. The Athenians extended the decree of execution to Mende. When the truce expired in 422, the Athenians refused to renew it and prepared an expedition under the command of Cleon to retake Amphipolis and the other Chalcidian cities.

Cleon had 300 cavalry, 1,200 hoplites, and a sizeable fleet. He recovered several rebel cities before he camped on the coast in the vicinity of his principal objective, Amphipolis, and there he waited for his ally, the king of Macedonia. Brasidas had a force of 1,500 Thracian mercenaries, about 2,000 hoplites, 300 cavalry, and several thousand light-armed troops. While Cleon waited, his troops ridiculed him for the delay, compared his inaction with the daring of Brasidas, and accused him of cowardice. Cleon decided he had to do something to shut them up, so he led a reconnaissance in force.

The Athenians marched up past Amphipolis. They could see into the city, and they could see that Brasidas had his army in formation. Cleon thought he had enough time to withdraw. He ordered his left wing (facing the city) to retreat, and he began to turn the right wing (under his personal command). This movement exposed the unprotected right sides of his troops to Brasidas and also threw the Athenians into confusion. Brasidas had the city gates opened, and he led a charge right at the center of the Athenian line. The Athenian troops closest to the sea immediately broke and fled to their camp. As Brasidas hit the center, the center, already afraid because they had been deserted by the left wing, broke and ran Brasidas turned on the right wing already under attack by his second in command. (Cleon ran and was killed by a peltast.) The Athenian right wing fell back, reformed up a hill, held out for a while, and then—under a storm of missiles—broke and fled. Six hundred Athenians were killed, seven of Brasidas's troops, and Brasidas himself.

The Amphipolitans gave Brasidas a state funeral and voted to honor him with religious rites and a shrine as hero and founder. They sent a delegation to Sparta to praise Brasidas. (His mother thanked them but told them Sparta had many men just as good as her son.) Of all the figures of the Peloponnesian War Brasidas made the greatest impression on those around him. He was quick-witted, had both strategic and tactical reach, and he was a leader who inspired his own men, the people he wanted to win over, and his enemies. Even after he died, he was influential: Athenian subjects believed that all Spartans were like Brasidas, selflessly fighting for the freedom of Greeks.

Brasidas was dead and Cleon was dead. For the moment only the peacemakers survived, and their leaders, Pleistoanax of Sparta and Nicias of Athens worked out the terms of a peace. A treaty, the Peace of Nicias, was signed in 421.

## 23. The Trireme: a Reconstruction and a Relief

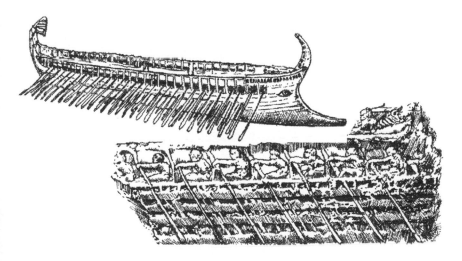

## 24. Trireme tactics

A. The triremes ram bow-on; the stouter, or better built, ship will win ... but both may be damaged in the strike and both may sink.

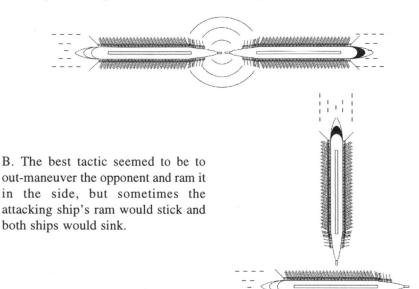

B. The best tactic seemed to be to out-maneuver the opponent and ram it in the side, but sometimes the attacking ship's ram would stick and both ships would sink.

C. The Athenians would feign a bow-on strike and sheer off at the last moment, boat their oars, and smash into the oars of the other ship, shattering them and battering the crew. The enemy ship would be helpless and the Athenians would row slowly into the side of the enemy ship and roll it over.

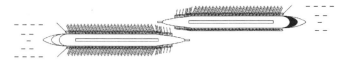

D. The opposing fleets would form in line and row through each other's line (if they did not strike bow on). The first to turn could catch the other in the stern or side. The Athenians could turn more quickly than their opponents; they would also employ the oar-shearing maneuver.

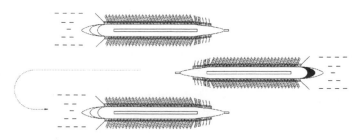

# 13

# The Peloponnesian (Decelean) War

## Suspicion, Poor Decisions, and the Persians

The Peace of Nicias was supposed to last fifty years: it enjoined the two powers to commit no acts of war against each other or each other's allies, to submit disagreements to arbitration, to allow access to shrines, to guarantee the independence of Delphi, to liberate all prisoners of war, to return all the places that either side had taken, or, at least, to remove all garrisons, and to make no changes in the terms of the treaty without the agreement of both sides. A majority of the council of the Peloponnesian League accepted the terms and the treaty was ratified, but peace never had a chance. Corinth, Megara, and Elis rejected the treaty and seceded from the Peloponnesian League; Thebes and the Boeotian League also rejected the treaty.

Sparta and Athens became allies, but the Athenian aristocrat and nephew of Pericles, Alcibiades, personable, wealthy, ambitious, and a general of real ability, assumed Cleon's role as the leader of the war party and rival of Nicias. He played upon the suspicions of the Athenians to gain prominence as the foremost opponent of Sparta, and (in 420) Alcibiades persuaded the Athenians to join a defensive alliance with Argos, Mantinea, and Elis. Between the years 420 and 418 the Spartans brought Megara and Corinth back into their alliance, checked the expansion of Elis, and in midsummer 418 cornered the Argive army, forced the Argive generals to admit defeat without a battle, and imposed peace terms on them. The Argives, however, once the army was safely back in Argos, trepudiated the terms. The Spartans were furious with the commander of their army, Agis, one of their two kings; the ephors (the highest civil magistrates of Sparta) publicly rebuked him and ordered him out anew, this time accompanied by a number of ephors.

Agis again brought the Argive army with its Arcadian and Athenian allies to battle. The Spartans were drawn up on the right of their battleline, with the troops of Brasidas and the neodamodeis, a class of Spartan without political rights, next to them and their allies to the left. Agis had about 3,600 Spartans, formed eight deep, with a front rank 448 men long. On the opposing side the Mantineans were on the right; next to them were their Arcadian allies, then a unit of 1,000 elite Argives (who were supported in their profession of arms by the city), then the rest of the Argives, their allies, and on the far left flank (directly opposite the Spartans), the Athenians.

The armies approached each other, the Argives and their allies shouting their war cries to rouse their spirit, the Spartans quietly and steadily, keeping in step to the music of their flutes. As the two armies approached each other Agis decided to change formation because he saw that his army extended too far to the right.

As two armies approach each other, their right wings extend to the right, and both armies tend to extend beyond the left wing of the enemy, because each man is motivated by his fear to place his unprotected side behind the shield of the man drawn up next to him on his right and he thinks that the compactness of the formation is his best protection; for this reason the rightmost man in the front line becomes the guide, as he strains always to get his unprotected side past the enemy and everyone else in the formation follows him.

The flank of the Mantineans extended far beyond the left of the Spartan line, and the Spartans were even farther extended past the Athenians, and Agis thought that the enemy might turn his left, so he ordered his leftmost units to move to the left, opening a gap in the middle of his line, and he ordered his two rightmost units to march down and fill the gap. The commanders on the right refused, because the lines were already advancing—later they were found guilty of cowardice—and Agis did not have time to close the gap before the two armies met. Agis's left wing was overwhelmed by the enemy, routed and driven from the field, but, on the right, King Agis and his elite guard routed the enemy before the lines even met. Some of the enemy were trampled to death in their panicked flight.

Agis wheeled his phalanx around to save his left wing, which by then was in flight. His advance across the battlefield caused the Argives, who had defeated Agis's left, to break and run, and he cornered some Mantinean soldiers, but he did not make a vigorous pursuit of the defeated—Spartans generally fought steadily and tenaciously until the enemy broke but then let them escape. Agis lost about 300 men, his opponents about 1,100. Sparta and Argos made a fifty-year treaty and Mantinea rejoined the Spartan alliance. The Spartan alliance was again intact and Sparta's prestige was restored. Alcibiades' reputation was damaged, and Nicias's support of peace was reaffirmed in Athens.

In 416 Alcibiades convinced the Athenians to send an expedition to the tiny island of Melos. The Melians were no threat to the Athenians, except that they did not want to give up their freedom and become part of the Athenian empire; Athenian policy, however, (and Alcibiades) allowed no room for neutrals—all Greeks were either with them or against them—and they presented the Melians with an ultimatum, enter the Athenian alliance or be exterminated. The Melians resisted, and the Athenians put them under siege for almost a year. Finally the

Melians capitulated, and the Athenians executed all adult males and sold the women and children into slavery.

In the spring of 415 the Athenians received sixty talents of silver and a request for an alliance against Syracuse from Segesta, a town in Sicily, the Athenians had always suspected that the Syracusans might help their mother city, Corinth, the ally of Sparta, and they believed (erroneously) that the Sicilians were enormously wealthy and would support the whole Athenian fleet for as long as it took for them to force Syracuse and the rest of Sicily into the Athenian empire. Alcibiades saw this expedition as his big chance. He spoke for it in the assembly, overrode Nicias's objections, and convinced the Athenians to approve a budget of 3,000 talents and a force of 60 triremes, 40 troop ships, 1,500 hoplites, 700 thetes as marines, 30 cavalry, and (if the ships had full crews) 10,000 oarsmen. The Athenian people appointed Nicias, Lamachus (a steady general), and Alcibiades to lead the expedition.

On the day the fleet was to sail the Athenians awoke to find that someone had mutilated the sacred herms (little busts of Hermes scattered throughout Athens and Attica). The people of Athens attributed the sacrilege to the opponents of democracy, that is, to the aristocrats, and, in particular, they suspected Alcibiades because, rumor had it, he had once held a mock religious ceremony. The Athenians allowed him to sail but then decided to send a ship after him to summon him back to stand trial.

When the Athenian fleet reached Sicily, they found no money and no allies—the western Greeks were terrified of them—and the generals could not decide what to do. Nicias proposed that they attack Selinus (the stated objective of the fleet), make a show of force along the coast, and return home. Alcibiades proposed that they send representatives to the native population and to all Greek cities except Syracuse and Selinus to determine who would help them. Lamachus proposed that they attack Syracuse, while the Athenians were at full strength and the Syracusans were most unprepared and most frightened. In the end the generals compromised: they made a reconnaissance in force and then returned to winter quarters.

At this point the ship arrived to take Alcibiades back for trial; on the way home he jumped ship, escaped to Sparta, and made himself as useful to the Spartans as he could—he advised them that the Athenians intended to conquer Syracuse as a first step in a renewed war against Sparta and that the Spartans should respond immediately by sending help to Syracuse and by invading Attica, and this time when they invaded Attica, they should build a fort and keep their army in Attica all year round. The Spartans did not want to confront the Athenians directly, nor send a Spartan army as far away as Sicily, so they decided to help the Syracusans by sending them one expert, a Spartan named Gylippus.

Meanwhile the Athenians had begun their campaign. They seized the plains to the west and above Syracuse, built a fort ("the circle fort") in the center of the plains and extended walls north and south, to blockade Syracuse by land while their fleet attempted to blockade Syracuse by sea. When the Syracusans began a counterwall to the south of the Athenian wall, an Athenian elite force of 300 stormed it and took it. The Syracusans counterattacked, killed Lamachus, and almost captured the circle fort, but the Athenian fleet rowed into the Great Harbor and forced the Syracusans to withdraw into their city. The Athenians went on to complete their southern walls (two of them to enclose the beach the fleet used and to protect supply lines from the sea to the circle fort).

The Syracusans were so discouraged that they debated whether to make terms with the Athenians, but in the midst of their debate, Gylippus arrived and put new heart into them. He cut off the Athenian wall to the north with a new counterwall, and he forced Nicias to move his camp to the Plemmachium (the southern jaw of the Great Harbor). Nicias fell sick, he became depressed—he had never had faith in the expedition and now he alone was responsible for it—and he sent a letter to Athens and asked to be relieved.

"Our fleet and men were in prime condition when we arrived, the timbers were dry and we had full crews. Now because of the time they have been at sea the ships' timbers are waterlogged and our crews are no longer at full strength. We cannot beach our ships and repair them because we need every ship in case of an enemy attack on us and we must keep watch night and day to prevent a surprise attack. And even if we outnumbered them and were not forced to keep watch everywhere, still we would be in trouble because we can barely get our supplies past them and we are continually losing oarsmen to enemy cavalry when they forage. Our slaves are deserting and the Sicilians are returning to their cities. In short, I am writing to inform you that the moment when we had full crews was brief, that those with the expertise and spirit to get the ships going are few, and that we have no place to recruit new crew members, and, Athenians, you are not easy to command because of your difficult nature."

The Athenian people (in that winter of 414) voted to send the generals Eurymedon and Demosthenes to reinforce Nicias, and, in addition to the Syracusan campaign, they launched attacks on Amphipolis and on the coasts of Laconia. The Spartans demanded redress (through arbitration) and the Athenians refused. The Spartans now believed that war had been forced on them unjustly and they were confident that heaven would aid them and they would win in the end. The Spartan king, Agis, invaded Attica in 413 and (following the advice of Alcibiades) constructed a fort at Decelea in Attica to maintain troops there year round and prevent the Athenians from ever setting foot outside their walls.

In the spring of 413 the Syracusan fleet attacked the Athenian fleet in the Great Harbor. The Athenian fleet barely held its own, and while the Athenians in the Plemmyrium were watching the battle, Gylippus made a surprise attack on them and seized the Athenian camp there. Then, in July 413, the Syracusan fleet, having reinforced the bows of their ships, attacked the Athenians in the Great Harbor, while Gylippus assaulted the southern walls. The Athenians were on the brink of destruction when Demosthenes and Eurymedon rowed into the Great Harbor with Athenian reinforcements, 73 triremes, and 5,000 hoplites. The Syracusans withdrew.

Demosthenes assessed the condition of the ships and men at Syracuse, and he advised Nicias to withdraw immediately. Nicias refused. He knew what happened to generals who did not fulfil the expectations of the Athenian people—they were executed—and he preferred to die fighting. Demosthenes then proposed that they try a night attack on the counterwall to the north, with the understanding that if the attack failed, the Athenians would withdraw. Nicias reluctantly agreed. The night attack did fail and Demosthenes finally persuaded Nicias to agree to withdraw, but their decision was undone by an eclipse of the moon (27 August 413). The soothsayers advised the Athenians not to move for thrice nine days, and Nicias took their advice, which agreed with his own inclinations.

Gylippus and the Syracusans were confident now that they could not only defeat the Athenians but annihilate them, and they began to construct a wall of ships across the mouth of the Great Harbor. The Athenians attacked with every one of their 110 ships; their first attack penetrated to the barrier of ships, but when they tried to break the line of tethered ships, the Syracusans attacked them from all sides. The Athenians had no room to maneuver. Ship crashed into ship, marine fought marine, ship to ship, the oarsmen and the steersmen held nothing back. No one could make sense of what was happening, or give direction, with the noise of ships crashing, and the shouts of so many men, and the confusion of 200 ships fighting in a crowded harbor. No one could hear orders. The army on shore shouted encouragement when they thought their fleet was winning and cried out in despair when they saw part defeated. In the end the Syracusans broke the Athenians' will to keep fighting and the Athenians rowed to the land, beached their ships, jumped out, and ran to safety. Panic infected the Athenian camp. The oarsmen refused to man the ships for another attempt, even to try a dawn attack to break out of the harbor and escape. The generals had never considered what to do if they were defeated, and they vacillated for two days before they decided to retreat overland.

The Syracusans pursued and quickly surrounded Demosthenes' division; they accepted Demosthenes' surrender, granting only one condition—they promised not to kill the prisoners on the spot. They pursued Nicias's troops to the banks of a river and there, when the Athenians and their allies broke ranks in their wild desire to drink, the Syracusans slaughtered them. The Syracusans executed the generals, sold the allies of the Athenians as slaves, and threw the Athenians into a quarry. Of the 40,000 men in the expedition the Syracusans took 7,000 prisoner and left them to perish. A handful escaped during the night and the Syracusans later released a very few.

The Athenians suffered an irreversible disaster at Syracuse. Later Athenians (and modern historians) blamed the democracy, in that the Athenian people preferred the promises of demagogues like Alcibiades to the measured advice of men like Nicias and, further, that the democracy held its leaders accountable for success at the threat of their lives, so that Nicias knew, if he withdrew from Syracuse, he would be condemned to death—he did not have the moral courage to ignore his own personal fate for the benefit of the whole. The democracy is also held accountable for the disaster because its suspicion of men with power caused it to divide up the command and deny any single person the authority to make binding decisions.

On the other hand, Athenian democracy was responsible for the high morale of the ships' crews and for the Athenian fighting spirit, and that fighting spirit predisposed the Athenians to favor aggressive action. Their fundamental error was not so much their overconfidence in the power of their fleet but in their failure to understand the need to operate from a secure base. In terms of the principles of war they violated security in the interests of the offensive. While the Syracusans could attack at a moment of their choosing or retreat to safety in their walled city, where they could live a fairly comfortable and regular life, the Athenians in camp before Syracuse deteriorated in health just as their ships deteriorated. The Athenians consistently undervalued the need for security.

At the end of 413 the news raced through the Aegean. The island members of the Athenian empire revolted, the Spartans reached a secret agreement with the Persians, to abandon the Ionians of Asia Minor to the Persians in exchange for Persian money to build a fleet and hire oarsmen; and the Athenians used their emergency reserve of money to commission the 100 hulls laid up in dry dock. From 413 to 411 the Athenians held their own at sea. Meanwhile, Alcibiades had to flee from Sparta—he had seduced the wife of King Agis—and in 411 he arrived in Persia, where, like a good sophist, he urged the Persians to let Sparta and Athens fight each other to exhaustion, while, in secret, he advised the Athenians that, if they would abolish the democracy, he could persuade the Persians to help them.

The Athenians believed him and they voted to institute a new government, the "government of 400" leading citizens, who would choose 5,000 citizens to be the sovereign body of Athens, to oversee the war and bring peace. (The Athenians in the fleet at Samos set up a government in exile but took no other action against the new government.) The "400" restored Alcibiades' rights and appointed him general. Alcibiades commanded the fleet with some success, but in 410, after the new government had not received Persian money nor ended the war, the Athenians restored the democracy. They continued to employ Alcibiades and by the beginning of 407 the Athenians had forced a standoff at sea, they had regained their confidence, they were becoming more aggressive—the Spartans had to pay their oarsmen three times what the Athenians paid theirs—and they welcomed Alcibiades back to Athens.

Alcibiades' first official act was to raise Athenian morale by leading the state procession along the Sacred Way to Eleusis (the first time the festival had been celebrated since Decelea was occupied), and then he returned to the fleet. There he found that the situation had changed. Early in 406 the Spartans had appointed a new admiral-in-chief, Lysander, and he had won the friendship and support of the son of the Persian king, Cyrus the Younger. Alcibiades returned to Athens to report the new situation and his fleet was defeated in his absence by the Spartans. The defeat turned the scales once more against Alcibiades—he had already disappointed the Athenian people by his failure to produce Persian money—and he was forced to escape into exile.

Nonetheless, the Athenian position was not hopeless. When they heard that the Spartan commander Callicratidas (Lysander's replacement) had blockaded their own commander, Conon, at Mytilene on Lesbos, the Athenians mustered every man old enough to row, slave and free, rich and poor, crewed 110 ships in thirty days, collected ten ships from Samos and thirty more from their other allies, and met Callicratidas with his fleet of 120 ships at the Arginusae Islands. The Athenians incorporated the islands into their line to extend their line still further and force Callicratidas to break his fleet into two divisions to engage the left and right wing of the Athenians. Callicratidas' navigator thought that there were too many Athenians, and he suggested that Callicratidas order a retreat; Callicratidas replied that Sparta would be no worse off with him dead.

The weather was stormy and soon after the two formations met, they scattered and fought ship to ship. Callicratidas's ship rammed an Athenian ship, Callicratidas fell into the sea, and he was never seen again; the Athenian right wing routed the Peloponnesians. The Peloponnesians lost more than seventy ships; the Athenians lost twenty-five ships. The battle of Arginusae was an Athenian victory, but because of the stormy weather, the generals could not rescue the 5,000 oarsmen thrown into the water and the Athenian people were so furious at the loss of these irreplaceable men that they condemned the generals to death.

Even so, the victory at Arginusae gave the Athenians one last chance for peace. They received an offer from the Spartans to evacuate Decelea and end the war, if the Athenians would accept peace on the basis of the status quo. The Athenians refused and soon found themselves facing a new fleet, commanded by Lysander (who had persuaded Cyrus to furnish the necessary money), and stationed at Lampsacus on the Asian side of the Hellespont, where it threatened Athens's grain supply. The Athenians sent their whole fleet (180 ships) to Aegospotami ("the River of Goats") on the Chersonese side of the Hellespont where the Hellespont is about one and three–quarters miles wide. Once again, as at Syracuse (and at Arginusae, where storms had prevented the Spartans from launching a surprise attack), the Athenians rejected a safe harbor (Sestos) in favor of an exposed position close to the enemy.

The Athenians were still confident that they could defeat the Spartan fleet, and for five days the Athenians rowed across the Hellespont and offered battle to Lysander. For five days he refused to leave his safe harbor, and the Athenians came to believe that he was afraid of them and would never come out. On the fifth day, when once more he refused to come out, the Athenians returned to Aegospotami, beached their ships, and scattered across the countryside in search of firewood and food. Lysander chose that moment to attack. He caught the Athenians totally by surprise and captured most of their ships still beached. He executed all Athenians taken prisoner.

When the news reached the Piraeus, the first people to hear it began to wail, and the wailing travelled along with the news all the way up the Long Walls to

Athens itself. The Athenians feared that what they had done to so many others would now be done to them, and not without reason, for some of Sparta's allies wanted to do just that, but the Spartans refused "to destroy the city which had served Greece so well in the Persian wars" and accepted its surrender—the Long Walls and the walls of the Piraeus were demolished, the fleet except for twelve ships was surrendered, all Athenian garrisons everywhere were removed, all exiles were recalled, and a new anti-democratic government was installed.

The Athenians lost the war for several reasons. They turned away from Pericles' conservative policy—to defend Athens and the bulk of the fleet while raiding the enemy. They had no clear objectives in the war. They overrated the power of their fleet and they never understood the necessity to secure the fleet in a safe harbor, not at Syracuse, Arginusae, or Aegospotami. While the democratic assembly voted to adopt the (ultimately) disastrous policies proposed by its leaders, the Athenian people can hardly be blamed for the strategic and tactical failings of those leaders, although they exacerbated those failings by their narrow intolerance of the setbacks inevitable in war.

The Athenians lost, and Greeks everywhere rejoiced because now, at long last, they believed they would be free.

## 25.  The  Spartan  Soldier

# 14

# The Demise of Hoplite Warfare
## *The Greeks Get What They Ask For*

While the other Greeks celebrated, the Spartans assumed Athens's place at the head of an empire. They were determined that they never would have to fight such a war again and, second, they rejected the traditional, conservative, and circumscribed Spartan policy that limited Sparta's interests to the domination of the Peloponnesus only; unfortunately for the Spartans they neither had the strength nor the unity of purpose to maintain such an empire and their new policy led to a revulsion of feeling against them. They established narrow oligarchic governments throughout the new empire, garrisoned by mercenaries under Spartan command, in Athens they installed the "Thirty Tyrants" (who began a reign of terror against the supporters of democracy and moderation) and then they stood by while the thirty tyrants were driven from Athens by the supporters of democracy. The Spartans tried to break all alliances and leagues which might be a threat to them, leagues in Arcadia, Elis, and Chalcidice. Their pretext was that, as "liberators," they supported the ancestral constitutions of Greece.

These "liberators" of Greece had promised the Persians that, in exchange for their help, they would return the Greeks of Ionia to Persian control. Instead they conspired with Cyrus, the younger brother of the Persian king, Artaxerxes, to help him overthrow his older brother in exchange for his promise not to insist that they fulfil the terms of the treaty. In 401, when Cyrus mustered his army of revolt (with 13,000 Greek mercenaries under the command of the Spartan exile Clearchus), the Spartans supported him with their fleet. Cyrus marched his army into the heart of the Persian empire and fought Artaxerxes at Cunaxa. He drew up his army with the Greek phalanx on the right, its right flank protected by the Euphrates River, he posted himself in the center with about 6,000 cavalry and placed his native infantry to his left. Artaxerxes' army was so large that his center extended past Cyrus's left wing. Cyrus asked the Greeks to shift their position more to the center, but the Greek commander refused to pull his flank from the river.

"When the two armies were about half a mile apart, the Greeks began to chant their warsong and they advanced. As they advanced part of the phalanx bulged forward and those who were left behind began to run and they all shouted and they all were running. Some clashed their spears against their shields to frighten the enemy horses. Before they reached arrow range the barbarians turned and fled. Then the Greeks pursued as hard as they could, but they shouted to each other not to run a race but to pursue in ranks."

Only one Greek was hurt, wounded by an arrow, and the battle seemed all but won, until Cyrus saw his brother, yelled, "I see the man himself," charged, and was killed. The news stunned the Greeks. Their generals went to negotiate with the Persians, the Persians executed them, the leaderless Greek army elected new leaders, and decided to march out of the Persian empire. Artaxerxes sent cavalry to follow them and harry them, but he saw no reason to fight another battle and suffer large casualties to annihilate a force already retreating from his kingdom. Eventually the army did reach the sea and home, and Xenophon wrote an account of the great adventure, Greeks everywhere learned of it and, because of it, believed that they could defeat Persians any time they pleased.

Artaxerxes ordered his satraps to occupy Ionia, and the Spartans sent their new (398 B.C.) king, Agesilaus, with an expeditionary force of 20,000 hoplites (mostly mercenaries) to guarantee the freedom of the Greek cities of Asia Minor. Agesilaus was an excellent tactician, but a poor strategist. His best course might have been to try to detach Lydia and Caria from the Persian empire and establish them as buffer states between the Ionians and the Persians, but in his campaigns of 396–395 he ravaged Lydia and Caria to raise money to pay his army, and he alienated the very people he needed to win over.

Tactically he was the master of his enemies (and thus offered more "proof" that Greeks could defeat Persians any time they chose). In 395 he defeated and routed the Persian army before Sardis and advanced without opposition until unfavorable omens convinced him to turn back. Strategically his campaign not only failed to accomplish his objective but, worse, it convinced the Persian king that this war was directed at him, and he sent envoys with bags of gold coin to Greece to furnish monetary support to Sparta's enemies. Persian money underwrote a new, anti-Spartan, League of Corinth, an alliance of Athens, Thebes, Corinth, and many Peloponnesian states eager to see Sparta defeated.

While the allies met (in 394) and discussed their plans, the Spartans recalled Agesilaus, summoned their allies, and marched on Corinth. They seized the initiative and forced their enemies to fight on rugged terrain (near the River Nemea on the border between Sicyon and Corinth) before they were ready. The Thebans and Boeotians on the allied right moved to their right away from the Spartans; their movement compelled the Athenians on the left to follow, and the Athenians were outflanked by the Spartans. The Spartans sacrificed a goat and charged. They broke the Athenians and held the battlefield, but their allies had been overwhelmed and pursued off the field. Now the enemy who had pursued the allies came marching back in column. As each section of the column appeared in front of the Spartans, the Spartans charged and routed it, so that the Spartans routed every single division of the enemy army.

Meanwhile Agesilaus was marching his troops through Thrace, Macedonia, Thessaly, past Thermopylae, and into Bocotia to the city of Coronea, where the Theban army was waiting for him. Agesilaus had two units of Spartans and the neodamodeis, the mercenaries, the Ionian Greeks, and some troops whom he had recruited on his return march. The Thebans and the Bocotians had their local allies and contingents from Athens, Argos, and Corinth. As at the battle of Nemea, so at the battle of Coronea, the Thebans routed the troops opposite them, Agesilaus and the Spartans routed the troops opposite them, and the Thebans attempted to retreat past the Spartans. Unlike Nemea, Agesilaus blocked their retreat with his phalanx and forced them to reform and fight him. The fighting was vicious and sustained, many Thebans were killed, but finally the Thebans fought their way through the center of the line and escaped. Agesilaus was so badly wounded that he was taken to Delphi to be healed by the god Apollo. (Other wounded soldiers from other battles went to be cured at the shrine of Aesclepius, whence we learn of the ghastly possibilities of hoplite battle: a chest wound which suppurated over a year and a half and filled sixty-seven basins with pus; blindness caused by a spear thrust to the face—the spear tip remained lodged in the bone.)

The Thebans did not meet the Spartans in a set battle again for twenty-three years. By 388 the war had become a stalemate. An Athenian named Iphicrates —and others—were beginning to recognize the shortcomings of the hoplite and to arm and train a new kind of soldier, the peltast. This soldier had a small round shield (a pelta), a leather cap, and several javelins The peltasts were used almost as cavalry, to rush in and throw their spears at the hoplites and then rush back out of danger. Iphicrates' greatest success came against a detachment of 250 Spartan hoplites who had been released at Corinth to return to Sparta to take part in a religious festival. The peltasts threw their javelins at the Spartans, ran away when the Spartans charged them, and then, when the Spartans resumed their march, reformed and attacked again and again. Each time they wounded or killed a few of the Spartans and, as the Spartans became weaker and more demoralized, the peltasts became ever bolder and more of them joined in the attack. Finally, they broke the Spartans and killed them almost to a man.

Greeks, demoralized by the constant warfare, accepted a peace (387) dictated in the name of the Persian king with the Spartans as his guarantors of compliance—all Ionia was to be under Persian control, all Greek states were to be autonomous except three islands possessed by Athens. Greek philosophers lamented the fallen state of Greece and they called upon the major powers, Sparta and Athens, to lead a crusade against Persia, to free the Ionian Greeks, to punish the Persians, and to unite Greece, but Agesilaus intended that Sparta under the cover of the peace would dominate Greece by military force and political intervention.

Agesilaus's philosophy was simple—to test each act with one question: is it good for Sparta? In 382 the Spartans violated the peace and seized the acropolis of Thebes. Another Spartan commander, entirely on his own initiative, tried, and failed, to seize the port of Athens. The Spartans lost Thebes within three years and drove the Athenians into a hostile alliance; in the next eight years the Thebans united Boeotia into a federal league, they reorganized their army under the direction of Epaminondas, one of the few military innovators of the classical age, and the Athenians refounded the Second Delian League. Still, the enmities, kindled by Spartan arrogance, burned down, and, as a series of fruitless campaigns brought neither the Spartans nor the Thebans and Athenians closer to victory, they all agreed to meet in Sparta at another peace conference (371) under the aegis of the Persian king.

The representatives agreed to the Persian king's terms—all Greek polises were to be independent and autonomous; all garrisons were to be withdrawn from Greek polises; all polises were to disarm. All the representatives signed the treaty, but the Thebans insisted that the conference recognize the legitimacy of the Boeotian League. Agesilaus refused. His refusal meant that the war between Sparta and Thebes continued, and it brought about the battle of Leuctra (a small town in Boeotia), at which the other Spartan king, Cleombrotus, met the Theban army commanded by Epaminondas. Epaminondas formed his Thebans fifty deep (against a Spartan phalanx twelve deep), he ordered his weaker, right wing to avoid battle, and he led the Thebans directly at the Spartan phalanx, where, he believed, the battle would be won or lost.

The Spartans were unsettled by the sight of a phalanx moving in a direction opposite to what it should, but they fought well. Cleombrotus and Epaminondas both tried to inspire their men by the example of their courage. Cleombrotus was wounded over and over again until he collapsed. The Spartans drove the Thebans back from his body, picked the king up, and removed him from the field before he died, but when the moment of crisis came, and the battle hung in the balance, the Theban leaders called upon their men to give one more push, and they broke the Spartan phalanx.

The Spartans had not lacked courage—400 of the 700 Spartan citizens at this battle were killed—but they had lacked manpower. If they could have fielded an army, such as they fielded during the Persian Wars, they would have won the battle, but there were now too few Spartans to hold an empire. The battle of Leuctra finished the Peloponnesian League (in its place the Arcadians founded their own league), revealed the mirage of Spartan invincibility, and ended Spartan domination of Greece. The Thebans invaded Laconia, freed Messenia, and on the northern border of Laconia founded the "Big City," Megalopolis, to be a watchdog over Sparta and a staging area for future invasions of Laconia.

Thebes, as leader of the Boeotian League, now attempted to replace Sparta as master of Greece and so precipitated Athens, Achaea, Elis, and some of the Arcadians into an anti-Theban alliance with Sparta. The two sides met in a battle at Mantinea in 362.

"When the Boeotians and Spartans joined battle, they struck at each other with their spears, and when the spears broke, they fought with their swords, and they seemed not to care whether they lived or died. Their bodies were tangled together, many were wounded, and many of the wounded were wounded more than once, but they continued to deal death to each other. For a long time the battle hung poised until Epaminondas realized that it was up to him; he selected his best men and led them into the middle of the enemy. He cast his javelin, struck the Spartan commander, fought hand to hand, killed some and terrified others, and he broke the phalanx of his enemies. The Spartans retreated from the battle, and the Boeotians pursued, killed the slowest, and piled up heaps of corpses."

Then, in the moment of victory, a Spartan thrust his spear into Epaminondas's chest, Epaminondas fell, and the Boeotians instantly halted. They carried Epaminondas to the rear and summoned physicians; the physicians told him that when the spear was removed from his chest, he would die.

"Then it is my hour to die," he said, and he gave the order to draw out the spear.

## 26. Diagram of the Battle of Leuctra

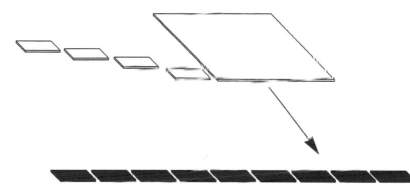

Note the massed formation on the Theban left, moving to their left, and the Theban allies in echelon, compared to **the battle of Mantinea (418)** in which the Sparta king attempted to redress his over-extended right by opening a gap in the middle and ordering the unit on the right to march behind his formation and fill the gap (which the subordinate commanders refused to do).

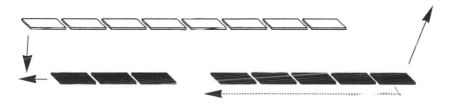

# Map 13: Macedonia and Philip

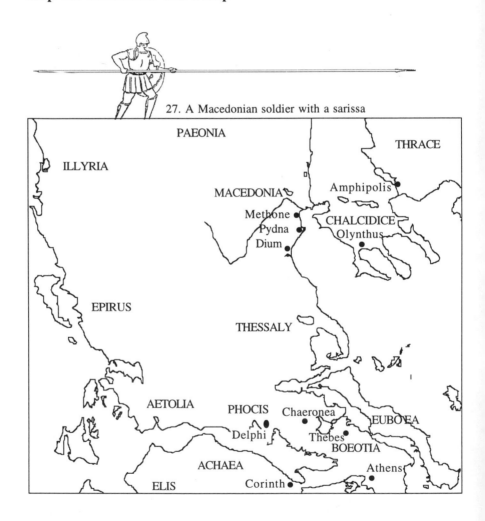

27. A Macedonian soldier with a sarissa

PAEONIA

THRACE

ILLYRIA

MACEDONIA

Amphipolis

Methone

CHALCIDICE

Pydna

Olynthus

Dium

EPIRUS

THESSALY

AETOLIA

PHOCIS

Chaeronea

EUBOEA

Delphi

Thebes

BOEOTIA

ACHAEA

Athens

ELIS

Corinth

# 15

# Philip and the Macedonians
## *One Man Restores a Nation*

Epaminondas and the Thebans had broken Spartan domination, but they had not been able to replace Sparta and dominate (and unite) Greece. Greeks believed that their polises should be autonomous (unless they voluntarily joined in a league) and free to conduct their affairs as they saw fit, and now, in truth, the Greek polises were free and autonomous. They expressed their autonomy by continuous inter–city warfare. A state of war existed between Boeotia and Athens, though they did not fight set battles; Thessaly was divided, so were Arcadia and Euboea; and the Spartans were determined to regain what they had lost; but, while the Greeks looked to their own affairs, to the north, outside the region Greeks considered Greek, events were about to overtake them.

Macedonia has two major rivers that form a great plain, good for horses. The plain is ringed by hills except to the east and provides both good agricultural land and good pasturage on the upland plateaus. Macedonia guards the high mountain passes into Greece and other passes into Illyria and Paeonia. The Macedonians were ruled by the royal house of the Argeads, who traced their ancestry back to Argos and claimed descent from Heracles; their claim had been recognized as valid by the presidents of the Olympic games and, thereafter, the Macedonian kings were considered to be Greek (ruling over barbarians).

By the time Philip came to the throne in 359, civil war, dynastic murders, and military disaster had brought Macedonia to the brink of dissolution. Philip had been sent in his teens to Thebes as a hostage (367–364), and there he came to know Epaminondas intimately and from him learned about Greeks, warfare, and diplomacy. In early summer 359, when Philip was twenty-two years old, the Illyrians invaded Macedonia, defeated the Macedonian army, and left 4,000 Macedonians and Philip's brother dead on the battlefield. Philip was elected king of a realm under attack from all directions. The Illyrians had already occupied the northwest territory of Macedonia; the Athenians, allied to the Illyrians, controlled the seacoast and intended to replace Philip with their own man. The

Paeonians in the north and the Thracians in the northeast—with their own candidate for the throne—were poised to invade. Some Macedonian cities had proclaimed their independence.

Philip subordinated his own ego to the needs of the state, he fought no unnecessary wars, he did not risk the lives of his soldiers needlessly, and he never lost sight of his ultimate objective, the security of Macedonia. In theory, Philip was an absolute ruler, commander-in-chief of the armed forces, high priest, treasurer, and chief justice, but in fact he depended upon the support of the army and the aristocracy; he could, and did, delegate his duties to the aristocrats in his court, his *hetairoi* ("companions"), but he, personally, was supposed to be accessible. Once, when he told an old woman that he did not have time to hear her petition, she yelled at him, "Then stop being king." He was addressed not as "your majesty," but simply as "king." The king and the Macedonians together formed the state—Philip and the Macedonians.

Philip relied upon two men, Antipater and Parmenion. Parmenion was the only general he trusted as much as himself. Antipater was the only man he trusted to leave as regent of the kingdom when he was on campaign. Philip had to be, and always was, at the forefront of battle: he received so many wounds that an essay was written "on the wounds of Philip"—he lost an eye, he fractured his leg, he broke his collarbone.

In the year 359, Philip's first goal was just to survive. He bought off the Paeonians and the Thracians, and he paid the Thracians extra to murder their candidate for his throne. In the breathing space he had purchased, he retrained his infantry and made them the bulwark of his army; always before the Macedonian king had ridden with the cavalry, but Philip chose to fight on foot with his infantry and leave the command of the companion cavalry to another. He modified the deep Theban formation by rearming the Macedonians with a small shield and a long spear (the sarissa), sixteen to twenty-six feet long. The spearpoints of the first five ranks, levelled, projected beyond the first rank and made the phalanx almost unbreakable.

Philip and his new army defeated a small Athenian army—they were attempting to put their own candidate on the Macedonian throne—and surrounded it. Philip did not want a war with Athens, so he offered the surrounded soldiers a deal, which they were glad to accept: he would let them all go if they would hand the pretender over to him. Philip not only kept his word, but he also helped them return to Athens, where they reported that the new Macedonian king was a charming gentleman, and when he, further, renounced his claim to Amphipolis (which the Athenians considered theirs), the Athenians made an alliance with him.

By 358, then, Philip had bought off two rivals and allied himself with a third, but he could not buy off the Illyrians; they intended to conquer Macedonia and resettle it. Philip met them in a battle lasting most of a day; at the end neither side could claim victory. Philip asked for a truce to collect the Macedonian dead—thus seeming to admit defeat—and the Illyrians relaxed.

Philip collected the bodies of his dead and then charged the Illyrians, caught them by surprise, routed them, pursued the fleeing army, and killed 7,000 of them.

This victory secured the western and northwestern border of Macedonia. Philip defeated the Paeonians on his northern border, and he secured his southwestern border (and brought his influence to the edge of the Adriatic Sea) by marrying Olympias, an Epirote princess whom Philip had fallen in love with when he saw her dancing with live snakes in a shrine in Samothrace. In 357 Philip struck a deal with the Athenians to trade Amphipolis (which the Athenians coveted) for Pydna (an Athenian possession on the Macedonian coast). Philip took Pydna, he took Amphipolis, and he kept both. The Athenians were outraged, but they were already fighting a war (357–355) to preserve their sea alliance (the Second Delian League) and they had neither the time nor the resources to fight Philip.

Thebes, the only other Greek state strong enough to have challenged Philip, became involved in a war with Phocis, a minor state located around Delphi. Philip turned his attention to the Chalcidian League, which had joined an alliance of Illyria, Paeonia, Thrace, and Athens. Philip lured the Chalcidian League out of the alliance by capturing the Athenian city of Potidaea and giving it to the Chalcidians. Philip then drove the Athenians off the coast of Macedonia. In August of 356 he learned on a single day that Parmenion, his general, had defeated the Illyrians, that his horse had won a victory at the Olympic games, and that his wife, Olympias, had borne a son: Alexander.

In his first three years Philip defeated his enemies, secured his kingdom, and built a new army, the best in the world at that time, considering his infantry, cavalry, and an innovation—the siege train. Siegecraft had recently been introduced into the Greek world by the Carthaginians. The Carthaginians were rivals to the Greeks in the west, and Carthage and Syracuse were fighting for the control of Sicily. Dionysius, the tyrant of Syracuse, gathered together weapons experts from Sicily, Italy, Greece, and Carthage itself, to invent and manufacture new weapons.

One expert invented a kind of crossbow, the gastraphetes, or "belly-bow," so called because it was braced against the belly when the string was drawn back with both hands. (Later a winch was added for better mechanical advantage.) The gastraphetes was essentially a compound bow with a pull beyond the strength of the ordinary man. It belonged to a category of weapons called catapults ("shield piercers"). The gastraphetes could have evolved into an individual, hand-held weapon (as in China) but, instead, Greek engineers concentrated on giving the catapult a larger payload and a longer range. Catapults, consequently, could seldom be employed in a battle (though when used they were effective).

Dionysius used these new devices and other innovations to attack the Carthaginian island stronghold of Motya (396). Dionysius built a mole out to the fortress and wheeled forward his siege towers, six stories high and equipped with catapults (to drive the defenders from the walls) and with battering rams (to break through the walls). His siege of Motya caught the attention of the eastern

Greeks and convinced them that they needed to study siege warfare, to employ it, and to defend against it.

As the siege towers approach and the attackers try to drive the defenders from their walls, the defenders (according to a short treatise, *Siegecraft (Poliorketike)*, written by Aeneas the Tactician) should raise sails or put up wicker screens to protect the defenders from missiles, burn materials that will emit clouds of smoke and conceal the defenders, build reinforcing towers of rocks and baskets of sand, suspend inflated skins or bags of wool between the battering ram and its target, or lasso the ram and drop a boulder on it. (The defenders should have put the boulder in place already.) If the defender knows where the enemy will use the ram, he can set up his own ram on the inside of the wall, tear away all but the outer crust of bricks, and deliver a counterblow.

The defenders should dig traps in the ground to catch the wheels of the siege towers, and they should build up their walls to top the siege towers. The defenders should pour pitch and sulfur on the siege towers and the sheds and then set them alight with burning sticks, or they could take a piece of wood, put spikes in the weighted end, attach inflammable material all over it, set it on fire, and drop it; it will stick to the sheds and set them on fire.

The defenders should also beware of tunnels; they should dig a trench outside the wall deep enough so that any tunnel will emerge into it, or, if a tunnel undermines a wall, the defenders should block the tunnel with rocks or cram it with wood shavings, set them alight, and drive the smoke down the tunnel (and smother the attackers) or drive bees or wasps into the tunnel, and they should build an inner wall to replace the outer (mined) wall. Defenders can also detect tunnels by putting the lip of a bronze vase to the ground and listening—digging will resonate in the vase—and they can countermine.

The defenders should cover all flammable points of access with felt (and keep it wet), but if the enemy do manage to set the gates on fire, the defenders should feed the fire and keep it so hot that it will hold the enemy at bay while the defenders dig a trench and build a defensive wall. They should demolish nearby houses if necessary. Defenders can extinguish fires with vinegar, but they are better advised to smear flammable surfaces with bird lime (which won't burn). Once they have thwarted the enemy's engines, tunnels, and fires, they may face an assault with siege ladders; if they are driven back from the edge of the wall by missiles, they can still push the ladders over with a wooden pitchfork, or if the ladder is even with or just below the top of the wall, they can push over the first man to appear.

Philip's siegecraft was crucial in his campaign to dominate the cities on his borders. Philip's contemporaries developed the oxybeles, a more powerful, fixed bow drawn by a winch and levers; the oxybeles gave way to a reinvention of the bow by breaking it in half, each half pulling against twisted sinews to create more pull, more payload, and more range: stones from ten to 180 pounds could be thrown one-quarter of a mile. When Philip brought up his siege train, few cities could resist, and as for the few which could, Philip asked if a donkey laden with gold could gain access where his siege train could not; he accomplished as much by his generous gifts as he did by assault.

Once he had secured his borders, he was determined to dominate those powers which had previously dominated Macedonia, and he seized an opportunity to enter into Greek affairs. The Thebans and the Thessalians were fighting a "Sacred" War with Phocis. The Thebans claimed that the Phocians had violated the sanctity of Delphi (hence, "Sacred" War), but their real purpose was to annex Phocis. They soon found that the easy war they had expected was grim and difficult because the Phocians seized the treasures of Delphi and used them to hire a mercenary army. When the Thebans killed the soldiers hired by the Phocians, the Phocians just hired more, but the Thebans who were killed could not be replaced. Thebes' allies, the Thessalians, were split into factions, and one of the factions asked Philip to intervene in the war. In 353 Philip led his troops into action against the Phocian mercenaries, but the enemy general drew Philip into a prepared position, flanked by catapults, and broke the Macedonian phalanx. Philip found himself for the first time having to regain the confidence of his army, but in 352 he defeated the Phocian forces, and the hostile Thessalians, at the Battle of the Crocus Fields. Because of this victory and his previous machinations in Thessaly—Philip and the Thessalian nobles all liked drinking and riding and hunting and carousing with young men and women, and, more to the point, Philip could drink them under the table—Philip was chosen hegemon of Thessaly, a position that entitled him to all the harbor and market dues (much needed money) and, more importantly, to the command of the fine Thessalian cavalry (which almost doubled the strength of cavalry at his disposal).

Still Philip was thwarted in his attempt to bring his army into Greece, and so he turned his attention to breaking the Chalcidian League. The Chalcidians appealed to Athens for help and the Athenian orator, Demosthenes, persuaded the Athenians, despite their suspicions of the Chalcidians, despite rival orators who told the Athenians that Philip wanted to be their friend, despite their circumscribed and limited resources, that Philip was their enemy and they should help the Chalcidians, but the Athenians were too slow. Philip had already corrupted the aristocrats of Olynthus, they deserted to him, and Olynthus fell into his hands. (Philip once said that the man he liked the best was the one who was about to betray his city to him and the one he despised the most was the one who had already done it.)

After Chalcidice fell, the Athenians and Philip signed a peace treaty (in 346). Philip bribed his way through Thermopylae, entered Phocis, and ended the Sacred War, for which service he received the Phocian seat on the Amphictyony (the Greek council concerned with the administration of Delphi). Philip returned to the north and attacked Perinthus and Byzantium (a city vital to Athens's supply system). When the Athenians reacted to the threat, sent a fleet, and forced him to lift the siege of Perinthus, he decided that the time had come to confront the Athenians directly. He marched his army down to the borders of Boeotia, where he offered the Thebans the only two choices he thought they had, to join him and share in the booty or to stand aside and let him pass. The Thebans, however, were persuaded by Demosthenes that Philip intended to conquer them as well as Athens, and they joined an alliance with the Athenians. Philip was astounded that one man's oratory could threaten everything the Macedonians had gained in Greece.

On 2 August 338, the two armies met at Chaeronea. The Macedonians were drawn up with their cavalry on the left under the command of Alexander (who was then 18 years old) facing the Thebans and the phalanx under the command of Philip on the right facing the Athenians. The Athenians pushed the Macedonian phalanx backwards, and for a time they thought they were winning the battle, but they advanced too fast, and a gap opened between the Athenians and Thebans. When Philip sensed that the Athenians were becoming tired, he ordered his men to push hard and the Athenians gave way. At the same time, Alexander led the companion cavalry in a charge into the gap in the Greek line. The Athenians broke and ran. Philip let them escape and turned to the destruction of the Thebans. Alexander annihilated the Theban Sacred Band.

By the victory at Chaeronea Philip became the master of Greece. In 337 he reconstituted the Greek League (sometimes called the Second League of Corinth) as a federal union, the aim of which was to guarantee universal peace, provide collective security, ensure the liberty and autonomy of existing constitutions, and to protect Greeks from unlawful execution, redistribution of land, and piracy. The Greeks swore to uphold an offensive and defensive alliance with the Macedonians as equal partners under the hegemony of the Macedonian king, so long as Philip or his blood descendants held the throne of Macedonia. The first act of the league was to declare war on Persia (and the Persian king Darius). In spring 336, a vanguard of 10,000 men crossed into Asia Minor to prepare the way for the coming campaign.

In July of 336 Philip held a great feast to celebrate the marriage of his daughter. He invited—it seemed—the whole Greek world, and he paraded before them at the head of a procession of statues of the twelve gods, and another statue as well, the statue of a thirteenth god, Philip himself. Philip ordered his bodyguard to keep their distance while he worshipped—to prove that he had no enemies and could move among his own people unprotected—and a Macedonian named Pausanias, who had nursed a grudge against Philip for many years, saw his chance and struck the king down.

When the news came to Athens, Demosthenes celebrated because it seemed to him, and to many others, that as Macedonian power had been built by one man, so on his death it would collapse again, and Athens could regain its place in the Aegean. He proposed that the Athenians decree a gold crown for the assassin. In Macedonia on the same day Philip died, the army saluted his son, Alexander, as king. Alexander was fully prepared to be king, he had no credible rivals for the throne, he was popular with the army (soldiers at Chaeronea had said, "Philip is our general, Alexander is our king"), and he had the support of Philip's two foremost supporters and friends, Antipater and Parmenion.

Alexander was twenty years old. He had been commander of the companion cavalry for two years, he had led them at the battle of Chaeronea in 338, he had been left as regent for the kingdom when he was 14 and he had conducted an independent campaign when he was 16. Philip had been determined to train his son to be a worthy successor; he had recognized his own shortcomings —principally a want of education and culture—and he decided that his son would be prepared, both in the qualities necessary to a Macedonian king and in the education that Greeks considered proper. Philip had hired Aristotle to tutor Alexander and Alexander had acquired a love of Greek culture and, in particular, a love of its greatest work, the *Iliad*; the *Iliad* appealed to him because of its warrior code and code of honor—the king rules because he is the foremost warrior of the kingdom. He also learned a system of logic—to look to the ultimate goal—and he used this system of logic and his inherent intelligence to devastating effect on the Persians. Philip's last service to the Macedonians had been to ensure that his successor would be worthy of them.

When Alexander learned that the Greek League had refused to recognize him as hegemon, he wasted no time. He marched into Thessaly, and the Thessalans recognized him as heir and hegemon of the Thessalian League; he occupied Thermopylae and ordered the Greek league to meet at Corinth, he marched on Thebes, and the Thebans recognized his rights, and in Corinth he was appointed general with unlimited powers. He then marched back to Macedonia and convinced his neighbors that he was as capable as his father, but the Greeks had seized upon a rumor of his death to renounce their oaths, and he marched from Illyria to Thebes in fourteen days, took Thebes by storm —while the other Greek states waited to see what would happen—and razed the city. His destruction of Thebes sent shock waves through Greece, but Greeks everywhere now knew what would happen to them if they rebelled while Alexander was campaigning in Persia—from that time on, not a single Greek state that had sworn loyalty to Alexander betrayed their oath.

Alexander was ready to invade Persia.

# Map 14: The Empire of Alexander the Great

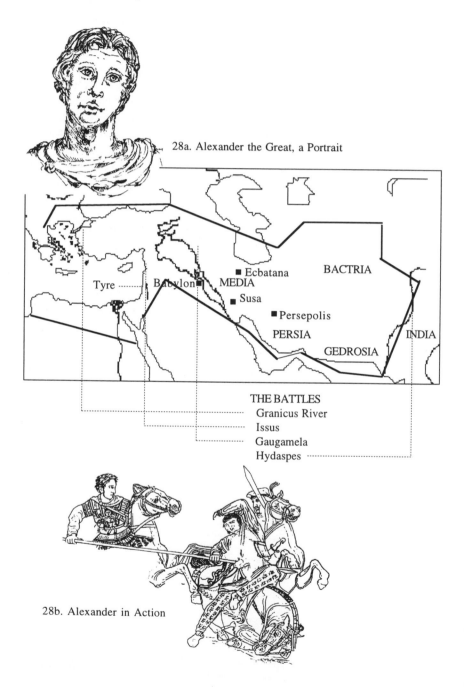

28a. Alexander the Great, a Portrait

■ Ecbatana

BACTRIA

Tyre

Babylon■    MEDIA

■ Susa

■ Persepolis

PERSIA

INDIA

GEDROSIA

THE BATTLES
Granicus River
Issus
Gaugamela
Hydaspes

28b. Alexander in Action

# 16

# Alexander the Great
## *One Man Changes the World*

In the spring of 334 Alexander crossed to Asia Minor. He brought 30,000 foot and 5,000 cavalry (of which 12,000 foot and 2,000 horse were Macedonian), and he left Antipater as regent in Macedonia with 9,000 troops. Alexander had to pay his troops 200 talents a month, he had a debt of 1,300 talents, and he had a war chest of 70 talents. The Persians had all the manpower of western Asia at their beck and call, and they also had a highly trained and highly motivated cavalry, 20,000 Greek mercenaries (who fought for pay but also for revenge againt the hated Macedonians), and a fleet much superior to Alexander's. (By the end of 334 Alexander had decided he would neutralize the Persian fleet by conquering those cities which provided them with ships, particularly the Phoenician cities along the eastern Mediterranean seaboard.)

The Persian commander, Memnon of Rhodes, a Greek married to Persian royalty, advocated a scorched earth policy—to retreat before Alexander, to deny him cities and provisions, and to let his expedition collapse around him. The Persian nobility opposed this plan. They were too proud to admit that they could not defeat the invader face to face, and they also found themselves in an anomalous position. If they listened to Memnon and lost, they would lose everything and they would be ruled by Greeks, but if they won, the credit would go to Memnon, and they would be ruled by Greeks. Therefore they preferred their own plan, which was to meet Alexander at the Granicus River and kill him in battle. (Alexander's plan had the same simplicity: he would force Darius to fight him, man to man, and the victor would be king of Asia.)

As Alexander approached the Granicus River, his scouts informed him that the enemy were drawn up on the other side of the river. The Persians had (by a rough estimate) 20,000 cavalry and slightly fewer than 20,000 mercenary infantry. Parmenion advised Alexander to camp and see whether the Persians would withdraw, but Alexander ordered an immediate attack with Parmenion in command of the phalanx on the left, himself in command of the cavalry on the right. Alexander was conspicuous in his bright armor and marked by the bodyguard around him, and he drew a mass of Persian cavalry to contest his crossing.

Alexander ordered the cavalry and one battalion of infantry to charge into the river; at the trumpet's signal, with battle cries resounding everywhere, Alexander entered the river. Some of the Persians were on top of the bank and some were down on the edge of the river; all of them threw javelins at the Macedonians, and cavalry met cavalry; the Persians had the advantage of position, the Macedonians had the advantage of experience and longer and stronger spears that they thrust and did not throw; gradually, despite heavy casualties, they forced their way up the bank.

Alexander charged into the thickest group of Persians, where their leaders were gathered, and there was a ferocious battle around him. The cavalry fought more like infantry: horse to horse and man to man in a wild melee. Alexander's spear broke in the fighting. He called on Aretes (one of the royal companions) for another spear but Aretes' spear had also broken in the struggle and he was fighting with the butt spike. Demaratus, a Corinthian, and another of the royal companions, gave Alexander his spear. Alexander seized it and charged Mithridates, the son-in-law of Darius; he struck Mithridates in the face with the spear and hurled him to the ground, but while Alexander was concentrating on Mithridates, Rhosaces charged him and struck him on the head with his sword. The blow of the sword cut off part of the crest of the helmet, but the helmet stopped the blow, and Alexander drove his own spear through Rhosaces' breastplate into his chest and knocked him from his horse. Behind Alexander, Spithridates raised his arm to strike the king with his sword, but Cleitus, Alexander's bodyguard, cut Spithridates' arm off at the shoulder.

Alexander and his men pushed the Persians back, and at last the Persians gave way and fled. About 1,000 Persians were killed, many of them nobles. Alexander's immediate attack had caught the Persians by surprise, and they never got their 20,000 mercenaries into the battle; Alexander surrounded them with cavalry and infantry and killed all of them, except for 2,000 taken prisoner. Twenty-five of the royal companions were killed in the first attack and about sixty cavalry and thirty infantry.

Alexander's victory opened the whole of Asia Minor; city after city came over to him and the few, like Miletus, which resisted, soon fell. In the spring he broke out of Asia Minor through the Cilician mountains to Issus. In Issus, however, he fell ill and had to delay his advance. When he recovered, he heard that Darius had entered Syria (333 B.C.), and so he left his wounded and sick at Issus and marched down the coast after him; Darius, however, was marching to Cilicia, where, he had heard, Alexander had stopped. The two armies passed each other on opposite sides of the Lebanon mountains. Darius occupied Issus, murdered all the Macedonians he found there and then followed Alexander down the coast to the Pinarus River. There he decided to halt, prepare a defensive position, and await Alexander's attack.

Alexander had to be convinced that Darius had gotten behind him, but once he accepted the fact, he wasted no time. He prepared his plan as he marched north. Darius had put his Greek mercenaries (30,000) to his right and tied the rest of his army into them. He set an ambush in the mountains south of the Pinarus to attack Alexander from the rear while Alexander was crossing the river. Darius, himself, was in the center. Alexander estimated that the greatest threat to his army would be a Persian cavalry thrust to the left, so he sent Parmenion and the Macedonian phalanx to his left and ordered Parmenion, no matter what, not to lose contact with the sea; Alexander sent a detachment of cavalry and archers to cover the Persian ambush, but the ambush fled as soon as they spotted Alexander's troops.

Alexander led his troops forward in step at first, so that the phalanx would not spread out or lose its formation in the advance, and he rode everywhere and called upon his men to be brave, and everywhere his men shouted back not to wait but to attack the enemy, and when they were within arrow range, the front ranks around Alexander and Alexander himself charged into the river at a run, so that they could close with the Persians, hand to hand, and neutralize the archers. That part of the battle went just as Alexander had conceived it—when he closed with the Persians, the Persians fled—but the Macedonian phalanx encountered steep banks everywhere, they lost their formation. Just when they were at their most confused, the Greek mercenaries charged them. The Greeks tried to break the Macedonians and pull out a victory even as their own side was fleeing; they fought in a vicious struggle in which 120 distinguished Macedonians were killed.

As soon as Darius saw his left wing collapse and Alexander charge towards him, he fled in his chariot. When the ground turned rough, he abandoned his chariot, his shield, his armor, his bow and quiver, and he continued his flight on horseback. The Macedonian right, seeing the Persians before them flee, turned on the flank of Darius's mercenaries, drove them back from the river and struck them down. The enemy broke. Alexander pursued the fleeing and panic-stricken enemy as hard as he could until he could no longer see the ground in front of his horse's hooves. Darius avoided capture.

The victory had several important consequences. Alexander captured Darius's mother, wife, and two daughters. (He treated them so well that Darius's mother eventually called Alexander "my son.") He also captured the Persian treasure train and put an end to his financial worries. Issus convinced many doubters that Alexander would win this war, and it enabled him to cut the Persians off from their fleet—though he still needed to conquer the coast and from their only source of heavy infantry, the Greeks. Darius had escaped, he had won time to recover, but he had also learned how formidable his opponent was; he offered terms to Alexander, and he offered to ransom his family. Alexander replied to Darius that, by virtue of the battle of Issus, Alexander, not Darius, was now king of Asia, and, if Darius wanted anything, he should approach Alexander as the king's subject, and it would be granted. Darius prepared to fight again.

Alexander continued his unimpeded march down the coast, until he reached the city of Tyre. The Tyrians thought that their island city (half a mile from the mainland), defended by a powerful fleet and by a combination of counter-siege machines along its walls, could hold out against even Alexander. Alexander drafted the local inhabitants and began to construct a mole 200 feet wide from the ruins of "Old Tyre" (on the mainland). At first the Tyrians were amused—*did the king think that he could conquer Poseidon, the god of the sea?*—but as the mole grew, so did their anxiety. They took to their ships and attacked the labor gangs. Alexander immediately ordered his fleet to cut the Tyrian ships off. He caught part of the fleet, and the Tyrians had to row for their lives.

As the mole approached the city, a storm arose; high winds destroyed a large part of the mole (an event which encouraged the Tyrians to believe that Poseidon *was* helping them), but Alexander refused to quit; the mole was swiftly rebuilt and when it was within missile range, he placed catapults on the end and knocked down a portion of the wall. The Tyrians built a new wall behind the original wall and shored it up with rocks and earth. Alexander lashed triremes together, put catapults on board, knocked down a part of the seaward wall, and stormed the city through the breach. The Tyrians met the storming party with a hail of missiles and only just turned them back; that night they rebuilt the fallen part of the wall.

The mole reached the city wall. The Macedonians rolled forward siege towers as high as the walls, dropped bridges, and attacked the Tyrians. The Tyrians jabbed huge bronze tridents into the shields of the Macedonians and hauled them in with ropes; the attacker then had to let the shield go and fight exposed or be pulled over the edge and plunge to his death. The Tyrians cast nets over the Macedonians, pinned their arms, and yanked them off the bridges. They filled bronze and iron shields with super-heated sand and poured the sand over the Macedonians leading the assault. The sand ran down into the breastplate and the undergarments, scorched the flesh, drove the victims mad with pain, and killed them. The Tyrians shot masses of blazing material into the throng of soldiers (and seldom missed a target), and they employed "crows" and "iron-hands" to grapple those taking cover behind the breastworks and hurl them to their death. The defenders took cover from the mass of incoming missiles behind large, spoked marble wheels, which, when spinning, caught the missiles and deflected or broke them and yet enabled the defenders to observe the attackers. They hung hides of double thickness stuffed with seaweed from the walls to break the force of the catapult stones. Some Tyrians ran onto the bridges and chopped at the Macedonians with axes, but always more Macedonians took the places of those who fell.

Alexander observed that the wall was weakest near the navy base, and he had the yoked triremes rowed there and the bridge of the siege towers dropped. He called upon his men to follow his example, and he ran across the bridge to the city wall by himself and fought hand to hand with the massed Tyrians; he killed some Tyrians with his spear, some with his sword, and some he knocked off with blows of his shield, and he drove the Tyrians back, and his Macedonians followed him. At the same time, in another part of the city, a ram knocked down a section of wall and the Macedonians charged through the opening. As the Tyrians fell back from the wall, they realized that their city could no longer be saved, but they resolved to fight to the death; they blocked the narrow streets and fought street by street until almost all of them—more than 7,000 men—had been killed. The 2,000 men of military age who survived Alexander hanged; he sold the woman and children (more than 13,000) into slavery.

The seven-month siege ended in July of 332.

Alexander continued his march to Egypt, where, late in November 332, he accepted the submission of the Persian satrap. Alexander sacrificed to Apis, the sacred bull, and was crowned Pharaoh. He traced out the boundaries of Alexandria (which was to become the first city of the Greek world). He visited the famous oracle of Zeus Ammon in the oasis of Siwa (and may have learned there that he was "the son of Zeus"). Alexander rested his troops, organized his supply, arranged affairs in Egypt (so that no one man could seize power there), and then he set out for his final confrontation with Darius. Alexander had about 7,000 cavalry and 40,000 infantry.

Darius had chosen a large plain near the little town of Gaugamela, a plain perfect for the maneuvering of cavalry, where he thought that his greater numbers, particularly his large force of fine cavalry, might overwhelm the Macedonians. He hoped an attack by a force of scythed chariots would disrupt the Macedonian phalanx—he was cut off from the recruiting ground for Greek mercenaries, and he had only a few heavy infantry. His chief concern was that Alexander might attack him in the dark, since he had no fortified camp, and he ordered his men to keep watch all night. The Persians spent a wakeful night wondering what would happen in the morning, while the Macedonians, after Alexander scouted the battlefield, rested.

On 1 October 331 the two armies fought the battle of Gaugamela. Alexander maneuvered his army on the oblique to the right across the plain, and the Persians followed. The Scythian cavalry tried to divert the movement with an attack, but still Alexander led to the right until he was close to the end of the land that the Persians had prepared. Darius ordered the cavalry on his left to ride around Alexander, attack his right, and stop his movement. The battle on the flank swayed back and forth, as each side sent reinforcements, but Alexander still continued his movement. At this moment Darius ordered the scythed chariots to attack Alexander himself and to disrupt his plans, but the Macedonian javelin men ran forward, caught the reins of the chariot teams, pulled the drivers out, and killed the horses. The chariots that escaped dashed through lanes formed by the Macedonians in their phalanx and were overpowered by specially designated troops behind the formation.

Darius advanced, but a gap had opened in his formation when the cavalry had left to attack Alexander's flank, and Alexander led the squadrons near him, and the phalanx drawn up with them, into the gap. Once in the gap, he formed a wedge with the companion cavalry, and they charged in close order, screaming their war cries and bristling with their sarissas; jabbing, thrusting, and striking at the faces of the Persians, they fought their way towards Darius. Darius turned and fled.

Alexander urged his men to their utmost effort, to catch and kill Darius and prevent the reforming of the Persian army, but a messenger brought a plea for help from Parmenion (who had seen a large cavalry force flank him on its way to the Macedonian camp), and Alexander had to turn back to rescue (as he thought) his phalanx. He ran the greatest risks of the battle, to fight his way back through the fleeing Persians to bring help, only to discover that Parmenion was safe. Alexander resumed his pursuit of Darius and continued all night, with only a brief pause at dusk, but in thirty-five miles he could not catch Darius.

Alexander dropped the pursuit and concentrated on winning over the eastern part of the Persian empire. He accepted the surrender of Babylon, and he appointed a Persian as satrap with civil powers, while a Macedonian held the military command. He captured the royal treasury at Susa and appointed a Persian as civil satrap. In the summer of 330, he took Persepolis, marked the conclusion of the war of revenge against Persia by burning the palace, released his Greek allies, and proclaimed himself King of Persia. He then returned to a relentless pursuit of Darius. Alexander's advance guard came upon Darius as he lay dying, where he had been stabbed by his own courtiers. One of the courtiers, Bessus, laid claim to the throne, but he was betrayed to Alexander in 329 and executed.

Between 330 and 327 Alexander subdued the hard-core resistance of the Iranian plateau. Alexander impressed them with his courage and his military ability, but he knew that he could not continue to rule the Persians as a conqueror: he intended to integrate the Macedonian and Iranian nobility, which he believed were much alike—they both loved hunting, riding, fighting, and feasting. He wore Persian dress for Persian ceremonies; he introduced *proskynesis*, the practice of bowing and touching the forehead as a salute to the king; he appointed Persians to positions of trust; he had Persian boys educated in Greek speech and Macedonian arms; he founded cities with Greek-Macedonian-Persian populations; he encouraged his Macedonians to marry Persian women; and he himself married into the Iranian and Persian nobility. He alone understood what he was trying to do and why, and he found that his Macedonians were suspicious, or outright hostile, to his plans.

In the autumn of 330, Philotas, the commander-in-chief of the companion cavalry and the son of Parmenion, heard of a plot to murder Alexander and did not report it to the king. (He said he did not think it was serious.) Alexander prosecuted him before the army assembly, convinced the army, and had him executed on the spot; Alexander ordered assassins to kill Philotas's brothers and father, Parmenion, Philip's most trusted commander. In the autumn of 328 Cleitus, the bodyguard who had saved Alexander's life at the Granicus, enraged Alexander at a drunken banquet by telling him that Alexander had forgotten who he was and who had put him where he was. Alexander ran Cleitus through with a spear. In the spring of 327 Alexander had the companions perform proskynesis. The companions complied, though they thought it ridiculous, but one man, Callisthenes, the nephew of Aristotle, refused. Alexander denied him the kiss of kinship. Callisthenes quipped, "So I go away, poorer by a kiss." Alexander was angry, and when he discovered that his pages were plotting to kill him, he blamed Callisthenes (their tutor). How Callisthenes died is unknown.

## 29. Persian against Greek (carved gem and seal)

# 30. Diagrams of Alexander's Major Battles

GRANICUS RIVER

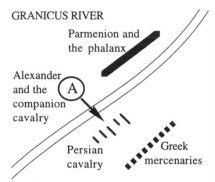

ISSUS

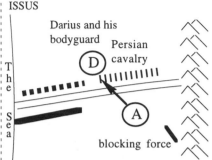

*Note the effects of the immediate evening attack: the Persians were caught by surprise and the Persian leaders did not bring their Greek mercenaries (heavy infantry) into the battle. Still, they had the chance they had sought, to end the war right there by killing Alexander*

*Alexander's scouts detected an ambush in the mountains and Alexander dispatched a blocking force. Alexander saw the key to the battle was the preservation of the left flank of his line, that Parmenion not be overwhelmed before Alexander had finished his business with Darius. With all else prepared he launched his charge directly at Darius.*

GAUGAMELA

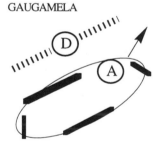

*Once again Alexander fought on a battlefield chosen by the enemy. The Persians outnumbered him in cavalry, but had only a few Greek mercenary infantry. Alexander secured his army on the field by using a reserve and flank guards to form a quasi-perimeter. Then he maneuvered obliquely off the prepared field. When the Persians tried to maneuver with him, gaps opened in their line and Alexander launched his charge into the gaps directly at Darius.*

*The Battle: Alexander knew that his horses would not face the elephants, so he used his cavalry to drive the Indian cavalry back and he used his light-armed soldiers and the phalanx to drive the*

HYDASPES RIVER

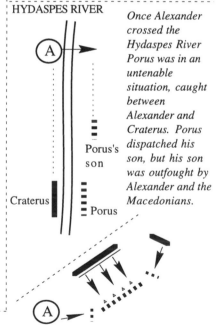

*Once Alexander crossed the Hydaspes River Porus was in an untenable situation, caught between Alexander and Craterus. Porus dispatched his son, but his son was outfought by Alexander and the Macedonians.*

*elephants back into the Indian infantry. He turned the Indians' elephants against them and he caused the Indian army to lose its cohesion.*

# 17

# Into India and Beyond

## *When Success Depends Upon One Man*

In the spring of 326 Alexander reached the Hydaspes River, where the Indian king, Porus, opposed his advance. Alexander had found allies in India and he believed, if he could conquer India, he would come to the Ocean and to the end of the inhabited world. First, though, he had to defeat Porus, an Indian king. Porus had light infantry, chariots, cavalry, and units of war elephants. Horses are naturally afraid of elephants, though they can be taught to work with them. Alexander had to cross a river in the face of the enemy, maneuver two independent wings, and then overcome the elephants. He planned an elaborate deception of the enemy. He had supplies gathered for a long encampment, as though he were going to wait for the river to drop enough to ford. He announced in public that he was going to wait, he placed pickets all along the river, and he instructed them to keep fires going and to make a lot of noise, and he led his cavalry up and down the river at night. Porus followed him on the other bank until, after many nights, he concluded that the movements were an empty threat.

Alexander made his move during a thunderstorm that masked the sound of the army on the march. He took his light-armed troops, the companion cavalry, and some infantry and left his second-in-command, Craterus, the rest (except for three units stationed along the way to maintain communications). He instructed Craterus to watch Porus and, if the king shifted his elephants against Alexander, Craterus was to cross. As he began the crossing, the scouts of Porus rushed off to inform the Indian king.

Once across the river Alexander drew up his army with the light-armed troops on the wings of the infantry and ordered them to follow quickly behind Alexander and the cavalry. Alexander wanted to fight his battle with Porus as close to Craterus as possible, to reduce the distance Craterus would have to cover to join the fight. Porus sent his son with 2,000 cavalry and 120 chariots to prevent the crossing, but his son arrived too late, the charge of the companion cavalry broke the Indian cavalry, the Indian chariots slid in the mud and proved useless, and Porus's son was killed in the fighting.

When word reached Porus, he determined to move as swiftly as he could and try to defeat Alexander before Craterus could cross. He left a small force to delay Craterus and he himself took 300 chariots, 4,000 cavalry, 200 elephants, and 30,000 infantry. He advanced through the soft ground until he found a place suitably firm for his cavalry. He drew his elephants up on a wide front, filled the gaps between them with infantry, and posted infantry on their flanks and the cavalry beyond them with the chariots in front. Alexander formed up his cavalry and waited for his infantry. He put his cavalry strength on his right, led by a thousand mounted archers, and he ordered his infantry not to engage the main army until they saw that the cavalry had thrown it into confusion. He sent a unit of cavalry to his left and ordered it to delay its attack until it saw the enemy cavalry leave its position in response to Alexander's attack on their left.

The horse archers attacked Porus's army first, and Alexander followed close behind. Porus ordered all his cavalry to swing around to meet this attack, and Alexander's cavalry unit on the left followed orders smartly and pursued the shifting Indian cavalry. The Indian cavalry split, part to defend the rear, part to fight with Alexander, but the confusion of the move threw them into disorder, and they fell back to their elephants. At that moment the Macedonian infantry advanced and came to grips with the Indian infantry. The soldiers threw all their missiles at the elephants' drivers, and many were killed. The elephants ran amuck and trampled Macedonian and Indian alike. The Indian cavalry returned to the charge, but Alexander beat them back again. The effect of Alexander's plan now became apparent. The Indian army was boxed in the middle, massed together, infantry, cavalry, elephant, without room to maneuver, while the Macedonians surrounded them and the Macedonian cavalry had room to charge and retreat. The Indian cavalry could not move and many were killed by the rampaging elephants. When the elephants finally became exhausted, Alexander ordered his infantry to lock shields and advance. The remnants of the Indian army that escaped through a gap in the cavalry had to face the army of Craterus, which had just moved up and which took over the pursuit. Two-thirds or more of the Indian army was killed or captured. Porus himself was wounded, taken prisoner, and brought to Alexander. Alexander asked him how he wanted to be treated and he replied, "Like a king." Alexander appointed him the satrap of India.

Alexander intended to continue the march, to come to the Ocean. His men, however, had heard that there were bigger and fiercer elephants over the next hill, and they refused to advance. They were supported by the soothsayers, who reported unfavorable omens, and Alexander, although he was furious, finally acquiesced. He turned his attention then to local campaigns, a punishing series of small battles in which he participated personally and recklessly. He was shot in the chest with an arrow and was near death; within days the rumor that he was dead had gained such currency that he had himself hoisted onto a horse so that the army could see that he was alive.

When he had recovered (September of 325), he decided to return to Susa through the Gedrosian desert, which no army had ever crossed. He ordered his fleet to follow along the shore with him and to bury barrels of water along the route, but the fleet was wrecked by ocean tides and delayed by monsoons and whales. The army ran out of water. Alexander shared the hardship, set the example for the rest of the army, and in the spring of 324 reached Susa.

There he discovered that many of the men he had appointed to power, many of them Persians, had believed that he was lost in the desert and they were free to do as they pleased. Alexander punished them: he replaced them with other Persians, he reorganized the empire, and he took a second wife in addition to his first, the Bactrian princess (chosen by policy and love) Roxane—now he married the daughter of Darius. Alexander gave the army its back pay, a bonus, and a release to anyone who wanted it, but the soldiers thought that the release meant that he was replacing them with Persians, and they shouted objections. He replied that he had raised them from nothing and made them wealthy men, but if they no longer wanted to keep good order, let them return to Macedonia and tell people there that they had deserted their king. The army sent representatives to him to beg his forgiveness, and he forgave them, but he continued to carry out a total reorganization of the army, to create a new ruling class and a new army, half Macedonian, half Persian, all imbued with Greek language and culture.

In 323 he returned to Babylon. There he caught a fever, and on 13 June 323 he died.

Some military historians believe that Alexander was the greatest military leader who ever lived. None dispute that he was one of the very best. He had unique advantages: he inherited an army that was an amalgamation of the best of the ancient world—cavalry derived ultimately from the Iranian plateau, heavy infantry from the Greeks, siegecraft from the Assyrians—and he was the son of one of the great military leaders and diplomats of the ancient world, the pupil of one of the greatest intellects and teachers of the ancient world, and he himself was gifted, physically and mentally. Alexander understood what are now called "the principles of war," his battles are masterpieces of planning and execution, and his mind reached much farther than the battlefield, much farther than the campaigns that made him king of Asia, to the very basis of rule. If he had lived longer, he might have fused the Iranians and Macedonians into one empire and one culture, but he died, and he left behind him no adult heir.

On his deathbed Alexander is supposed to have said, "The whole world will be filled with my funeral games." He was right. His generals fought each other first in the name of Alexander's posthumous son (by Roxane) and then in their own names. Some fought to reunite the empire (under themselves), and some fought to control a piece of it. They dismissed the Persian successors and made themselves competitors for the limited supply of Greek and Macedonian men; they settled Greeks and Macedonians in their territory, to be "citizen-soldiers," and they hired Greek and Macedonian mercenaries. They retained phalanx and cavalry, and they added an elephant corps.

We have one good description of what their battles were like (Raphia between the kings Ptolemy and Antiochus)—"The men stabbed and struck at each other with sarissas, while the elephants locked their tusks together and thrust and pushed with all their might and stamped all over the place, until the elephants of Antiochus overpowered Ptolemy's with their strength and pushed them sideways and when they had entirely taken them sideways, they gored them with their tusks; Ptolemy's elephants were panicked by the battle because African elephants cannot abide the smell and sound of Indian elephants, and also they were cowed by their size and strength. Some were badly wounded and they stampeded through their own formations, and disrupted Ptolemy's left."

On foot, horse, and elephant, the successors and the successors of the successors fought each other for forty years. The last chance of reuniting Alexander's empire died at the battle of Ipsus (301 B.C.). A father and son (Antigonus and Demetrius) had victory in their grasp when the son routed the cavalry opposite him, but he threw away the chance by pursuing the enemy off the field and leaving his father to be overwhelmed and killed. The successors displayed a high level of tactical skill and some strategic ability, but they were driven solely by individual ambition, and they committed the most despicable acts: they murdered Alexander's son, they swore oaths to each other and broke them, they sought asylum and then murdered their benefactors, brother killed brother, sons threatened their fathers, and their internecine war cost them India first and then the other eastern provinces and so weakened Macedonia that for the first time since the Persian invasion, two centuries before, an enemy broke through the borders.

In 279 B.C. a band of Gauls invaded Macedonia, smashed the Macedonian army, placed the Macedonian king's head on a pike, and plundered Macedonia. Another band of Gauls under the leadership of their chief, Brennus, joined in the plunder and then headed for the richer spoils of Greece. The Thessalians bribed Brennus to pass through their territory and attack other Greeks, Aetolians and Boeotians stopped him at Thermopylae, and Brennus sent a band of Gauls into Aetolia to draw the Aetolian troops away from Thermopylae.

"The Gauls captured the town of Callium and the fate the inhabitants suffered is the most unholy I have ever heard of and unlike anything humans beings have ever dared to do. They cut down all the males, the old and the young, even including babies at their mothers' breasts. The Gauls drank the blood and ate the flesh of the plump babies. The married and unmarried women who had their wits about them killed themselves when the city was taken. Those who lived were raped, but they did not live for long, as they received no food, nor any sleep, and were passed from one barbarian to another; the barbarians even raped the dying and the dead."

The Aetolians marched from Thermopylae to Aetolia. All men of military age were called up, and the older men came too because of the crisis, and women went with them—they were angrier about the barbarians than the men were. The Aetolian men and women harried the Gauls along their whole line of retreat; they threw missiles at the Gauls (and few missed because the Gauls had no protection except for their shields). When the Gauls charged them, they fled and, when the Gauls resumed their march, they returned to the attack. Less than half returned alive to their camp and Brennus.

Brennus decided to divide his forces, one to break into Greece at Thermopylae and the other, under his personal command, to raid Delphi. (It was now winter.) Brennus failed in his first attempt to break into Delphi. More Phocian troops arrived in the evening, and that night there was a snowstorm. (Apollo had made a promise through his priest that "white maidens" would help the defenders.) The Greeks shot arrows at the Gauls. Brennus was wounded and the Gauls had to carry him. They retreated, but they were blinded by the snow, harassed by arrows, wounded and killed, and only a few returned to the main band. The Greeks were more confident now. The Aetolians followed the main band and continually attacked them, the Thessalians joined in the attack, Brennus committed suicide, and the Gauls scattered.

In 277 Antigonus, the grandson of one of Alexander's generals, lured the Gauls into a battle in which they had their backs to the sea, and he annihilated them. Antigonus used the prestige of his victory to establish himself as king of Macedonia and to secure the kingdom for his descendants. Egypt was firmly under the control of the Ptolemies (and remained under their control until the Roman emperor Augustus removed the last Ptolemaic ruler, Cleopatra). The Asian empire was held by the descendants of Seleucus (one of Alexander's generals) and named after him: the Seleucid Empire.

Three Gallic tribes had invaded Asia Minor—they may have numbered no more than 20,000, but they inspired a terror as though they were inhuman monsters. They divided Asia Minor into three districts, so they would not interfere with each other's looting. Some cities defended themselves—as Pergamum did—but many paid the Gauls to leave them alone or hid behind city walls and let the Gauls plunder their land. Antiochus (the Seleucid king) used elephants to drive the Gauls out of his territory, and he defeated them in what was known as "the elephant victory." The Gauls settled in central Asia Minor—a place that came to be known as Galatia ("the Gauls' place")—and forced the local population to feed them, while bands of Gauls regularly raided throughout Asia Minor or extorted protection money.

A new ruler of Pergamum, Attalus (related collaterally to the Seleucids), refused to pay the Gauls not to raid his territory, and he defeated the tribe who "owned" the plunder rights to his territory. They appealed to the other Gallic tribes. Attalus stopped the combined invasion at the temple of Aphrodite in the outskirts of Pergamum, and there he decisively defeated them and routed them and annexed most of Asia Minor, which he subsequently lost to the Seleucid king. He commissioned a series of sculptures that depicted the defeat of the Gauls and glorified himself as the champion of Greeks against barbarians. Attalus established Pergamum as a power in the world of the Greek East, but it was to reach its greatest power and prosperity by its alliance with Rome.

## Map 15: Sequence Maps of Asia

THE WORLD OF ASOKA, CA. 250 B.C.

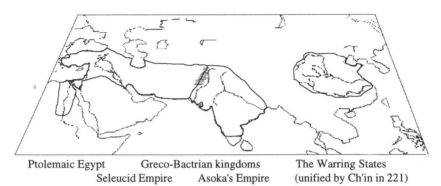

| Ptolemaic Egypt | Greco-Bactrian kingdoms | The Warring States |
| | Seleucid Empire      Asoka's Empire | (unified by Ch'in in 221) |

ASIA AT THE END OF THE FIRST CENTURY B.C.

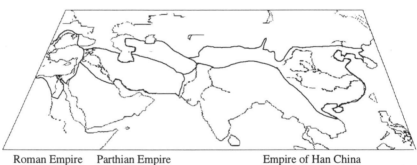

| Roman Empire | Parthian Empire | Empire of Han China |
| | Kushan Empire | |

ASIA IN THE MIDDLE OF THE THIRD CENTURY A.D.

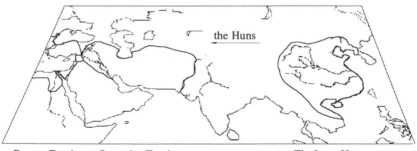

the Huns

| Roman Empire | Sassanian Empire | The Later Han |
| | Palmyra | |

# Part Three
# The East

I refer to the nomadic horsemen known to the Chinese as the Hsiung-Nu anachronistically as the "Huns." By and large East and West did not meet and did not influence each other, but the West sent the chariot East and the Iranian plateau sent cavalry both west and east and so may be responsible for the Huns who raided across the Chinese border for centuries until the Chinese expelled them and drove them west, where they sent the Goths fleeing into the Roman Empire and thence to the battlefield of Adrianople, a catastrophe, the effects of which were responsible for the fall of the western Roman Empire.

## 31. Depictions of Combat

CHINESE BRONZE FROM THE LATE CHOU

GREEK VASE PAINTING FROM THE EARLY ARCHAIC PERIOD

Note the similarity of gesture: each warrior wielding a sword has his enemy by the top of his head, whether a topknot or the crest of a helmet. The scenes must reflect a reality of individual combat and not an artistic convention.

## Map 16: The Warring States

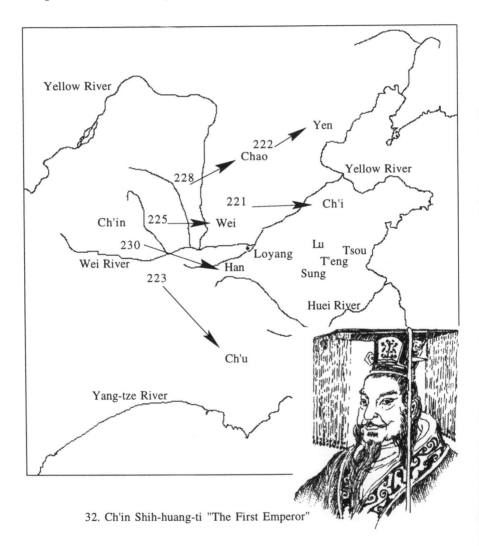

Yellow River

Yen

222
Chao

228

221

Yellow River

Ch'i

Ch'in 225 Wei

230 Lu Tsou
T'eng
Wei River Han Sung
Loyang

223

Huei River

Ch'u

Yang-tze River

32. Ch'in Shih-huang-ti "The First Emperor"

The arrows (with dates) indicate the kingdoms attacked and conquered by Ch'in.

# 18

# India: Chandragupta
## Empire and Remorse

When Alexander withdrew from India, he left the defeated king Porus as vassal of an expanded kingdom. Porus remained loyal to Alexander and his successors, but he encouraged the Indian prince, Chandragupta, who emulated Alexander himself. Chandragupta had met Alexander and had been introduced to the Macedonian way of war, though he, and other Indian kings, preferred to continue using war elephants and chariots in a four-part division of their armies—elephant, chariot, cavalry, foot. After the death of Alexander Chandragupta raised an army and defeated the Macedonians in India. Buoyed by this success, he overthrew the king of Magadha—Magadha, centered on the Ganges and patron of the Buddha, was the most powerful state of some 120 independent kingdoms in India.

Chandragupta (reigned 321–297) expanded his power along the Ganges and into the Indus valley, where he had to contend with Seleucus Nicator in 305. The details of their battles are lost, but Seleucus ceded all territory east of the Indus and the western provinces of Arachosia and Gedrosia. In return Chandragupta presented Seleucus with 500 war elephants and took a daughter in marriage. (Seleucus was forced to keep his attention on his wars in the west and prepare for an impending battle—Ipsus—with his rivals.) Chandragupta founded the Mauryan Empire. His empire encompassed the whole of northern Indian and Afghanistan. A curious story relates that when a famine struck his kingdom, Chandragupta joined the religious sect of the Jains, abdicated, and accompanied a party of Jains south in search of better conditions. There he starved himself to death. His son (who took the title Slayer of the Enemy) increased the size of the empire and passed it on to his own son, Asoka.

Chandragupta organized his empire around the central point of his capital city, Patna. He maintained a standing army (according to contemporary reports) of 300,000–600,000 infantry, 30,000 cavalry, and 9,000 elephants. By now the chariot, though still a royal status symbol, was obsolete. Indian rulers lived a life of warfare, hunting, gambling, and sports (a race between chariots pulled by combined teams of horses and oxen was popular). Chandragupta feared assassination, as he was quite ready to encourage the assassination of rival kings, and so he did not sleep in the same bedroom two nights in a row. He was an absolute monarch at the head of a fully organized and closely controlled bureaucracy. One bureau had charge of the military and was divided into six boards controlled by five men each: navy, quartermaster, infantry, cavalry, chariot, and elephant. The army was to be recruited from "robbers, mountain men, gangs, forest people, and warrior clans." Soldiers were to receive a regular salary and their equipment, but they had to be mindful of the guiding principle of Mauryan government—the art of government is the art of punishment.

Chandragupta's right-hand man, Kautilya, is the supposed author of a work on politics and war (the *Arthasatra*) that describes, summarizes, and advises on the situation of the time of Chandragupta. There are sections on the duties of the ministers of the boards of elephants, boards of chariots, and boards of infantry—to inspect the troops, to check their equipment, their proficiency in training ("in shooting arrows, throwing clubs, wearing armor, fighting seated in a chariot, controlling the team of horses"), and their pay. Among sections on organization and punishment (appropriate tortures) are chapters on when and how to attack, to make and betray allies, to feign peace, and to use spies to gather intelligence. "If you face two enemies, one strong and one weak, which should you attack first? The strong, because once he is defeated, the weak will capitulate without a fight."

Part 10 offers advice on war. The king's camp should be sited by the commander, an astrologer, and the engineer. It should be divided into nine parts with six roads. The quarters for the king should be surrounded by trenches, parapets, and a wall with gates. There should be a place for his harem and the harem guard, his financial officials, the gods and their priests, stables for the royal mounts (elephants and horses), quarters for infantry, chariots, cavalry, elephants, and free labor, for merchants, prostitutes, hunters, spies and guards. People should not be allowed to come and go. Drinking, parties, and gambling are prohibited. Wells should be dug in advance all along the way.

"Armies in good locations will defeat armies in bad." The best rate of march is ten and a quarter miles a day. There are different formations for marching. Provisions and water must be supplied in advance. "Strike the enemy when he is caught in unfavorable terrain." Deceive the enemy, feign defeat. Look for places to put ambushes. Harass the enemy at night to prevent his sleeping. Before a pitched battle the king says to his troops, "I'm being paid just like you. You and I will both profit from this conquest." The priests encourage the army. Priests (and poets) should say that heroes go to heaven and cowards go to hell. Offer cash rewards for acts of bravery.

The army's back should be to the sun. "When a defeated army resumes its attack, it cares not whether it lives or dies, its fury cannot be resisted; let a defeated army flee." The different divisions of the army do better on different terrain. The best terrain for the chariot is dry ground that is firm, level, and free of wagon ruts, trees, plants, vines, and thorns. The duties of the four armies is described in detail. The order of the army arranged for battle is: the strongest troops will lead the attack from center, left, and right. Once the enemy is broken, the weaker troops in reserve will destroy the enemy. The king should station himself with the reserve. "Never fight without a reserve."

The moral of the *Arthasatra* is to deceive and divide your enemies without allowing them to deceive and divide you. "When an archer shoots an arrow, he may miss his target, but intrigue can kill even the unborn." In part the *Arthasatra* is a manual of organization of the army. Chandragupta relied on a core of trained men supplemented by levies of militia and by mercenaries (independent war guilds that sold their services to the highest bidder). There were mercenary corps (guilds) of elephant troops.

The elephant was now the royal mount of the kings. Elephants were armored, had neck ropes and bells, and they carried hooks and quivers, slings, and lances. Seven men rode their backs, employing the different weapons. The elephant was used to connect different elements of the army, to guard the flanks when advancing and to guard the rear in retreat. An army might have 8,000 chariots, 1,000 elephants, 60,000 horse; an ideal division of an army would have 10,000 horse, 2,000 elephants, 10,000 foot, and 500 chariots. A unit organized to care for the wounded followed the army.

Asoka (reigned 274–232) began his reign as his father and grandfather before him — an autocrat devoted to the hunt, feasts, gambling, and war—but the campaign he led against the Kalingas (a people on the middle of the southeast coast) changed his life and the life of the whole of India. He wrote (paraphrased), "I conquered Kalinga in the eighth year of my reign (261 B.C.) and had 150,000 people carried off as prisoners, I was responsible for 100,000 slain, and many times 100,000 died. Then I suffered remorse for having conquered the Kalingas because conquest of an independent country necessitates the slaughter and the capture of the people. I regret this. Now I desire that all living creatures—even the people of the forest who I wish would mend their ways—live in peace without fear."

True conquest (according to Asoka) depended upon the conquest of men's hearts. Among these true conquests he included disparate people in his own domains, neighbors, and the kings of Ptolemaic Egypt, Cyrene, Asia Minor, and the Seleucid empire. Such conquests win favor in the next world, too. Asoka sponsored Buddhist missions to the Hellenistic kingdoms, to Ceylon (where they rapidly converted the inhabitants), and to east and north. As the unity of the Roman Empire in the future was to contribute to the rapid spread of Christianity, so the Mauryan unity contributed to the rapid spread of Buddhism. Asoka intended to inculcate in his people—by being accessible to them and by showing them through his own example—the three virtues, reverence to authority, respect for life, and truth. After his death in 232 the empire began to disintegrate, because of both the lethargy of his successors and the increased aggressiveness of the Seleucids.

Details of specific battles do not survive, but in the epic of the battle between the Kurus and the Pandavas an elephant battle is described. Elephant was used against elephant, but in the melee an elephant would trample and crush anything that got in its way. The most feared elephant was a male in rut. Its musk glands discharged a noxious substance that warned other elephants to give it wide berth (unless they, too, were in rut). The difficulty with elephants in rut is that they are impossible to control.

## THE ELEPHANT BATTLE

On both sides there arose a clamor, shouting, the blare of cow horns, beating drums and cymbals and tabors, and the two sides rushed upon each other. The prince's shouts rose above the noise made by the thousands of neighing horses and filled the enemy with fear. Horses and elephants all lost control of their bladders and bowels. The sun himself was shrouded by the dust raised by the warriors.

Huge elephants with wounded temples attacked other huge elephants, and they tore one another with their tusks. They had castles and standards on their backs, they were trained to fight, and they struck with their tusks and were struck in turn, and they shrieked in agony. They were goaded forward by pikes and hooks, and so they fought each other, though it was not the mating season. Some elephants uttered cries like cranes and fled in all directions. Many elephants, bleeding from temple and mouth, torn by swords, lances, and arrows, shrieked aloud, fell down, and died.

One warrior turned his elephant with upraised trunk and rushed upon a chariot. The elephant in his anger placed his foot upon the yoke of the chariot and killed the four large horses, but the chariot warrior stayed on his chariot with the dead horses and threw a lance, made entirely of iron and resembling a snake, and he hit the elephant-warrior. The lance pierced his coat of mail; he dropped the hook and his lance and fell down from his elephant's neck. The chariot warrior drew his sword, jumped down from his chariot, swung with all his strength, and hacked off the elephant's trunk. The elephant's coat of mail was pierced all over with arrows, his trunk was cut off, and he uttered a loud shriek and fell down and died.

# 19

# China: Spring and Autumn
*The Search for Unity and Social Order*

China is a land of mountain, river, and plain. It is not a geographical unity as Egypt is, but once it was united under one ruler, it rather looked to defense and isolation than to conquest and expansion. The early history of China is a history of internal warfare leading to unity in 221 B.C., broken by civil wars, and finally leading to a system of bureaucracy that could control the land as it controlled the military. The first priority was social order.

From the fall of the Shang dynasty to the rise of the Ch'in the Chou dynasty "ruled" China. The king was the "son of Heaven" and was responsible for the balance of heaven and earth. When the Chou overthrew the Shang dynasty, the new rulers parcelled out the conquered land to their kin and to their supporters. These divisions over time became permanent, and the leaders of these parcels of land (some great, some small) acted independently while giving lip service to subordination under the Chou emperor. The attempt of the Chou to reestablish control of these nobles ended disastrously.

In 771 B.C. the Chou king was defeated by a coalition of northern nobles and killed in battle. A Ch'in noble salvaged a Chou prince to act as king, and the Chou dynasty continued in name, but the king retained little power. He was dominated by whichever noble (the hegemon) ruled the most powerful district. The later Chou period comprises two periods, the "Spring and Autumn" (722–481)—when China was divided into as many as 170 independent districts—and the "Warring States" (403–221). The land-holding nobles rode in chariots, lived under a code of chivalry, and pursued glory and domination. A king's highest duties were worship (sacrifice) and war; his virtue was calculated by his military success, since success was a mark of heavenly favor: the successful man used the balance of heaven and earth to succeed, the unsuccessful missed the balance.

The wars they conducted were governed by rules. They fought only in the season when the crops were not being sown or reaped, and not in the winter when it was too cold, and not in the period of mourning for the death of a noble.

They did not lift their hands against the elderly nor slay the wounded, they did not put cities to the sack, lay ambushes, keep their armies out in the field past the standard campaigning season, and they did not attempt to deceive their enemies.

This Chinese chivalry fought, like Homeric heroes, in two-wheeled chariots drawn by four horses, two harnessed on the shaft, two harnessed at the wings. Three men fought on board: the driver, the lancer, and the archer. They wore breastplates, armlets, and knee pieces, and they carried shields. The great chieftains fought under standards, the Red Bird of the south, the Black Tortoise of the north, the White Tiger of the west, and the Green Dragon of the east. The greatest of all virtues was courage, and they expressed courage through bravado. It was customary, when invaded, to send provisions to the invading army, and in some cases to send messengers who would come into the presence of the enemy general and then cut their own throats . . . to show the enemy their contempt for death. Before they met in battle, the heroes might drink together and even exchange weapons. In battle a vanquished enemy would be spared if he had exhibited bravery. Battles assumed the nature of a duel, between individuals and between armies, so that subterfuges were condemned as unworthy: "The thousand chariots charge, banner against banner, honor against honor."

The Chou emperor was the creature of the hegemon, the most powerful noble; the object of the nobles in their constant wars with each other was to control the Chou emperor and become hegemon. Duke Huan of Ch'i (686–643) fulfilled several of the duties of the hegemon. He defended the middle kingdom from the nomadic barbarians. (The nomads responded to Chinese attacks that were responses to their attacks. In the process they became more nomadic, giving up all agriculture and so becoming harder to fight; they depended upon Chinese products, acquired through trade and war, and they became more Sinicized.) Huan promoted agriculture through the control of the rivers and through irrigation. He attempted to stop the constant wars by holding conferences, by staying within established boundaries, and by open trade. Upon his death his sons quarreled over the succession and lost the hegemony to Duke Siang of Sung (643) who quickly lost it to Duke Wen of Chin (635–628). The greatest threat to the hegemon was the southern, semibarbarous power of Ch'u.

Early Chinese battle descriptions follow a certain pattern (which may relate actual practice or may idealize it). First the leaders attempted to divine who would win or who had the advantage. They sought the answer with omens, dreams, and divination using turtle shells. They attempted to determine who had heaven's favor on the basis of past events. As with all divination the results could be ambiguous and open to interpretation. The leaders sought to avoid ambiguity by accepting the results of one, and only one, divination (particularly if the divination was favorable) or they might even refuse to divine if they thought the battle was not in doubt. The results of divination might be used in diplomacy. Singers (or music masters), especially if they were blind, were considered gifted seers.

They made an estimate of the situation by gathering intelligence about the enemy through reconnaissance and espionage. They analyzed the terrain, enemy and friendly forces, arms, morale, and the enemy commander. They estimated who would be their allies, who would remain neutral, and who would oppose them. Then they would select the field of battle and decide how to deploy their own troops, provide special equipment, and cover their own weaknesses. Once their preparations were complete, they decided whether to fight— would they win, could they force the other side to fight, could they force him to retreat? They summoned the officers to hear the plans. They pitched a tent in which to hold the divinations and then took it down. They issued orders. They levelled the ground on which they formed ranks. The various units heard their orders, they made a battle prayer, and they were ready.

Just before the battle they fed the army and raised morale with speeches, prayers, and appeals to the ancestors and the gods. Individuals would boast, raid the enemy, make a heroic display. The forces were deployed and the final decisions ratified—to attack or to await attack and then counterattack. To attack is to gain the initiative, but to defend is to be secure. When the battle is won, or lost, there is pursuit, or surrender or flight. (In one case a commander examined the chariot tracks of the fleeing enemy. When he saw that they were disordered, he knew that they were not luring him into an ambush.) Prisoners are taken, some sacrificed to provide blood for the drums, some are held for ransom, some are enslaved. Then the victors feast on the enemy's provisions and return home in triumph (or defeat). Political decisions are made then—to seize new territory, to garrison new cities, build forts, to gain new allies, and to seek advantage in the changed circumstances, and finally to judge the new spiritual situation.

In the battle of Ch'ang–p'u (632 B.C.) Duke Wen of Chin has both moral and spiritual doubts about fighting Ch'u. The omens, and his dreams, suggest that the moral balance lies with the army of Ch'u. His chief of staff has to convince him that the omens and dreams can be explained as auspicious. The herald of Ch'u brings a challenge to Duke Wen to fight, and Wen replies that he will be ready at the crack of dawn. Duke Wen had identified the weakest point of his enemy's army as his right wing (comprising his somewhat reluctant allies). He knew that the commander of the enemy left wing was bold and impetuous. Therefore he determined to attack the enemy right wing strongly and to feint against the left wing, draw it forward, and attack it from two sides. He considered his center army to be his weakest and the enemy center the strongest elements of the combined forces.

Consequently he ordered his left to launch an all-or-nothing attack on the enemy allied right. The attack was completely successful and routed the enemy allies. The right was then ordered to feint. (Duke Wen's banner was carried by the right wing to give the impression that this was the main attack.) After it had closed enough to have taken some casualties, it was to withdraw, seemingly in panic, while the chariots on its left flank were to rush forward and sweep between the friendly and enemy army. Brush had been tied to the rear of the chariots to raise enough dust to obscure what the right was doing (that is, re-forming). An elite unit drawn up in the center army now launched an attack on the enemy left while the chariots reformed and attacked the flank; the right reformed and attacked. The enemy left was broken. The battle was won. For subtlety of planning, coordination and execution, the battle of Ch'ang p'u must take its place next to the other great battles of antiquity.

Duke Wen now gained control of the Chou king and became hegemon, but he was unable to build upon this victory. In three years Chin lost the hegemony to Ch'in (629). The primary task of the leader of Ch'in after the defeat of Chou had been the defense of the western border. The Ch'in were considered semibarbarian themselves, the leader descended from a barbarian horse trader. In the face of constant threats they had grown strong and soon developed a reputation for their fighting men; at this time, however, Chin was the dominant power of the north, the semibarbarous Ch'u was the dominant power of the south.

Duke Chuang of Ch'u became hegemon (613–591) and was the victor of the battle at Pi in 595 B.C. Before the battle of Pi the chariot nobles rode out to duel each other—three to a chariot, driver, archer, spearman. A single Ch'u chariot was pursued by several Chin chariots. As the Ch'u fled, a deer leaped up in front of the chariot and the archer killed it with his last arrow. They stopped and presented the deer to the Chin pursuers, who accepted the deer and allowed the Ch'u to withdraw unscathed.

After the battle, while the Ch'u were pursuing the Chin, one of the Chin chariots got a wheel stuck in a rut. A Ch'u chariot man gave the Chin driver advice on how to get it unstuck, and the man replied, "Thank you—we do not have the experience you have of running away so often."

Ch'u dominated until its own generals, exiled by the Ch'u court, trained its enemies. One (e.g., Wu Ch'en 584) trained the army of Wu to wield its weapons and fight in formation.

Chin was victorious at the battle of Yen-ling in 575 B.C.

## TWO TYPICAL CAREERS

### Wu Tzu-hsü

At the court of Ch'u an adviser to the king, King P'ing, rose to prominence by driving a wedge between the king and his son, the heir apparent. When the father of Wu Tzu-hsü tried to reconcile the king with his son, the king had him arrested, and he sent men to arrest the two sons. One was taken, but Wu Tzu-hsü fled. The king executed the two men he had in his power (in 522).

Wu Tzu-hsü escaped to Wu and was introduced to the king. He advised the king that he could defeat Ch'u, but the king refused. When King P'ing of Ch'u died, the king of Wu sent two armies in a surprise attack during the official period of mourning for the king. The armies were cut off and destroyed, and the prince regent of Wu took that opportunity to have his father assassinated and he became king (King Ho-lu of Wu). He made Wu Tzu-hsü his minister of foreign affairs.

Nobles from both sides deserted to the other. In 512 King Ho-lu attacked Ch'u and defeated two rivals to his throne (who had deserted to Ch'u). Wu Tzu-hsü then commanded expeditions against Ch'u (511), against Yueh (510), and against an invasion from Ch'u (509). In 506 King Ho-lu asked Wu Tzu-hsü if the time was ripe to attack the capital (Ying) of Ch'u. Wu Tzu-hsü replied that the Ch'u commander-in-chief had antagonized two neighboring principalities. If he could win these over, he could defeat Ch'u. He succeeded, and then he faced the Ch'u forces across the Han River. The Ch'u army was routed.

Wu Tzu-hsü developed a navy and a strong infantry. He defeated the Ch'u in five battles. The Ch'u king fled for his life from his capital. Wu Tzu-hsü and King Ho-lu entered the capital of Ch'u. Wu Tzu-hsü had the corpse of King P'ing dug up and had it whipped 300 times in vengeance for his father's murder. The chief minister of Ch'u fled to Ch'in and begged the reluctant king to aid Ch'u. The minister wailed in mourning for seven days before the king agreed to send an army with 500 chariots. This army defeated the army of Wu. While King Ho-lu of Wu was in the field, his younger brother seized the throne, and Ho-lu had to return and drive him out.

In the end Wu crushed Ch'u, overawed Ch'i and Chin, and defeated Yueh, but in a subsequent invasion of Yueh, Ho-lu was wounded in the toe and died. The new king of Wu came to terms with Yueh and turned to the conquest of Ch'u. Wu Tzu-hsü advised against it, and the king ordered him to commit suicide. In 471 Yueh launched a surprise attack and overran Wu.

## Wu Ch'i

Wu Ch'i was a native of Wey. He bit his arm and swore that he would never return to Wey until he had won fame as a general. He followed the profession of arms and became recognized for his genius, but also for his lecherous and avaricious nature. He sought employment with the Duke of Lu, then fighting a war with Ch'i (408 B.C.), but the Duke of Lu was suspicious of his loyalty because Wu Ch'i was married to a woman from Ch'i, so Wu Ch'i killed her. The Duke of Lu hired him and Wu Ch'i defeated the army of Ch'i, but courtiers convinced the Duke of Lu that he could not trust Wu Ch'i, and he dismissed him.

The leader of Wei hired Wu Ch'i when he was informed that there was no better commander of troops in the world. Wu Ch'i dressed the same as a common soldier, slept on the ground with them, ate the same food they ate, marched on foot, carried his own pack, and he once drained the abscess of a private soldier with his own lips. He had the complete loyalty of his troops. He served the leader of Wei until the leader's death, and then he served his son. The new leader took a river trip with Wu Ch'i and boasted of his fortifications along the river. Wu Ch'i told him of the dukes who had depended upon their fortifications and not upon virtue— they had all been defeated and slain. The new leader was so taken with the advice that he gave Wu Ch'i his own domain within Wei.

Wu Ch'i prospered for a while, but a new prime minister was jealous of him and suggested to the ruler that Wu Ch'i's ambitions would lead him to desert the tiny state of Wei and seek service with the mighty neighbor state of Ch'in. When Wu Ch'i realized that he was under suspicion he took a position as prime minister to the king of Ch'u (who reigned 401–381 B.C.). He trained the Ch'u army, dismissed bureaucrats, revised the laws, and got rid of travelling orators who advised on the changing of alliances.

While he was prime minister, Ch'u was the strongest state in China, but he had made many enemies and when the king died, the nobles formed a mob against him. Wu Ch'i fled from them and threw himself on the body of the king lying in state. The nobles shot him with arrows and struck him with knives, but in attacking him they also struck the body of the dead king. The heir and new king ordered all those who had struck the king to be executed along with their families. More than seventy families were wiped out.

Wu Ch'i was not without a stratagem, even in death.

The foremost philosopher and religious sage of this period was Confucius. The traditional date of his birth is 551 B.C., which places him in the period of Buddha and Zarathustra. Confucius left no work written by his own hand, but he founded a school of wisdom that taught a kind of universal ritual. There is a cosmic order, balance between *yin* (representing shadow, moisture, earth, contraction, and the female) and *yang* (representing light, heat, sky, expansion, and the male). He taught filial piety and piety towards the ancestors, a piety expressed actively in ritual, a courtesy towards the living and the dead, an expression of a feeling of humanity towards others and human dignity within oneself, and always self–control.

Recognize that you know what you know and that you are ignorant of what you do not know. . . . If you do not know about the living, how can you know about the dead?
Individual morality, however, is no different than collective morality.  One can be good only under a good prince.
It is the moral power of the sovereign, the supernatural influence which he draws from the mandate of Heaven, which makes for the good or evil conduct of his people.

Sun-Tzu (c. 400–320) was to the military art what Confucius was to the political/social art. When Sun-Tzu went to work for his royal patron, the king of Wu, the king decided to test the expertise of Sun-Tzu. He ordered him to teach the manual of arms to his harem of 360 concubines. Sun-Tzu divided them into two companies, put the king's two favorite concubines in command of the companies, ensured that they knew their front from their back, their left from their right, and explained the first maneuver. When he gave the order to face right, the women giggled. He told them that when the troops do not understand the maneuver, it is the fault of the general, and he explained the maneuver again.

Again they giggled. So, he said, when the troops understand but do not obey, then it is the officers' fault, and he ordered the execution of the two concubines in charge. The king was horrified and begged him to spare them, but Sun-Tzu told him that once the general was appointed, he must carry out his mission regardless of the commands of the king. The concubines were executed, new officers were appointed, and the harem learned the manual of arms perfectly.

According to the biography of Sun-Tzu he put his theory into practice on the battlefield (and passed his ability down to his grandson). Drawing on his own experience and a long history of military conflict Sun-Tzu wrote *The Art of War*, a treatise on military practice. After the introduction, which establishes the bona fides of both Sun-Tzu and his treatise, the text begins. It is divided into thirteen chapters:

1. *Estimate of the Situation:* The five key factors of victory are morale, weather, terrain, command, and organization—"Victory is won by deception."

2. *Waging War:* Campaigns should be short, for if resources fail, the war is lost—"Use the enemy's resources to strengthen your own."

3. *Offensive Strategy:* How and when the enemy should be engaged (only when you are stronger, never against walled cities)—"To defeat the enemy without fighting is the greatest test of strategy."

4. *Formations:* The successful commander is one who makes every preparation for victory—"Defense is security, attack is victory."

5. *Situation:* The successful commander has mastered timing and organization of the battle—"Compel the enemy to conform to your plan."

6. *Subtleties:* The successful commander makes his plans based on the situation of the enemy, the terrain, and his own strength—"The successful commander seizes the initiative."

7. *Movement:* Move lightly, where the enemy does not expect, and never corner him or drive him to desperation—"Attack when you are rested and fed and the enemy is not."

8. *Nine Variables:* Employ your army in different ways in different circumstance—"The five faults of character in a general are brashness, cowardice, anger, honor, compassion."

9. *Marches:* How to estimate what the enemy intends and what the state of his morale is—"Numbers alone do not guarantee victory."

10. *Using Terrain:* How to use terrain and how to judge the condition of your own army—"Know the enemy and yourself."

11. *Nine Types of Terrain:* The different types of terrain and the qualities of generalship are defined—"Speed is the key to victory."

12. *Fire:* How fire should be employed in an attack—"Never act out of anger."

13. *Espionage:* How agents should be used, what information to collect, how to turn enemy agents and use double agents—"Knowledge of the enemy leads to victory."

Unlike the extant military treatises of Greeks and Romans, which are more compilations of examples than discussion of theory—and despite the degree of mysticism found in this treatise (the divisions of five, seven, and nine, the goal of earthly and heavenly balance)—Sun-Tzu's *Art of War* contains solid theory supported by example, and it is still studied and used.

## 33. Siege Warfare (Bronzes from the Warring States Period)

These scenes of siege warfare from the period of the Warring States show various instruments of war: grappling hook, sword-dagger, bow and arrow (but not the crossbow introduced in the fourth century), siege-ladders (one on wheels), halberd, and the combination ax-grappling hook. Shields appear to be used only by the attacking forces. Decapitation is common. One figure appears to be dropping rocks on the attackers. Neither side appears to wear helmets and the figures of the lower course may be wearing quilted jackets.

# 20

# China: The Warring States
## *The Offensive of Ch'in Unites China*

By the beginning of the period of the warring states the constant wars had consolidated the 170 districts into eight major powers, none of which was strong enough by itself to dominate the king—and the aristocracy was giving way to professional generals who maneuvered massed infantry. This confused period is marked by shifting national and personal alliances. Deceit was a way of life and treachery became a self-fulfilling prophecy. As the rulers distrusted their subordinate nobles, so those nobles, conscious of the suspicion, were quick to forestall punishment by switching their loyalties.

In 453 the leaders of the Wei, Han, and Chao formed an alliance and attacked the leader of Chin, defeated him at the battle of Ching Yang, made his skull into a drinking cup, and divided up his realm among themselves. Thereafter six states fought continually among themselves for domination—Ch'i, Ch'u, Ch'in, Wei, Han, and Chao. The drive to dominate led to almost constant warfare between 450 and 300. Philosophers decried the situation—if a man should steal from another, it would be considered a crime, but should one nation attack another, no one comments upon it; the armies march out in the planting season, destroy crops, cause starvation, take the resources of the land, and do not bring them back. All suffered—but no one had any other solution than war until one power had conquered the others.

By 335 B.C. the courtesies and chivalry of the feudal period were dead. The barons no longer paid even lip service to the king of the Chou dynasty, but assumed the title *king* themselves. They developed state bureaucracies, both to administer their realms better and also to control the power of the nobility. Their ideal became a compartmentalization so strict that each individual would know his own duties, do only those duties, and dare do nothing else (so that the appointed "crown keeper," who dared to cover a sleeping king with the king's coat, was executed for usurping the "coat keeper's" duty). In Ch'in the land was divided into thirty-one administrative districts led by administrators appointed directly by the king.

The crossbow was introduced in the later fourth century B.C. and iron was used for weapons. The chariot gave way to horse cavalry in 307, a change forced on the Chinese by their wars with the Huns (Hsiung-nu) of Mongolia, whose mounted archers would dash in and shoot down the soldiers on the slow-moving chariots. Each "king" had his cavalry—the Chinese adopted the barbarian horseman's trousers—and a standing national army drafted from the common people. This period sees the development of siegecraft, movable towers, and catapults. Defeated heroes were no longer pardoned, but prisoners were executed en masse, and the soldiers of Ch'in (the district that eventually came to dominate China) received pay only for severed heads. The towns that were taken were put to the sword—man, woman, and child—and the kings to "increase their prestige" would boil their enemies and drink the soup . . . and also force the kinsmen of their victims to partake.

The growth of power of Ch'in took several hundred years. Their inner stability, geographical position, and policy all contributed to their victory. One regent, Wei Yang, was described as "bad for the people but good for the state." Discipline reached from the highest to the lowest and was severe. The power of the nobility was checked by the growing bureaucracy, which was loyal to its boss.

## THE LORD OF SHANG

Yang Kung-sun was born in a noble family in Wey. He had studied political philosophy as a youth, and he served on the staff of the prime minister to the king of Wei. When the prime minister fell ill, he recommended Yang to the king, but he added that if the king could not find a place commensurate with the young man's ability, he should kill him and not let him leave the country to serve someone else. When the prime minister died, Yang left Wei and sought service in Ch'in, where, he had heard, the duke was seeking talented men from abroad.

The youthful Yang required four meetings with Duke Hsiao before the duke could be convinced of Yang's ability. At the fourth meeting they talked all night. Yang was soon involved in an argument over whether to follow precedent and respect the past or to break with it. He argued that great deeds can be accomplished only by men who create something new and are not tied to the past.

Following his advice, Duke Hsiao allowed peasants to own land; consequently, peasants flocked to Ch'in to get land (and in turn were drafted into the army). He centralized the administration of Ch'in and made the law more important than the position of the offender. He weakened the ties of family and replaced the extended family with groups of five or ten nuclear families. He established eighteen ranks of honor, mostly gained by military service. To attain the first rank ("official gentleman") a soldier presented the head of an enemy killed in battle. The reforms were intended to create a stable agrarian society loyal to the king and only to the king. Yang attempted to exclude merchants from positions of power. The strength of Ch'in depended upon the promotion and rewarding of men for their military prowess, of welcoming immigration at all levels, and of the stability of the reign and the succession.

At first there were thousands of complaints about the new law code, but after the heir to the throne was punished for an infringement of the code, complaints died away. (The heir could not be punished himself, but one of his tutors was mutilated and the other tattooed on the face.) When the heir again violated the law, Yang had his nose cropped.

Yang commanded an army in an attack upon the king of Wei, the king he had once served. The king's principal son commanded the army of Wei. Yang sent him a message that said that he could not bear to fight against someone he had known so well. Could not the two of them meet and have a drink and come to an agreement? The prince agreed. Yang ambushed him, captured him, made a surprise attack on his army, and routed it. After the victory Yang was made prime minister and given land and the title Lord of Shang.

As long as his protector, Duke Hsiao, lived, the Lord of Shang prospered, but when the duke died and the mutilated heir became king, he wanted revenge. Shang fled to Wei, but they returned him to Ch'in, and he was torn apart by two chariots as an object lesson to others.

The armies and leaders of Ch'in were both efficient and merciless. It is recorded that in 331 Ch'in defeated a neighbor and "cut off" 80,000 heads, in 318 in a victory against a coalition they cut off 82,000 heads, in 312 80,000 heads, in 307 60,000 heads, in 297 240,000 heads, in 275 a mere 40,000 heads (but that was an unsuccessful campaign, and they came back the same year and redeemed themselves with 150,000 heads), and in 260, although the king had promised to spare the lives of the conquered, more than 400,000 were decapitated. The kingdom of Ch'in was known as "the wild beast."

In 325 the Duke of Ch'in took the title "king" (as did the other leaders of independent states in China). In 256 the king of Ch'in eliminated the royal house of Ch'ou. Ch'in had a geographical advantage—it was protected from invasions from the east by rivers and mountains. Twenty thousand men could defend it successfully from an attack by a million. (It had already subdued the barbarian Jung to the west). As the Chinese historian put it: "When it poured out its soldiers it was like a man emptying a jug of water from the top of a high house."

In 316 the king of Ch'in attacked Ch'u and annexed two small territories, thus weakening Ch'u and strengthening Ch'in. From 364 to 234 Ch'in fought fifteen major campaigns in which (they record) 1,500,000 enemy were killed. The first emperor, born Cheng in 259, became king of Ch'in in 246 at the age of thirteen; he would be one of the greatest conquerors the world had ever seen and the first emperor of the Ch'in dynasty——Ch'in Shih-huang-ti.

The story of his rise to the kingship is a twisted tale. A merchant named Lü Pu—wei became wealthy through the sale of pearls and jade. While travelling in the capital of Chao, he met the son of the heir apparent to the Ch'in throne, a son by a concubine, sent to Chao as a hostage. The merchant made friends with this son—perhaps too close a friend because the prince fell in love with the merchant's concubine and insisted on having her for his own. The merchant went on to Ch'in and there he convinced the heir apparent to accept his concubine's son as his successor. The heir apparent became king in 251 and died within the year. His son, the concubine's child, became king but died in 247, and his young son became king—that is, Cheng, the future "First Emperor." Lü Pu-wei became the most powerful man in the realm next to the king, but when Cheng assumed the cap and sword of manhood in 238, he banished him from the court and Lü Pu-wei committed suicide.

Lü Pu-wei had started a circle of intellectuals that grew to 3,000 men. Among them was Li Ssu. Eventually he rose to the highest position in Ch'in, chancellor of the left. The First Emperor (Ch'in Shih–huang–ti) conquered Han in 230, Chao in 228, Wei in 225, Ch'u in 223, Yen in 222, and Ch'i in 221. With the conquest of Ch'i the First Emperor had united the whole of China. As the rulers of these states realized they could not resist the Ch'in advance, they tried assassination. In 227 the ruler of Yen sent an envoy to the First Emperor on the pretext of submitting. The envoy brought a map of Yen and the head of a Ch'in general who had deserted to Yen. The envoy pulled a dagger from its place of concealment in the map and almost succeeded in assassinating the First Emperor before the imperial bodyguard struck down the would-be assassin and cut him into little pieces.

When Cheng had completed the conquest, he had his councilors invent a new term for his position—huang-ti ("august emperor") and the complete title Shih-huang-ti (First August Emperor) was to be his alone. His successor would be Second August Emperor. His chief adviser convinced him not to appoint his sons to rule the newly conquered territories—because such policies had ruined the Chou. The First Emperor had his empire divided into thirty-six command areas, each run by a board of three men—a civil governor, a military commander, and an imperial inspector—who were the eyes of the emperor. The command areas were further divided into counties so that the whole of his land was divided into more than a thousand counties. The county administrators were appointed directly by the imperial bureaucracy, were salaried, and were subject to recall. This system was adopted by all later emperors.

The emperor had all the royalty of the defeated kingdoms moved to the capital of Ch'in and pensioned there. In addition, he had all opposition weapons collected and melted down, and he had the walls of all strategically important towns torn down. He standardized the Chinese written characters, absolutely essential in a country in which people spoke mutually unintelligible dialects. The standard written language ensured that what was written in the south could be understood in the north and vice versa.

Ch'in Shih-huang-ti standardized the coinage, weights and measures, and even the length of the axles of carriages (so that they could use the imperial roads). He built a system of roads, (more than four thousand miles of them) radiating out from his capital, to unite his kingdom. As he was the proponent of centralization and monarchic authority and the enemy of feudalism, so he was the enemy of the literati (as Confucius had been a proponent of feudalism). He ridiculed the pretensions of the literati (but later emperors were to use the literati as a counterweight to the nobles) and had almost 500 executed and their books burned. He wanted only one version of the past to survive . . . his.

Ch'in Shih-huang-ti was the Chinese Alexander the Great (except that his conquests and his program endured, first because he was uniting a homogeneous people, and second because he lived long enough to carry out his program).

His last great project was completed in 215. He ordered his foremost general, Meng T'ien, to build a road to the north (with an army of 300,000 men or 30 divisions), to subdue the barbarians to the north, and to build a wall 2,600 miles long. Meng T'ien constructed the Great Wall of China, and if he did incorporate other defensive walls and fill the gaps in the permanent wall with a temporary wall of earth, still he planned and built the wall, transported the building materials, and commanded and supplied an enormous army. In the end the Great Wall defined agricultural China and separated, if it did not defend, China from the barbarian nomads. The other great work of the First Emperor was to have his own tomb prepared, guarded by an extensive terra-cotta army.

The army of Ch'in fought against the Huns (Hsiung-nu) in the north—always a holding action—and added three new "commands" in the south. Where land could be irrigated and farmed, the Chinese way of life could be introduced. The First Emperor went on five extensive tours of his empire—to unite it by resettling it. He travelled from one palace (of the 270 he had constructed around his capital) to another so that no one would ever know where he was. When he suspected that a member of his entourage was carrying information about his location to the chancellor, he had his whole entourage executed. He was encouraged by the magicians to seek for the elixir of life along the seacoast. He believed (on the basis of a dream) that he would kill a large fish and then receive the elixir. In July or August of 210 B.C. he killed the prophesied big fish with his crossbow and soon after fell ill and died.

While the councillors and the kin contended for the control of the throne, two men outside the imperial household led a rebellion. One was Hsiang Yü, a giant of a man and a general, the other was Liu Pang, who founded the Han dynasty.

**34. Chinese Soldier and Horse**

# 21

# China: The Former Han
## *When Unity of Command Breaks Down*

At the death of the First Emperor rebellions broke out all over China, and when the Second Emperor's attempts to suppress the rebellions were ineffective, the rebellions spread farther and farther until they overwhelmed Ch'in. Two of the rebels were Hsiang-Yü and Liu Pang (also known as Liu Chi or Kao Tsu). Hsiang-Yü grew up in a military family. He excused his poor swordsmanship by saying, "Swordsmanship is good only against one foe. Teach me to defeat ten thousand." He was hot-headed, impetuous, self-confident, and physically strong—over six feet tall. Once he saw the First Emperor and his entourage crossing a river, he realized that the First Emperor was but one man, and he said to his uncle, "He could be overthrown." His uncle clapped a hand over his mouth and said to him, "Silence. Such words could get us all executed."

The first to begin the revolt (Ch'en She) was a common soldier who had risen to a position of command by his character alone. He was defeated and put to death in 208. When word of his revolt spread to the district where Hsiang-Yü lived, the governor of the district called in the uncle of Hsiang-Yü and told him that if they took the initiative, they might wind up leading the revolt. The uncle agreed completely, summoned Hsiang-Yü, had him murder the governor, and the two of them took over the district. They raised Wu in revolt and reconstituted the kingdom of Ch'u. The uncle became governor, Hsiang-Yü became the commanding general of 8,000 picked troops, and in a short time the two rebel leaders attracted commanders of other armies and a force of some sixty thousand men.

The other rebel, Liu Pang, came from a good family. He had a good education, but he was not rich. He was a village head under the emperor's regime and as village head he was ordered to march a gang of forced labor to their place of employment, but on the way he lost many to desertion and knew he was in serious trouble; he started drinking and told the rest they might as well run away, and he would take care of himself. The remaining men, however, were impressed with his personality and with the divine aura about him, his dragon features, the greatness predicted for him, and omens along the way, and a dozen of them volunteered to stay with him. He became a bandit and attracted a considerable gang. When the rebellions began, the leading citizens of Liu Pang's district murdered the governor and chose Liu Pang as their leader. (They chose him because they did recognize his ability, but they also feared that if they took the lead and lost, they and their whole families would be executed.)

Meanwhile the uncle of Hsiang-Yü had defeated the Ch'in forces in several battles, but they retaliated with a surprise attack, caught him by surprise, defeated and killed him, and left the rebel forces with no clear leader. Hsiang-Yü and the others agreed that whoever entered the capital of Ch'in first should rule Ch'in. In the ensuing campaign of 207 Hsiang Yü won enough victories over the Ch'in leader to establish his reputation as a master tactician and to win for himself the position of commander-in-chief of the rebel armies, but Liu Pang attacked the heart of Ch'in, broke through the chain of defense in November of 207, and fought his way into the capital of Ch'in, where he accepted the surrender of the emperor.

Liu Pang rescinded the harsh laws of Ch'in. He expected (according to the prior agreement) to be named king of the territory he had conquered, but Hsiang-Yü had agreed to that deal only because he expected to be the one to fulfil it, and, when he heard that Liu Pang had beaten him into Ch'in and planned to rule there, he was enraged and he was determined to break into Ch'in with his army and drive Liu Pang out. Liu Pang recognized that he could not hold the passes or hope to win against Hsiang-Yü (who outnumbered him four to one), so he submitted. Hsiang-Yü entered the capital of Ch'in, executed the former emperor, massacred the inhabitants, and razed the city.

Hsiang-Yü was now the most powerful of the leaders. He may have intended that he himself, established as king of his own kingdom, would also be the overlord of a confederacy of smaller kingdoms. In 206 B.C. he delineated eighteen kingdoms. He divided the territory of Ch'in into three and assigned Liu Pang a neighboring territory, Han-chung. (Hence forward Liu Pang was known as the king of Han.) Whatever Hsiang-Yü's vision might have been, Liu Pang had quite different ideas of the future of post-Ch'in China. After establishing himself in his assigned territory, he invaded the three kingdoms of Kuan-chung and organized them into commanderies. Liu Pang won over the population by a two-year remission of taxes, a relaxation of the harsh Ch'in code, and other generous measures.

In 206 and 205 he invaded Hsiang-Yü's home territory, but Hsiang-Yü turned the tables, cornered him, and defeated him in a battle from which Liu Pang only escaped with a few cavalry. In the debacle Hsiang-Yü captured Liu Pang's father and other members of his family and held them hostage. Liu Pang renewed the offensive, he took the majority of the troops of his best general,

Han Hsin, for his own campaign and sent the general to attack the district of Chao in 205. To reach the enemy army Han Hsin had to march through a gorge. The Chao commander rejected the obvious—to ambush Han Hsin on the march and destroy his supply train, deny him local supplies, and starve him out—because the commander's reputation would suffer if he seemed to be afraid of fighting this tiny Han army in a fair fight.

Han Hsin had developed a plan based on his knowledge of the opposing general (that he would not attack until Han Hsin himself was on the battlefield)—Han Hsin sent 2,000 cavalry to steal their war up the mountain sides above the Chao camp, to wait for an opportunity and then to storm the camp, and raise the Han banners (red flags) if they had the chance, while the main army emerged from the gorge and occupied the attention of the Chao forces. He sent half his army (10,000 men) out first to deploy with their backs to the river, in "dead" ground, that is, ground from which there would be no retreat if they were defeated. The opposing army laughed to see them, as it were, committing suicide. Then Han Hsin marched slowly from the gorge and placed his drums and his flags, the symbols of command, in front of his first unit. The Chao army attacked, and Han Hsin abandoned his drums and flags and retreated in seeming rout. The Chao troops left in camp were so excited by the rout that they rushed out to join the main attack, whereupon the 2,000 cavalry seized the deserted camp, they raised their red flags and the Chao army, finding the Han army tougher than expected and their camp taken, panicked, broke, and ran. The king of Chao was captured and beheaded.

Liu Pang's general Han Hsin won the strategic city of Hsing–yang for him, but Hsiang-Yü put Liu Pang under siege there. Once again Liu Pang escaped with only a few horsemen. While Hsiang-Yü was occupied with Liu Pang, however, Han Hsin campaigned in eastern China and won it over. Liu Pang made him king of Ch'i as a reward (203 B.C.). Hsiang-Yü was so frustrated by his inability to knock Liu Pang out that he offered to fight him in single combat to settle who would rule, but Liu Pang declared that the issue could only be settled by a battle between their armies. The two compromised and divided China between them, but Liu Pang soon renewed the attack and this time surrounded Hsiang-Yü and defeated him. Hsiang-Yü committed suicide in 202. When Liu Pang was proclaimed emperor, he issued a general amnesty.

Individually Liu Pang was no match for Hsiang-Yü as a military commander. His ultimate victory is one more lesson in the paramount importance of strategy. Several times he escaped from battle only with his life, but he recovered and used Hsiang-Yü's personality defects against him. Once the king of Han challenged his councilors to explain to him, how, after so many defeats at the hands of Hsiang-Yü, he had won, and they told him that he was arrogant and Hsiang-Yü was sweet, but Hsiang-Yu insisted upon controlling everything himself while the king of Han presented whatever his subordinates won to them as a reward. (After the final victory, however, he attacked them one by one until none were left.) The king replied that he could attract and trust men of unusual ability, while Hsiang-Yü was jealous of others and unable to trust men of ability.

Liu Pang adopted the bureaucratic strategy of the Ch'in. He ensured that power never was concentrated in one man (except himself). The emperor chose—and could dismiss—his ministers. Liu Pang divided central China, the area he had conquered, into thirteen commanderies, but those supporters whom he had confirmed as kings he left as kings in ten separate kingdoms, subject to their sending taxes and maintaining order. Liu Pang accepted the kingdoms, but not the kings. One by one he replaced them with members of his family (whom he thought he could trust).

The greatest external threat were the Huns (Hsiung–nu). While China was locked in its civil war, the Huns of the north were being united in a confederacy under one leader, Mao-tun. Liu Pang was unable to stop Hunnic raids, and his one campaign against them ended disastrously—Liu Pang was allowed to escape only because the wife of the Hunnic leader convinced him (after Liu Pang had sent her gifts) that he could not hope to rule China, nor could Liu Pang rule the Huns, so the two should cooperate. The Huns welcomed Chinese immigrants at all levels, as farmers, as scribes, as masters of military drill, and as high-level advisers. The Huns remained a threat to China.

Liu Pang was aware of this threat, and he agreed to pay a yearly tribute to keep the peace. The Chinese envoys who brought the tribute tended to be chauvinistic and outspoken about the barbarian customs of the Huns. The Hunnic king replied to them, "Less conversation! Your words mean nothing. If the list of goods you bring us is complete, then we are happy. If it is not, all your words cannot prevent our attacking you."

The problems of the Han empire were the balance between a central government and semi–autonomous Chinese kingdoms, between China and the Huns, and China and its disorganized western and southern neighbors. Han policy, as it came to be formulated, was to create a buffer zone against its enemies, to protect trade, and to increase revenues. The Han, living in the only authentic, heavenly sanctioned kingdom in the world, the center of the world, the "middle kingdom," did not believe that they were invading and conquering foreigners but rather forcing intransigent barbarians to recognize the rights of the middle kingdom. The Han might have expressed their philosophy, as the Romans did of the unconquered Germans—so they shall live in their savage, barbarian way never knowing the benefits of civilization.

Liu Pang died in 195. Between Liu Pang (195) and Wu Ti (141) the Han emperors spread their control along the Yellow and the Huai Rivers, collected taxes, and amassed the resources of the empire, but the first crisis of the Han was almost its last, a fifteen-year struggle between the descendants of Liu Pang for the throne. His wife, the empress Lü, tried to set her own family on the throne. During the struggle China was raided by the Huns and by the independent southern kingdom of Yueh. (In 196 Chao T'o, a former general of the First Emperor, had become king of Yueh and was confirmed by the Han—an attempt to subdue him in 181 failed). The surviving sons of Liu Pang reestablished the dynasty in 180 and nominated Wen Ti, a son of Liu Pang renowned for his character (and his mother's character).

The Huns made massive raids into Han territory in 177. The Han paid the Huns off. In the decade from 176 to 166 the Huns defeated the Yüeh-chieh tribes in the area of Kansu and western Mongolia and drove them into Central Asia where they forced out the Scythians, who then fought for the control of Bactria with the Parthians and the Greeks at Gandhara. In 166 the Huns made another massive raid and continued with minor raids and another massive raid in 160. The Chinese were unable to stop these raids with military force, but they attempted to control them by setting up defensive structures and a system of beacon signals. The Han army was simply not mobile enough to reach the point of the raid before the Huns had withdrawn or to follow them and to force them to battle.

A Hunnic chieftain told a Chinese envoy, "The business of the Hun is war. In time of war we ride and shoot arrows, in time of peace we follow our flocks, eat their flesh, and drink their milk, and relax and enjoy ourselves. Our laws are simple. Our relations with our king friendly. We are easy to govern. While you Chinese wear yourselves out building houses and raising crops and building walls and never having time to practice the attack."

Wen-ti and his successor, Ching-ti, continued to expand the number of commanderies, isolating and surrounding the kingdoms. In 154 the Han army put down a rebellion of seven kings; the emperor divided up their kingdoms into new commanderies, limited the staff of the remaining kings, appointed their senior officials, and, when the kings passed away, the emperor appointed the new kings so that eventually all the kings were sons of Ching-ti.

Wu-ti, the great conqueror, came to the throne when the Han dynasty was fully established, the economy was sound, and the treasury was full (the money could not be counted and the strings holding the coins together had rotted away). He (as emperor he was given all credit and all blame) shifted the policy of the Han to accelerate the changes to a controlled kingdom and to be more aggressive towards externals threats. His predecessor had been told to his face, in the old days, when the kings sent their generals off to war, the kings knelt before them and said, "I will manage the affairs of the palace, you manage what lies beyond." When the generals had completed their campaigns, they submitted a report in which they detailed what rewards should be given to their officers and men. They had complete control over revenues for the army and all supplies.

"But under your reign, so I have heard, the governor of the northern province uses all his revenues to support his army, but his privates are common people recruited from the field who do not know how to submit proper reports—they just tell their officers how many enemy they have killed—and so the clerks criticize them for filing improper reports and do not forward any requests for rewards and you put this governor on trial because there was a discrepancy in his reports of enemy killed."

Under Wu-ti the system of examination was begun that was to determine administrative rank in the imperial bureaucracy. In one sense the empire was reduced to writing—tax records, census records, imperial decrees, maps. Commanderies and kingdoms were reduced in size for better control and new commanderies (in new territory) added. By 108 B.C. the Han comprised eighty–four commanderies and eighteen kingdoms. The great question of Wu-ti's reign came to be the balance of the expense of foreign campaigns and loss of life against the profit.

In the period 135–119 the main thrust of their foreign policy was directed against the Huns. The Huns had crossed the Great Wall, and the first objective was to control those Huns who had setttled south of it. To better fit the imperial army for the struggle against the Huns, Wu-ti undertook a massive breeding program of horses and enlistment and training of cavalry. The Han strategy was to retaliate against Hunnic raids with massive (30,000 cavalry) raids of their own to break the strength of the combined Huns and to recover, settle, and secure the line of the Yellow River. In 127 the Chinese defeated the Huns between the Great Wall and the northern bend of the Yellow River. During the later 120s Chinese generals leading forces of 30,000 cavalry raided Hunnic lands and drove off "hundreds of thousands" of horses. The horses would mount the Han cavalry and dismount the Huns.

One general (Wei Ch'ing) led seven campaigns against the Huns, in the course of which he killed over 50,000 of them. In 121–119 Ho Ch'u Ping (20 years old) led an army of 100,000 cavalry in an invasion of Kansu. He defeated the Huns and drove them north of the Gobi Desert. He opened routes to the west for invasion and trade. He led four campaigns against the Huns and killed or captured 110,000 of the enemy. By 119 the Huns' capabilities had been reduced to occasional small-scale raids. The successful completion of this operation enabled the Han to turn its attention elsewhere.

## THE CAREER OF LI KUANG

Li Kuang came from a noble family and served as a young man against the Hun incursions of 166. He made a name for himself with his courage and his marksmanship with the bow. He rose to the position of general of palace horsemen. He then was transferred to the northern districts as director of dependent kingdoms. There he frequently fought the Huns, so frequently that the emperor came to believe that he would soon be killed and transferred him to the governorship of the province of Shang. Emperor Ching sent a favorite eunuch to Shang province to train and lead troops. One day while out with some thirty cavalry the eunuch came upon three Huns eagle hunting. The Huns attacked the eunuch and routed his force. Li Kuang gathered 100 cavalry, rode out, surrounded the Huns, and shot down two with his own arrows and captured the third. Then in the distance he saw a force of several thousand Huns. The Huns thought that Li Kuang's small force was a decoy to lead them into an ambush, and they took up a defensive position on a hill. Li Kuang's men begged him to flee. Rather, he advanced on the Huns and by convincing them that he had nothing to fear, prevented them from attacking him. They withdrew during the night.

When Li Kuang was on campaign, he selected a campsite with water and grass and did not put out sentries or keep records or bother his men. They had a relaxed life in the field and were rested and ready to fight. A fellow general who kept a strict camp said that he preferred to avoid surprises and have a less loyal and effective army in battle. In 129 Li Kuang was given command of an army and sent to campaign against the Huns. He encountered a force much larger than his own, was defeated, wounded, and captured alive. He pretended to be more seriously wounded than he was. The Huns put him in a litter between two horses and were carrying him back to their own leader when Li Kuang sprang from the litter, knocked a boy off his horse, and fled. He rejoined the remnants of his army after a pursuit of ten miles and escaped from the Huns. When he returned to the capital, the emperor's advisers recommended that he be executed for losing so many men. The emperor instead fined him and reduced him to the rank of commoner.

When the Huns invaded Liao-hsi, killed the governor, and defeated the general, the emperor sent Li Kuang there to be governor. The emperor reminded him that the general is the fangs and claws of the nation—when he goes out, he spreads terror for a thousand miles. He became known as the Flying General, and his presence curtailed Hunnic raids. (In his spare time he hunted tigers.) He was rewarded for his efforts by being promoted to chief of the palace attendants. In 123 he was sent out with an army against the Huns. In 120 he was sent out again with 4,000 cavalry. He ran into a force several times larger than his own and was surrounded. His men were terrified, so he sent his son with a small band to ride through the Huns. The demonstration gave his men heart and he formed them in a circle. The Huns surrounded them, and the two sides traded fire. Li Kuang killed several of the Huns with his famous yellow crossbow, and they fought until nightfall; the next day a relieving army arrived, and the two forces fought their way to safety. Li Kuang was charged in the capital with having lost his army. The emperor decided that failure and success canceled each other out, and he gave him neither reward nor punishment.

Li Kuang participated in more than seventy campaigns, large and small, against the Huns. When he was over 60, he was given command of a division and ordered to take it by a circuitous route to join the main army. He lost his way and upon reporting to the commanding general was ordered to give an explanation for his failure to join the army on time. He told his staff that he was over 60 years old, unlucky, too old for campaigning anymore, and he cut his throat.

## THE CAREER OF LI LING

Li Ling was the grandson of Li Kuang. The emperor believed that he saw in him the same capabilities that his grandfather had, and he sent him in command of a force of 800 cavalry on a raid against the Huns. Li Ling covered almost 700 miles and never caught sight of the Huns. In 99 B.C. when the emperor sent 30,000 cavalry to attack the Huns, Li Ling requested that he be allowed to take an infantry force armed with crossbows and make a diversionary attack on the Huns. He was ordered to survey the country he passed through and send the information back to the emperor. When he had penetrated Hunnic territory, the Hunnic chieftain surrounded him with a cavalry force of 30,000. Li Ling drew his wagons up in a circle. He drew up his force in line with the men with shields and lances in front and bows and crossbows behind. Then he advanced on the enemy and drove them off. The Huns got reinforcements and regrouped. Li Ling conducted a fighting retreat, using the wagons to form a perimeter and to carry the wounded. Those who had been wounded three times could ride, those who had been wounded twice pulled the carts, those with one wound carried the weapons and fought. As he noticed that his men's energy and enthusiasm seemed to be flagging, he searched the camp and found that some women had been hidden in the wagons; he had them all killed. The Huns started fires and Li Ling started counter fires. When the cavalry attacked, he had his men take shelter in the trees and shoot at them. The Huns were discouraged—on the one hand, they believed that they had to defeat and destroy this small force or they would never be able to fight the Han again, while on the other hand, they believed that a larger army must be coming to the relief of Li Ling, or his men would not be fighting so fiercely. Then a deserter from Li Ling's force brought the Huns the news that the army was fighting so well because of Li Ling and that they expected no relief. The Huns renewed the attack and at last Li Ling's men (3,000 then surviving) ran out of arrows after firing "half a million." They broke off wagon spokes to use as clubs. The army was brought to bay about thirty miles from the border. In the night the army dispersed. About 400 finally made their way home. Li Ling was cornered, and he surrendered. He had conducted a fighting retreat of some 350 miles.

Li Ling lived with the Hunnic chieftain. The emperor rewarded the survivors of the retreat, but he was angered against Li Ling and when he heard rumors that Li Ling was training the Hunnic army he had his family executed. (Li Ling, innocent of the charge, hired an assassin to kill the actual culprit, Li Hsü.) Eventually Li Ling was appointed a subchieftain of the Huns. He lived with the Huns until his death in 74 B.C.

In 138–126 the emperor sent his envoy Chang Ch'ien to look for allies against the Huns. He was taken prisoner by the Huns and held for ten years. In the process he became an expert on them. He took a Hunnic wife, and they had a son, but in the end he escaped and continued his mission. He travelled to Ferghana (where he reported seventy cities and men armed with bows and halberds and cavalry who could shoot their bows from horseback). He also reported that here could be found a breeding stock of the "heavenly horses." He continued his travels through Sogdiana and Bactria, where he met the leaders of the Yüeh-chieh (the Indo-European tribes—known in the west as the

Kushans—driven out by the Huns). He was expected to be able to convince neighboring kingdoms to submit to the emperor (who would then use them to contain the Huns). He failed in this mission, but, nonetheless, by 106 B.C. the Chinese had driven the Huns from the Kansu corridor and opened a caravan route (the Silk Road) from China to Parthia through Bactria.

After 112 the Han advanced into Korea, south and southwest, and into Central Asia, and in 111–109 reconquered the kingdom of Yueh (with Tonkin and Annam) and established fourteen new commanderies on the southern and southwestern borders of the kingdom. In 108 the Han annexed the kingdom of Ch'ao Hsien, southern Manchuria and northern Korea, and in the period 105–102 the Chinese penetrated into Central Asia.

Wu Ti sent envoys to demand tribute (horses) from Sogdiana. When the tribute was refused, the Chinese envoys stole some horses. They were pursued, captured, and executed, so in 104 B.C. Wu Ti sent Li Kuang Li to lead an army into Ferghana in the Jaxartes Mountains. He won a number of victories but was defeated by a coalition of independent tribes in Ferghana. He withdrew, reorganized, and invaded again. This expedition defeated the army of Sogdiana and laid siege to its capital. The Sogdianians bought off the siege with rations and 3,000 horses and acknowledged Chinese overlordship. Of an invading army of 60,000 only half reached Ferghana, and only 10,000 returned to China. The Chinese emperors then left well enough alone in that area for over 100 years. (They felt less urgency to seek allies against the Huns when the Huns split into two bands and one band submitted to China.)

In 99 the Hunnic raids began again, and two campaigns against them ended badly. Han and Hun were coming to realize that neither could defeat the other without tremendous losses. The Han enjoyed organizational advantages. They could collect men, train them, and supply them, both as an army and as a labor force. They could coordinate operations. The Huns' strength was their mobility and, of course, their large numbers and the large number of horses they bred. The Han, despite strenuous efforts, could not match the Huns in cavalry. Nor did the Han expansion pay for itself. The population of Han China may have been somewhere around 50,000,000, a base that allowed a maximum call-up of troops (for two-year service) of about 1,000,000 men. Men were liable to call-up between the ages of 23 and 56, for one year of training and one year of service. Generally an army was raised for a specific campaign from the districts bordering the area of operation.

The latter part of the reign of Wu-Ti consisted of the consolidation of the conquests of the emperor and the extension of the Great Wall to the northwest and the formation of new commanderies to protect the northern trade routes and to dominate the numerous small tribes along the route. The Great Wall also stopped large numbers of Chinese from deserting to the Huns.

When Wu-ti died in 87 B.C. he left a succession in turmoil. The mothers of candidates for the succession and their powerful families vied for the throne. The existence of an efficient bureaucracy, the degree of independence granted generals on campaign, and the normal isolation of the emperor meant that the empire could be run quite well by the imperial staff. The emperor was not expected to go out on campaign and lead the army, nor even to put in an appearance before the army. The men who held the highest offices, then, preferred that the emperor be a minor who could be controlled or who would play a passive role. Two powerful families fought for control of the throne and placed and deposed emperors.

Within the decade after the death of Wu-ti his expansionist and aggressive policies were being questioned and criticized. Could the state afford such policies? Was not the purpose of government to cultivate the prosperity of the people? To that end was not a combination of defense and diplomacy preferable to aggressive war? Such a debate was possible only because the aggressive policies had broken the unity of the Huns, at one point into five rival factions, and the imperial government had kept them split by founding new agricultural colonies.

Nonetheless, in 73 and again in 54 B.C. the Huns tried to occupy Turkestan and the Tarim Basin. The Chinese formed an alliance with the Wu Sun (an Indo-European tribe of the Yüeh-Chieh who lived northwest of the Jaxartes River) and repelled the Huns. By and large, the last eighty years of the Former Han was a period of peace and stability for China and its neighbors.

## 35. A Chinese Chariot

# 22

# China: The Later Han

## *The Dangers of Universal Military Training*

As the emperor became more a creature of the great families, opportunities opened for adventurers. Wang Mang, a man from the lesser nobility, rose to power through the influence of the empress (his aunt). He became regent to two underage emperors and in A.D. 6 he named himself acting emperor for an infant emperor. In A.D. 9 he declared that the heavenly cycles had turned and brought down the red empire (the Han) and replaced it with the yellow, the New Dynasty. Under the pressure of new Hunnic aggression Wang Mang mobilized 300,000 men divided between twelve stations. This show of force was enough to deter the Huns (Hsiung-nu) and the two sides teetered between threats of force and diplomatic professions of peace. By sending an expedition along the Tarim Basin in A.D. 16 he maintained the Silk Route. He encouraged innovations in the military and in A.D. 19 at a conference on military matters one inventor demonstrated (not very successfully) an attempt to fly.

Between A.D. 4 and 11 the Yellow River shifted its course. The consequent flooding was a disaster before which the government of Wang Mang was helpless. Famine and disease spread. Bands of starving peasants roamed the countryside, stealing and plundering. Those who had not suffered from the flood suffered from the depredations of the refugees. In Shantung the ranks of the desperate swelled and overwhelmed the local militia. Wang Mang mobilized the army in A.D. 18 but failed to put down the uprising. In the winter of A.D. 22 he dispatched a large army, which failed miserably against the rebels. The rebels smeared red paint on their foreheads, to tell them apart from the imperial troops, and so were known as the Red Eyebrows. (Red was the color of the Han dynasty.) The rebel army (if it may be called so) had only the most basic discipline—if two soldiers fought each other and one died, the other was executed; if one was wounded, the other had to pay compensation. Their leaders, at least in the modest titles they took, had no wide ambitions. Leaders and led alike were peasants, but peasants who had received military training. When the army of rebellion became so large that it could not feed itself, it split apart into three divisions. The nobility in their path kept themselves behind walls protected by their followers, but one division of the Red Eyebrows moved towards the rich agricultural land of Nan-yang, and other armed bands arose.

In Nan-yang two brothers, Liu Po-sheng and the younger Liu Hsiu, both descendants of the first Han emperors, organized resistance to the Red Eyebrows in the name of the Former Han dynasty. They convinced two of the armed bands roaming the countryside that the real (and common) enemy was Wang Mang. Liu Po-sheng was defeated by Wang Mang's army and his own army almost wiped out, but even in defeat he was able to convince another division of rebels to join him, and in the beginning of A.D. 23 he defeated an army of Wang Mang. In a third battle he again defeated Wang Mang's forces, and he sent messengers through China to call for the overthrow of Wang Mang and the reinstatement of the Han dynasty. The nobles in the army knew that the crisis had arrived, and if they acceded in the leadership of Po-sheng he would become emperor, and they would be out. In secret they found their own candidate, a nonentity who was a third cousin of Po-sheng and likewise a descendant of the first Han emperors. The troops assembled and proclaimed Liu Hsuan emperor—a man the nobles thought they could dominate.

The peasant army became the army of Han and the younger brother of Po-sheng was sent as commander of a detachment against Wang Mang's newly recruited army. In July of 23 Liu Hsiu defeated the imperial army. His reputation was won and Wang Mang's power was broken. (Po-sheng was executed on a trumped-up charge to get rid of this threat to the new regime). The army moved towards the capital, but before it arrived, mobs attracted by their hatred of Wang Mang and their expectation of loot broke into the palace and cut off Wang Mang's head. His supporters had either been killed in the fighting or had committed suicide.

The victors then threw away the victory in their ambition to control the new emperor and the spoils. They dispatched Liu Hsiu to the north on an independent mission. They did not reach an agreement with the Red Eyebrows. They dismissed the leaders of the military units who had won them their victory but did not replace them in the army. They moved to a new capital that isolated them without protecting them. The Red Eyebrows moved on the new capital, entered it, and sacked it, while Liu Hsiu in the north proclaimed himself emperor (A.D. 25) and took the new name Kuang-wu-ti. He is the founder of the Later Han (A.D. 25–220). He had to put down almost a dozen rivals in the decade after he proclaimed himself emperor.

Kuang's policy towards the Huns was to rebuild and defend the line of the Great Wall, to fill in the gaps in the defensive line, and to build watch towers.

When the leader of the Huns died in 46, a dynastic dispute arose. The loser appealed to the Chinese and offered his submission to them. A drought aggravated the political situation. In 49 the Huns split into a northern and southern division, each ruled by one of the rivals. In 50 Chinese envoys visited the ruler of the southern confederation and ordered him to prostrate himself. He did, and the envoys gave him a gold seal and other gifts and permitted him to settle within the empire in the Ordos region. The Great Wall was still manned by Chinese troops. The emperor's advisers advised him to join with the southern Huns in an attack on the northern. The goal would have been to force the northern Huns to accept the leadership of the southern ruler (who had submitted to the emperor) and to move the southern Huns out of the empire. The emperor refused. Given the subsequent history, this decision appears mistaken, but such a campaign would have been risky and expensive, and the situation must have seemed stable and manageable to the emperor. The Hunnic ruler sent a son as hostage to the Chinese capital each year, and the system continued to the end of the Later Han.

In A.D. 73 the imperial government, together with the southern confederation, attacked the northern. In A.D. 89 a massive joint effort by the "general of cavalry and chariots" Tou Hsien routed the northern Huns and divided the northern confederation. The northern Huns began a massive migration that eventually brought them to Europe, while two subject peoples (one of whom was the Mongols) moved into their territory. The southern confederation remained in Chinese territory to vex the Han for a century and eventually to bring down the successor dynasty to the Han (A.D. 308) and usher in two and a half centuries of disunity.

The defensive policy of Kuang-wu-ti had led to the loss of control over the Silk Route. The defeat of the northern Hun provided an opportunity exploited by the general Pan Ch'ao. He spent three decades (73–102) in western Asia. He recovered Han control of the oasis states and the Silk Route (which they maintained until the middle of the second century). With a small army he conquered the Tarim Basin. He crossed the Tien Shan mountains into western Turkestan, defeated the various nomadic tribes between the Hindu Kush and the Aral Sea, and forced them to accept Chinese overlordship. He received tribute from Kushan India. Reconnaissance parties reached the Caspian Sea. In 166 (in the wake of Roman victories over the Parthians) envoys arrived in the Han court from Marcus Aurelius, "king" of Rome. The envoys offered presents of ivory, rhinoceros horn, and tortoise shell. Thus the Romans briefly opened communications with Han China.

In the southeast Chinese were infiltrating and settling the Red River valley (in opposition to the local inhabitants). Ma Yüan was given the command in A.D. 42. He put down an uprising led by two sisters and set out to destroy local culture and force the natives to live as the Chinese did. As the Chinese expanded and settled, the native population rose in opposition. The imperial government considered this act rebellion and sent in the army. As always the emperor had to deal with factions around him. Ma Yüan ended his life in the conquest (suppression of rebellion) of Hunan. Denounced by opposing factions, he was at first denied burial.

Kuang-wu-ti died in A.D. 57 and was succeeded by a number of ineffectual emperors. The early second century was a time of debate over Han military policy—what could they afford? Wasn't the defense of the Silk Route too expensive? The opening of the Silk Road also opened China to the influence of Buddhism. Hadn't the attack on the Huns been wasteful? The response was that lands that had once belonged to the Han should be protected regardless of the cost.

The later emperors of the Han dynasty were an ineffectual lot whose lack of character was enough to inspire a wide-spread belief that the mandate of heaven had been withdrawn from the Red (Han) and turned to the Yellow. In Szechwan a family of Taoist magicians—Taoism was the third religion of China—organized a secret society. They worked wonders, healed the sick, remitted sins, and rebuilt roads, distributed free rice, and thereby they gained hundreds of thousands of followers: in the year 184, which they proclaimed the beginning of a new millennium, they led a revolt, the revolt of the "Yellow Turbans." The imperial army—which had become a place to settle palace favorites—was as ineffectual as the emperor.

In the court the eunuchs controlled the regents and the child emperors. In A.D. 189 the officers of the army conspired together and slaughtered the eunuchs, but the general in charge, Tung Cho, set himself up as dictator, and the generals of the different provinces followed his example, which led to military anarchy. Tung Cho finally was murdered. Civil war followed and then the Huns invaded. In the period 190–200 the Han empire was ruled first by Tung Cho in the name of a puppet Han emperor; he was assassinated in 192, and two rival generals, Ts'ao Ts'ao and Liu Pei in 194 fought for the control of the empire. In 196 Ts'ao Ts'ao was successful and proclaimed himself protector of the empire; the emperor was his puppet, and between 196 and 204 he reunited the Yellow River valley and eventually founded the Wei dynasty. At the same time a second empire was formed in the south under Sun Ch'üan, and a distaff member of the Han dynasty—so poor he had supported his mother by selling straw sandals—seized the province of Szechwan, and the three fought it out.

Then the Turco-Mongolian horde invaded the empire. One of their kings claimed descent from the Han dynasty and in 308 Liu Yüan proclaimed himself emperor of all of China. His son, trained in the Chinese capital and reputed a fine scholar, led the invasion. He took the capital and slaughtered its 30,000 inhabitants. He killed the heir to the throne and sent the emperor back to be cupbearer to his father (until the father had a fit of rage and killed him). A second Chinese emperor was captured and sent to succeed his predecessor as cupbearer. The north fell to the barbarians and the Chin dynasty fled to the south and set up their capital in Nanking and there for nearly three centuries (318–589) they remained. The north was fought over by the barbarians—truly barbarians: from time to time the king would have one of the girls of his harem beheaded, cooked, and served to his guests, while the uncooked head was passed round on a plate to prove that he had not sacrificed an ugly one. The farm lands were so devastated that wolves and tigers came back to regions where they had been exterminated. When the Chinese people asked for protection by their barbarian masters from marauding animals, one king replied, "When the beasts have satisfied their hunger, they won't eat anyone else."

In the south the Chin dynasty was overthrown by the Sung dynasty and it, in turn, after a bout of murders and debaucheries, was overthrown by the Ch'i dynasty. The first act of a new emperor all too often was to murder every other member of the royal family so that he would have no rivals. The Liang dynasty followed and then the Ch'en until in 589 the south was conquered by the north.

In the north a Turkish tribe, the T'o-pa, between 396 and 439 destroyed or absorbed all other tribes in north China. They preserved their own culture for a long time, but gradually they were sinicized. They also gained acceptance by the Chinese by successfully defending them from the Mongols. T'o-pa T'ao (424–452), sometimes called the Oriental Charlemagne, adopted Confucianism and changed his culture enough that it became acceptable to the Chinese. He did maintain some of the old ways, for instance, to put to death the mother of the new king to spare his wife, the new queen, arguments with her mother-in-law. A new dynasty of the T'o-pa, the Sui, reunited the empire in 589.

## Map 17. Han China

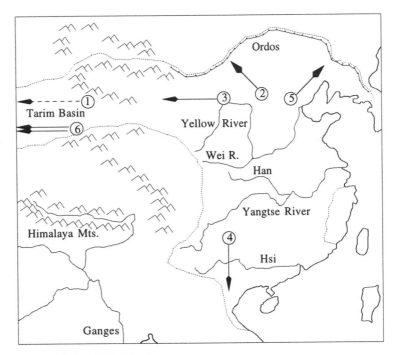

..... Limits of Han Empire
└┘ The Great Wall

### MAJOR CAMPAIGNS DURING THE REIGN OF WU TI

1. Embassy of Chang Ch'ien, 138-126
   to the Yueh-Chih (Bactria)
2. The Huns (Hsiung-nu) 127
3. The Huns (Hsiung-nu) 121-119

4. Yueh 111-109
5. Ch'ao Hsien 108
6. Ferghana, two campaigns
   105-102

### THE SILK ROAD

Antioch     Ecbatana     Samarkand
Palmyra     Hecatompylos    Tashkent
     Merv      Kashgar     Loyang

Han China controlled the road from Loyang to Samarkand.

# 23

# The Parthians

## *A New Power Moves Into a Power Vacuum*

When Seleucus succeeded in wresting control of the Asian empire from his rivals, he made the fateful decision to move his capital to Antioch on the Mediterranean coast. With a need to recruit mercenaries from Greece and Macedonia he could hardly have done otherwise, but he left the defense of the eastern borders to those living in the east, a power vacuum developed in Bactria and Parthia, and a central Asian tribe, the Parni, entered this region. In the mid-250s the Seleucid governor of Bactria, Diodotus, rebelled and established a kingdom including Bactria and parts of Parthia and India. He forced Arsaces, the leader of the Parni, into western Parthia, where, under the cover of the rebellion of Diodotus, Arsaces established a kingdom (247 B.C.). He defeated the Seleucid governor of Parthia and expanded his kingdom to include both Parthia and Hyrcania. Diodotus and Arsaces cooperated to defend themselves from Seleucid attempts to bring them back into the empire. Diodotus, though successful, was assassinated and replaced by Euthydemus (a Greco-Macedonian).

The Seleucid king, Antiochus III, was determined to recover the eastern provinces of Alexander's empire. The Parthian king was taken by surprise—he sent cavalry to choke the wells along Antiochus's line of advance, but Antiochus's cavalry outrode them. The Parthians' second line of defense was the mountainous and broken terrain of Parthia itself. They abandoned their capital and tried to guard the passes. Antiochus's troops, however, were well used to mountain warfare, and they scaled the cliffs the Parthians thought were impassable. In the last pass into Hyrcania a pitched battle was fought between the Seleucid phalanx and the Parthians. The Seleucids won and marched into Hyrcania. The Parthian king agreed to peace terms that left him as vassal king to the Seleucids.

Thus by 208 Euthydemus was isolated. He determined to hold the line of the Arius River, but Antiochus stole a march on him. When he was one day's march from the river crossing, he made a forced march at night with his cavalry and arrived at the undefended crossing, seized it, and held it until his phalanx arrived. As he continued his advance, the Bactrian cavalry fell on his point guard, while his army was still in march formation. Antiochus personally led the charge against the Bactrians. He had a horse killed under him and several teeth knocked out in the battle, but then the rest of his cavalry appeared and the Bactrians were routed. Euthedemus asked for, and received, generous terms.

After Antiochus's successes, however, Seleucid policy was reduced to holding the line against Parthia. In the middle of the second century the Seleucid king tried to prop up the east through an alliance between the governor of Media and the Bactrian (Greco-Macedonian) king. The new Parthian king, Mithradates I, utterly shattered that scheme. As the Seleucids devolved into dynastic conflict, Mithradates entered Media (early 140s). In 141 Mithradates invaded Babylonia and took Seleucia (on-the-Tigris). His generals took Susa. The Seleucid king raised an army and advanced on Babylon, but he was defeated and captured in 139, paraded as a captive, and sent to Mithradates (who treated him as a brother king and gave him one of his daughters as wife).

By the time of Mithradates' death in 137, the Parthian kingdom extended from the Euphrates to the Indus River. The extent of the empire brought its own problems. Mithradates' successor (Phraates) faced a movement of people (the Sacae) who were impelled by the turmoil on the steppes of central Asia—the Tochari (Yueh-chi) had been attacked and defeated by the Huns (Hsiung-nu) and in their turn had attacked and defeated the Sacae, who had entered the Parthian empire. As the Sacae entered in the east (and into Bactria, where they overthrew the last Greek settlements), a new Seleucid king attacked from the west.

The Seleucid defeated Parthian generals in three battles in 130, entered Media, and sent his men into winter quarters to wait for spring and complete victory. The Medes, forced to supply these soldiers, had a revulsion of feeling, and they attacked the separate garrisons. When the Seleucid king rushed out with his personal guard to go to their help, he ran into the main Parthian army. He was overwhelmed and killed. The Parthian king Phraates annihilated the Seleucid army of 80,000 by killing many and by accepting the surrender of the rest, but he foolishly refused to pay some Sacae mercenaries (because they had arrived too late to do any fighting). The Sacae decided to collect their pay by turning to plunder, Phraates decided not to waste his own troops against the Sacae, he enlisted the Seleucid prisoners as mercenaries, and they promptly decided to join the Sacae (in 128). The combined force overwhelmed the Parthians and killed Phraates.

Phraates' successor was killed in a battle with the nomadic Tochari (wounded in the arm by a poisoned arrow), but his successor, Mithradates II (124–87 B.C.) stabilized the eastern frontier and moved the administrative capital to Babylonia (out of reach of eastern raiders). Under Mithradates' successors the

Parthian empire first came into contact with the growing Roman Empire and the ambitious Roman Crassus. Crassus was the wealthiest man in Rome, but he had not earned the reputation that came to those who had won a major victory and had conquered new land for the Rome. While Caesar was conquering Gaul, Crassus was given the mandate to conquer Mesopotamia and Alexander's empire. The pretext was the defense of the Romans' eastern frontier. The fact was that the same impetus that drove the whole of Roman imperialism also drove Crassus.

In 53 B.C. he set off with his army into the interior of Mesopotamia. He had seven legions and 4,000 cavalry. His son commanded the cavalry. Crassus was so confident of the superiority of the Roman legions that he rejected the protected routes through the foothills or through Armenia and crossed the plain where the Roman legions would be most at risk and the Parthians would have the greatest advantage if, contrary to his expectations, they did have heart for the fight.

The Romans began to cross the plain in a square formation. When they came to a little stream, the Balissus, the staff advised that they camp there for the night. Crassus's son, however, urged that they advance against an enemy thought to be retreating. Crassus ordered a forced march that finally brought them within sight of the enemy. The Parthians now began to beat their battle drums and the strange noise caused consternation among the Romans. The Parthian general had intended to charge the Roman formation with his heavy cavalry (armored horses and men with long lances), but he estimated that he could not break through the line of shields, so he had his formation split and surround the Roman square.

The Parthians fired arrows at the Romans, shooting them at an angle up into the air so that they would fall on the ranks behind the shields. The Romans suffered, but they expected that they could endure until the Parthians ran out of arrows. The Parthian general, however, had organized a camel train loaded with arrows and horsemen to ride back and forth to supply the warriors. Crassus ordered his son to launch an attack on the enemy and his son led 1,300 cavalry, 500 archers, and 8 cohorts in the attack. The Parthians fled and the Romans pursued. They thought they had driven the enemy off, but when they were a long way from the main force, the Parthians circled around them and shot arrows at them. The arrows were barbed and impossible to pull out—they pierced the feet of the Romans and pinned them to the ground. Young Crassus tried to relieve the distress of his infantry by a cavalry charge, but his Gallic cavalry was at a disadvantage. They wore no body armor, and the lances they used were lighter and shorter than the Parthian lances. They dismounted and stabbed the Parthian horses in the belly, they grappled with the enemy, seized their long lances, and pulled them off their horses, but they were overcome by superior numbers, and young Crassus was badly wounded. The survivors of the cavalry and infantry took refuge in a tight formation on a small hill, where they tried to protect themselves with their shields. Arrows found their way above and below the shields and killed all but 500. Young Crassus killed himself rather than be taken prisoner.

At first the elder Crassus thought that his son had defeated the Parthians and driven them off because the attacks against him lessened, but soon the main force of the Parthians returned with his son's head on a spear. Roman morale plummeted. All day the Parthian light cavalry rode around the Roman force and shot arrows at them, while the heavy lancers attacked from the front and caused the Roman cavalry to fall back on the infantry formation. At nightfall the Parthians withdrew (since they had a difficult time conducting operations at night). Crassus was in shock, and his subordinate officers had to take matters into their own hands. They organized a retreat and made the decision to bring all the wounded with them. A unit of 300 cavalry reached Carrhae about midnight, called out to the sentries on the wall that Crassus had fought a great battle with the Parthians, and then they moved on, but the column was far behind them. The Parthians harassed the retreating army, killed about 4,000 stragglers, surrounded a force of four cohorts that had gotten separated from the main body, and killed all but about twenty who continued to resist so bravely that the Parthians withdrew and allowed them to march into Carrhae without further attack. Crassus and his demoralized army took refuge in Carrhae.

The Parthians surrounded Carrhae and learned from their agents that Crassus intended to set out at night to retreat into Armenia. Guides friendly to the Parthians led him astray, and the army fragmented. Some cavalry made their way to Syria. The troops remaining with Crassus were surrounded on a mountain refuge, but they fought so fiercely that the Parthian attack began to slack off. The Parthian commander feared that the Romans might yet escape with one more night march, so he offered to negotiate with Crassus. Crassus suspected deception, but his soldiers forced him to talk with the Parthians. The Parthians seized him, cut off his head, and sent it to the Parthian king; they informed the Romans that their general was dead and that they should come down off the moutain and surrender. Ten thousand did, the rest scattered in the night, and most of them were hunted down and killed. Twenty thousand Romans died in Crassus's campaign.

After the battle of Carrhae the 10,000 Roman prisoners were sent to Margiana on the eastern border of Parthia (1500 miles from Carrhae). In 36 B.C. two Chinese generals attacked the principal city of a Hunnic chief in the vicinity of Sogdiana. An eyewitness describes soldiers at this city in a "fishscale formation" behind a double palisade—an apparent description of the Roman tortoise and a typical Roman fortification. These troops—145 of them—who stopped fighting when their paymaster died, were settled in a frontier town given the name Li-jien ("Roman").

Thus the Parthians, as they expanded west and east, came into contact with the Romans and the Chinese. With dynastic disputes, an empire of disparate peoples, and pressures from the great empires to their west and east, Parthia seldom enjoyed a period of stability.

The qualities of a successful empire seem to be unity, stability, and justice. What would have been the result, if Alexander had lived and the center of gravity of his empire had not been the point closest to Macedonia, but a point in the center of the empire? What if the settled Greek colonies had not been called upon to support the ambitions of the dynasty, but the dynasty rather had supported the colonies? And what if the Iranians had not been exploited as subjects, but had been partners in the empire? Two centuries of cooperation might have created an empire more powerful than the Roman or the Chinese.

## 36. A Parthian Horse Archer

## Map 18: Maps Illustrating the Expansion of the Roman Republic

THE ROMAN REPUBLIC ON THE EVE OF THE FIRST PUNIC WAR

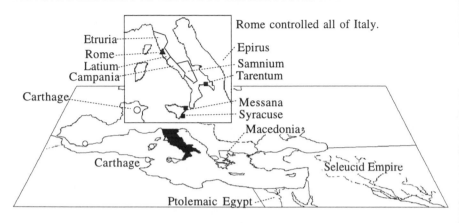

Rome controlled all of Italy.

Etruria
Rome
Latium
Campania
Carthage

Epirus
Samnium
Tarentum

Messana
Syracuse
Macedonia

Carthage

Seleucid Empire

Ptolemaic Egypt

THE MAJOR ROADS OF THE ROMAN REPUBLIC
(name in italics with the date the road was begun)

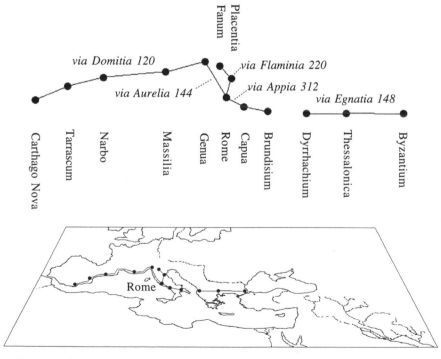

Placentia
Fanum

via Domitia 120
via Aurelia 144
via Flaminia 220
via Appia 312
via Egnatia 148

Carthago Nova
Tarrascum
Narbo
Massilia
Genua
Rome
Capua
Brundisium
Dyrrhachium
Thessalonica
Byzantium

Rome

The roads, built to speed the movement of the Roman legions, reflect the stages of
Roman domination of southern Europe.

# Part Four
# The Roman Republic

The Romans develop a system that insures individual rights within an organized and disciplined society. The Roman society gained a military and moral advantage over its neighbors, but its true advantage lay in its ability to organize the peace its soldiers won.

**37. An Italian Hoplite: a. Palestrina ivory plaque, 300-250; b. Bronze, Fifth Century**

a.

b.

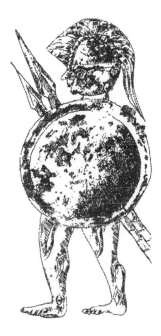

## Map 19: The First Punic War

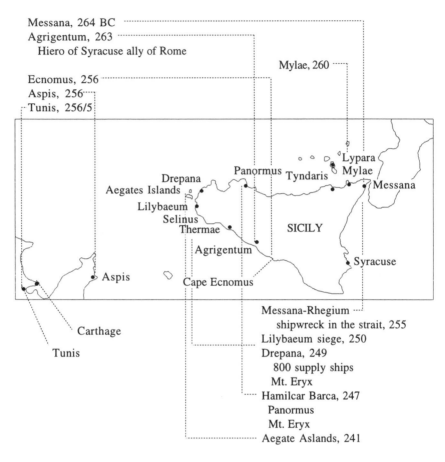

Messana, 264 BC
Agrigentum, 263
  Hiero of Syracuse ally of Rome

Mylae, 260

Ecnomus, 256
Aspis, 256
Tunis, 256/5

Lypara
Panormus  Tyndaris  Mylae
Drepana
Aegates Islands
Lilybaeum
Selinus
Thermae
Agrigentum
SICILY
Messana
Syracuse

Aspis
Cape Ecnomus

Carthage

Tunis

Messana-Rhegium
  shipwreck in the strait, 255
Lilybaeum siege, 250
Drepana, 249
  800 supply ships
  Mt. Eryx
Hamilcar Barca, 247
  Panormus
  Mt. Eryx
Aegate Aslands, 241

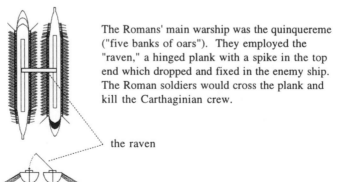

The Romans' main warship was the quinquereme
("five banks of oars").  They employed the
"raven," a hinged plank with a spike in the top
end which dropped and fixed in the enemy ship.
The Roman soldiers would cross the plank and
kill the Carthaginian crew.

the raven

# 24

# The Development of the Roman System

## The Supreme Organizers of War and Peace

Until 390 B.C. Rome was just one of a number of moderately powerful states in Italy; its army, like its neighbors, fought in a phalanx, and the Romans had only a slight military advantage over them. Then, in 390, the Romans fought the battle of the Allia against an invading band of Gauls. The Gauls seemed not to care whether they lived or died; shrieking their war cries, they threw themselves, some of them naked, into the Roman phalanx and shattered it. The victorious Gauls pursued the fleeing Romans all the way to Rome, they occupied the city, and they refused to leave until the Romans had paid them a huge indemnity. The Romans, however, now at their lowest point, proved the truth of the adage that they were most to be feared when they themselves had the most to fear.

They gave their foremost citizen, Camillus, full power to reform the army and the state. As in Greece military, social, and political status were determined by property and by family. The Camillan reform organized Roman citizens into centuries: those who had horses—the highest property class, the equites—were apportioned to eighteen centuries. The class-one centuries (eighty centuries) comprised those who could afford the panoply: helmet, shield, breastplate, greaves, sword, and spear; class two, all but the breastplate; class three and four, shield and weapons only; class five, slingers. Centuries of armorers, trumpeters, and horn blowers and a single century of those without property brought the total number of centuries to 193. Each century had one vote; the eighteen equestrian centuries and the eighty class-one centuries held the majority of votes.

The Romans also reached a social accord within Rome. The aristocracy (the patricians) recognized the plebs (the people) as having a corporate identity and individual plebeians with property as having the right to hold the highest office. (Eventually a custom was established that one consul should be patrician, one plebeian.) The reforms produced a unified, stable state with a growing

population, a flexible system of command, an organized army, and a purpose . . . to secure themselves forever from Gallic attack.

From this core of citizens Camillus created the flexible, tripartite, manipular
army that, in essence, was to be the army of the Scipios and the Caesars. The
first lines drawn up in formation were the *hastati* ("spearmen"), organized by
maniples of two centuries (thirty men each) armed with the oval shield and spear.
(In front of the hastati and attached to them were the *leves*—the light-armed
soldiers.) Behind the hastati were the *principes*, men in the prime of life,
organized in maniples. Behind them were the *triarii, rorarii,* and *accensi*
(considered one "line"). The triarii were the older (veteran) soldiers, the rorarii
were younger, less experienced, the accensi the least dependable. The Roman
soldiers were armed with an iron helmet, a wooden shield reinforced with bronze,
and, by the end of the fourth century, the characteristic Roman throwing spear,
the *pilum*. The Roman tripartite army could now sustain the initial assault of
the Gauls and fight, if need be, not for twenty minutes, but for three times
twenty minutes.

The Romans believed that divine powers (*numina*) resided in everything and,
with the proper ritual, men could compel the numina to perform their duty,
whether that duty was to formalize marriage, to fertilize a field, or to bring
victory in war. So long as the priests used the proper ritual, the numina were
constrained by a binding contract to bring the Romans victory. As the Romans
fought man to man on the battlefield, so also did the numina fight for them in
the spirit world.

As the Camillan army defeated one enemy after another—the Etruscans, the
Latins, and other neighboring Italic peoples—the Romans offered to the defeated
peoples a form of citizenship that bound them to the Roman state. The
Latins—and many other Italic peoples—considered that they had much more to
fear from the Gauls than from the Romans, and they accepted the Romans'
terms. The Romans used each victory to forge bonds that made them stronger for
the next war. Tactically the Romans were sound; strategically they were
brilliant; politically they were unique.

Three decades after the sack of Rome, the Gauls returned. At a bridge over
the Anio River (a barrier along the approaches to Rome), a Gaul of immense
size, "naked except for his shield, two swords, neck chains and armlets,"
challenged the Romans to a duel. No Roman dared accept the challenge until an
officer named Manlius "took an infantry shield and a Spanish sword, ran forward,
and smashed his shield into the Gaul's shield so that the Gaul could not get a
full swing at him with his sword. The Gaul gave ground, and the Roman hit his
shield again and drove the Gaul backwards, knocked him over, and cut off his
head."

The Romans won no decisive victory, they continued to face the threat of
powerful Gallic tribes, but they held the line of the Anio, they defended themselves and their confederates from the Gauls, and they felt free enough to expand
their power to the south despite the Gallic threat. They defeated the Latins (338)

and dictated terms: some Latin cities became separate and independent allies; others were annexed and incorporated into the Roman state. (These Latins became Roman citizens.) The Romans now dominated central Italy, and they were determined to control Campania to their south—they conferred Roman citizenship (without the vote) on Capua and four other Campanian cities—and they resolved to break the strongest power left in south Italy, the Samnites.

The Samnites were organized as a confederation of independent villages under the command—in an emergency—of a chief with absolute authority. The Samnites were armed like the Romans (they may have introduced the pilum to the Romans), but their tactics, to fight in maniple-sized units, were adapted to the mountains, while the Roman legion was adapted to the plain. When the Romans received a report that the Samnites had massed their troops for a campaign in Apulia, they send their army to cross Samnium, cut off the Samnite army, and force a battle in the plain, but the report was a ruse. They were ambushed in the mountains (the battle of the Caudine Forks, 321 B.C.), defeated, driven into a box canyon, and starved into submission. The Samnites compelled the whole of the Roman army to walk under the yoke—a symbolic act to show Roman inferiority—and they held 500 equites hostage until the Romans had fulfilled the terms of the peace treaty—to abandon all forts in territory claimed by the Samnites and to swear not to make war on the Samnites ever again.

The Romans lived up to the letter of the treaty, but they formed alliances in the territory to the north of Samnium, they trained their army to fight in independent maniples—the better to fight the Samnites—and in 316 they sent one of their consuls to found a colony in the north while the other kept the Samnites occupied in the south. The Samnites reacted violently and, at first, successfully to this attempt to encircle them, but then the Roman army inflicted 10,000 casualties on the Samnites at the battle of Terracina (in Campania) in 314. The Romans' success, however, drove their northern neighbors, the Etruscans, into an alliance with the Samnites, and the Romans had to fight them as well as the Samnites. For ten years the Romans engaged in a multifront war. The Romans isolated the Samnites by controlling the passes into Samnium, and they raided Samnium continually until, in 304, the Samnites agreed to peace on the basis of the pre-war status quo.

The Romans now used a combination of colonies, grants of citizenship, and binding treaties to push their control through central Italy to the Adriatic, but no sooner had they attained their long-sought domination of central Italy than they faced their greatest challenge—the Gauls again crossed the Po and invaded Italy. The Gallic invasion awoke new hope in the Etruscans and the Samnites. A Roman double-consular army had to fight all three allies at the battle of Sentinum. The Roman consul Publius Decius offered his life to the gods in exchange for victory, he died in the battle, and the Romans won. The consul Papirius invaded Samnium. The Samnites swore an oath to die before giving ground; Papirius vowed, if he won, to give Jupiter the first drink of wine. The

Romans crushed the Samnite army, and in 290 the Samnites surrendered. The Romans defeated the strongest of the Gallic tribes, the Senones, and expelled them from Italy. The other Gauls they restricted to the valley of the Po.

The Greeks of south Italy and the Adriatic now looked to Rome as their protector rather than to the Spartan colony of Tarentum. The Tarentines believed that Rome had usurped the position that was rightfully theirs and, in 281, they attacked a small Roman fleet en route to the Adriatic to suppress piracy. Roman ambassadors sent to Tarentum to demand redress arrived during a festival when the Tarentines were drunk. A large crowd gathered and mocked the Romans. One drunk flung his own feces at the Roman ambassador. The Roman ambassador departed but left in the air the ominous remark, "You will wash my garment clean with your blood."

When the Tarentines sobered up, they realized that they had made a bad mistake, but they then made a worse one. They appealed to Pyrrhus, the king of Epirus, to protect them. Pyrrhus knew little of the Romans, but he was an experienced general who was confident in his own abilities and in his phalanx, cavalry, and elephants. He came west not to champion the Tarentines, but to fulfill an old ambition, to unite the Greeks of Italy and Sicily in a league with himself as hegemon (as Philip and Alexander had been hegemons of the Hellenic League). Pyrrhus had been told 300,000 Italic natives stood ready to serve him. To prevent this fiction from becoming reality, the Romans garrisoned south Italy and sent a consular army to winter in Samnium.

In the beginning of the campaigning season of 280 B.C. the Roman consul forced an engagement on Pyrrhus at Heraclea. On the eve of the battle Pyrrhus observed the Romans pitching camp. When he saw the fortified camp they built, he exclaimed, "These are not barbarians." In the morning he stationed his elephants on his flanks to frighten off the Roman cavalry and used his phalanx to break the legions. The Romans lost 7,000 men; Pyrrhus lost 4,000. The master tactician, upon being congratulated for his victory, said, "Yes, one more like it and we are done." Pyrrhus marched on Rome, but he found few allies, and forty miles from Rome he turned back. He offered the Romans what he thought were generous terms: the Romans would guarantee Greek autonomy, and they would withdraw from the territory of the Samnites, Lucanians, and Bruttians. The Senate rejected the terms.

In the spring of 279 a double consular army met Pyrrhus at Asculum near the Aufidus River. The battlefield was rugged and unsuited to a phalanx, but Pyrrhus had created a flexible phalanx by putting maniples of Samnites and Lucanians between units of his phalanx. The two armies fought all day without a decision, but early the next morning the king seized favorable ground and broke the legions. The Romans retreated to their camp and defended it successfully. One consul and 6,000 Romans had been killed. Pyrrhus lost 3,500 men and was himself wounded. He had won a battle, but his next step was not clear.

At this point he was invited by Sicilian envoys to come put Sicily in order. Sicily was in turmoil because of the death of the Syracusan tyrant Agathocles

—Pyrrhus was the son-in-law of Agathocles—and because the Carthaginians had launched an invasion, Pyrrhus offered the Romans a truce with but one demand—that the Romans recognize the territorial integrity of Tarentum. The Senate might have agreed, had a Carthaginian admiral (with his whole fleet of 120 ships) not appeared and offered to subsidize the war against Pyrrhus, to use his fleet to blockade Pyrrhus in Tarentum, and to transport Roman troops to Sicily, if they wished, to carry on the war against Pyrrhus there. The Romans accepted the Carthaginian treaty, and the two consuls with their armies advanced on Tarentum. Pyrrhus sailed for Sicily and left the Romans with a free hand to regain control of southern Italy.

After some initial successes in Sicily Pyrrhus's schemes collapsed, and in the spring of 275 he gave up and returned to Tarentum with a much-reduced force. The two Roman consuls were operating separately against Pyrrhus's former allies—none of them would help him now—and Pyrrhus tried to defeat one consul before the other could come to his aid. At Beneventum he fought his third grim battle against the Romans; the day ended without victory for either side, but that night the other consul reached the battlefield, and Pyrrhus withdrew. Pyrrhus left a garrison in Tarentum and returned to Epirus with but a third of the forces he had brought to Italy. The Romans won this war without ever having defeated Pyrrhus in battle.

The Roman victory brought them to the attention of the eastern courts. The court poet of Ptolemy, king of Egypt, identified the Romans with the Trojans who escaped from the sack of Troy under the leadership of Aeneas, and Ptolemy made a pact of friendship with them. The victory also gave the Romans a free hand in south Italy. They subjugated the native peoples, confiscated territory, and settled colonies to further divide these people from each other and from themselves. In 272—Pyrrhus was killed in a skirmish in Argos: an old woman threw a roof tile which stunned him, and a Gallic mercenary cut off his head—the Romans laid siege to Tarentum. The consul in command made a private deal with the Epirote garrison by which they handed over the citadel to him and were allowed to leave unharmed. The Romans treated the city with decency, accepted it as a naval ally, and permanently garrisoned the citadel with a legion, both to watch Tarentum and to protect southern Italy. The Romans were now masters of the greatest resource of military citizen manpower in the western world: a quarter of a million citizen-soldiers.

As their reputation grew, so did requests for their aid. An Italic people calling themselves the Mamertines ("devoted to Mamers," their god of war) had seized the Sicilian town of Messana, appealed to the Carthaginians to help them against the tyrant of Syracuse, Hiero (who wanted to expel them), and then had second thoughts about the garrison the Carthaginians imposed on them. They sought help from the Roman Senate, but the Senate referred the question to the Roman people: Carthage did not threaten Rome's control of Italy, and it had the greatest monetary resources of any city-state in the Mediterranean—an annual tribute of 12,000 talents. The Roman people voted to accept the alliance.

The consul of 264 B.C., Appius Claudius (nicknamed "the Log"), mobilized his forces and dispatched an advance party, which fought its way into the harbor of Messana. The Mamertines ordered the Carthaginians to leave, the Carthaginian commander complied (he had no orders to fight the Romans), and he returned home, there to have his decision repudiated with a death sentence. A Carthaginian army under the command of Hanno was sent to cooperate with Hiero's Syracusan army and put Messana under siege.

The First Punic War (264–241) had begun.

The Romans had a clear and simple strategy—gain a foothold in Sicily, expand their control (and limit Carthaginian control) throughout the island, and then invade Africa and knock Carthage out of the war. Up to a point all went exactly as they planned. Appius Claudius ferried his army across the straits of Messana at night, forced Hiero to retire to Syracuse, drove Hanno from the field, and thus, in two quick operations, accomplished Rome's primary objective—to preserve its new ally, Messana, and to acquire a base of operations.

In 263 B.C. two new consuls convinced Hiero to sign a fifteen-year treaty: the Romans recognized him as "king" of Syracuse, and Hiero paid the Romans an indemnity of 100 talents. At first the Romans were able to win support in Sicily by spreading the Ptolemaic story that they were the descendants of the Trojans—they granted freedom and autonomy to two Sicilian cities that asserted a connection with Aeneas—but soon they committed an act that repulsed Sicily.

The Carthaginians had retired to their base at Agrigentum, and the Romans wasted no time in putting them under siege; they built a double wall around the city, to blockade it and to protect themselves from a Carthaginian relief force of 50,000 infantry and 6,000 cavalry, which soon besieged the Romans besieging Agrigentum. The siege of Agrigentum demonstrated Roman tenacity and confirmed Hiero's loyalty: the Romans ran out of food but did not lift the siege; Hiero broke through the Carthaginian lines to resupply the Romans; a massive Carthaginian assault on the Roman siege works was beaten off with heavy losses, and the Carthaginian garrison inside the city decided to use the cover of the assault to abandon Agrigentum. The Roman commanders occupied Agrigentum and then shocked Sicilian Greeks by giving the city to their troops to sack and by selling the entire population into slavery.

Although the Romans had been successful so far, they now realized that the war would require them to subjugate the whole of Sicily and to neutralize the Carthaginian outposts in Sardinia and Corsica. Consequently the Roman Senate authorized the construction of a fleet of 20 triremes and 100 quinqueremes (a captured Carthaginian ship was the prototype), and they drafted 30,000 oarsmen to "sit and sweat" at rowing machines on land—the trick to rowing with banks of oars is to train the quinquereme's five-man tier to pull together. The Carthaginians' long experience at sea seemed to give them the upper hand, but a simple invention, the "raven," a boarding plank with a spike at one end and a hinge at the other, changed the nature of war at sea. The consul, Duillius, in command of this new Roman fleet, found the Carthaginians near Mylae.

Duillius had thirty ships fewer than the Carthaginians, and he was the first Roman ever to fight a sea battle. The ravens, however, worked perfectly. They locked Roman ships to Carthaginian, and Roman soldiers crossed the planks and slaughtered the Carthaginian crews. Duillius eliminated fifty Carthaginian ships. (The Romans were never to lose a sea battle to the Carthaginians.)

By the end of 257 the Romans had confined the Carthaginians to the western third of Sicily, they had neutralized the Carthaginian forces in Sardinia and Corsica, and they were ready to invade Africa. They organized a fleet of 300 ships with crews of 300 oarsmen and 120 marines each (a total of about 100,000 men) and two legions of about 15,000 men. The invasion force of 256 B.C. was commanded by Marcus Atilius Regulus. Regulus had to fight for his passage against a Carthaginian fleet lying off Cape Ecnomus. The Roman "ravens" worked again, and the Romans captured fifty Carthaginian ships and sank thirty.

The Romans landed in Africa, seized the coastal city of Aspis, and ravaged the neighboring area. Regulus advanced into the Carthaginian hinterland (apparently he intended to cut Carthage off from its allies and revenues and force it to come to terms). When he was confronted by a much larger Carthaginian army, well supplied with cavalry and elephants, he feigned retreat, lured the Carthaginian army after him into rugged terrain (where their cavalry could not operate), and smashed them. Regulus then went into winter quarters at Tunis, from which he ravaged Carthaginian territory and persuaded Carthage's Numidian allies (or subjects) to join him in ravaging Carthaginian territory. Regulus had every reason to be confident. The Romans outside Africa had won all but two (minor) engagements against the Carthaginians, he himself had defeated them in Africa, and he expected to defeat them again in the spring. Consequently, when he offered them terms, he named terms so harsh that he seemed to be goading them to further resistence rather than trying to settle the war.

During the winter, therefore, the Carthaginians sought, and found, help in a mercenary general, Xanthippus of Sparta; Xanthippus retrained and reorganized their army to fight the legion, and in the spring he met Regulus in battle. Xanthippus used 100 elephants to break the Roman formation and trample the soldiers while his cavalry encircled the Roman army and forced Regulus to surrender. The Carthaginian army killed or captured all but 2,000 Romans.

The defeat was severe but need not have been decisive; the Romans still held Aspis and their fleet of 350 ships defeated a Carthaginian fleet off Aspis and captured, or destroyed, over a hundred ships, but chance, and the Roman unfamiliarity with the sea, wrecked their plans. As their fleet was returning to Rome by way of the Messana strait, an enormous storm struck, hurled almost 300 of their ships on the rocks, strewed wreckage for fifty miles, and drowned the crews, perhaps as many as 100,000 freeborn Italians, a large number of whom were Roman citizens.

The Romans raised taxes and in three months built and manned 200 new quinqueremes, but in the next ten years the Romans suffered one disaster after another. In 253 they lost another 150 ships in a storm off Africa, and they abandoned the campaign there. In 249 the consul Claudius ignored bad weather and the consequent ill omen that the sacred chickens wouldn't eat ("let them drink, then," he said, and had them thrown overboard), and he lost 100 ships and 20,000 men in an attack on the Carthaginian fleet at Drepana. Nonetheless, Roman tenacity, leadership, and their enormous resources drove the Carthaginian forces in Sicily to the westernmost reaches of the island where the Romans overcame storms, poor judgement, counterattacks, hunger, and the loss of naval support to cling to the siege of the great Carthaginian stronghold in the west, Lilybaeum. The Romans had suffered huge losses of men (the census of 247 B.C. shows a *drop* of 50,000 citizens) and materiel—a total of 1,500 warships and transports—and their treasury was depleted. The Carthaginians had suffered even more. They had lost their revenues from Africa and from their trading empire, they were about out of money to hire mercenaries (rumor had it that they had murdered Xanthippus because they could not afford to pay him), and they could no longer afford to man their fleet.

The Carthaginians sent a commission to Rome to discuss peace terms and a prisoner exchange. When the Romans rejected both, the Carthaginians attempted to put pressure on the Romans in Sicily. In 247 they send a new commander, Hamilcar Barca, to command the forces in Sicily. He was convinced that he could use his limited resources to force the Romans to agree to terms. Hamilcar Barca was a brilliant tactician, and the Romans did feel the pressure, but they responded with new determination. The Senate voted to lend money as individuals to the state to build a new fleet of 200 modern warships.

In 242 the consul Lutatius Catulus sailed the fleet to Drepana, there to confront the Carthaginians, but the Carthaginians did not have the money to pay their crews except in an emergency, and the Carthaginian fleet lay unmanned at home. They needed most of 242 to find the crews, and in March of 241 the fleet sailed—manned by raw crews—with the intention of picking up Hamilcar and his men to use as marines, but Catulus intercepted them at the Aegates Islands. The Romans sank fifty ships and captured seventy. The Roman victory totally isolated the Carthaginians in Sicily, and the Carthaginians were compelled to accept Roman terms—to evacuate Sicily, to return all prisoners, to pay an indemnity of 2,200 talents over ten years, and to make an immediate payment of 1,100 talents; each side was to hold its possessions without interference from the other.

The First Punic War was over.

The Romans formed Sicily into a province (their first province) and soon took advantage of a mutiny of Carthaginian troops on Sardinia to seize that island. (The Romans captured Corsica in the First Punic War and never relinquished it.) When the Carthaginians protested—and prepared a fleet—the Romans declared war on them, and the Carthaginians had to buy their way out with 1,200 talents in indemnity and an agreement to cede Sardinia and Corsica. Hamilcar Barca, already convinced himself, now convinced a majority of Carthaginians that they must either find new sources of money and men or accept that the Romans would be their masters. Hamilcar's target was Spain. Under the leadership of the Barca family in Spain, first Hamilcar himself, then his son-in-law, Hasdrubal, and finally his son, Hannibal, Carthage did acquire wealth, manpower, a professional (if mercenary) army, and a leader whose genius emerged in the training ground of Spain.

If all these consequences can be attributed to the Romans' opportunistic seizing of Sardinia—and would not have happened without it—the Romans certainly made a mistake, but their annexation of Sicily, Sardinia, and Corsica was consistent with the Roman policy of a hundred years, to seize the barriers between themselves and their enemies with the object of denying their enemies bases while also isolating them and dividing them, and ultimately incorporating them or annihilating them.

## 38. One of Pyrrhus' Elephants (Campanian Painted Dish)

## Map 20: The Second Punic War, 218-201 B.C.

THE THEATERS OF WAR

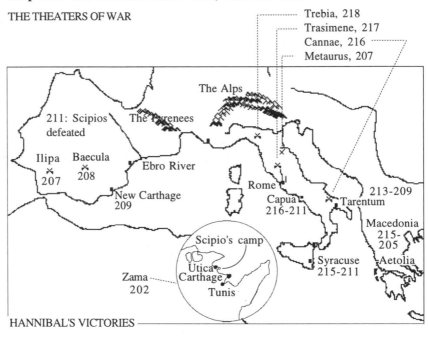

Trebia, 218
Trasimene, 217
Cannae, 216
Metaurus, 207

The Alps

211: Scipios defeated

The Pyrenees

Ilipa 207

Baecula 208

Ebro River

New Carthage 209

Rome

Capua 216-211

Tarentum 213-209

Macedonia 215-205

Scipio's camp

Utica

Carthage

Syracuse 215-211

Aetolia

Zama 202

Tunis

HANNIBAL'S VICTORIES

### TREBIA RIVER

Po River

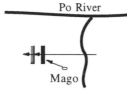

Mago

Hannibal lured the Romans across the icy Trebia River, past an ambush under the command of Mago, on to ground prepared by Hannibal. The Romans nonetheless repelled Hannibal's war elephants and broke through the center of his line ... to escape.

### LAKE TRASIMENE

the ambush

Roman Camp

Lake Trasimene

Hannibal's Camp

Hannibal lured the Romans into the killing zone he had prepared.

### CANNAE

Hannibal drew the Romans into his prepared formation. His cavalry drove off the Roman cavalry and circled back to envelop the Roman infantry, while Hannibal's center held under intense pressure.

One theory is that the Romans deployed the double-consular army, not to double the front of their army, but to pack their ranks doubly thick, as ...

instead of ...

# 25

# Hannibal

## *When Individual Genius Meets Collective Genius*

The Romans were concerned about the Barcas's subjugation of Spain, but they had more immediate threats to worry about. The Illyrians had consolidated into the most powerful kingdom in the Greek peninsula, they were determined to subjugate the Adriatic coast, their pirate vessels ravaged shipping, and no one seemed ready, or able, to stop them, until 230, when the Illyrian queen, Teuta, rejected Roman demands for redress for the murder of some Italian merchants, and ordered one of the Roman envoys, whose forthright speech had annoyed her, to be intercepted and murdered. In response, two consuls appeared with a fleet of 200 ships, an army of 20,000 infantry, and 2,000 cavalry, and fought and conquered their way up the Adriatic coast, until in the spring of 228 Queen Teuta agreed to pay an indemnity, to recognize the freedom of all the places that had submitted to the Romans, and to confine her fleet to the northern Adriatic.

With the Illyrians chastened, the Romans responded to the threat of a Gallic invasion across the Po. In 225 the Romans took a census to determine what their resources were for the coming war: 250,000 male citizen infantry, 23,000 citizen cavalry, and 350,000 allied infantry. They sent three separate armies under the command of the two consuls and a praetor to defend Italy from the Gauls, but the Gauls defeated the praetor and his army (killing about 6,000 Romans), plundered northern Italy, and then tried in vain to elude the consuls pursuing them. The Gauls were brought to bay between the two consular armies and they prepared for battle. The Roman soldiers were disconcerted by the Gauls' dreadful appearance—some naked except for their weapons, their huge, muscular bodies apparent, some blowing trumpets and horns, some giving the war cry, clashing their weapons against their shields, and moving so that their gold ornaments flashed—but the legions remained steady as the Gauls charged. The Romans threw their spears and met the berserk Gauls in hand-to-hand combat. Roman infantry weapons held their own—the Gallic sword could slash, but not thrust, and the iron was so soft that the blade would bend after one blow—until the Roman cavalry charged the flank of the Gauls and broke them. The Romans killed 40,000 Gauls and captured 10,000. One of the consuls was killed in the fighting.

Two years later (223 B.C.) the consul Flaminius defeated an army of Insubres 50,000 strong. The Romans in the front line armed themselves with the triarii's spears, charged the Gauls, and, when the Gauls had rendered their own swords useless by striking the spears, the Romans drew their swords and thrust into the chests and faces of the Gauls. In the next year the consul Marcellus defeated a Gallic chieftain in single combat and routed the surviving Gauls The Gauls of the Po River valley now surrendered to Rome, and the Romans considered the area pacified. In 219 the two consuls brought a fleet up the Adriatic and drove the new Illyrian king, Demetrius of Pharos, from his kingdom.

With these two threats neutralized, the Romans now felt themselves free to handle the situation that had developed in Spain. When Hamilcar Barca landed at Gades in 237 B.C. with his nine-year-old son Hannibal, he had almost the whole of Spain to reconquer. Spain's rugged terrain and lack of food and water made ambush easy, movement difficult, and supply for an army often impossible. Hamilcar fought for control of the river routes into Spain, defeated the major tribes, and established Carthaginian dominance, but in the winter of 229–228 he drowned in a river. His successor, Hasdrubal, signed an agreement with the Romans that he would not advance across the Ebro River under arms. When Hasdrubal died in 221, Hannibal (25 years of age) became commander. His world was the army camp, his enemy was Rome, and when he concluded that war was inevitable, he seized the initiative despite having no fleet and five major barriers to traverse before he could get at the Romans—the Ebro, the Pyrenees, the Rhone, the Alps, and the Po.

The Romans planned to send one consul, Publius Scipio (and his brother, Gnaeus), to Spain to fight Hannibal while the other consul, Sempronius, invaded Africa. Their strategy was impeccable, but Hannibal had already crossed the Rhone River by the time Scipio's fleet reached Massilia (at the mouth of the Rhone). Publius Scipio returned to Italy to organize the defense (while he sent his brother Gnaeus, the fleet, and the army on to Spain) and there he met Hannibal in a skirmish (the battle of the Ticinus). Scipio was defeated and wounded, and he decided to retreat across the Po and hold the line of the Po against Hannibal, but Hannibal outmarched him and crossed safely. Scipio made the prudent decision to avoid battle and wait for his colleague, but his prudence convinced many of his Gallic allies that the Romans were finished, they murdered their Roman officers, and they joined Hannibal.

Sempronius marched his army of 26,000 men up Italy approximately 700 miles in two months and joined Scipio as winter was setting in. Scipio advised caution—he had tested the abilities of Hannibal and his army—but Sempronius was a man of action, and he was determined to fight Hannibal as soon as the opportunity arose. Hannibal offered him the opportunity. Hannibal sent cavalry through the frigid waters of the Trebia to provoke Sempronius and to lure him across the icy river, now swollen to the height of a man's chest, and into a battlefield of Hannibal's choosing, where he had placed his brother Mago in ambush. Sempronius could not resist the challenge and he crossed without feeding his troops or preparing them for the cold.

Hannibal had fires going, hot oil to rub on cold bodies, and hot food. His army was ready and eager to fight. He placed the light-armed men, about 8,000, in front of his heavier-armed men. On the flanks he placed 10,000 cavalry, and he dispersed his elephants on both wings. Sempronius had 18,000 Roman troops, 20,000 Latin allies, and some Gallic auxiliaries (who had not yet deserted). The Roman cavalry on the wings was soon dispersed, but the Roman legions, although they were weakened by hunger, exertion, and cold, nonetheless were advancing when the Numidian cavalry attacked their flanks and Mago charged from ambush in their rear. Hannibal expected his elephants to break the Roman front and complete the annihilation of the Roman army, but the Roman light-armed troops dashed forward and speared the elephants under their tails and turned them. Hannibal withdrew his elephants and used them to break Sempronius's Gallic allies.

About 10,000 legionnaires broke through the middle of the Carthaginian line (held by Hannibal's Gallic allies) and made directly for Placentia. Other survivors scattered in the fields and followed the tracks of those who had retreated to Placentia, others returned to the river where some of them were killed as they hesitated on the banks, some drowned, a few managed to cross the river and find their camp. The Carthaginian pursuit stopped at the Trebia River. A sleet storm and icy wind carried off many men, animals, and almost all the elephants.

The victories of the Ticinus and Trebia delivered northern Italy and the Gauls to Hannibal. Hannibal understood his Roman opponents, "an enemy blind to this kind of war," but he did not understand the Roman system: he expected to use the aspirations for independence of the people under Roman domination to break apart the Roman confederation and to diminish the power of Rome. He did not understand the extent to which many Italians identified with Rome and considered Hannibal to be a hideous and inhuman monster, he did not understand the depth of Roman resources, and, most of all, he did not understand or appreciate the tenacity of the Roman character.

Sempronius returned to Rome and calmed fears with a self-serving statement that the weather, not the Carthaginians, had won the battle. Neither he nor the Romans yet understood the quality of the Numidian cavalry or the genius of Hannibal, but the Romans judged that Sempronius had been responsible for the defeat, and they did not entrust him with another command. Scipio's command in Spain was extended and he was sent to join his army. Two new consuls were elected, Gnaeus Servilius and Gaius Flaminius, and they had every confidence that the Roman legions would prove more than a match for the Carthaginian army.

Hannibal wintered at Bologna. The consuls moved to block the approaches into central Italy; one consul, Servilius, with two legions and 4,000 cavalry was stationed at Ariminum to watch the eastern route; the other, Flaminius, was at Arretium to watch the western route, but Hannibal took a more difficult route, through passes just cleared of snow and across a marsh. "For four days and three nights the depth of water prevented them from sleeping. The beasts of burden dropped dead and provided thereby the only place where the men could get out of the water and snatch a short nap during the night. Many of the horses lost their hooves through the continual submersion. Hannibal got through on the back of an elephant (the only one to survive), but he suffered an eye infection and lost the sight of one eye."

Hannibal rested his army and then marched past Flaminius's camp at Arretium to provoke him to battle, but Flaminius was not to be diverted from the Roman plan, to track Hannibal until the two consuls and their armies could converge on him. Hannibal, however, had his own plan. His scouts had found the perfect place for an ambush, an extremely narrow passage between the mountains and the north shore of Lake Trasimene. As Hannibal marched through the pass, he concealed his cavalry at the entrance and all his light-armed troops on the slope, and he had his Africans and Spanish troops set up a camp on the other side of the pass; Flaminius reached the lake too late to reconnoitre the pass and, as he could see the enemy in camp, it never occurred to him that an ambush had been set. At dawn a mist covered the hills, but Hannibal seemed to be breaking camp and moving on, so Flaminius hurried after him. The first the Romans knew of the ambush was the war cry of the enemy.

"Flaminius was completely surprised. As the enemy rushed down in the heavy mist, the centurions and tribunes could not see what was happening, and they were not able to help those who most needed their help. The enemy was everywhere, missiles struck the Romans from every side, and most of the men were killed still in marching formation. During the melee a group of Gauls charged Flaminius and killed him."

About 6,000 men who were at the point of the column broke through and fled to a nearby hill. There they listened to the clamor and noise of the armed conflict, until the rising sun burned off the mist and the soft light revealed Roman dead strewn everywhere. The 6,000 Romans surrendered to a Carthaginian general who promised to release them, unarmed, with a single garment; Hannibal disavowed his general's agreement and kept the Romans prisoner. The Romans were completely taken aback at the news of the disaster—15,000 Roman soldiers killed and 15,000 captured—but "the Romans are most to be feared, collectively and individually, when they have most cause to be afraid."

Hannibal crossed the Apennines into the district of Picenum along the Adriatic and plundered his way south into Apulia. He issued an order to his army to kill any adult found on the way. If he hoped to win allies, he failed. The Romans appointed a dictator, Q. Fabius Maximus. Fabius enrolled two new legions and marched north to meet the other consul and to take command of his legions. He camped five miles away from Hannibal in Apulia. Hannibal crossed into Samnium and then into Campania, and Fabius followed Hannibal as he ravaged the countryside. Fabius understood a simple truth—that the Romans need not defeat Hannibal in a battle in order to defeat his intentions. They could use the natural barriers between the different regions of Italy to confine Hannibal, deny him recruits and supplies, depend upon the stability of the Roman system to deny Hannibal allies and thus to destroy him by attrition, but Fabius was unable to convince the Romans that Hannibal was a new kind of opponent, one whom the Romans were incapable of defeating on the battlefield, and Fabius was given a nickname, Delayer (Cunctator), which was meant at the time to be a slur. When his six months as dictator were up, the new consuls of 216, Paullus and Varro, set out to fight the one great battle—surely a double consular army properly handled could defeat Hannibal—and win the war.

Hannibal broke from winter quarters in 216, moved south, and seized the Roman supply depot at Cannae. The new consuls followed and prepared to give battle. Varro drew up his cavalry on his right (next to the river), the legions next to them and then the allied infantry, and on the left the allied cavalry. The front he covered with light-armed troops. Varro commanded the left wing, Paullus the right. Hannibal placed the Gallic and Iberian cavalry on his left by the river opposite the Roman cavalry; on his right wing he placed his Numidian cavalry, he split his Africans between the two flanks, and he placed the Gauls and Iberians in the center. The African troops were armed with captured Roman equipment. The Gauls fought bare from the waist up and the Iberians in brilliant white tunics with purple borders. The Gauls used long, slashing swords, the Iberians short, stabbing swords. Altogether Hannibal had 40,000 infantry and 10,000 cavalry. The lines were placed so that the Romans faced south and the Carthaginians north, while the sun shone obliquely on both. The prevailing wind blew dust into the faces of the Romans.

On the Roman right the cavalry clashed head to head with no room to maneuver. After a short, fierce battle, the Romans turned and fled. On the left the Numidians quickly drove the Roman allied cavalry off. In the center both sides were equally determined, but the Romans, densely packed, pushed the wedge of the Iberians and the Gauls in and finally broke through, only to face the African reserves. While the Romans pushed these back as well, the cavalry on the flanks encircled the Roman lines and attacked the Roman rear. The Romans became so densely packed that they could not wield their swords, and the slaughter began. The Romans reported that 45,500 infantry and 2,700 cavalry (about half citizen, half allied) were killed and among them both quaestors, twenty-nine military tribunes, eighty senators (who had voluntarily served in the ranks), and the consul Paullus. Varro escaped, and so did about 20,000 Romans and allies.

The victory gave Hannibal tactical control of most of southern Italy. He offered generous terms to anyone who would declare for him—no conscription and complete independence—and in the five years after the battle of Cannae he won over Capua and Tarentum (and many lesser cities), the regions of Lucania and Bruttium, Syracuse in Sicily, and he concluded a treaty with King Philip V of Macedonia. As soon as the news of Cannae hit Rome, the Romans began to marshall their forces. They had two legions in Spain, two in Sicily, two in the valley of the Po (which were destroyed by the Gauls in November 216), and two legions of recruits in Rome. They formed two weak legions from the survivors of Cannae and sent them to Sicily to replace the two full-strength legions there, which they brought back to Italy for service in Apulia. They purchased slaves and filled legions with them and used them as garrison troops. They appointed a dictator.

The Romans now accepted that they could not hope to defeat Hannibal in open battle, and they determined to follow the strategy of maneuver and attrition. The heart of the Roman system held firm, and the routes through central Italy were kept open by strongly held fortresses. The Romans raised enormous numbers of soldiers, so that by 212 they had twenty-five legions in being. They assigned three armies (of two legions each) to follow Hannibal, they sent one army to retake Capua, and another to Sicily to retake Syracuse. In all they had sixteen legions in Italy to contain Hannibal and to retake the places he had taken but could not defend.

First and foremost, the Romans intended to reduce Capua. In 213 they prevented the Capuans from putting in or harvesting crops, and Hannibal was forced to command one of his generals to deliver supplies to Capua. That general failed, and Hannibal himself had to come to Capua; he raised the siege temporarily, but when he retired, the Romans closed the lines around Capua with a double wall to protect themselves from sudden attack. Hannibal tried to catch them by surprise and failed, and he tried to lift the siege by marching on Rome, but the Romans would not meet him in battle nor lift the siege, and he broke off the advance. Capua surrendered. In the same year Syracuse was taken and by the end of 211 the Romans had recovered most of the cities of Samnium and Apulia and had closed the barrier across central Italy.

Roman strategy was vindicated, their tenacity was proven, but they had not defeated Hannibal, and in 211 Gnaeus and Publius Scipio were killed in separate battles in Spain, their armies were almost wiped out, and all their successes to that point were undone. The Roman survivors held the line of the Ebro River, while an experienced commander, Gaius Claudius Nero, was dispatched with a full legion and a half legion (to form a second legion with the survivors), but the Senate decided that more was required, and they acceded to popular demand and personal lobbying to support the election of Publius Cornelius Scipio (the son of the Publius Scipio killed in Spain—he was then about twenty-five years old), and to confer the *imperium* and the command of the combined army of about four legions in Spain. When he arrived at the Roman port of Emporium towards the end of 210, he inspired his troops with his own confidence and conviction.

Scipio conceived a bold stroke. He would seize New Carthage, the enemy's main base—it contained all their war materiel, it was the only base that had a suitable harbor, it was lightly garrisoned (perhaps 1,000 troops), not one of the three Carthaginian armies in Spain was within reach of the city, and although its position seemed impregnable, surrounded on three sides by water and on the fourth by a high wall atop a ridge, in fact, the water barrier to the north was a fordable lagoon under certain conditions (a strong north wind at low water). Scipio grasped the three most important principles of war—the objective: to cut the Carthaginians off from their supply fleet, to raise Roman morale and depress the Carthaginians, and to give the Romans a secure base; the offensive: to seize the initiative; and surprise: whatever the Carthaginians expected, it was not this.

With the proclamation *Neptune leads our way*, Scipio set out with the fleet and his army (about 25,000 infantry and 2,500 cavalry) early in the spring of 209. He ordered his forces to attack New Carthage by land and sea, he pushed the attack throughout an entire morning and drove the defenders into their city, he replaced tired troops with fresh, and, after a midday break, he continued the attack in the afternoon. The Romans formed a tortoise and were hacking at the timbers of the gate, while at sea troops from the ships were trying to scale the walls. The exhausted defenders concentrated on the points of attack.

Meanwhile, 500 Roman troops with scaling ladders waited behind the lagoon for its waters to drain and, when a strong north wind pushed more water out through the channel, the Romans waded across, scaled the unguarded walls, and ran along the top of the wall, throwing the enemy off, until they reached the gates, where they dropped from the walls and broke the bolts holding the gates closed. More Romans scaled the walls from land and sea and Scipio ordered his army to spread out and kill everyone they met while he personally led a force of about a thousand men to the citadel where the remnants of the Carthaginian garrison had taken refuge. The Carthaginian commander surrendered with only one condition, that his own life be spared. Scipio ordered the slaughter to stop and the looting to begin. (It was Roman custom to have half the army collect all the booty in one place—while the other half stood guard—and to have the loot distributed by the military tribunes throughout the whole army.)

Scipio's bold stroke paralyzed the Carthaginians. He held New Carthage, and they were not strong enough to retake it. He gained control of the Iberian silver mines, their source of revenue to pay the mercenaries, and control over the coast road. He encouraged the Iberian tribes to revolt and thus compelled the Carthaginians to divide their troops to keep the Iberian tribes in line, but Scipio still needed to meet and defeat the Carthaginians in the field and to that end he reformed the inflexible Roman army so that the hastati, the principes, and the triarii, trained in maniples, could operate independently of each other and could maneuver to the flank.

Scipio also improved the individual skills and conditioning of the Roman soldier with a regular training regimen: on day one the army would double-time four miles in full armor, on day two Scipio would inspect the equipment of the army (he armed his soldiers with the "Spanish sword"), on day three the army would rest and recuperate, and on day four they would have sword and javelin practice, the edges and points wrapped in leather. Then the routine began again. Scipio created the new Roman army.

"The Roman formation and ranks are hard to shatter, for each soldier and each unit can fight in any direction as a unit, for the maniples can turn to the closest point of danger and their equipment gives them confidence because they have a large shield and the sword remains true even after many blows. They are hard to fight."

In 208 Scipio marched into the interior of Spain to force Hasdrubal (the brother of Hannibal) to fight him. Hasdrubal occupied a strong position near Baecula on a hill, flanked by two arroyos and fronted by a stream. He intended to keep Scipio in play until the other Carthaginian armies could converge and overwhelm the Romans, but Scipio had no intention of postponing the decision. He sent his light-armed soldiers forward across the stream to climb the hill and attack Hasdrubal. The light-armed troops made a ferocious attack on the Carthaginians light-armed; even the camp personnel joined in. They threw their javelins, they hurled rocks picked up from the slope, they closed with the enemy and fought hand to hand (a kind of fighting the Carthaginian light-armed troops had no stomach for), and they thrust the enemy back to the main Carthaginian battleline.

Scipio, meanwhile, sent half his remaining troops under the command of Laelius up the arroyo to the right of the hill, while he himself led the other half up the arroyo to the left. They burst out of the arroyos on Hasdrubal's flanks, and Hasdrubal fled with as many troops as he could disengage. Scipio's new army had enveloped the Carthaginians and smashed them—8,000 enemy were killed and about 12,000 taken prisoner—but he had not had complete success; his center had not been strong enough to fix the Carthaginians, nor had the legions been quick enough to complete the envelopment of Hasdrubal. Hasdrubal retreated north and, after a conference with the other two commanders in Spain, he took all the Iberian troops—now of suspect loyalty—to cross the Pyrenees and the Alps and join Hannibal. Scipio informed the Senate that Hasdrubal was coming.

Hannibal badly needed reinforcements. At the same time Rome's allies were becoming heartily sick of the war. Each side needed a victory. Into this situation in 206 came Hasdrubal leading an army of some 20,000 men with cavalry, elephants, and Gallic recruits. Both sides knew he was coming, but not exactly where and when.

The Romans placed four armies (of two legions each) across the passes into central Italy under the overall command of the consul M. Livius Salinator. The Roman commanders in the south, under the overall command of the other consul, C. Claudius Nero, kept Hannibal in play, so he could not move north to join his brother. Hasdrubal crossed the Alps in the spring, when the passes were clear. He recruited Gauls in the Po valley and sent a party of six to link up with Hannibal and tell him where and when they should meet. The messengers crossed the whole length of Italy safely only to take the wrong road and wind up prisoners of the Romans. The consul Claudius Nero at once realized that this opportunity had to be seized, even if it meant violating the overall tactical scheme formulated against Hannibal. He selected 6,000 of his best infantry and 1,000 cavalry and set out for the proposed meeting place. Throngs of people lined the way, cheered the troops, prayed for them, and told them to help themselves to whatever food and drink they wanted. The soldiers marched night and day and never broke ranks.

The two consuls planned to move Nero's troops into Livius's camp to double up with Livius's troops and to seek battle the next day. Hasdrubal was ready to fight, but then his scouts reported seeing unfamiliar shields and blown horses in the Roman camp and hearing two trumpet calls, and Hasdrubal realized that both consuls were present. He tried to escape that night, but he could not find a ford across the Metaurus River, he exhausted his army with march and countermarch, many of his Gauls straggled or deserted, and in the morning he was brought to bay by the Romans.

Livius commanded the left, Nero commanded the right, and a praetor commanded the center. Hasdrubal put his elephants out in front, his Gauls opposite Nero (he believed the Romans were afraid of them). He put the Ligurians in the middle behind the elephants, and he led the Iberians on the right opposite Livius. The elephants at first disrupted the Roman formation, but as the noise increased and the struggle grew more intense, the beasts panicked, trampled men on both sides, and were killed by their own handlers. (Their drivers carried a mallet and spike, they placed the spike on the vertebra where head and neck join, and they drove the spike home with a blow.) Nero, blocked out of the fighting by a hill on the right, called to his men, "Why did we rush so far to get here?" He led some of his cohorts behind the battle line around to the left and attacked the enemy's flank. The Romans were attacking the Iberians and Ligurians from all sides—front, flank, and rear—and they carried the fight to the Gauls. As the Gauls broke and ran, Hasdrubal realized the battle was lost and he charged into the middle of the Romans to his death.

The consuls reported to Rome that they had killed 57,000 enemy and taken 5,400 prisoners and four elephants. They also reported that 8,000 friendly troops, Roman and allied, had been killed. They wildly exaggerated the size of Hasdrubal's army, but the basic fact was correct: they had destroyed his army. The Romans found Hasdrubal's body, cut off the head, and Nero carried it back as he rushed to return to his proper area of operations against Hannibal. He had the head thrown in front of Hannibal's pickets, and he released two prisoners from Hasdrubal's army to carry the news to Hannibal. Hannibal is supposed to have said, "Finally I see the fate of Carthage."

Hannibal, however, was still Hannibal, and, as the Roman historian Livy wrote, "The Romans left him in peace, for, although everything around him was falling in ruins, they still thought that he, in himself, was the Carthaginians' greatest strength. And I do not know what is more to be wondered at, how he was, when he was winning, or how he was, when things were going against him, since he had maintained himself for thirteen years in hostile territory, so far from home, waging war with varying success, and with an army not from his own country but mixed together from the runoff of every people, for whom there was no common law, or custom, no common language, but they each dressed in their own way with their own weapons, their own ritual, their own religion and their own gods; these he bound to him so tightly that there was no unrest directed at him or even among themselves, although rations and money was often lacking, And even now, shut up in Bruttium with only the resources of an impoverished and denuded land to support them, still there was no unrest in his camp."

Once the Carthaginians in Spain heard the results of the battle of the Metaurus, they realized that their only hope of victory was to clear Spain of the Romans and marshall Iberian resources to help Hannibal. Consequently, the Carthaginians sought out Scipio and offered him battle at Ilipa. The Carthaginians outnumbered the Romans, both sides had Iberian allies in whose loyalty they were not confident, but Scipio worked out the winning strategy—every day in the middle of the afternoon he presented his army, the Romans in the center, the allies on the flanks, prepared for battle (if the Carthaginians advanced on him), and the Carthaginians drew up their army accordingly, Africans in the center, allies on the flanks. Once he had accustomed the Carthaginians to the routine, he broke routine and advanced on their camp at dawn in a different formation—allies in the center, Romans on the flanks. The Carthaginians rushed from their camp and formed their army exactly as they had day after day. Scipio sent his skirmishers to keep the enemy busy and in ranks, while the hot sun, hunger, and thirst worked on the Carthaginians. Then he advanced.

As he advanced, he extended the Romans on the left and right farther and farther until they outflanked the enemy, while the threat of the advancing Iberian troops in the Roman center fixed the African troops in position. The Romans enveloped the enemy army and overbore the weaker allied troops on the flanks. The enemy fell back to the foothills, the Romans dislodged them; they sought protection in their camp, the Romans drove them out, they retreated, the Romans cornered them, they resisted, and the Romans annihilated them.

Scipio had won Spain. In 205 the victorious Scipio returned to Rome, he was elected consul, and he convinced the Romans to invade Africa. He sent Laelius to judge the state of affairs in Africa; Laelius reported that many of the native peoples would welcome a Roman attack on Carthage, but that Syphax, the Numidian king (married to the seductive Carthaginian Sophonisba) remained true to his alliance with his wife's city. Scipio's firmest African ally, Masinissa, had lost his kingdom but might regain it with Roman help and thus furnish them with cavalry to rival Hannibal's.

In the spring of 204 B.C. Scipio landed with about 25,000 men at Cape Farina and put Utica under siege. When he learned that the Carthaginians were near with about 4,000 cavalry, he sent Masinissa to lure them out of their camp past a line of hills where the Roman army waited. The Carthaginians fell into the trap, their commander was cut off and killed with about 1,000 men, and 2,000 more were killed or captured in the thirty-mile pursuit. Scipio then retired into winter quarters in the *castra Cornelia*, a camp built by the Romans on a promontory where their fleet could threaten Carthaginian shipping and their army could have access to land and sea.

When the winter was over and Scipio was preparing to lay siege to Utica, and the Carthaginians and Syphax (the Numidian king) occupied separate camps seven miles away from Scipio, Syphax proposed peace on the terms that the Romans would quit Africa, and the Carthaginians would quit Italy. Scipio used the pretext of negotiations to reconnoitre the two enemy camps; then he broke off negotiations, that night set the camp of Syphax on fire, and attacked both camps. Syphax's men believed that the fire was accidental, and they were totally unprepared to fight the attacking Romans. The Carthaginians, too, believed that the fire was accidental and, when they ran—unarmed—to help, they ran right into the Roman army. Syphax and the Carthaginian leader escaped, but both camps were destroyed, almost 40,000 men were burned to death, and 5,000 were captured (among whom were many Carthaginian nobles).

The two leaders raised another army, but Scipio struck them before they could train and organize it, drove off the enemy cavalry, enveloped the enemy army, and defeated them in the Battle of the Great Plains. Once again Syphax escaped, and Scipio sent detachments to pursue him while he completed the subjugation of the Carthaginian hinterland. Scipio lifted the siege of Utica, caught the Carthaginians by surprise, and took Tunis. These Carthaginian disasters prompted them to send envoys to Hannibal to ask him to return. Meanwhile Masinissa and Laelius brought Syphax to bay, defeated him in battle, and wounded and captured him. Masinissa then was able to regain his kingdom among the Numidians, and Numidia was lost to Carthage.

When the Carthaginians heard that Syphax had been captured, they sent a delegation to Scipio to ask for terms. Scipio named them: to return all prisoners of war, deserters, and runaway slaves, to evacuate Italy and Cisalpine Gaul, to give up all claim to lands outside Africa, to surrender all their ships except twenty, and to supply a quantity of rations to his army and pay an indemnity. The Carthaginians accepted the terms and agreed to an armistice while their envoys went to Rome to ratify the treaty, but in the interim the Carthaginians violated the truce and Hannibal landed in Africa and convinced the Carthaginians to renew the war.

Hannibal organized an army and then sought battle with Scipio. At the moment Scipio was weak in cavalry because Masinissa had left for a visit to his kingdom and had not yet returned. Scipio fell back before Hannibal to avoid battle and to move towards Masinissa. At last Masinissa rejoined the Romans at Zama and Scipio was ready to fight (the battle of Zama). Hannibal asked for a conference before the battle, and the two commanders met. Hannibal offered to accept the terms the Romans had given the Carthaginians before they broke the armistice. Scipio rejected the offer, "Let me speak clearly—either you must surrender unconditionally to us or you must defeat us in this battle."

Scipio drew up the hastati first, behind them the principes, and then with a space the triarii. He put Laelius and the Italian cavalry on the left, Masinissa and the Numidians on the right. Hannibal put his elephants—eighty of them, the most he ever had—in front, and behind them he placed the mercenaries. Behind the mercenaries he put the heavy infantry of Carthaginian citizens, he put the Carthaginian cavalry on the right, the loyal Numidians on the left, and he held the veteran troops from Italy in reserve. Hannibal intended that his elephants would disrupt the Roman formations, his mercenaries and the Carthaginian citizen army would wear the Romans down, and then his veterans would advance on them and defeat them. Scipio, however, made lanes for the elephants to pass through his formation, and he held the triarii in reserve.

"As the battle began the Romans blew trumpets and horns; that noise combined with the uproar of battle panicked the elephants on the far left wing so that they turned on their own side. In the confusion Masinissa easily cleared the battle line on the left of enemy cavalry. The Roman light-armed troops fell back on the maniples where they made an unobstructed lane for the elephants and from both sides of the lane they struck at them with spears and hurled their pila and they forced the elephants to run down the lanes or to turn back on the right wing of the Carthaginians. Laelius charged when he saw the enemy wing opposite him in disorder.

"The battle was fought man to man, hand to hand, and both sides used the sword; the mercenaries had the advantage at first in dexterity and quickness, and they wounded many of the Romans, but the Romans, confident in their formation and armament, advanced, and the Roman troops behind the front lines supported them, while the Carthaginians would not come to the support of the mercenaries (because Hannibal wanted them to stay fresh for the next phase of the battle) and the mercenaries tried to fight their way back through the Carthaginian ranks. Into this confusion the Romans advanced, but, as the hastati were beginning to weaken, the leaders of the principes brought their formations forward through the ranks of the hastati, and the fresh troops cut down most of the mercenaries and the Carthaginians and routed the rest."

Hannibal had his veteran troops present their arms and force the fugitives to retreat to the flanks. Scipio was at a momentary loss how to move his formation across the morass of discarded weapons, blood, body parts, and corpses; he recovered his wounded and ordered the advance to halt. He made a deep formation of the surviving hastati (they had taken most of the casualties) on the enemy side of the battlefield opposite the center of the enemy's lines, and he deepened the ranks of the principes and triarii and placed them each on the flanks of the hastati.

When Scipio had formed his army, he ordered them to advance, and the two armies threw themselves on each other with the greatest enthusiasm. Men rushed willingly to their deaths in the killing ground, and the battle raged without decision, until the cavalry of Masinissa and Laelius returned from the pursuit. They fell on Hannibal's army from the rear and killed most of them, still fighting in their ranks; of the few who fled fewer still escaped, for the cavalry was at hand, and the ground offered no cover. Of the Romans about 1,500 were killed, of the Carthaginian forces about 20,000, and about the same number were taken prisoner. Hannibal escaped, the Carthaginians surrendered, and the Second Punic War was over.

### 39. Diagram of the Battle of Zama

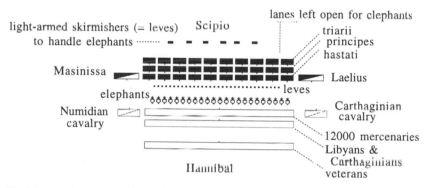

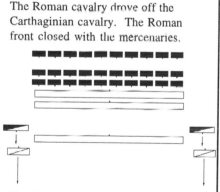

The Roman leves turned back the elephants (which were supposed to disrupt the Roman ranks) into their own troops or forced them to run through the lanes to be dispatched by the leves in the rear.

| | |
|---|---|
| The Roman cavalry drove off the Carthaginian cavalry. The Roman front closed with the mercenaries. | Both armies paused as they surveyed the carnage between them. Hannibal had hoped that the Romans would have committed all their troops by now and would be exhausted, but Scipio had fought the battle to this point with his hastati and leves alone. Now he reformed his army and advanced. |
| |  |
| The Romans drove the mercenaries back into the Carthaginian ranks. Using this disruption they broke the Carthaginians and drove them to flight. | The final battle was even until the Roman cavalry returned and attacked the veterans from the rear |

## 40. The Development of the Roman Legion

THE EARLIEST ROMAN LEGION AS DESCRIBED BY LIVY

Vexillum (later the Maniple) = 60 men, 2 centurions. The different ranks were armed with different equipment. "Hastati" means "spearmen," "principes" means "first."

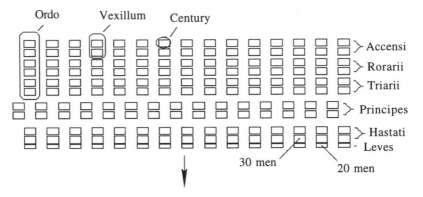

THE ROMAN LEGION OF THE TIME OF SCIPIO

Scipio armed his soldiers with the "Spanish sword" and trained the Principes and Hastati to act as separate units.

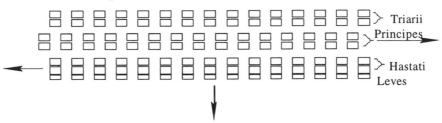

THE ROMAN LEGION OF THE TIME OF MARIUS

Marius issued all ranks standarized equipment: pilum, sword, and the rectangular shield (scutum); he introduced the legionary eagle and signa to the cohorts.

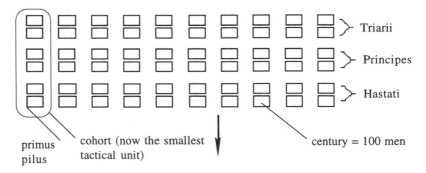

# 26

# The Conquest of the Mediterranean

## *Roman Ambition and the Legions*

In the century after the Second Punic War the Roman republic came to dominate the Mediterranean, but the necessity to provide, train, and field armies and the necessity to control the ambition of generals (who won wealth and power through their conquests) put an inordinate strain on the republic. In the end, the Romans were unable to find an answer consistent with a free republic.

Campaigns in northern Italy and the west revealed the strengths and weaknesses of the Roman system, as the Romans set out to reduce Cisalpine Gaul and Spain. In a series of campaigns (197–191) they resettled, expelled, or exterminated the Gauls north of the Po, introduced Roman colonists, and by the 140s had completely romanized Cisalpine Gaul and connected it to Massilia by roads.

The Romans found Spain to be a different proposition altogether. The Celtiberian tribes reacted to the Roman threat and to the ambition and rapacity of the Roman governors by waging a fierce war (197–179) won by the Romans only after the consul Cato combined terror and pledges (to respect their territory) that induced the tribes to agree to pay tribute and furnish auxiliaries. Cato's successors, ambitious and rapacious Roman governors, soon broke the agreement, and the Romans had to fight a series of wars in Lusitania (154–133) and against the Celtiberians (153–133).

In Lusitania, after the Romans had lost two battles and 16,000 Roman soldiers, the Roman commander offered a pardon to anyone who came and requested it. Thousands took the bait. He murdered them all except for a very few who escaped; one of the few to escape was Viriathus, who led the Lusitanians to four victories over the Romans, until the Romans put a large enough bounty on his head to tempt an assassin.

Against the Celtiberians, Roman consuls took turns for twenty years (153–133), each consul campaigning for a two-year term. As the consuls entered office in March and thus lost much of the campaigning season before they could reach Spain, the Romans reformed their calendar to begin the year in January. The consuls faced vicious fighting, high casualties, and ever-diminishing rewards. They won few victories and suffered a multitude of disasters. To avoid the difficulty of recruiting Roman citizens they drafted noncitizen Italians. In 137 a Roman commander surrendered his army of 20,000 to a Celtiberian force half his size. His chief of staff, Tiberius Gracchus, reached an agreement with the Celtiberians to release the army in return for guarantees about their territory, but the Senate refused to ratify the agreement and returned the commander—without the army—to the Celtiberians.

The Senate sent its best commander, Scipio Aemilianus, to Spain. Scipio could not trust his thoroughly demoralized army (20,000 Romans and Italians and 40,000 Iberian auxiliaries) to fight a pitched battle; instead he put Numantia, the chief city of the "revolt," under siege in October of 134, first with a trench and palisade, and then with a siege wall that included seven camps and towers. Roman tenacity overcame Celtiberian élan, Scipio burned Numantia to the ground, and the Romans built a road from the Pyrenees to the Straits of Gibraltar, finally to complete the pacification of Spain.

If Roman tenacity, despite the incompetence of individuals, subdued the west, first-rate leadership won the east. In the Second Macedonian War (200–196)—fought to punish Philip V for his treaty with Hannibal—the consul of 198, T. Quinctius Flamininus, pursued a vigorous diplomatic policy, to appear to the Greeks as their champion against Philip by demanding that Philip withdraw totally from the whole of Greece, including Thessaly (which had been under the control of the Macedonian kings for a century and a half), and at the same time pursuing a vigorous military campaign. In his first year of campaigning he broke through the passes into Thessaly and isolated Philip. (Flamininus had an army of some 18,000 Romans and 8,000 allies, and a small elephant corps; Philip had enlisted youths of 16 to raise his army to about the same number.) In 197 Flamininus made first contact with Philip around Pherae in Thessaly; Philip decided to withdraw to a more open country, suitable for his phalanx, and Flamininus was determined to cut him off. By chance the two armies marched parallel to each other for two days, separated by a line of hills; on the third day a violent storm and thick mist impeded Philip's advance and he pitched camp on the hills called Cynoscephalae (Dog's Heads).

Flamininus's reconnaissance force (ten units of cavalry and 1,000 light-armed troops) ran into Philip's rearguard; after a moment of shock both sides sent runners to their commanders, and then they engaged. As soon as Flamininus received the message, he ordered his Aetolian allies to help his reconnaissance force; the Aetolians arrived just in time to stop its retreat and force the Macedonians, in turn, to retreat up the slopes of the hills. Philip sent his cavalry and mercenaries to reinforce his rearguard while he dispatched runners to recall the troops out foraging (a large part of his army). The reinforcements pushed the Romans and Aetolians back.

"King!" the Macedonians called to Philip, "the enemy are running. Don't throw away this opportunity. The barbarians cannot hold us. This day belongs to you, this is your chance."

Philip was worried about using his phalanx in this broken terrain of hills and valleys, but he was carried away by the reports he was hearing and so, even though half his army was still foraging, he ordered his chief of staff Nicanor, called the "Elephant," to gather the rest of the force, and he took what he had, drew his battleline up on the crest of the hills, pushed forward, and drove the Roman advance guard back. He was convinced he was winning, and he ordered his phalanx to lower their sarissas and advance. At the same time Flamininus led his army out in battle order, he recovered his advance guard by pulling them back through the lanes in his formation, and then he advanced.

Flamininus soon realized that his left wing—the half of his army that was engaged—would not be able to stop the advance of the phalanx, but he could see that his right wing was poised precisely in position to smash the other half of Philip's army, which was just now marching up to the crest of the hills. Flamininus moved to the right, placed his elephants in front, and ordered the right wing to advance. He caught the Macedonians on the hills completely by surprise and routed them. When he topped the crest of the hills, he stopped because he saw the Macedonians holding their sarissas straight up, and, although he had never seen Macedonians do this before, he understood they were trying to surrender; he ordered his men to halt, but his advance guard got among the Macedonians and killed most of them (see diagram, p. 197).

As the Romans were charging up the line of hills, a tribune commanding the third line (the triarii, about twenty maniples) looked to his left across the slope of the hill, where the mists had risen, and saw the rear of Philip's formation. He immediately grasped the opportunity, ordered his maniples to follow him, charged across the slope of the hill, and smashed into the rear of Philip's phalanx. The Macedonians in the rear threw down their shields and ran. The Roman left wing sensed the change, stopped their retreat, held their ground, and then began to advance. Suddenly Philip, who had thought he was winning, saw Macedonians run past him and saw the enemy behind him; Philip rallied what troops he could and fled from the battlefield. The tenacity of the Romans, their ability to fight for a prolonged period, the flexibility of the legions, and their excellent leadership were too much for Philip and the Macedonian phalanx.

Flamininus dictated the terms of peace (without consulting his allies): Philip was to remain king of a reduced Macedonia; Greeks were to be free and to be under the protection of Rome. The Romans understood what they meant by "free," but they soon learned that Antiochus, the king of the Seleucid empire, had misunderstood their message and thought that he could use the turmoil in Greece to expand into Europe. The Romans judged Antiochus trebly suspect—he was a king, he had interfered in a Roman sphere, and he had taken as his adviser Rome's greatest enemy, Hannibal. (Hannibal advised Antiochus either to wage total war on the Romans or avoid conflict altogether.) Antiochus brought a small army (10,000) into Greece, the Romans declared war in November 192, and by the spring of 191 they had driven him back to his kingdom.

Lucius Scipio was chosen consul for 190 and given command of the war in Asia with the understanding that his brother Publius (Africanus) would accompany him. Antiochus sought terms, Lucius demanded that he withdraw from the whole of Asia Minor, and Antiochus prepared to fight. His army outnumbered the Romans two to one, he had some fifty elephants, scythed chariots, and over 10,000 cavalry, and he lured the Romans onto ground of his own choosing, a flat, open plain near Magnesia where his cavalry and chariots could maneuver. On a rainy day in January 189 the two armies met.

Antiochus led his cavalry in person, broke the Roman left, and advanced on their camp, but the Pergamene king, Eumenes, commanding the cavalry and light-armed troops on the Roman right, routed Antiochus's scythed chariots, pursued them into their own formation, broke Antiochus's left, and then turned and attacked the flank of Antiochus's phalanx (16,000 strong, 32 men deep), while the legions threw their pila, charged the front of the phalanx, and forced the phalanx to give ground. The phalanx was withdrawing in good order, when the elephants (posted between sections of the phalanx), now wounded, went on a rampage and trampled their own men. The Romans saw the confusion and pushed into the phalanx, to fight man to man, where the sarissa was useless and the sword was deadly; they destroyed the phalanx.

Antiochus agreed to abandon Asia Minor, and he acceded to all Roman demands. Greece, Macedonia, and Asia Minor were now open to Roman ambition—one campaign among the Galatians netted 40,000 slaves. In 170 B.C. the Romans declared war on the new king of Macedonia, Perseus, and in 168, after two fruitless years of campaigning, the Roman commander, Aemilius Paullus, broke through Perseus's chain of defenses and cornered him at Pydna. On the night before the battle of Pydna (21–22 June 168) there was an eclipse of the moon; the Macedonians believed that the eclipse portended the fall of a king.

The Romans were disconcerted by the appearance of the Macedonian army, the glittering of the shields and the long sarissas, the war cries, and the quickness with which the phalanx moved towards the Romans. The Macedonians swung their shields around to protect themselves, couched their spears, and drove them into the shields of the Romans. Later the Roman commander Paullus would tell his friends that he was as frightened as he had ever been (and he had forty years of experience), when he saw his soldiers pinned out of reach of the Macedonians, but at the time he pretended that nothing was amiss, and he rode among his men with a confident look on his face. The Romans tried to smash the spears with their swords or knock them aside with their shields or to grab them and pull them, but the Macedonian phalanx held firm and pierced Roman shields and armor with their sarissas.

As the two sides fought on the uneven terrain, part of the phalanx pushed forward, part gave ground, and the phalanx gapped. Paullus ordered his men to concentrate on the places where the phalanx had split and to attack the breach.

Once the Romans broke into the ranks of the phalanx, the Macedonians had to fight against them with short swords and small shields, and the battle became a slaughter In one hour of battle the Romans, at a cost of about 100 men, destroyed the Macedonian army; Paullus had Perseus march in his triumph. The Romans divided Macedonia into four republics and in 148 (after an impostor arose and had to be put down) the Romans annexed Macedonia, Illyria, and Epirus and organized them into provinces. They built the via Egnatia (535 miles of road, with every mile marked) to link the new provinces with Rome.

The Romans now interfered freely in the Seleucid empire, they broke Rhodes for its lukewarm support in the war against Perseus, they removed 1,000 Achaean hostages to Rome in 168 (only 300 survived to be released in 151), and when they found further grounds for displeasure with the Achaeans, the Romans sacked Corinth (in 146). In 148 Cato succeeded in his personal project to convince his fellow Romans that Carthage must be destroyed; the two consuls with four legions and 4,000 cavalry landed at Utica and demanded that the Carthaginians surrender themselves to the will of the Roman Senate. The Carthaginians acceded, turned over their weapons (200,000 personal sets of arms and 2,000 catapults), and then were told that they were to abandon their city and resettle "wherever they liked" as long as it was ten miles from the sea.

The Carthaginians refused. Scipio Aemilianus was elected consul (though he was under age). He was able to close the siege only after he had defeated a Carthaginian army of 20,000 operating outside the city and driven the survivors inside the walls. The Carthaginians fought desperately, but at last the Romans broke into the inner part of the city. The Carthaginians set their houses on fire. Scipio delegated detachments to clear the streets of debris so that his men could advance. For six days the Romans fought from street to street and rooftop to rooftop. They killed everyone they met; many more died in the burning wreckage. On the seventh day the Carthaginians surrendered, and Scipio turned the city over to his soldiers to loot.

The Romans had no serious rivals left around the Mediterranean, but the constant wars and the enormous profits (won by a few commanders) broke the republic. The Senate lost control of the commanders and of the army. Senators had already profited from the wars, or they hoped to profit, so they refrained from establishing limits on the power of the commander that might someday apply to themselves; further, they did not recognize, or they did not care, that the system of farmer/soldier was dead. Ordinary citizens no longer served for part of the year and then returned to their farms. Spurius Ligustinus, who first became a soldier in 200 B.C., described his career to the Senate.

"I served for two years as an ordinary soldier against Philip the king. In my third year because of my courage Titus Quinctius Flamininus promoted me to centurion in the tenth maniple of the hastati. After Philip and the Macedonians were defeated and we were brought back to Italy and dismissed, I set out as a volunteer soldier with Marcus Porcius Cato to Spain. Nobody with much military experience knows of any general who was a fiercer witness and judge of courage. This general made me centurion of the first century of the hastati. When for the third time I went as a volunteer in that army that was sent against the Aetolians and Antiochus I was made centurion of the first century of the principes. After we had driven out Antiochus and subjugated the Aetolians we were brought back to Italy. And subsequently I served two one–year terms in the legions. Twice more I campaigned in Spain, first with Q. Fulvius Flaccus, again with Tiberius Sempronius Gracchus praetor (180–178). I was allowed to march in the triumph of Flaccus, among those specially chosen by him for their courage. I was asked by Gracchus to accompany him. Four times in a few years I was primus pilus. Thirty–four times I have received awards for bravery. I received six civic crowns. I have served twenty–two one-year hitches and I am more than fifty years old."

As citizens served year after year, their farms fell to ruin, the land was bought up by wealthy landowners who then worked it with gangs of slaves or turned it to pasture, and the discharged soldiers had nowhere to go but to Rome and to the army. When the younger Tiberius Sempronius Gracchus was on his way to the wars in Spain in 137 B.C., he passed through whole districts empty of free farmers, worked by gangs of slaves, and he was struck by the magnitude of the transformation of the Roman state. Tiberius Gracchus had saved the Roman army at Numantia and had been repudiated by the Senate; he had lived through a massive slave rebellion in Sicily, and he was determined to restore the Roman state to the ideal, citizen-farmer state of his ancestors.

He was elected tribune of the people and entered office on 10 December 134 B.C. He proposed an agrarian law in the Senate to divide the public land among the urban dispossessed (army veterans). Tiberius Gracchus had powerful supporters in the Senate, but he had more powerful opponents who feared the loss of land they held, and his plan was defeated. Tiberius then brought the law directly to the people's assembly and the people passed the agrarian law. An agrarian commission was established to identify and distribute public land, but when Tiberius announced his intention—against all tradition—to stand for reelection, his opponents took to the streets, attacked Tiberius, and clubbed him to death with 300 of his supporters.

Perhaps Tiberius had had noble intentions, but he circumvented tradition and showed less scrupulous men how to bypass the Senate, he gave the popular assembly a taste of power, he introduced violence to the streets of Rome, and in the end he did not solve the problem he had set out to solve; the agrarian commission awarded land to veterans, but the veterans still had to leave the land to serve in the army. What the situation required was senatorial action to protect the soldiers' private interests and to provide them with benefits and pensions so that the soldiers would give their loyalty to the Senate, and the Senate could control the army.

Ten years later—ten years in which the agrarian commission was allowed to do its work—Tiberius's brother Gaius became tribune. Gaius Gracchus addressed the roots of the main grievances of the Roman people: he set a minimum age—perhaps seventeen—for the draft, and he had the state provide clothing to the troops, a reflection of the poverty of recruits. He extended to Latin soldiers the Roman soldier's right to appeal a capital sentence. He attempted to continue the distribution of land. He proposed that the Latins and the Italian allies—who had done their share, or more, by the side of Roman troops—be granted Roman citizenship.

Gaius Gracchus was reelected for a second term without violence, but the Senate had a partisan tribune of their own, and their tribune outbid Gaius Gracchus for the affections of the people by offering them greater benefits and by advocating that citizenship not be extended further (one of Gaius's unpopular measures). When Gaius Gracchus failed to win a third term, he became involved in a riot, the Senate invoked the right to restore public order, and Gaius Gracchus was killed in the subsequent brawl.

In the period 125–121 the Romans defeated the Gauls in the vicinity of Massilia, linked Spain to Rome by the via Domitia, and organized the transalpine region into a province (which was so thoroughly romanized that it was called "Italy rather than a province"). For the moment the Senate had preserved its prerogatives and Roman supremacy in the Mediterranean world, but the next generation would pay the price.

## 41. Diagram of the Battle of Cynoscephalae

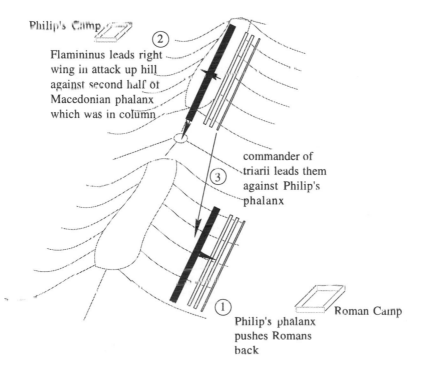

Philip's Camp

② Flamininus leads right wing in attack up hill against second half of Macedonian phalanx which was in column

③ commander of triarii leads them against Philip's phalanx

① Philip's phalanx pushes Romans back

Roman Camp

**42. Second Century Soldiers (Ahenobarbus relief)**

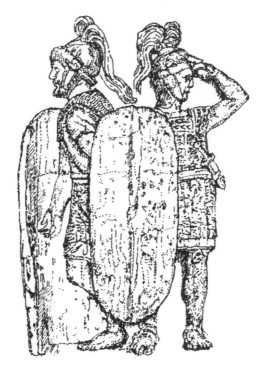

**43. Attacking Legionnaire (Mainz relief, I A.D.)**

# 27

# The Breakdown of the Roman System

## *Who Controls the Army? Who Is Controlled By the Army?*

By 121 B.C. Rome seemed to be a power without significant rivals, but in the next sixty years the Romans were shaken by scandals, incompetence, catastrophic defeats by two German tribes, by civil war, first between Roman and Italian, then between Roman and Roman, by a slave uprising, by pirates, and by a petty but persistent Eastern king. By the end of the period the Roman army was no longer an army of landholding citizens, who wanted to serve their time and return to their land, but an army of professionals whose only means of livelihood was their military service and whose only loyalty was to their commander, whether their commander used the new army to further the interests of Rome or of his own personal ambition.

The reorganization of the army grew out of a minor affair in Africa. Upon the death of the king of Numidia in 118 B.C. his nephew, Jugurtha, assumed control of the kingdom, murdered his rivals (sons of the king), and, when some Italian merchants intervened, murdered them as well. Summoned to Rome to explain himself, Jugurtha let his wealth do the talking (and win him powerful friends), and for the moment he escaped the consequences of his actions, but, as he departed Rome, he remarked—"All of Rome could be purchased, if someone had enough money"—and that remark infuriated the Roman people. They declared war on Jugurtha.

The first Roman commander made a fortune in booty but could not win a battle, and he was replaced. The new commander, the consul of 109 B.C., Q. Caecilius Metellus, was competent enough to defeat Jugurtha in battle, but thereafter he could not force Jugurtha to fight another battle, and Metellus had to wage a long, drawn-out campaign to reduce Jugurtha's strongholds, one by one, and he had to garrison them. His war required time and a large number of troops. The Roman people grew impatient, and their impatience was inflamed by reports from one of Metellus's staff officers, Marius—reports that Metellus was prolonging the war for his own benefit. Marius promised, if the people appointed him to the command, he would end the war in one campaign with half the troops.

The Roman people elected Marius consul for 107 B.C. and by their own authority gave him the command against Jugurtha. Marius fulfilled his promise to reduce the size of the present army by opening the ranks (officially) to citizens without property; the landless saw the army as an opportunity—pay for the moment, booty on campaign, and, at the end of service, perhaps, a grant of land. Thus Marius stilled the voice in the ranks demanding an end to the war and a return to their farms, and he created a large body of Roman citizens who made their living entirely from military service.

Marius also reorganized the army to incorporate changes that had evolved and been put to practical use in Numidia: the maniple had proved to be too small to sustain itself in combat and had been replaced by the cohort (a unit comprising three maniples). The cohort could operate as an independent tactical unit or could fight as part of a legion. Marius eliminated the distinctions within the cohort of hastati, principes, and triarii. He had all soldiers armed and equipped alike, he issued to each soldier the new and improved pilum, and he eliminated light-armed troops (as an integral part of the cohort).

By the end of 107 Marius had reduced the eastern half of Numidia, and in the next year (106) Marius defeated the combined armies of Jugurtha and his ally, Bocchus (the king of Mauretania), and he sent his cavalry commander, Lucius Cornelius Sulla, to negotiate with Bocchus. Bocchus offered to withdraw from the war in exchange for a Roman pardon. Sulla told him that the Romans wanted deeds, not words, and Bocchus handed Jugurtha over to Sulla. The war was over. Marius had proven his worth as a commander and fulfilled the expectations of the Roman people, but Sulla's romantic tale of his adventure in the court of Bocchus made him the hero of the hour and stirred Marius to a combination of envy and spite.

Against Jugurtha the shortcomings of the Roman army—annual command, short-term enlistments, ambitious, rapacious, and incompetent commanders—did not matter so much, but a different kind of threat now shook the Republic. Two German tribes, the Cimbri and Teutones, had set out—men, women, and children—to find a new home. They fought their way through different Gallic tribes to the borders of Roman territory, where the consul of 113 B.C. ordered them to retire; the Germans obeyed, but the consul attacked them anyway. He thought, with the usual Roman contempt for the Germans (a people regularly defeated by the Gauls), that he would have an easy victory, plentiful booty, slaves to sell, and glory. Instead the Roman army was saved from annihilation only by a provident thunderstorm. The Germans, fearful of Roman retribution, avoided Roman territory and continued their migration into Gaul (111 or 110 B.C.). In Gaul the Cimbri and Teutones were joined by a Celtic people (from Helvetia) the Tigurini.

Incompetent Roman commanders in Gaul were defeated by the Germans in 109 B.C., 107 B.C., and 106 B.C., and on 6 October 105 at Arausio on the Rhone River, while the two consuls were feuding, the Germans defeated the Romans in detail and annihilated the Roman army (80,000 Romans and Italians). The Romans immediately issued emergency orders—men of military age had to swear an oath not to leave Italy, and officials at the ports of Italy were instructed not to let any man age 35 or younger leave, but once again the Germans did not press their advantage; instead, they split, the Cimbri turned to Spain, and the Teutones turned to Gaul. At this critical juncture, with no certainty that the Romans could defeat the Germans, Marius returned from the war against Jugurtha, celebrated a triumph, and entered office as consul for 104 B.C.

Marius had time to recruit experienced staff officers (one of whom was Sulla), to raise, and to train an army of slightly more than 30,000 men. He worked his men so hard—digging a canal for Massilia to bypass the silted-up mouth of the Rhone River—and he loaded them with so much equipment, that they became known as Marius's mules. Marius was reelected consul for 103 B.C. and again for 102 B.C. By then the Germans had concluded that they did not like Spain or Gaul, and they decided to conquer Italy. They adopted a plan that would have had a devastating effect on the Romans immediately after Arausio. They left all their baggage in Gaul to be guarded by a force of 6,000 men (who later formed a tribe known to Caesar as the Atuatuci), and they prepared a three-pronged invasion of Italy—the Teutones were to come from the west along the coastal road, the Cimbri were to cross the Brenner Pass, and the Tigurini were to cross the Julian Alps and attack Aquileia.

Marius built a camp on the Rhone in the path of the Teutones. When the Teutones were unable to take the camp by storm, they marched past it; for six days they streamed by the camp and shouted insults at the Romans—"Do you have any messages for your wives? We will see them before you do."

When they had passed, Marius followed at a safe distance. Every night Marius had his men build their fortified camp in defensible terrain, until they drew near to Aquae Sextiae, close to the passes into the Alps; there Marius had his men build their camp in a place without a secure approach to water. They complained that they were thirsty, and he told them that there was water next to the Teutones, but they would have to buy it with their blood.

"Then lead us out," they replied, "before our blood dries up."

He ordered them to fortify their camp first. While they were working on the camp, the soldiers sent their servants to fetch water; the servants drew water in safety at first because the Germans were swimming, relaxing on the other side of the stream, and eating dinner, but one tribe of the Germans, the Ambrones, shouted their war cry, "Ambrones!" and began to cross the stream. The Ligurian Gauls (Roman allies) responded with their war cry, the same word, "Ambrones!" and rushed down to meet them. The two sides met while the Ambrones were still crossing the stream. The Roman army formed up and rushed down to help the Ligurians and drove the Ambrones back across the stream, crossed it, and pursued them to their wagons. The German women charged into the Roman ranks like berserkers and hacked at Roman and German alike with axes and swords. The Romans withdrew in good order and night fell.

Throughout the night Marius kept his troops on alert—they had not finished their palisade—and they listened to the war cries and the lamentations of the Germans across the stream. Marius sent an ambush force of 3,000 men to hide themselves and be ready should the enemy attack in the morning. At first light Marius drew his army up on the slope before his camp, and the Germans came on at the charge. The Romans threw their pila, and the two sides closed and fought hand to hand with their swords. Marius himself fought in the front ranks of the army. The Romans forced the Teutones back down the slope, but the Teutones rallied and held at the bottom of the slope. At that moment Marius's ambush force of 3,000 charged the rear of the Teutones. The Teutones broke and fled, and the Romans killed or captured "100,000" of them. (The local inhabitants used the bones to build fences and enjoyed a remarkably fertile soil for years after.)

Marius had annihilated the Teutones, but Catulus, the other consul, failed to stop the Cimbri. The Cimbri seemed so ferocious—they ran naked in the snow and used their shields as toboggans—that the Roman army broke and fled at the sight of them. Catulus seized the standard and ran ahead of his army, so that the fault would be his alone. In 101 B.C. Catulus (his command prorogued) and Marius (reelected as consul) linked their commands. (Marius is supposed to have redesigned the pilum for this battle. He replaced one of the two iron rivets—which held the head in place—with a wooden peg. On impact this peg broke and the shaft swung down, so that the pilum could not be thrown back, but the shaft would still impede its victim.)

The armies met at Campi Raudii. The Cimbri refused to fight because they were "waiting for their brothers." When they demanded land for themselves and "their brothers," Marius replied that the Teutones had been given land enough for their needs, land they could keep forever. Then he brought out the captured Teutonic kings so that the Cimbri could see them. The king of the Cimbri challenged Marius to name a day and a place when the two armies would meet in battle. The day they met was hot and dry; a huge dust cloud obscured the field of combat so completely that Marius and his men missed the Cimbri on their first rush forward. The Romans were in such good physical condition that they easily withstood the hot and dry climate, but the Cimbri were exhausted. The men in the front line of the Cimbri had linked themselves together with chains, and none were able to escape. The rest fled back to their wagons and were killed by their wives, who then killed the children, and cut their own throats. (Nonetheless 60,000 were taken prisoner.) The Cimbri were annihilated. (The Tigurini, who had not taken part in the battle, withdrew back to their homes in Helvetia.)

Marius had crushed the enemy and saved Rome. In the process he created the army with which Caesar conquered Gaul and the early Roman emperors established the Pax Romana. The Marian army, competently led, was unrivalled, but the Roman people were convinced that the whole of the nobility was incompetent and corrupt; the nobles were using the army—and thus the Roman people—to fulfill their own ambition for political advancement and their own greed for the wealth to be won in war. In 103 B.C. the people created a special (people's) court to try individuals who had "diminished the majesty of the Roman people." The crime could be anything a prosecutor made of it, but the intention was to control the officials exercising the imperium.

Marius soon frittered away his prestige with inept political schemes, and he retired to Asia. If the Senate had now established a fund to provide benefits to discharged veterans, it could have seized control of the army; if the Senate had satisfied the grievances of the Latins and Italian allies—that they fought in equal numbers, side by side with the Romans in all their wars, and received none of the rewards—it could have avoided a civil war that threatened the very existence of Rome, but the last prominent Roman advocate of Latin rights was murdered and Roman arrogance towards the Italians became unendurable. The citizens of the Italian city of Asculum massacred all the Romans within their city, and the civil war between Rome and Italy began.

The Roman army faced its mirror image—soldiers every bit as good as themselves, trained and armed the same, and totally familiar with Roman leaders and methods. The Romans recalled their armies in the provinces, selected their most experienced commanders, and used their central position in Italy to divide the rebels. Nonetheless casualties in this avoidable war were so high that the Romans could not bear the sight of the dead brought back to Rome, and they directed that henceforth the dead would be buried on the battlefield.

Marius was brought from retirement, the consul Lucius Julius Caesar (the father of the famous Julius Caesar) commanded one army, and Sulla another. The Romans survived the first year, and Lucius Caesar sponsored first a law that granted citizenship to the Italian communities that had remained steadfast in their loyalty and then a supplement that granted citizenship to any Italian who applied within sixty days to the praetor in Rome. This act, combined with Roman successes, contained the rebellion and in the end broke it. All free (surviving) Italians were now Roman citizens.

The enemies of Rome—and Rome's exploitation of its provinces had created many enemies—had seen opportunity in the civil war. In the east, they coalesced around Mithridates, the king of Pontus; he traced his descent from the king of Persia, but he and his nobles spoke Greek, intermarried with Seleucid royalty, and generally created a fusion of Greek and Iranian culture. Mithridates was nominally an independent ally of Rome, but he dreamed of an empire centered in Asia Minor and extending to the Greek peninsula. He defeated the one Roman legion stationed in Asia, captured its commander, led him around on a donkey, and then, "to at last quench his thirst for gold," had molten gold poured down his throat. Mithridates issued orders for the murder of the thousands of Romans in Asia Minor, and he sent his foremost general, Archelaus, to drive the Romans from the mainland of Greece and bring the Greeks into Mithridates' empire.

The Senate voted to give Sulla the command, and Sulla had already joined his army and administered the oath, when he learned that Marius (then seventy years of age) had convinced the Senate to transfer the command to himself. Sulla marched his army to Rome, drove Marius and his supporters into exile, and forced the Senate to repudiate the change of command. Sulla was the first Roman commander to march his army on Rome and, conversely, but just as important, his army was the first Roman army to follow its commander in a march on Rome. Sulla retained his command and departed with his army for Greece. (After Sulla's departure Marius returned to Rome and murdered Sulla's supporters.)

Sulla arrived in Greece with his army—five legions and some cavalry—and all too soon learned that Marius had cut him off from Rome. (Marius died of old age, but his followers clung to power.) Sulla looted the shrines of Epidaurus, Olympia, and Delphi to pay his troops and raise a fleet. He invested Athens and the Piraeus, where Archelaus had established his headquarters. Sulla dug a trench and built a ring of forts around Athens, interdicted the supply columns from the Piraeus (where his supporters slung lead balls with messages on them out to him), and, when he judged that starvation had sufficiently weakened the Athenians (there were reports of cannibalism), he assaulted the city (1 March 86). He forbade his troops to burn any property, but otherwise he let them loose to loot and kill as they pleased. They slaughtered men, women, and children. Archelaus fled from the Piraeus to Thessaly, Sulla burned the Piraeus to the ground, and then he followed Archelaus into Thessaly; there, however, Sulla demonstrated such a peculiar disinclination to fight that Archelaus grew careless. Near Chaeronea he camped on the edge of a rough and broken country dominated by a gentle slope which the Romans promptly seized. Sulla led his legions in a charge down the slope and caught Archelaus completely by surprise.

Archelaus tried to divert the Romans with some cavalry and his chariots, but the Romans drove off the small force of cavalry and opened their ranks to let the chariots through. Archelaus led out his whole army and dispatched a massed cavalry charge which penetrated the Roman formation and broke it in two. The Romans formed squares and fought on all sides, until Sulla, who had held back a mixed reserve of cavalry and individual cohorts, charged directly at Archelaus. Archelaus tried to reform his disorganized army to meet the charge, but Sulla struck before he could, the enemy army panicked, broke, and ran. Archelaus tried to rally them, but his unit leaders were killed, wounded, or missing, and the Romans broke his army once again, followed the fugitives into the camp and slaughtered them. Archelaus escaped with about 10,000 troops; the rest were killed or captured. Sulla lost thirteen men.

Sulla returned to Athens, Archelaus raised a new army of some 80,000, and the two commanders met again in the plains of Orchomenus (in Boeotia), where Archelaus thought he would have room to maneuver his cavalry and chariots and where his superior numbers would overwhelm the Romans. Sulla, once again, outthought him. His troops dug a trench in front of them on the plain, the trench broke Archelaus's cavalry charge, and Sulla ordered his men to attack immediately, before the cavalry could recover, but his men were hesitant to leave the protection of the trench, and Sulla had to get off his horse, take a standard, and lead them in person. The enemy fled to their camp. Sulla enclosed Archelaus's camp with a trench and advanced his men to the wall in a tortoise formation. The Romans breached the wall, but Archelaus's men jumped down from their palisade, fought hand to hand with the Romans, and held the breach until a military tribune personally killed one of the defenders and led the Romans into the breach. Archelaus once again evaded capture.

Mithridates sent his general back to propose to Sulla that, if Sulla would accept the status quo, the king would furnish Sulla with ships, money, and troops to use against the Marians in Rome. Sulla, in turn, invited Archelaus to desert Mithridates, turn over his fleet, and join Sulla. By August 85 B.C. Mithridates finally was convinced that Sulla would not bend, and he accepted Sulla's terms: he would hand over his fleet, give up all his conquests, and pay 2,000 talents indemnity; in return he was named "friend and ally" of the Roman people. The Romans once again proved the superiority of their legions when led by men such as Sulla and his subordinate commanders.

Sulla took time to organize Asia—and to exact an indemnity of 20,000 talents—and then in 84 B.C. he brought his army back to Italy to deal with the Marians. Sulla fought a two–year civil war that culminated in a massacre of the Marians at the Colline Gate of Rome and the murder of 4,000 Samnite prisoners. Once he was in control, Sulla issued a proscription list of all his enemies, hundreds of them, who could be (and should be) murdered. The murderers, as their reward, got a part of their victims' property. Thus Sulla eliminated his opponents (and his two subordinates, Crassus and Pompey, founded their fortunes and established themselves as men of power).

Next Sulla set out to reform the republic (so that there would be no more men like Marius or himself). As Sulla understood the problem, a consul or a praetor would obtain an army and an area of operations, where he would endeavor to make his fortune regardless of policy or the good of Rome. Even worse, he would have but *one* year of command in which to make his fortune. Under Sulla's reform the provinces would each receive an ex-consul or ex-praetor as governor (regardless of whether there was a threat of war there or not), and the duties of the magistrates and the governors were specifically described (and their actions circumscribed). A governor committed treason if, without the orders of the Senate and the Roman people, he left his province, moved his army outside his province, started a war on his own initiative, or invaded the territory of a client king. In short, Sulla attempted to put the Senate back in charge.

Sulla did not live long after his reforms passed, and the men who succeeded him—Pompey, Crassus, and Caesar—chose to follow his example rather than his precepts. Crassus had the greater wealth, Pompey the greater reputation, and the two, despite their personal differences, were firmly in control of the Roman state, but Mithridates, that persistent enemy of Rome, believed once again that Rome's problems gave him an opportunity to unite all the enemies of

Rome—the kings of Armenia and Parthia, the tribes of Thrace and the Danube, the pirates of Cilicia, the Marian rebels in Spain and, within a year, the gladiator Spartacus.

The Romans responded vigorously. One by one they eliminated, or neutralized, the putative members of the hostile coalition. Pompey defeated one Marian rebel who invaded northern Italy and defeated another in Spain. His victories made him the Senate's champion and the most powerful man in Rome, but while he was in Spain (in 73 B.C.), the gladiator Spartacus with seventy-three fellow gladiators broke out of a training school at Capua, defeated the first troops sent against him, and used the captured arms to equip a mass of men large enough to be formed into two armies. Spartacus commanded one of the armies (the other was defeated by the Romans) and was so successful—he defeated both consuls—that he altered his initial plan to march his army out of Italy (and allow the slaves to disperse to their homelands) and turned back towards the toe of Italy, where he may have planned to find ships (with the help of Mithridates and the pirates) and transport his army to Sicily.

In this moment of crisis the Senate turned to Marcus Licinius Crassus, then a praetor, and the only man in Rome willing to accept the assignment, to command an army of eight humiliated legions. Crassus stiffened their shattered morale by decimating them—"an army should fear its commander more than the enemy"—and by avoiding battle. He intended to wall Spartacus into the toe of Italy and starve him out, but Spartacus broke out and tried to escape; Crassus brought him to battle, defeated him, and crucified the 6,000 slaves he captured. Crassus might have been hailed as the savior of Rome, but in a moment of panic he had sent a plea for help to Pompey (en route from Spain). Pompey caught some fugitives and used this modest success to claim, "Crassus pruned the rebellion, but I pulled it out by its roots." His conceit made Crassus his enemy and Crassus refused to disband his army until Pompey had disbanded his. Pompey likewise refused, and the crisis was avoided only when both Pompey and Crassus were elected consuls for the year 70 B.C.

Pompey wanted the command in a new war against Mithridates (even though the commander, Lucullus, was doing an exemplary job), but he was diverted by an assignment to rid the Mediterranean Sea of pirates. Pirates had assembled a fleet of 400 ships and sacked Delos. They raided the nobles' summer villas on the coasts of Italy, and they captured so many ships bringing grain to Rome that they drove the prices up. (They had even held the young Caesar for ransom.) Pompey was given a three-year command, with authority over the whole of the Mediterranean Sea and the power to command within fifty miles of the sea, to have 6,000 talents, 500 ships, 24 legates (with the imperium), and 20 legions. He divided the Mediterranean Sea and the Black Sea into thirteen areas of operation. All the straits were closed—to block the pirates in the Adriatic, for instance, and to keep the pirates in Cilicia in play.

At the beginning of the sailing season, spring 67 B.C., Pompey's fleet of sixty ships drove the pirates of the western Mediterranean from their refuges into the fleets of the various commands of the west. Pompey cleared the west in forty days. Following this success Pompey swept the pirates of the east towards their strongholds in Cilicia. Pompey defeated them at sea and then with siege engines forced the capitulation of their strongest fortress, Coracesium. He cleared the eastern seas in three months.

As a reward he was given the command he wanted, against King Mithridates. The Romans had used the death of the king of Bithynia (in 74 B.C.) to declare Bithynia a province and to send both consuls, Lucullus and Cotta, to operate against Mithridates. Cotta was defeated, but Lucullus trapped Mithridates, reduced his troops to eating grass (and each other), and, when Mithridates used the cover of a snowstorm to try to escape, Lucullus caught him and annihilated his army. In the next three years Lucullus harried Mithridates until he fled his kingdom and sought refuge with the king of Armenia. In 69 B.C. Lucullus invaded Armenia with a force "too large for an embassy and too small for an army," drove the Armenian king from his capital, caught him and his army by surprise, struck the Armenian heavy cavalry, armored men and horses, on the flank, where they were vulnerable, drove them into the rest of their army, and routed them.

Lucullus, however, did not understand that the Roman commander and his troops (drawn from those without property) were now partners in an enterprise of war for profit. Senators, too, and their business partners expected some return from this war, but Lucullus had refused to let his soldiers plunder, and they rather believed that he was keeping everything for himself. The Senate appointed Pompey to supersede Lucullus. Pompey promptly ordered Mithridates to turn himself over to the pleasure of the Roman people, and when Mithridates refused, Pompey negotiated an alliance with the king of Parthia and so knocked Armenia out of the war. He annihilated Mithridates' last forces and hounded him through his dominions; Mithridates, with a price on his head, deserted by his friends and even by his own son, finally committed suicide. Pompey made a tour of the Near East and settled all questions of frontiers and rulers. (He besieged and captured Jerusalem in 63 B.C.)

Pompey understood war, Roman style. He made a distribution to his own troops of 384 million sesterces (400,000 sesterces qualified a man to be a senator) and paid even more into the Roman treasury, but his very success awoke the envy and fears of the Senate, and the Senate tried to curtail his power by not voting pensions for his soldiers and by encouraging his rivals. Julius Caesar, one of those rivals, was elected consul for 59 B.C., but when the Senate also tried to cut Caesar down to size by allocating him the province of the "woodlands and pastures" of Italy, he made a political alliance with Pompey— who married Caesar's daughter Julia—and Crassus, "the first [and secret] triumvirate."

Caesar's first act was to propose a bill to provide land for Pompey's veterans. When the Senate voted down the bill and then attempted to prevent the assembly of the people voting on it, Caesar rallied Pompey's veterans to drive their opponents from the forum. Caesar was allotted a different province (for a period of five years)—the province of Cisalpine Gaul, Illyricum, and, by a later addition, Transalpine Gaul.

## Map 21. Caesar's Gaul

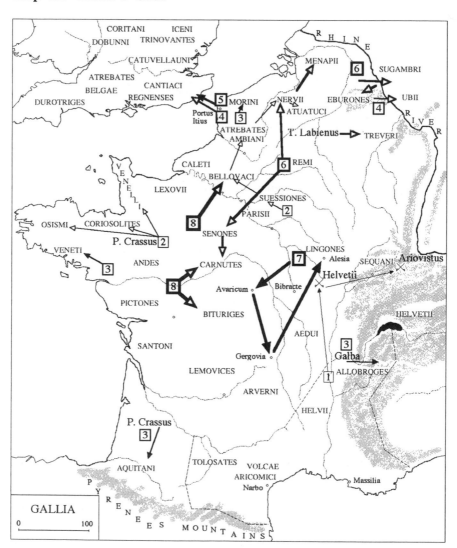

The numbers refer to the years of the campaign and the book of the *Gallic Wars*, so ①  = year one and book one.

# 28

# Julius Caesar

## *The Only Ancient Commander Whose Accounts of His Campaigns Survive*

Gaul, on the eve of Caesar's conquest, was divided into more than 200 separate tribes, great and small; the tribes were settled in agricultural communities under the leadership of a narrow circle of aristocrats. They lived in three regions, so famously defined by Caesar: Aquitania, Belgium, and Gaul proper. They had general knowledge of each other, but they had no sense of common identity or common interest. One of the two great tribes of the Gauls, the Aedui, had been defeated recently by the other great tribe, the Sequani, who had obtained the alliance of Germans led by King Ariovistus. Ariovistus had occupied part of their territory in payment, and he had invited other German tribes to cross the Rhine and join him.

This troubled scene was troubled further by the Helvetians, a tribe in the region of Lake Geneva; they decided as a group to leave their restricted and threatened territory and to conquer and settle a safer, more fertile, and less restricted region in the heart of Gaul. They asked Caesar for permission to pass through his province, but Caesar concluded that the interests of Rome would not be served by letting 92,000 armed and ill-disciplined men loose in the rich lands of the Province; the Helvetians tried to force their way, but Caesar defended his borders and diverted them to another route, through Aeduan territory. When the Aedui asked Caesar to help them, Caesar seized the opportunity. He pursued the Helvetians, caught a detachment before it could cross the Saone River, and annihilated it. He continued to shadow the larger body until short rations forced him to turn back towards his supply base, whereupon the Helvetians, who believed that they had scared him off, turned and forced a battle on him. As soon as Caesar realized that the Helvetians intended to attack him, he drew his army up on the slope of a hill, with his more experienced legions in their triple formation and the baggage defended by the other two legions (who also built a fortification). He removed all the officers' horses.

Caesar writes, "The soldiers, in their higher position, threw their pila, drew their swords and charged. The Gauls were seriously encumbered in this fight because many of their overlapping shields were pierced and fixed together by single pila and they could not pull them apart (since the iron bent back on itself after piercing) nor could they fight very well with their left arms pinned. Many preferred to drop their shields and fight with their bodies exposed."

The Romans forced them to retreat, but the Helvetian rear guard attacked the Roman flanks, and the Romans had to form a square and fight on all sides. The battle was fought from about midday until the sun went down, face to face and hand to hand. Finally the Helvetians broke and fled to their laager. The Romans stormed the line of wagons and finally carried the camp. The Helvetians surrendered and Caesar had a census made: he estimated that of the 368,000 people who had set out, 110,000 survived to return to their homes.

As a consequence of the Roman victory the Aedui asked Caesar (secretly) to help them against Ariovistus and the Germans. Caesar acceded to their request and sent Ariovistus an ultimatum that made the Roman position clear—Rome had become the protector of the whole of Gaul west of the Rhine River. Ariovistus rejected the ultimatum and Caesar prepared to attack him, but Caesar's troops had heard stories told by the Gauls—the Germans were of monstrous size, inhumanly courageous, and so fierce that no one even dared look them in the eyes. Some Romans deserted; the rest made out their wills and prepared to die. Caesar summoned his centurions and his staff, berated them for their lack of faith in him and in themselves, and told them that, if they refused to go, nevertheless he would go himself with just the tenth legion. His words won the army over.

Caesar advanced on Ariovistus, built (as always) a fortified camp, and offered battle for five days in a row. Ariovistus refused to engage with his infantry, though his cavalry proved more than a match for the Gallic allies of Caesar. (The Germans employed pairs of men, one mounted, one on foot; if the cavalryman should fall from a wounded horse, the foot soldier would protect him; if they had to advance or retreat quickly, the cavalryman would offer his bridle to support the foot soldier.) If Caesar was to defeat Ariovistus, he would have to force an infantry battle on him, and so, as he would do again and again in his career, Caesar put pressure on the enemy by building a fort about six–tenths of a mile (in this case) from the enemy camp. Ariovistus attacked the smaller camp and continued the attack until dusk. The Romans took some prisoners and the prisoners told Caesar that German witches had announced that the fates would not allow the Germans to win if they fought a battle before the new moon.

"On the next day Caesar drew up his triple battle line and advanced on the enemy camp. Thus the Germans were forced to bring out their own troops from camp; they formed up in front of their wagons and carts (to block any retreat). The women behind the carts implored the men with outstretched hands not to let them become the Romans' slaves. Our troops charged and so did the enemy, so quickly that our men had no time to throw their pila; they dropped them, drew their swords, and fought hand to hand. The veteran Germans formed a tight phalanx and warded off the blows of the swords, but many of our soldiers wormed their way into the phalanx, tore the shields away, and wounded the Germans from underneath. We drove back the enemy line on the left, but on the right we were pressed hard by a mass of the enemy. When Publius Crassus observed this—he was a young man in charge of the cavalry and so somewhat removed from the fighting—he sent the third line to help those troops of ours who were in trouble. Now all the enemy turned their backs and fled, and they did not stop until they reached the Rhine River (about five miles away)."

Caesar's men never doubted him again. While Caesar was no military innovator, he was competent in all facets of tactics, he had supreme confidence in himself and in the legions, both as soldiers and as engineers, and he was quick, decisive, imaginative, and tenacious. As a strategist he had no peer.

Because of his victories over the Germans and the Helvetians, he now considered himself master and patron of Gaul, and he intended to punish any resistance as rebellion. Caesar established winter quarters at Vesontio. There envoys from various tribes appeared to seek alliance with Caesar; one of the Belgian tribes, the Remi, informed Caesar that the other Belgian tribes believed, quite correctly, that Caesar intended to conquer Gaul, and they were planning a summer campaign against him. The Remi estimated the Belgian fighting force as close to 300,000 men.

As soon as the weather allowed, Caesar advanced on this force and pinned it down, while his Aeduan allies were let loose to ravage the Belgian homeland. The Belgian army split into its constituent tribes, each determined to defend its own homeland. Each tribe set out on its own, the withdrawal soon became confused, Caesar struck, and the retreat became a panic rout. One by one, Caesar visited the tribes in their homelands and, one by one, his siege engines, often by their appearance alone, forced the tribal strongholds to surrender. When he had knocked the weaker tribes out of the war, he turned against the stronger—the Nervii and their immediate allies—and he marched into their territory.

Deep in their territory one evening, as the Romans were preparing their camp, the Nervii, and their allies, burst from ambush, charged across a shallow stream, and were on the Romans before they could remove the covers from their shields or put on helmets or find their own standards; still, Caesar had issued standing orders to his officers to stay with their men until the camp was entrenched, the men were experienced, and they formed lines wherever they stood. The ninth and tenth legions threw their pila at the Atrebates, the tribe attacking them, broke the impetus of their attack, drove them back down the slope into the stream, and killed a large number of them, but the Atrebates rallied on the other side of the stream; the ninth and tenth crossed and broke them again. The eleventh and eighth legions had also driven their enemies back and were fighting on the edge of the stream.

In the center the assault force of the Nervii divided. Half attacked the twelfth and the seventh legions—they had a gap between them—and the Nervii killed or wounded almost every centurion in the twelfth legion; the Romans, without leadership, packed themselves so tightly together that they did not have room to use their swords properly. Caesar ran among them and called upon them to open their ranks. He infused courage into his men, they fought harder, and he ordered the military tribunes to bring the seventh and twelfth legions together and form them in a square. This they did despite being engaged at the time by a mass of Nervii. Meanwhile the other half of the Nervii rushed the camp, which had been left exposed by the confused fighting, and they scattered the baggage handlers, the camp followers, the light-armed soldiers, and the cavalry. Some Gallic cavalry, newly arrived, saw the Roman camp in the hands of the Nervii, saw the hard-pressed twelfth and seventh legions and fled with the news that the Roman army had been destroyed.

At this moment the two reserve legions, which had been guarding the baggage column, arrived and drew up on the hill where the enemy could see them, while on the other side of the stream the tenth legion had reached the top of a hill, had looked back, and had seen what was happening to their own camp. Both the reserve legions and the tenth legion rushed into the battle, the Roman cavalry regrouped and rejoined the fight, and even the camp followers resisted the attack of the Nervii. The surrounded Nervii continued to fight, the living on top of mounds of their own dead, until, in Caesar's words, these "men of tremendous courage" were almost exterminated from the face of the earth. The surviving Nervii accepted the results of this battle and submitted. Those of their allies who did not, were conquered and sold, man, woman, and child, into slavery. Caesar's strategy—and general Roman practice—was to administer a sharp lesson: if the enemy then capitulated, gave hostages, and proved their loyalty by fighting against their former friends, they would gain the status of allies. Caesar had no tolerance for second thoughts: "rebels" were annihilated as an example to others; rebel booty and slaves became rewards for the new allies and, of course, the Romans and, in particular, Caesar.

In the third year Caesar (in person and through his lieutenants) conquered Aquitania and the tribes of the far north. He repelled a German invasion, he built a bridge (in ten days) across the Rhine—the bridge, by itself, overawed the Germans—and he made a show of force on the German side of the river. Once he had secured his main objective—to deny the Gauls German allies or a place of refuge—Caesar crossed the Channel (in late August 55 B.C.) and invaded Britannia. The Britons massed on the shore, but Caesar sent his warships in, their strange appearance caused the Britons to retreat a little, and (Caesar writes) "a standard bearer of the tenth legion called upon the gods and said to his comrades, 'Jump out, soldiers, unless you want the enemy to have your eagle—for I intend to do my duty for the state and for my commander.'"

The troops followed, but the Briton cavalry came into the water and harried the small groups of Romans until Caesar sent scout boats loaded with soldiers to help the struggling men. At last the troops reached dry land, drove off the Britons, and established a base camp. A month later they returned to Gaul. In 54

Caesar invaded Britannia anew with 2,000 cavalry and five legions, and he forced the Britons' strongest king to agree to let Caesar keep the spoils of the campaign, receive hostages, and be paid an annual tribute. Caesar returned to Gaul. He had acquired a good amount of wealth from the invasion, and if he had not added Britannia to the Roman Empire, he had denied the Gauls any chance of help from the Britons.

In the winter of 54–53 the separate Roman camps came under attack, one was destroyed, and the Roman reputation for invincibility was shaken, but the Romans responded vigorously, broke up the other attacks, and killed the "rebel" leaders; Caesar completed the winter by raising his forces to ten legions. In the spring of 53 he concluded a campaign against the last Gauls—it seemed—to hold out. Caesar conducted a formal inquiry into the situation in Gaul and a seditious chieftain was scourged and beheaded.

During the winter the Gauls united behind Vercingetorix, the newly chosen king of the Arverni. Vercingetorix planned to secure central Gaul by defending the mountain passes and then to strike at the Romans before Caesar could collect his troops from their winter quarters. Caesar repelled the attacking force, broke into the homeland of Vercingetorix himself, drew Vercingetorix there, marched to his two legions in winter quarters among the Lingones, reunited his army despite the Gauls' best efforts, and replaced his absent Gallic cavalry with German mercenaries. Then Caesar set out in pursuit of Vercingetorix.

Vercingetorix hoped to draw Caesar after him, deep into the heart of Gaul, to deprive him of supplies and then to destroy him in a campaign of movement, but Caesar attacked Avaricum (one of the most beautiful and important towns in Gaul), and the Gauls refused to obey Vercingetorix's order to abandon it. The Gauls were still convinced that élan, courage, and individual prowess could defeat the Romans, but the Romans (in twenty-five days) threw up a terrace (330 feet by 8) equal to the top of the walls of Avaricum. They drove the defenders from the walls, the Gauls panicked, dropped their weapons, and ran for the gates; of the original garrison of 40,000, only 800 escaped.

Vercingetorix's hopes were dashed: he could not control the other tribes, his cavalry was far inferior to Caesar's Germans, and he had failed to cut off Caesar's supplies. He determined to win or lose the war in one great battle—to retreat to the stronghold of Alesia and there accept a siege which, he hoped, would fix Caesar while a Gallic host gathered around him. Caesar accepted the challenge. His troops constructed double walls around Alesia, and when the Gallic host—according to Caesar 250,000 infantry and 8,000 cavalry—did gather, they found themselves facing a well-constructed Roman fortification that thwarted their first, ill-coordinated attacks.

The struggle for Gaul's independence came down to this one last trial of strength which culminated in a coordinated attack from both sides on as many points of the Roman line as possible. The Romans were stretched as thin as could be and, as they fought, they could hear their fellow soldiers fighting behind them. Only their confidence in each other, and in Caesar, kept them from losing their nerve. Caesar from his observation point dispatched units to the greatest points of danger. At last the Gauls lifted their general assault and concentrated on one portion of the walls. Three times Caesar sent reinforcements, and the last time he led the troops in person. When Caesar broke the attack from outside the fortification, the Gauls inside lost hope and returned to Alesia.

Then "Vercingetorix selected the best of his arms and armor, he groomed his horse, rode out through the gates, and rode in a circle once around the place where Caesar was seated and he leaped down from his horse, tore off all of his equipment, seated himself at the feet of Caesar, and offered no resistance as he was taken into captivity to adorn Caesar's triumph."

In the ensuing winter and following year Caesar broke the final Gallic resistance. An ancient writer summed up Caesar's conquest: "Of the 3,000,000 inhabitants of Gaul, Caesar killed one million, enslaved another million, and pacified the last million."

Meanwhile, in Rome the Senate voted that Caesar must lay down his command or be declared a public enemy. When Caesar refused, the Senate turned to Pompey. Pompey had stated that he need only stamp his foot, and ten legions would spring from the ground, but Caesar had one legion ready to march, and on 11 January 49 B.C. Caesar ordered his troops to cross the Rubicon River (the boundary of his province) in contravention of Roman law. He seized control of the passes into central Italy, and—although he was unable to prevent Pompey from transporting the recruits he had raised to Greece (where the recruits could be organized and trained)—on 25 January, Caesar held Rome.

He took possession of the treasury (which the Pompeians had not had time to remove), and he reconstituted the government; henceforward he claimed to be acting for the Senate and People of Rome. He granted citizenship to the whole of Cisalpine Gaul, which at once gave him a recruiting ground and a block of citizens personally loyal to him. Caesar secured Italy, he appointed a successor in Gaul, and, while he was waiting for a fleet to be collected to transport his army to Greece, he undertook a campaign against Pompey's troops in Spain.

Pompey's commanders in Spain agreed that two of them with a combined force of five of the seven available legions plus eighty cohorts of auxiliaries, and about 5,000 Spanish cavalry, would await Caesar north of the Ebro River, in the vicinity of Ilerda (see diagram, p. 220). Ilerda, a fortified town on a height on the western bank of the Sicoris River—where the rivers Cinga and Sicoris divide the terrain as they flow south to the Ebro—commanded a stone bridge over the Sicoris and dominated another height nearby; there the Pompeians placed their camp. There they intended to hold Caesar until Pompey could join his forces to theirs, and the combined army could mass against Caesar.

Caesar assumed command of his advance force of six legions and 6,000 Gallic cavalry (3,000 veterans and 3,000 recruits) on 23 May 49 B.C. and immediately seized the initiative. As the Pompeians planned to use the river as a barrier against Caesar, so he saw that it could as easily be used against them. He let his Gallic cavalry loose on the east bank, while he led his army over his newly constructed bridges directly to the Pompeian camp on the west bank. The Pompeians refused to meet him in battle—they had everything to lose and little to gain—and so he set his third line, screened by the first two, to work digging a trench, fifteen feet broad, with the earth mounded behind it. Ordinarily the Romans would have put in a palisade, but this time Caesar could not do that because the Pompeians would have noticed it and immediately forced the issue. In the evening Caesar withdrew his force behind the trench. The trench was vulnerable to attack, and the troops had to stand under arms all night. The next day Caesar drew up three legions behind the trench and set the other three legions, one legion to a side, to complete the entrenchments. Now the Pompeians did offer battle, but Caesar refused it, and on the third day he completed the camp. Caesar's legions had cut the Pompeians off from the west, and Caesar's cavalry had gained the ascendancy on the east bank.

Then, suddenly and unexpectedly, a heavy rainstorm, combined with melting snow, flooded the Sicoris and the Cinga, swept away Caesar's bridges, flooded his camp, and marooned him and most of his cavalry between the rivers. He was cut off from food and from his allies, while the Pompeians still had access to the eastern bank over the bridge at Ilerda. They meant to keep Caesar isolated. When the flood waters receded, the Pompeians guarded the bridge sites, but Caesar had his men construct light boats and in the night transport them twenty miles upriver to a suitable site; he put enough men across the river to build a fort on an adjoining hill before the Pompeians discovered his move. Once he had secured the bridgehead, he transferred a full legion across to the fort, and in two days completed the bridge (11 June 49). So quickly did his men complete the work that Caesar got his cavalry across before the Pompeians realized the bridge was finished. Caesar's cavalry terrified the Pompeians to the point that they would drop whatever forage they had collected and run at the first sight of a horse. The neighboring Spanish tribes, sensing the shift of power, switched their support to Caesar; the Pompeians found themselves increasingly isolated.

When Caesar began work on a ford near Ilerda (by digging channels to divert the river and lower its depth), the Pompeians decided to cut their losses, withdraw, and join the other Pompeian forces south of the Ebro. Once they had made the decision, they wasted no time—they marshalled their forces, crossed the stone bridge to the east bank, and began their march south. Caesar's cavalry attacked the Pompeian rear guard. At times it cut off the rear guard and forced it to form up in battleline. If the rear guard counterattacked, the cavalry fled to safety, but, as soon as the rearguard rejoined the main body, the cavalry reformed and renewed the attack.

The slow advance of the Pompeians was noticed in Caesar's camp. Caesar's troops, veterans all, understood the situation and demanded of their centurions that they be allowed to cross the river (where the water still came up to their chests) and pursue the Pompeians. Caesar acceded to their wishes, led them across, and they caught up to the Pompeian army in midafternoon. The Pompeian commanders were appalled—they were just five miles from the mountains, two hours (unopposed) march to terrain where cavalry could not operate, but their troops were too exhausted to continue, and they encamped.

That night Caesar's cavalry foiled an attempted breakout, and the Pompeians took a day to rest and reconnoitre; on the following day the Pompeians abandoned their baggage (and the few cohorts appointed to guard it) and set out for the mountains—if they did escape, it would be with their individual arms and rations, no more. The Pompeians had a direct route to safety, Caesar a circuitous route to block them, but Caesar's cavalry attacks forced the Pompeian commanders to abort their advance and seek refuge on an isolated hill. Four of their cohorts were wiped out in a futile attempt to reach the foothills.

Suddenly Caesar was confronted with an unexpected situation. All the experienced men in his army, the legates, tribunes, and centurions, saw that the Pompeians were caving in. They had not gone to the rescue of their four cohorts, they were not moving from the hill, they were not keeping their ranks or legion integrity, and they could hardly beat off the cavalry attacks. Caesar's subordinates were sure of victory, they were ready to fight, and, almost certainly, their assessment was correct, but Caesar made a risky and courageous decision—to destroy the Pompeian army without fighting a battle. As he wrote, "It is the duty of a general to win as much by planning as by fighting"; true words, but military history is filled with generals who lost opportunities because they did not seize the moment.

Caesar allowed the Pompeians to recover their camp. There, he believed, in not so long a time, his complete domination of the field would induce the Pompeians (unable—except when they led out their whole army—to forage or fetch water) to capitulate. The Pompeian commanders, however, undertook the construction of ramparts all the way from their camp to the water. Their tenacity was not shared by their troops and centurions, and the centurions met with Caesar's centurions to negotiate terms of capitulation. Some of Caesar's centurions crossed to the Pompeian camp and stated the terms of capitulation Caesar offered—to discharge all Pompeians who wished, to enlist all volunteers on the same terms as his own men, and to allow the centurions who came over to keep their rank. A number of the centurions accepted on the spot, and the centurions of both camps were working out details when the Pompeian commanders learned of the negotiations, returned to the camp, and executed those of Caesar's soldiers they could catch. They required their men to swear a new oath of loyalty, and they decided to return to Ilerda, but an attempted subterfuge failed, and they could not fight their way through Caesar's cavalry. They offered battle, but Caesar refused. When Caesar began to encircle them with siege works, the Pompeian commanders admitted that they were beaten.

The Pompeian army capitulated on 2 July 49 B.C. and Caesar returned to Italy. The victory of Ilerda and another victory at Massilia guaranteed the security of Italy, but Caesar still needed to defeat Pompey in Greece. Caesar collected transport, caught a favorable wind, eluded Pompey's fleet, and crossed to Greece with seven legions. Pompey had nine legions—with two more marching to him from Syria—36,000 men, 3,000 archers, 1,200 slingers, 7,000 cavalry, and about 300 ships, and he had the greater logistical resources, but Caesar had a veteran army used to his style and imbued with the conviction that they could not be beaten.

Pompey had fortified a position along the coast south of Dyrrhachium, thus securing his resupply by sea. Caesar interposed his army between Dyrrhachium and Pompey and set about investing Pompey's army with his own, smaller army. The two sides raced to occupy and fortify the hills—Caesar to close Pompey in, Pompey to force Caesar to spread his forces out as thinly as possible—and then to connect the hill forts with walls. Pompey built twenty-four forts and enclosed an area large enough to graze animals. Caesar had to construct trenches and walls fifteen miles long, that is, about one legion for every two miles. Each construction put his men in extreme danger as Pompey would occupy an adjacent hill with archers, slingers, light-armed troops, and artillery.

Caesar's troops had to fight and build at the same time. If Pompey could bring enough force to bear, he would assault their position. Attack provoked counterattack, and Caesar's troops were fighting continuously, they were outnumbered, and their supplies ran short, but their morale was high because they were working for victory, and they considered that they had the moral edge over their more numerous opponent, who avoided open battle. Caesar's soldiers on sentry duty called to Pompey's troops that they would sooner eat the bark from the trees than let Pompey slip from their hands. Deserters brought the news to Caesar that Pompey's horses were at the point of death, the rest of the animals were being slaughtered, and the men were not in good health because of the confined space, the noxious odor of rotting corpses, and the daily labor of those unaccustomed to labor, and—since Caesar had diverted or dammed all the rivers and streams that made their way to the sea through Pompey's zone—they were affected by lack of water.

As the siege worked its effects on Pompey's army, Pompey ordered a general attack all along the line. Six battles were fought in one day, three at Dyrrhachium, three along the line of fortifications. Pompey lost some 2,000 men, many centurions, and six military standards. Caesar lost only twenty men, but in one fort every man was wounded, four centurions in one cohort lost an eye, 30,000 arrows were fixed in the fort, and the shield of one centurion had 120 holes in it. Pompey's situation continued to worsen until two Gallic deserters brought to him the complete details of Caesar's dispositions, commanders, and units and revealed that the lower end of Caesar's line of fortifications had not been completed. Pompey sent sixty cohorts by land and sea in a dawn attack on the exposed fortifications. He drove Caesar's troops back, and only Caesar's personal intervention saved the situation. Caesar's counterattack failed, and he decided to break contact and march inland.

Pompey believed that his victory had infused his men with enough confidence to fight Caesar, he took the title *imperator*, and he set out in pursuit of Caesar. The two armies met in battle at Phar̄ ̠̠̠ on (by the Roman calendar) 6 June 48 B.C. Pompey anchored his right on a river and stationed himself on the left with two legions and all his cavalry, archers, and slingers. Caesar estimated Pompey's forces at 45,000 men. Caesar put his tenth legion on his right and his ninth legion, combined with the eighth, on his left. He had eighty cohorts (22,000 men) drawn up in line. He left two cohorts as a garrison for his camp. His commander on the left wing was Antonius. When Caesar had reconnoitred the enemy, he drew individual cohorts from his third line and formed a fourth line to prevent Pompey from outflanking him.

When the two sides had advanced just so far apart, Caesar's troops charged, but Pompey's did not move. Pompey had given the order to his men to await Caesar's charge. He expected that Caesar's troops would wind themselves by running all the way, and their line would be dispersed, but when they saw that the Pompeians were not running to meet them, they halted (being veterans), caught their breath, and then charged anew, threw their pila, and drew their swords. The Pompeians did not hold back: they received the thrown pila, threw their own pila, drew their own swords, met the charge of Caesar's legions, and fought hand to hand.

Pompey's massed archers poured out a cloud of arrows, his cavalry charged, they forced Caesar's cavalry to give ground, and then they broke through. Now they would have fallen on Caesar's flank, but his "fourth" line attacked so fiercely that they routed Pompey's cavalry, slaughtered Pompey's light-armed skirmishers, and fell upon the rear of Pompey's legions. At the same time Caesar ordered his third line, which had remained in reserve, to advance. These fresh troops and the troops in the rear broke the Pompeians. Caesar estimated that as many as 15,000 Pompeians were killed and more than 24,000 taken prisoner.

Pompey escaped on horseback, found a ship, and fled to Egypt, where he thought he might find a small Roman force. The Egyptians, however, persuaded by the dictum *dead men do not bite,* murdered him. Three days later Caesar arrived in Alexandria (early autumn 48 B.C.) with two under-strength legions. Pompey was dead, but his followers were determined to continue the war. Caesar soon became embroiled in a civil war in Alexandria between Ptolemy XII and Cleopatra, a brother and sister, for the throne of Egypt. He had to hold out on the island of the lighthouse Pharos until help could arrive. Then he defeated Ptolemy and established Cleopatra on the throne. She named their son Caesarion.

After he settled affairs in Egypt, he returned to Italy. His troops demanded their discharge, land, and a bonus. He faced them down and convinced them that the wars were not over. He had to defeat the ten legions and 15,000 cavalry of the Pompeian rebels in the province of Africa and their chief ally, the Numidian king Juba, who had formed 30,000 men into four "Roman" legions. In early October 47 Caesar risked autumnal storms to get his force of ten legions (five veteran, five recruit), 4,000 cavalry, and 3,000 light-armed troops to Africa.

Storms scattered his fleet. He landed at Hadrumentum with only 3,000 infantry and 150 cavalry, he occupied the harbor of Leptis and slowly gathered in his stragglers until he had raised his strength to eight legions (three veteran). His opponents had missed their opportunity to crush him while he was weak, and now he set fire to his camp and moved on his enemy's principal supply depot, Thapsus.

The Pompeians had to fight to protect their base. Caesar's troops wanted to fight despite his orders to hold their ground and they forced "a trumpeter to give the signal to charge and all the cohorts began to carry their standards forward towards the enemy, while the centurions, standing chest to chest with them, tried to stop them and hold the troops, so that they would not attack without the orders of their commander." Caesar let them go, they drove the enemy in panic before them, and Caesar cleared Africa.

He returned to Italy to put his affairs in order there, but then he heard that Pompey's son, Pompey the Younger, had organized resistance in Spain—he had gained control of the Baetis valley, but he had neither the troops nor the money necessary to defend it, and his brutal treatment of his troops turned even Pompey's old supporters against him. In the end Pompey the Younger made a stand at Munda on the slope of a hill. Once again Caesar's troops took matters into their own hands and charged up the hill without orders. The tenth legion on the right, although understrength, pushed back the enemy opposite them. Caesar's troops, in particular, his cavalry, were making such an aggressive attack upon the Younger Pompey that he could not support his left, and it broke. Then the whole enemy army broke and fled. Caesar attacked and eliminated the remnants of the Pompeian forces wherever they might be found, he granted Roman citizenship to those who had proved their loyalty to him, and he returned to Rome, the one dominant figure still alive.

The question for him was, how would he rule? He had been chosen *dictator* and *dictator for life*. Could he transform *dictator for life* into a permanent office? Would he insist on the title *king*? Would he try to leave his power to a successor? If so, who? And would his successor have the loyalty of the army? Many senators believed that he would kill the republic. Fewer, perhaps, believed that the republic could still be saved; they joined a conspiracy against him, and on the Ides of March 44 B.C. they struck him down.

Gaius Julius Caesar is considered the greatest Roman commander and one of the greatest captains of all time. Had accounts written by Scipio, Cato, Marius, Sulla, or Trajan, to name a few, survived, we might not be so quick to give Caesar primacy among Roman commanders. He used his army to the extent of its abilities, but he was not an innovator, and he never appreciated the power of cavalry. He is the epitome of the later republican commander who used his command to satisfy his own ambitions. (Satisfying those ambitions did add Gaul to the Roman Empire.) Julius Caesar is no Alexander, nor even Hannibal, but he is one in a long line of Roman commanders who knew how to get the job done.

# Map 22: Civil War Campaigns of Caesar

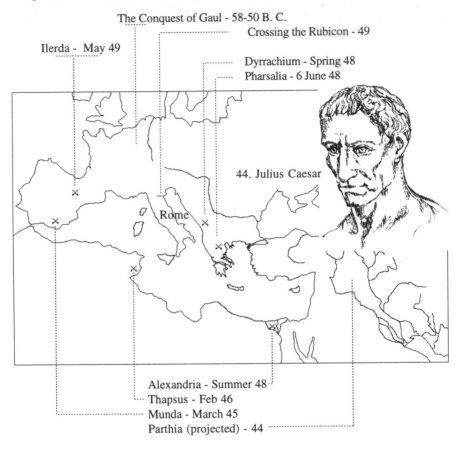

The Conquest of Gaul - 58-50 B. C.

Crossing the Rubicon - 49

Ilerda - May 49

Dyrrachium - Spring 48
Pharsalia - 6 June 48

44. Julius Caesar

Rome

Alexandria - Summer 48
Thapsus - Feb 46
Munda - March 45
Parthia (projected) - 44

DETAIL MAP OF THE ILERDA CAMPAIGN

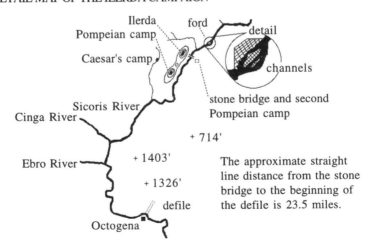

Ilerda
Pompeian camp
ford
detail

Caesar's camp

channels

stone bridge and second
Pompeian camp

Sicoris River
Cinga River

+ 714'

Ebro River

+ 1403'

+ 1326'

defile

Octogena

The approximate straight
line distance from the stone
bridge to the beginning of
the defile is 23.5 miles.

# Part Five
# The Roman Empire

The period of the Roman Empire is characterized by a sharp decline in extant descriptions of military affairs, while, at the same time, we have an increase in extant monuments and inscriptions, so that a greater knowledge of the inner workings of the Roman army and the appearance of the soldiers is balanced by a diminished knowledge of the campaigns and battles.

## 45. The Siege

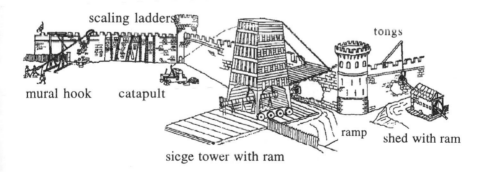

scaling ladders

tongs

mural hook    catapult

ramp    shed with ram

siege tower with ram

## Map 23: Sequence Maps of the Roman Empire

THE ROMAN EMPIRE IN THE TIME OF THE PRINCIPATE
(with the legion disposition of A.D. 23 marked by the symbol o).

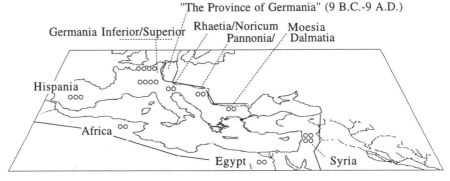

"The Province of Germania" (9 B.C.-9 A.D.)

THE ROMAN EMPIRE IN THE TIME OF TRAJAN
(with the legion disposition of A.D. 107 marked by the symbol o).
Trajan added the provinces of Dacia, Armenia, and Mesopotamia.

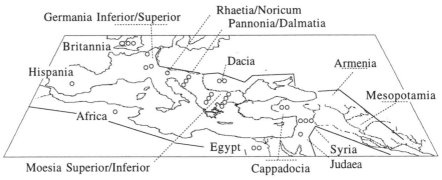

THE ROMAN EMPIRE IN THE TIME OF DIOCLETIAN

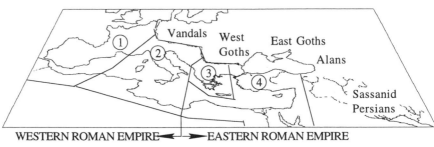

WESTERN ROMAN EMPIRE ◄─┼─► EASTERN ROMAN EMPIRE

1 Prefecture of Gaul - Dioceses: Britain, Gaul, Spain
2 Prefecture of Italy - Dioceses: Italy, City of Rome, Africa
3 Prefecture of Illyricum - Dioceses: Dacia, Macedonia
4 Prefecture of the East - Dioceses: Egypt, Thrace, Asia, Pontus, "The East"

# 29

# The Creation of the Empire
## *One Man's Ambition Supercedes All Others*

Julius Caesar was assassinated on the Ides of March (15 March) 44 B.C. His assassins, Cassius and Brutus, proclaimed their intention to restore the republic. They were too confident—they allowed Caesar's protégé, Marcus Antonius, to address the crowd; the ensuing riot drove the conspirators from Rome and established Antony as Caesar's avenger. Antony also expected that he would be Caesar's heir, in fact if not in law, but Caesar had posthumously adopted his great-nephew Octavius, then nineteen years old, and appointed him his heir and executor. (Because of the adoption, Octavius became Gaius Julius Caesar Octavianus; "Octavianus" is the adjectival form of the name "Octavius," but only his enemies—and modern historians—called him Octavian.) The new Caesar was warned by his family that he would be murdered if he accepted Caesar's legacy, but Octavian had the character, intelligence, and ambition of a Julius Caesar.

When Octavian arrived in Rome, Antony belittled his claims and refused to release Caesar's property. Octavian borrowed money to pay the promised legacies to Caesar's veterans and so won their loyalty, first by discharging his obligation to them but second, and more importantly, as the "son" of their beloved commander; Octavian never failed them. With the support of the veterans, he won allies in the Senate, the Senate declared Antony an outlaw, and it appointed Octavian to the command of the army that was to destroy that outlaw. Some senators believed that once Octavian had rid them of Antony, they could be rid of Octavian. Instead, once he had driven Antony to the brink of destruction, he struck a deal with him, and the two of them agreed to a partnership to assume control of Rome and to eliminate the conspirators who had assassinated Caesar. The senators who had thought to use Octavian had to flee for their lives.

On the first of January in the year 42 B.C. the Senate officially accepted the portends and declared that Julius Caesar had become a god. The young "Julius

Caesar" issued coins on which he asserted the divinity of his "father" and depicted himself bearded—he had sworn that he would not shave until he had avenged his "father's" death, but he had almost no military experience, and he had to depend upon Antony to conduct the operations. Caesar Octavian and Antony (with twenty-eight legions) brought Cassius and Brutus to bay in the vicinity of Philippi in northern Greece, where the two assassins had established their camps close to the sea along the via Egnatia and within easy communication of each other. As Brutus raided Octavian's camp (and slaughtered a detachment of 5,000 Spartans who had just arrived), Antony routed Cassius and plundered his camp; Cassius despaired needlessly and committed suicide. Brutus assumed command of all the troops, but he found his grip on the loyalty of his soldiers beginning to slip, and so he determined to fight as soon as possible. In late October 42 B.C. he was defeated at the battle of Philippi. He too committed suicide.

Antony and Octavian had attained hegemony over a divided, impoverished, and confused domain. Antony, now the senior partner, claimed what he believed to be the greater spoils: the Greek-speaking east and Gaul; he left Italy and the west to Octavian and so, too, the problem of reducing the army and finding land for the discharged veterans. Antony took the bulk of the army and turned to the east, where he intended to humble, if not conquer, Parthia, and avenge the defeat of Crassus, but in 41 B.C. his plans went awry. He met Cleopatra, he became infatuated with her, and within a few years, he discarded his wife, the sister of Caesar Octavian, and married Cleopatra (in 37).

Octavian, meanwhile, took the west in hand; he confiscated the land of his opponents (and supporters of Antony) and distributed it among the veterans, so that he won their loyalty and scattered his enemies. Then he launched a propaganda campaign by which he convinced Italians that Antony was the tool of an Eastern despot, a queen, a woman, Cleopatra, who now ruled Antony and expected soon to rule Rome. The result, Caesar Octavian wrote, was that "the whole of Italy voluntarily took an oath of allegiance to me and demanded that I command in the war."

Octavian met Antony at Actium in 31 B.C. to fight the battle that would decide the leadership of the Roman world, but the issue had already been decided: Antony's army and navy deserted to Octavian, Cleopatra ordered her flagship to flee, and Antony followed her. Caesar Octavian pursued Antony to Egypt, Octavian rejected Antony's offer to meet in single combat for the rule of the empire, and Antony committed suicide, Cleopatra committed suicide, and Octavian was the sole master of the Roman world.

"I had about 500,000 Roman citizens under military oath to me. I settled about 300,000 in colonies or I returned them to their own communities, and I allotted land or I paid money to everyone of them as a reward for military service." In all he paid out over 1 billion sesterces to settle the veterans, and he established—as the Senate should have done a century before—a soldiers' fund to provide retirement benefits for soldiers who had completed their service. He established a standing army of twenty-eight legions and he set the terms of service at twenty years for the legions, sixteen for the Praetorian Guard. Octavian opened a military career path for young men of good families, to enter service as military tribunes and eventually rise to command a legion.

Octavian's new regular army also regularized the centurions' path of promotion. Although some centurions were appointed directly from the equestrian class by Octavian, most centurions rose from the ranks and then were promoted to the different centurion posts in the legion or to a more senior position in another legion. Those who rose from the ranks to the highest position, the *primus pilus,* could receive equestrian status, move on to a provincial career, to command in Egypt or in the Praetorian Guard, rise in the financial service, and set a son on a senatorial track.

Octavian understood that he was the master of Rome because he was the master of the armies, but if he did not want to live his life surrounded by conspiracies against him, he had to find a way to appease the Senatorial class. In 27 B.C., "when I had the greatest power and I received accolades everywhere, I refounded the republic. The Senate decreed that I be given the title *Augustus.* The people decreed that my person be sacrosanct and that I possess the tribunician power for life. From then on I had no more power than anyone else, except that I was first in moral authority."

Augustus (as he was now called) had identified the two essential powers, the *tribunician power,* which protected his person and gave him the right to intercede in state business, and the *greater imperium* in the provinces, which meant the power to command the armies of Rome. He designated his successors by conferring these two powers on them (although, one by one, they all died except for his very last choice, his adoptive son, Tiberius).

By and large Augustus ruled in peace—"The temple of Janus, which our ancestors would close whenever the whole of the Roman Empire was at peace, and which before I was born was closed only twice since the founding of the city, during my lifetime was ordered by the Senate to be closed three times"—but in 19 B.C. the Iberian tribes in "Baetic Spain," once more, rose in revolt. Augustus gave orders to an expeditionary force to destroy any construction that could be used as a fort, to disarm the whole population, and to execute every man of military age. The three-year campaign transformed Baetic Spain into another Italy: men lived in cities, they wore the toga, they spoke Latin; the campaign became a paradigm for Roman brutality—"they make a desert and call it peace."

Augustus sought stability within and without the empire. He estimated that the empire could afford and could be protected by twenty-eight legions. He used diplomacy to establish a secure border with the Parthians and to recover the eagles captured from Crassus. He authorized a campaign to pacify the Illyrians (a people within the Rhine-Danube line of defense) and another to pacify the Germans between the Rhine and the Elbe River (a better defensive line).

During the years 12–9 B.C. Augustus's stepson, Tiberius, conducted a series of lightning campaigns in Illyria, he overawed the Illyrian tribes, and he forced them to capitulate. When he declared the area pacified, Augustus sent him to complete the pacification of Germany. Tiberius conducted a flawless campaign, he defeated the separate tribes of Germans, one by one, and his army of twelve legions was converging from three different directions on the last independent German king, Maroboduus, when Tiberius learned that Illyria had risen in revolt. Tiberius immediately struck a deal with Maroboduus—the German was recognized as king and a friend of the Roman people—and then Tiberius turned back with his army towards Illyria.

Tiberius conceived the perfect strategy: first, he contained the rebellion—he blocked the passages out of Illyria, protected bordering provinces, and isolated the rebels—second, he ravaged the Illyrian land, destroyed the crops, and brought the rebels to the brink of starvation; third, he forced battle on them. The battle was close, but the Romans won, and the victory gave Tiberius the power to split the Illyrians and to compel them, district by district, to surrender. Tiberius had to pull legions from all over the empire to put down the revolt, but Augustus's twenty–eight legions proved sufficent to do this job and still protect the security of the empire.

In other areas of the empire Augustus established the fundamental principles of control that his successors would employ: in Africa, for instance, he placed Roman settlements within provincial cities, he settled veterans in colonies (eleven colonies in one vassal state) to guard the frontier and to romanize the inhabitants, he constructed frontier fortifications, he build aqueducts and, in the end, he brought about an empire-wide prosperity (and made Africa the breadbasket of Rome).

In Egypt in 29 B.C. he appointed Cornelius Gallus governor with command of one legion quartered near Alexandria. The governor had to solve the many problems of Egypt, a complicated tax system (with a head tax, trade licenses, the corvée, and corrupt tax farmers), the requirement to find land for veterans, confiscations of religious property, fines for impropriety (a priest could be fined for neglecting his hair cut), and the gradations of class as defined by the *ideologue:* Egyptians had to register as members of different classes (it was illegal, for instance, for a non-Greek to take a Greek name). The governor cleared the channels of the Nile, raised agricultural production so that Egypt regularly furnished Italy with one-third of its required grain supply, put down two revolts and a riot, and stabilized the southern border.

Cornelius Gallus was a first-rate governor, who in the days of the republic would have returned to Rome a wealthy and powerful man, but not under the Augustan "republic"—Gallus returned to stand trial for treason; Augustus declared him guilty, confiscated his estates, and banished him. The ambition of the emperor, and only of the emperor, would now define Roman foreign policy.

Augustus was determined—despite the Illyrian revolt—to pacify the German tribes between the Rhine and the Elbe. Many Germans served in the legions, learned Latin, and seemed romanized. The most trusted of them, a German prince named Arminius, convinced Augustus's legate Varus to follow him into the

Teutoburg Forest to put down an uprising of the last unpacified Germans in the area. Arminius led Varus and his three legions into an ambush. The Germans had prepared the kill zone by sawing through trees; they pushed the trees over on the marching troops, broke from cover, and massacred them.

Augustus wandered through his palace for days, crying out in agony, "Varus, give me back my three legions," and then, once again, Augustus sent his adopted son, Tiberius (in command of eight legions), to put out the fire. Tiberius this time (A.D. 10–12) had the most formidable task—he had no trustworthy allies across the Rhine and no bases. Tiberius crossed the Rhine and ravaged the adjacent German land, but after he had made a good start, Augustus sent his nephew Germanicus to supersede Tiberius. Germanicus apparently planned to attack the smaller tribes in the German confederation first and, in particular, to concentrate on those tribes which had acquired a Roman eagle from the ambushed legions. Before Germanicus could carry out his plans, Augustus died, in A.D. 14.

Augustus transformed the Roman state. He created an imperial family at the head of an imperial system, but one consonant with Roman institutions and sensibilities, he created a professional army under the control of the imperial family, he achieved a balanced budget, and he promoted policies which made the empire prosperous. At his death a census recorded almost 5 million Roman citizens, an increase of 1 million in the years after Actium.

The emperors who succeeded Augustus—Tiberius (14–37), Caligula (37–41), Claudius (41–54), and Nero (54–68)—were descendants of his family and so are called the Julio-Claudians. By and large they preserved the borders Augustus had established, they held the size of the army to Augustus's limits, and they accommodated their neighbors. They maintained the fiction invented by Augustus that each presided over a republic as the first citizen, the *princeps* (and so the early empire is called the principate). The Julio-Claudians defined the relationship of emperor and Senate and emperor and empire. They limited the Senate to a role as junior partner at best. They established that the inhabitants of the empire were to show their loyalty to Rome by showing their loyalty to the cult of the emperor. The emperor was the commander-in-chief of army, people, and Senate.

The first successor, Tiberius, allowed Germanicus to continue the campaign against the Germans, but before Germanicus could lead his army across the Rhine, the army mutinied in protest against the brutal conditions of service. (One centurion had the nickname "Get Another"—after he would break a rod over the back of a soldier, he would say, "Get another.") Germanicus put the mutiny down and led the army into Germany. He buried the remains of Varus's army, he defeated the lesser German tribes, he recovered two eagles, and he brought the main German tribe to battle, but he could not defeat these Germans, and he had to withdraw back across the Rhine. In the next year (A.D. 16) Germanicus again led his army into German territory and fought two battles, but again he could not deliver a decisive defeat to the Germans, and again he had to retreat across the Rhine. Tiberius concluded that the effort required to subdue the Germans—

fighting constantly without any allies, building and manning forts, laying and maintaining roads—was all out of proportion to the gains. Germanicus had recovered the eagles; he had punished the Germans; he had done enough to restore Roman prestige.

Germanicus had proved his right to succeed Tiberius, but he died in suspicious circumstances, and Tiberus grew disillusioned with his own position; he withdrew from Rome and left the day-to-day administration of the empire in the hands of his praetorian prefect. Almost too late he recognized that this praetorian prefect intended to become emperor himself or, at least, to see his son become emperor. Tiberius saved himself by executing the prefect. (Future emperors would face similar problems with their own praetorian prefects and the praetorian guard.)

Tiberius's successor, Caligula, unbalanced, if not insane, tore down the facade of the principate to reveal that the emperor had all the power, and the Senate had none. He had his horse appointed consul; he executed senators without trial; he ordered the army to muster on the shore opposite Britain, and he gave the command "Gather seashells." His position was invulnerable, but his person was not. He was murdered, and in the ensuing riots the praetorian guard found Caligula's uncle, Claudius, hiding behind a curtain, took him to their camp, and there hailed him emperor.

In 43 Claudius led 50,000 troops in an invasion of Britain. He found allies, the legions performed admirably, and the conquest proceeded apace. Claudius, gimpy-legged, ill-coordinated, and not young, arranged somehow to kill the British chieftain in single combat and thus become one of the few Romans ever to win the *spolia opima* (awarded to a Roman commander who kills the enemy commander in single combat). Claudius and his successor Nero expanded the empire to stabilize their borders, to complete the plans of their predecessors (Julius Caesar in Britain), and to enclose the Mediterranean. Nero had to solve the tricky problem of Armenia. A Roman emperor could not accept a Parthian Armenia, a threat to Asia Minor and Syria; the Parthian king could not accept a Roman Armenia, a threat to Mesopotamia. Nero's general Corbulo (in 55–61) drove the Armenian king, supported by the Parthians, from his throne. By 61 Corbulo had convinced the Parthians to agree to a compromise—the Parthian king could choose the candidate for the Armenian throne, but that individual then would have to travel to Rome, where he accepted Roman suzerainty in exchange for his crown. This compromise kept the peace between Rome and Parthia until 115.

Nero showed little interest in the administration of the empire. He never visited his armies, he did nothing to win their loyalty, and the rumors about his character earned their contempt. Opponents arose, in 68 the legions on the Rhine rebelled, and Nero thought an appropriate response was to take some flute girls, run up to the Rhine, and quell the rebellion by singing to the soldiers. Instead he died in a hut outside Rome, a fugitive, alone except for one slave whose hand helped plunge a dagger into Nero's throat—the last descendant of Augustus.

The praetorian guard chose Galba as their emperor, but when they did not get the large payoff he had promised, they lynched him and chose another candidate, Otho. Meanwhile the legions on the Rhine proclaimed their own emperor, their commander, Vitellius. His army crossed the Alps and defeated the forces of Otho, who committed suicide. Vitellius entered Rome and proceeded to outrage his own soldiers by spending on himself the bonuses he had promised to them, and he outraged soldiers everywhere by executing the centurions of Otho's army.

A general in the east, Vespasian, who had been given command against a Jewish uprising—Nero had given him the command in 66 because he thought he was not intelligent or ambitious enough to be a potential rival—suspended operations against the Jews while the situation in Rome was in flux. When the prefect of Egypt and the governor of Syria declared for Vespasian, he allowed his troops to acclaim him emperor. Vespasian stopped the grain shipments from Egypt to Rome to increase the pressure on Vitellius, and he prepared for a march on Italy, but before he could act, the legions on the Danube declared for him, marched on Italy without his orders, and defeated Vitellius's troops at Cremona. (Neither Vitellius nor any of his senior officers were present at the battle.) The governors of the provinces of the western empire declared for Vespasian. Vitellius, isolated in Rome, wanted to negotiate with Vespasian, but his praetorian guard—all too conscious of their role in this debacle—would not let him; the Danube legions broke into Rome, annihilated the guard, and lynched Vitellius. The secret of the empire was secret no more—the man who ruled the army ruled the empire.

Vespasian established the Flavian dynasty—himself (69–79) and his two sons, Titus (79–81) and Domitian (81–96). He faced two immediate problems: first, the treasury was empty, and, second, the Jews were in revolt. As to the first, he practiced personal frugality, itemized every expense, and found new sources of revenue. As to the second, once Vespasian felt himself to be in firm control of the government, he ordered his son Titus to suppress the insurrection. The campaign included two notable sieges, Masada and Jerusalem. Masada is more famous because the site seemed to be impregnable, because the Romans spent so much effort on it, and because it is so well preserved. Jerusalem, however, was the more important siege. Titus spent six months investing Jerusalem before he broke in. The fighting continued within the city, and Jerusalem was largely destroyed. The surviving population was sold into slavery. The Judean council was abolished. The temple was razed. A legion was stationed in Jerusalem. Titus returned to Rome to hold a triumph and then to assume sole command of the reconstituted praetorian guard, the immediate support—or otherwise—of the emperor. Titus had the complete loyalty of the guard, and so did Vespasian.

A Jewish writer of this time, who threw his fortunes in with Vespasian, has left us a description of the Roman army as he knew it; "The infantry have a breastplate, a helmet, and two swords, one on each side. The sword on the left is much longer than the one on the right, which is about nine inches long. The commander's personal guards have a shield and a heavy spear. The rest of the legions carry the pilum and a large shield. In addition to these, they also carry a saw, a basket, a pick and axe, a strap, a sickle, a chain and three days rations."

By the time Vespasian died, he had restored the sound financial basis of the empire, restored the close relationship of the emperor and the army, and given the empire a sound administration. His older son, Titus, ruled for two years. His younger son, Domitian, ruled for fifteen years. Domitian introduced the imperial title, *dominus et deus* (master and god). The emperor, indeed, was the master. Under Domitian the Roman general Gnaeus Julius Agricola completed the conquest of the region of Wales, invaded Scotland, sent an exploratory fleet to Ireland, and circumnavigated Britain as the last step to the complete conquest of Britain. Agricola could be called the "father of Roman Britain," not just because of his conquests, but more because he established the administration of the province and convinced the native leaders of the superiority and desirability of the Roman way of life. From that time forward the Britons rapidly became romanized. In the republic Agricola's success would have won him a triumph; under Domitian it earned him the emperor's suspicion; Domitian recalled Agricola in A.D. 84.

Domitian had other problems. Although the Rhine defenses were firmly established, and the Flavians had solidified the frontier (the *limes*) by adding forts and watchtowers to a wall gradually being extended around the whole of the Roman Empire, the Suebi broke into Rhaetia on a raiding expedition, and a band of Roxolani armored horsemen crossed the frozen Danube on a raid. The Romans reacted quickly, caught the Roxolani as the frozen ground thawed and turned to mud, and annihilated them. The Suebi, the Roxolani, other Germans, and the Dacians were reacting to the movement of a people from the eastern steppes unknown to the Romans, the Alans. The Alans had invaded Parthia. (The Parthian king asked Vespasian to help in the war against these people, but Vespasian fortified his borders and declined.)

A new Dacian king, Decebalus, used the threat of the Alans to unite the whole of Dacia behind him; he raised a national army; and he trained it in Roman fashion. In A.D. 86 he crossed the Danube. Domitian sent two expeditions, which invaded Dacia and defeated Decebalus. Domitian himself had to take command of a campaign against a coalition of German tribes along the Rhine, which may have been incited by Decebalus or perhaps just by his example. Domitian was able to hold the line of the Rhine by force, but he held the Danube by agreeing to recognize Decebalus as king of Dacia and by paying him a subvention; in return, Decebalus acknowledged that he was a vassal of the Roman emperor. Domitian built and manned massive fortifications along the Danube.

In 96 Domitian—"No one will believe there are conspiracies against me until one succeeds"—was murdered in his bedroom. The Senate chose his successor, an aged, childless senator named Nerva. Nerva solidified his position by naming as his heir the commander of the army of the Upper Rhine—Trajan.

# 30

# The Army of Trajan

## *An Emperor Conquers New Territory*

In the winter of 97 Nerva formally adopted Trajan as his heir and successor. Trajan was a Senator, he had served ten *stipendia* as military tribune, and he was the commander of the army of Upper Germany. He was in every way an admirable choice and well able to handle the problems he inherited upon the death of Nerva in A.D. 98. Rome's neighbors had grown used to the idea of a Rome on the defensive and Rome's principal enemy, Decebalus, king of the Dacians, thought he had taken the measure of the Roman emperor when he had compelled Domitian to recognize him and pay him a subsidy. Decebalus planned to unite all of Rome's enemies, including the Parthians, to act in concert against Rome.

The Dacians organized themselves, trained themselves, and armed themselves like the Romans except that they preferred a huge scythelike sword and heavily armored cavalry. They believed that the terrain of their homeland—mountain barriers and hills and forests made for ambush—would protect them. Decebalus had their complete loyalty and was an able man, but like so many rulers before him, he totally misread Roman abilities and intentions.

Trajan had added two legions to the twenty-eight of his predecessor (180,000 men), he had ten cohorts of the praetorian guard (5,000), four cohorts of the city guard of Rome (6,000), and some 300 auxiliary units (200,000); that is, he had something like 200,000 Roman citizens in regular units, and he had another 200,000 men, mixed citizen and foreigner (enlisted individually), in auxiliary units, for a total somewhere near 400,000 men under arms. His soldiers had been recruited in their late teens or their early twenties to serve an enlistment of twenty-five years (less in the elite units). His auxiliaries would be granted Roman citizenship upon the honorable completion of their tour (when their children were also granted Roman citizenship). Trajan could give whole units citizenship if they earned it on the battlefield. Some of his auxiliary units had a specialty as archers or slingers.

In addition Trajan began the practice of recruiting barbarian allies, who served together, divided into units of some 300 men under Roman officers, with their own equipment and organization. One of the key units of the campaign was cavalry from Mauretania, commanded by Trajan's friend, Lusius Quietus.

The legion of Trajan's time comprised (on paper) 6,000 men divided into ten cohorts, each cohort in turn comprising three maniples of two centuries each and the centuries, at least for the purpose of encampment, were divided into "tents" of eight men each. Each legion had a mounted force of 120 cavalry plus engineers, medical personnel, and supply personnel. The commander was a legate of senatorial rank, and he had a staff of five or six military tribunes. The cohorts were commanded by senior centurions (the highest position a man beginning in the ranks could expect to attain).

As far as manpower went, Trajan had an overwhelming advantage. He also had the organization to deliver that manpower to the area of operations and to supply it. His army excelled all other ancient armies in logistical support and engineering; his enemy was totally unable to appreciate or to duplicate the skills that made the Roman army superior.

Trajan crossed the Danube and launched the invasion of Dacia in A.D. 101. Of Trajan's written account of his campaign, one sentence survives, "We proceeded to Berzobim and then to Aizim," but fortunately he commissioned a monument, the column of Trajan (dedicated in A.D. 113), to commemorate the war. Scenes of the war are carved into the marble and curve in a ribbon about three feet high, twisting in twenty-three spirals around a column 100 feet high, comprising seventeen column drums; if unwound, the ribbon would be about 670 feet long. More than 2500 figures are found in the reliefs.

This graphic story begins with the spectator looking from the Dacian bank across the Danube to the Roman side in Moesia. He sees Roman watchtowers, material for fire signals, and Roman guards. In the next scenes he visits (from the same perspective) the town where the army has marshalled and sees Roman troops crossing the Danube by bridge to begin the invasion of Dacia (**46**).

Soon after crossing the Danube Trajan was brought a giant mushroom upon which was written the warning "Go back." Undaunted, he divided his army into three columns and he advanced into Dacia along the western approaches. As he forced the enemy back, and they destroyed whatever they thought he would need to sustain his campaign, Trajan constructed a network of forts, roads, and bridges to secure his supply line and ensure his logistical support (47).

He built roads (48):

The most formidable barrier to the advance of the Romans was the pass at Tapae known as the "Iron Gates" and there the first battle was fought. The battle was so fierce that Trajan tore his own clothes into strips for bandages. The Romans won **(49)**.

Trajan continued to advance and drive the Dacians before him **(50)**.

At the end of the first year Trajan took his troops into winter quarters. During the winter the Dacians raided the Roman positions (**51**).

He fought a cavalry battle (**52**).

In the spring of 102 Trajan began to advance by an eastern route. He divided his army into three columns as he advanced on the Dacian capital, Sarmizegethusa. His own mission was to capture the main forts guarding the approach while the other columns guarded his flanks and harried the enemy (**53**).

He broke down the last resistance with the help of his auxiliaries and in a number of skirmishes (**54**).

Once he had defeated the enemy and broken through, Decebalus capitulated.

Decebalus believed that the cost of the war had been so high that Trajan would never fight Dacians again, and he broke the accord. In June 105 Trajan began his second campaign against Decebalus. Decebalus tried to prevent Trajan's crossing the Danube by attacking the Roman positions along the river. Trajan defeated him, crossed the Danube, advanced on Sarmizegethusa from two sides, and laid siege to the Dacian capital (**55**).

Decebalus rallied for one last battle. He lost (**56**).

He tried to escape, was cornered, and committed suicide in 106.

The column's story ends with scenes of a skirmish under a farflung town, the entrance of veterans (who will colonize the area), the surrender and enslavement of the population, and finally free Dacians gathering up their belongings and fleeing before the Romans. The Dacian war was over. Dacia became a province of the Roman empire.

Trajan also added to the eastern limits of the Roman empire by annexing the territory of the Nabataean Arabs (who controlled the caravan routes). The new Parthian king, Chosroes, had decided to get rid of his nephew, the most likely rival for the throne, by sending him to supplant the king of Armenia. The Armenian king, who lost his throne, had had his crown conferred upon him by the Roman emperor. Now Trajan appeared with an army. He gave no hint that he did not accept the fait accompli, and the new king of Armenia offered to submit. When the king appeared in person before the emperor, Trajan declared him deposed, annexed Armenia, and advanced into Mesopotamia with his army and with one fleet on the Tigris River and another fleet on the Euphrates River. After taking Chosroes' capital, Ctesiphon-on-the-Tigris (Chosroes fled without resistance), Trajan continued down to the Persian Gulf. He divided Mesopotamia: he organized the region from Ctesiphon to the Gulf into a vassal kingdom under a dissident member of the Parthian royal family and he organized the rest into a Roman province. Trajan foresaw that Mesopotamia would be a troubled province and he appointed an able governor, but he did not foresee that he himself would die suddenly (A.D. 117) nor that his successor, Hadrian, would have other priorities. Hadrian abandoned the new province.

## 57. A Portrait of Trajan and a Detail from the Column of Trajan

"a soldier carries a basket ... and three days rations (p. 230)"

# 31

# The Ascendancy of the Army

## *Some Weak Emperors Contend With a Strong Army*

Trajan's successor, Hadrian (117–138), lived out his reign working for the inner unity of the empire by touring continuously and showing himself to all, civilians and soldiers, and by authorizing the construction of massive border fortifications (like the wall in Britain that bears his name) manned by well-trained professional soldiers. Hadrian's new walls were to delimit the empire, to check free passage, and to fix a line that, if crossed, meant war. His strategy was to stop any invasion before it could enter Roman territory, or, failing that, to deliver the nearest troops by way of the frontier road to the point of attack. He assigned the troops to the points where the greatest threats existed, but should those troops prove insufficient, the emperor had his personal guard and his authority to raise troops as he saw fit.

The frontier system was one part of a larger network administered by a central bureaucracy that maintained supply points, built and repaired roads, and dispersed money; this bureaucracy ensured that the man who entered the Roman army would be taken care of for the rest of his life. Its expenditures were well within the regular income of the imperial government, and its organization of the military forces and fortifications of the Roman Empire made the empire far stronger than any of its neighbors, stronger, even, than any ordinary combination of its neighbors.

Antoninus Pius (138–161), increased the efficiency of the central administration of the empire. When Marcus Aurelius (161–180)—and Aurelius's co-ruler, Lucius Verus (161–169)—became emperor after almost four decades of peace, the Parthian king, Vologases III, declared war on Rome. His general, Osroes, marched into Armenia, installed a new king, defeated the Roman governor of Cappadocia, and routed the Roman legions in Syria. Osroes advanced so quickly that he caught the inhabitants of Antioch outside the walls, peacefully enjoying a performance in the theater; their first intimation of the invasion came when an actor exclaimed, "Isn't that a Parthian horseman?"

In the spring of 162 Marcus Aurelius dispatched his co-ruler, Lucius Verus, with legions drawn from the Rhine, the Danube, and Africa to fight the enemy. Lucius Verus did not arrive in Antioch until the spring of 163. In his absence the local commander, Avidius Cassius, reorganized the army, replaced incompetent officers with competent and experienced men, restored morale, and pushed the enemy out of Syria. In early summer of 163 the Romans invaded Armenia, sacked the capital, and reestablished control.

In the summer of 164 the Romans converged on Parthia. One army group moved from Armenia south to threaten upper Mesopotamia, a second army group advanced along the line Dausara–Edessa–Nisibis and threatened the main Parthian army on the Euphrates, while the third army group, the main Roman army under the command of Avidius Cassius, defeated the Parthians at Doura and again at Sura; the converging Romans cleared Upper Mesopotamia, destroyed the Parthian army, advanced down through Mesopotamia, and took Ctesiphon by siege. The satraps surrendered. The Parthian king fled. The next year the Romans advanced into Media. The Romans could at last make real the dream of Crassus, Caesar, and Marc Antony, to duplicate the feats of Alexander and extend the Roman Empire to the borders of India, but, alas, at the very moment of success the army was struck by a terrible plague and had to retreat. The army brought this plague back from Syria to Asia Minor and Europe.

Added to the devastation of the plague was another war brought about in part by the movements of new tribes into Europe. The Germans were pressed, and they had nowhere to go except across the Roman limes, and the limes was undermanned: troops had been removed to fight the war in the east, veterans had retired and not been replaced, and now many of the remaining troops had died from the plague. In the summer of 167 an attack by the Marcomanni and Quadi, aided by the Vandals, the Langobardi, and the Charii, broke through the limes along the Danube, overwhelmed a Roman army of 20,000, and advanced into northern Italy as far as Aquileia.

Marcus Aurelius had little money and no reserves to meet the crisis. He sold his personal possessions to raise money, he drafted slaves and gladiators to form two new legions, II Pia and III Concors, he drafted bandit gangs and city police, he paid the German tribes not participating in the attack to attack the Germans who were, and he hired Scythian mercenaries. He ordered towns in Italy to fortify. He created one zone of operations along the whole of the Danube (across provincial lines) to unite the whole area under one command.

In 168 Marcus Aurelius and Lucius Verus marched at the head of their army to fight the Marcomanni and Quadi still in Italy. They fought a battle so fierce that both the praetorian prefect and the king of the Quadi were killed. Lucius Verus panicked and advised Marcus Aurelius to break off the battle and retreat, but Marcus Aurelius and the army fought on and finally routed the Germans. The emperors received a delegation of defeated Germans who declared to them the "conspirators responsible for the revolt" were dead, and henceforward the Germans would accept a king only if he were approved by the Romans.

In 169 Marcus Aurelius lost his co-ruler, Lucius Verus, to the plague. In 170 he had to marshall the resources of the empire to drive out the Costoboci, who had crossed the lower Danube, invaded Greece, and sacked Eleusis. Marcus Aurelius recruited the men, managed the resources of Rome, and restored the empire's borders and defenses, but he knew that the security of the empire demanded more than the passive defense of the limes, and he set out to complete the logical next step in the expansion of the Roman Empire, the subjugation of Germany.

Once he had brought the limes back up to strength, he organized an independent command and advanced from Carnuntum up the March River into the territory of the Quadi. All his former bad luck now was compensated with good—the Quadi attacked his camp with a siege tower, but the tower was destroyed by lightning and later, just when the Germans appeared to have the upper hand in a battle, a sudden storm so demoralized them that they capitulated. Marcus Aurelius marched east to the Gran River and then back to the Danube and effectively split the allied Germans.

In 173 he occupied the country of the Marcomanni, and the next year he continued their pacification by resettling them within the borders of the empire, an experiment that was only partially successful, as the Marcomanni whom he had settled at Ravenna seized the city and had to be expelled. He then (175) subdued the Costoboci and turned on the Sarmatians, but he was forced to cut short his operations against the Sarmatians because a false report of his death had induced his general in the east, Avidius Cassius, to claim the empire. Marcus Aurelius marched his army to the east and Cassius's head was brought to him in a sack. Marcus Aurelius did a tour of the east to ensure its stability and then (in 178 and 179) he returned to the attack against the Quadi and Marcomanni and defeated them.

His strategy is clear, to defeat them in battle, to occupy their land, to resettle some of them within the empire, and to resettle their land with colonies, thus ultimately to romanize the Germanic land and the Germans. By the end of 179 he needed perhaps one more year to complete the pacification and annexation of "Germany," but in the winter of 180 Marcus Aurelius died in camp. His son Commodus was proclaimed emperor (180–192). He was nineteen years old and completely unfit. A system that had provided first-rate leadership and stability to the empire for over eighty years—that the reigning emperor choose as his successor a mature, experienced man whose character was already known—fell before the claims of a son and the affections of a father. Although Commodus was surrounded by the staff his father had put together, and he had been associated with his father in the rule, he repudiated his father's design to create a province and instead declared the wars won, accepted the German rulers as client kings, and returned to Rome to enjoy life.

He allowed the imperial staff to squabble and scramble for position and he bolstered the frontier defenses, not by bringing the legions up to strength, but by settling more warrior tribes inside the Roman frontier to defend the frontier.

Neither Commodus nor any Roman of his time (when the Roman army was supreme) dreamed that a policy of using one set of barbarians to defend the empire from another set of barbarians would ever undermine the security of the Roman Empire; in Rome Commodus was greeted with rejoicing that the Romans had peace for the first time in twenty years. Commodus gilded the celebration with a budget–breaking donative to the people.

Commodus let his generals conduct the defense of the frontier in Dacia, Africa and Britain. When, on the last day of the year 192, Commodus was murdered in his bath, his successor, Pertinax, insisted that the Praetorian Guard return to their ancient discipline; they marched down the streets of Rome with his head on the end of a pike, and then they auctioned off the empire. In response three army commanders—Niger in the East, Albinus in Britain, and Severus in Pannonia along the Danube—allowed their armies to hail them emperor. Severus entered Rome without opposition when the Praetorian Guard declared for him and abandoned their candidate, the highest bidder, to his fate; Severus summoned the Praetorians, surrounded them with his own soldiers, who despised the privileged Praetorians, disarmed them, and dismissed them. He reconstituted the Guard as an imperial fighting force, the emperor's personal army, of 15,000 men drawn from the best units in the whole Roman army.

Once Severus had consolidated his position in Rome, he satisfied the ambitions of Albinus in Britain by naming him caesar (and thus Severus's heir and successor) and he concentrated on Niger in the east. Severus ordered detachments from Numidia to move towards Egypt and keep the legion stationed there from joining Niger. Severus lost the race to seize Byzantium, but he was able to cross into Asia Minor, to force Niger to withdraw before him, and to break through the Cilician Gates (as Alexander had before him) into the plain of Issus. Severus had not yet met Niger in battle, but his rapid advance had convinced many of Niger's supporters that Niger's strategic withdrawal was a defeat, and they rushed to make their peace with Severus. Severus's veteran troops were more than a match for Niger's local recruits, Niger's scheme to seek Parthian aid failed, and Severus was handed Niger's head. Severus crossed the Euphrates in September 194, and by the end of 195 had punished those vassal states that had either favored Niger or used the situation to throw off Roman control. He could do no more than punish them because he had learned that his British caesar, Albinus, had invaded Gaul.

While Albinus tried to win over the Rhine legions and enlist new recruits for his army, Severus sent his army ahead to block the passes from Gaul into Italy, and he himself went to Rome to encourage the Senate to condemn Albinus. Severus commandeered the city garrison and joined his army in Gaul. He outmaneuvered Albinus, confined him to the area around Lyons, and defeated him in battle. Albinus committed suicide.

Septimius Severus understood the reality of the imperial system: he commanded the army's loyalty and the man who commanded the army's loyalty commanded the empire. He intended to make the army the center of the empire, to staff the imperial bureaucracy with senior, or retired, centurions, and thus win complete control of the imperial bureaucracy. He encouraged the loyalty of his army by distributing a donative, by increasing pay, by granting permission for soldiers to marry while on active service, and by granting centurions the golden ring of the equestrian order. He increased the standing army to thirty legions, but he had learned from his experience, particularly with Albinus, that the legions had developed local loyalties that superseded any greater loyalty to the emperor, and so he divided larger provinces into smaller and apportioned the troops between them; if he did not put an end to local loyalties, at least he provided local commanders fewer troops, and he created a central army of about 30,000 men, to overawe local ambitions and to reinforce the local troops, should they prove insufficient to defend the frontier defenses.

While Severus was occupied in the west, the Parthian king invaded Roman territory and laid siege to Nisibis. In 197 Severus returned to the east, he forced the Parthians to lift the siege, and he marched south along the Euphrates. He entered Seleucia and Babylon without a fight and took Ctesiphon after the briefest of struggles. Severus used this triumphal progression as an occasion to secure the succession (and himself) by appointing his son, Caracalla, as Augustus and his younger son, Geta, as caesar. He returned to Roman territory by way of the Tigris (as he had stripped the Euphrates of supplies in his march down the river). He reestablished the prestige of Rome in the east and secured the Roman borders by this demonstration of Roman power, and he discredited the Parthian royal dynasty—it was replaced by a Persian Sassanian dynasty.

In 202 he returned to Rome in triumph, but in 203 he had to go in person to stop the desert tribes of Africa from raiding Roman territory. He extended the Roman defensive line to the oases and the caravan routes in the desert, he had forts constructed, and he improved conditions for the soldiers along the African frontier. In 204 he returned to Rome. While he was in Rome the free tribes of northern Britain raided across Hadrian's Wall. In 208 Severus went to Britain to restore the northern border. He advanced by land and sea, built bridges and roads, and fought ruthlessly for three years in an unremitting guerilla warfare. Exhausted by the strains of the campaign Severus died in 211, and Caracalla and his brother Geta became co-emperors.

Caracalla did not allow his brother to share the imperial throne for long. On the return to Rome he had his brother struck down as he cowered in the lap of his mother. Caracalla compensated the Praetorian Guard for whatever outrage they felt by giving them a generous donative. (As his father had told him, "Satisfy the army and everything else can go to hell ") Caracalla continued the policy of his father to ensure the security of the frontier by aggressive action against Rome's neighbors. He made a demonstration in force against a new German confederacy—the German cantons along the Rhine had coalesced into one confederacy called the Alemanni—he repaired the limes, and returned to Rome in triumph. There, to enlarge the tax base and the pool of manpower (and because he, as his father, did not consider Italy to have any special status)

Caracalla passed an act that was to have profound consequences for the Roman Empire—the *constitutio Antoniniana* (212) which granted citizenship to every free person living within the Roman Empire.

Caracalla drafted separate units of 5,000 Macedonians and 300 Spartans for a new campaign against the Persians. He had a personal desire to emulate Alexander, and he intended to annex the whole of Mesopotamia as the logical, but not necessary, next step of his father's policy. His campaigns of 215–217 did not encounter serious resistance, but neither did they subdue Persia, and any future campaigns were cut short by his own superstitious and suspicious nature. He had astrologers cast horoscopes on each member of his staff, and he executed any member of his staff whose horoscope intimated an imperial future. On the last day of his life he handed a batch of unread reports over for the inspection of Macrinus, his Praetorian prefect, and the prefect found himself listed as suspect.

Macrinus murdered Caracalla and was proclaimed emperor by the troops, but he soon alienated the army by leading it into a defeat against the Parthians and by cutting its pay; the army switched loyalties to Elagabalus, a priest of Baal and the grandson of the sister of Caracalla's mother. Elagabalus's beauty, revealed as he danced in Baal's temple, and his resemblance to Caracalla—and the wealth of his family—won the support of the army. In 218 Elagabalus was proclaimed emperor, the army marched on Macrinus, most of Macrinus's troops deserted him, and Macrinus was executed. The new emperor and the imperial family made a slow tour of the east on the way to Rome and entered Rome late in 219, but when Elagabalus shocked the Romans by entering Rome in the regalia of a priest of Baal and continued to shock their sensibilities, his mother's sister sought to conciliate the favor of the Romans, in particular, the Praetorian Guard, with her own son, a Roman, so it seemed, trained in the traditional values of ancient Rome, Severus Alexander.

### 58. Two Soldiers in Scale Armor (III A.D., from Dura-Europas)

# 32

# The Awful Third Century

## Thirty Emperors on a Single Day, But a Great, Great Army

Soon enough the Praetorian Guard murdered Elagabalus and his mother and then proclaimed Severus Alexander emperor. The new emperor's mother rewarded the Praetorian prefect with senatorial rank, she organized a ruling council, and, in the emperor's name, she, the prefect, and the council ran the Roman Empire. The first test of this arrangement came when a new regime, the Sassanian Persians, overran Mesopotamia and lay claim to the whole of the ancient Persian empire. Negotiations failed, and the emperor was compelled to raise troops and invade Persia. He followed earlier Roman strategy and launched his invasion (in 232 when he was about 22 years old) with three army groups, one in Armenia and Media (which was completely successful), one in the center under his own command (a failure), and one to the south (a disaster); despite these mixed results, he accomplished his objective, recovered Mesopotamia, and restored the eastern frontier.

In 233 he celebrated a triumph in Rome, but the triumph was short-lived: the Germans crossed the Rhine and the Danube (and threatened the families of the soldiers who had marched east). In 234 Severus Alexander took command of operations along the northern Rhine, but in a short-sighted attempt to avoid battle he offered the Germans money to withdraw; his troops were disgusted, and one of his generals, Maximinus—a man of great physical strength, who had risen from the ranks to command the army—claimed the imperial purple in March 235. He ordered the troops to let the "mama's boy" go, they obeyed, and Maximinus put him to death.

Maximinus was the first barbarian emperor (a Thracian), he was the first to rise from the ranks, the first whose only qualification was his military experience, but he compelled the Senate to acknowledge reality, he survived the first two plots against him, and he had no viable rival. Maximinus oversaw extensive road building (to ensure rapid deployment), increased army pay, and sent officers to collect the taxes that had been raised to provide for the armies. (Some provinces were unable to meet their obligations.) Maximinus invaded Germany, burned crops, destroyed villages and, when his army hesitated to cross a river in the face of the enemy, the emperor jumped into the water first and led his army across. He campaigned on the Danube for two years. Maximinus was a leader, a good commander, but he had the soldier's contempt for civilians, and he treated them as though they had no significance except to support the army.

Maximinus had nominal control over thirty-two legions (two each in twelve provinces, single legions in eight), but the legions of Syria and Britain maintained their neutrality and when in 238 Maximinus's procurator in Africa was assassinated, Gordian, 81 years old, a noble Roman and a proconsul, accepted acclamation as emperor and took his son, also named Gordian, as his colleague. The Gordians were joyfully embraced by the Senate and by all but three provinces; Maximinus was declared a public enemy. Gordian II, however, was defeated in battle and killed by Maximinus's general in Africa, and Gordian I committed suicide (after a twenty-eight-day reign). The Senate chose Balbinus and Maximus coequal emperors but had to placate the Roman mob and the Praetorian Guard by adding Gordian III, grandson of Gordian I, as caesar. Maximinus invaded Italy and laid siege to Aquileia, but, when he ran out of food for his troops, he lost control of them, they murdered him, and they paid homage to the portraits of the Senate's three emperors. In Rome, meanwhile, the Praetorian Guard murdered Balbinus and Maximus and proclaimed Gordian III (13 years old) their emperor.

The Praetorian prefect (in 241), Timesitheus, father-in-law of Gordian III, ran the empire. With Gordian at his side he fought the Goths on the Danube and then led the army east against Sapor I, the Persian king, who had invaded Syria in 242 and put Antioch under siege. In 243 emperor and Praetorian prefect arrived on the scene, saved Antioch, defeated the Persians in a decisive battle, and invaded the new Persian empire, but in the winter of 243–244 Timesitheus died of disease; his second in command, Philip the Arab, became Praetorian prefect, and in 244 Philip the Arab convinced the army to put Gordian to death and acclaim Philip emperor. Philip concluded a favorable peace with Persia and marched in triumph back through Thrace to Rome. He established good relations with the Senate, he ensured the loyalty of army commanders by appointing them from his own family, and, all in all, he would have had a rosy future ahead of him, had it not been for the Germans.

The Germans had occupied Scandinavia originally as a group but then had divided into three. One group, the North Germans (Norsemen, the Vikings, the Danes, Norwegians, and Swedes), stayed in Scandinavia. The second group, called the West Germans, in the first millennium B.C. expelled the Celtic inhabitants from the territory between the Rhine and the Elbe. (Without the intervention of Caesar and the Romans they might well have occupied the whole of Gaul.) They were fierce warriors, with particularly good cavalry, and they lived by a pastoral, warrior code, to acquire wealth in raids on their neighbors, each tribe surrounded by woods and marsh, their power reflected in the extent of the no-man's-land around them, but their numbers increased, they could not expand into Roman territory nor could they expand east, where other German tribes barred the way, and so, to survive, they were forced to turn to farming.

The Germans' conversion to farming (by the end of the first century A.D.) did not ameliorate their fierceness but rather concentrated their power in three large, loose confederations: the Alemanni, the Franks, and the Saxons. Their war leaders (variously called kings or judges by the Romans) were chosen from a royal family to carry out the decisions reached by an assembly of the fighting men. The third group, the East Germans (the Goths) settled east of the Elbe and gradually moved south. The West Goths (the Visigoths) moved towards the Danube and the East Goths (the Ostrogoths) moved towards the Black Sea. By 235 (the last year recorded by the Greek colony of Olbia) the Ostrogoths had occupied the north coast of the Black Sea. In the middle of the third century German attacks pushed the Romans to the brink of destruction.

In 245–246 the Carpi crossed the Danube and raided Macedonia. In 247 Philip won a major victory on the Danube and on 21 April 248 in Rome he celebrated the 1,000-year anniversary of the founding of Rome. No sooner had he concluded the celebration then he learned that the legions on the Danube and in Syria-Mesopotamia had declared their own emperors and the Goths, Carpi, and Vandals had invaded the province of Moesia and were besieging the capital. Philip was so shaken by the crisis that he offered to abdicate, but the Senate refused to accept his abdication, and a senator named Decius advised him not to worry, that the soldiers themselves would murder the false emperors, and that he, Decius, would go to the Danube and restore order.

In autumn 248 Decius restored order among the Danube legions and forced the Goths out of Roman territory. He was so popular with the troops that in 249 they insisted that he take the purple . . . or be lynched. He accepted their offer, led them into Italy, and defeated and killed Philip in battle. Decius understood the problems of the empire: heavy taxation, loss of faith in the old gods amid increasing Christian influence, instability in the succession, and poor discipline and disloyalty in the army. He ordered that each and every citizen was to prove his loyalty by performing sacrifice before an image of the emperor, he set the army to building roads, he appointed a censor, and he appointed a senator named Valerian to be regent when the emperor was absent from Rome.

In 250 his troops on the Rhine frontier drove back an attempted invasion, but the Danube froze, and the Goths under their king, Kniva, crossed into Moesia and besieged Philippopolis. In 251 Decius defeated two detachments of Goths, but his ambitious general, Gallus, colluded with the Goths to lure Decius into an ambush, where he was killed; Gallus seized the purple and rewarded the Goths by allowing them to withdraw with all their booty and their Roman captives.

In the period 251–268 the empire almost went under, every European and Asian province was under attack, plague struck, as many as thirty men at a time proclaimed themselves emperor, and no one was able to assert control. While Gallus was emperor (251–253) the Persians invaded Syria, and the Goths crossed the Danube and raided Moesia, Thrace, and Asia Minor. In 253 the governor of Moesia, Aemilian, defeated the Goths, crossed the Danube, ravaged their territory, and was hailed emperor by his troops. Aemilian invaded Italy, Gallus's troops deserted him, Gallus was murdered, and Aemilian seemed secure until his troops heard that Valerian in the province of Rhaetia had been proclaimed emperor. They murdered Aemilian.

Valerian induced the Senate to make Gallienus, his son, caesar, and then both were proclaimed Augustus. Gallienus spent three years (254–257) fighting Germans along the Rhine and in the third year he made a pact with a German chieftain that temporarily restored the Rhine limes, but the limes collapsed in 257–258 under an onslaught by the Franks, who broke into Gaul, Spain, and Africa, and the Alemanni, who broke into Italy. Gallienus won a great victory over the Alemanni at Milan, but the governor of Pannonia rebelled and the Marcomanni, Quadi, Sarmatians, Goths, and Carpi were poised to breach the line of the Danube. Gallienus defeated the rebel governor in Pannonia, put down a second rebellion in 260, and averted one assault on the Danube by making an alliance with the Marcomanni chief (and accepting his daughter as a concubine), but the legions of the west acclaimed their own emperor, Postumus, the so-called Gallo-Roman emperor.

Meanwhile, Valerian had gone (in 256) to restore the situation in the east; in 257 he repelled the Persian invasion, but his momentary success came as the Goths raised fleets, crossed into Asia Minor, and looted indiscriminately. Other tribes imitated them, city after city fell, the Roman army was struck by a plague, and the Persians renewed their offensive. In 260 Valerian drove the Persians back once more and invaded Mesopotamia, but there he was trapped and taken prisoner (never to be released). Antioch fell. New emperors, proclaimed in the east, had fleeting success, but in the end they all were defeated and killed, and the Persian king was poised to extend the new Persian empire to the boundaries of the old. Only one obstacle remained in his path: the king of Palmyra who preferred an alliance with a distant and weakened Rome to a vassalage under a near and powerful Persia. And after his superb, heavy-armored cavalry had defeated the Persians, he received his reward—he was entrusted by Gallienus with the command of all Roman forces in the east. In 262–265 the king invaded Persia.

In the west Postumus (the Gallo-Roman emperor) consolidated his position in Gaul. Gallienus did not recognize Postumus, but amid his greater problems— plague in Rome, earthquakes in Asia Minor, a Gothic invasion of Greece and attack on Athens, raids in Asia Minor, and his own mental and physical exhaustion—he ignored him. In 263 Postumus crushed the Franks and Alemanni, but in 268, after he had put down a Gallic rival, Postumus refused to allow his troops to plunder the rebel city, on the grounds that the city was Gallic, and the disappointed troops murdered him.

Gallienus attempted to defend the borders of the empire by developing a system of a rapid reaction force (a substantial and mobile cavalry) backed by a reserve, and he attempted to eliminate rivals for the purple by depriving senators (his chief rivals) of the right to command an army and by depriving the provincial governors of command of the provincial legions. He opened a legal career track for a man to rise from the ranks to command an army; he organized a staff college to train centurions for high command. In 268 Gallienus fought the Goths and routed them, but he was unable to finish them off because of an uprising behind his back in Italy. He returned to Italy, laid siege to his rivals, and seemed to have the situation in hand, when his Illyrian officers joined in a conspiracy and assassinated him.

Gallienus preserved the heart of the empire, but at the time of his murder (in 268) there was an emperor (Victorinus) in Gaul, an independent queen (Zenobia) in Palmyra, a usurper in Milan, the Alemanni all but occupied the province of Rhaetia, the Goths were preparing a new offensive, the treasury was empty, the soldiers were exhausted, and their morale was shattered. The new emperor Claudius (later Claudius Gothicus) was a career officer from Illyria. He proceeded one step at a time: he accepted the surrender of the rebel in Milan and had him executed, he ordered the deification of Gallienus, and he appealed to the desire of his troops for unity, victory, and peace. When the cavalry he sent to fight the Alemanni was defeated, he cashiered all the officers and appointed his fellow conspirator, Aurelian, to command. In 269 the Goths sailed from the Black Sea with 2,000 ships, attacked Byzantium, looted its territory, and marched overland; Claudius cornered them and defeated them in a close battle in which his cavalry was decisive: 50,000 Goths were reported killed, but the German onslaught continued. The Jugunthi invaded Rhaetia, the Vandals invaded Pannonia, and in the east the queen of Palmyra, Zenobia, stretched her hands out to snatch Asia Minor and Egypt from the faltering—she thought—grasp of the Roman Empire.

Claudius's success enticed some of the western provinces back to Rome, the Gallo-Roman Empire began to break up, and in 270 the western "emperor," Victorinus, was murdered; by then Claudius had died of the plague (in January 270). Claudius's brother was elevated by his troops and then murdered by them as soon as they heard that Aurelian had been proclaimed emperor by *his* troops. Aurelian's nickname was "Drawn Sword." He was an Illyrian from Sirmium, of humble birth, strong mentally and physically, a disciplinarian, blunt, and successful. He defeated the Goths, he defeated the Jugunthi in Rhaetia at the Danube and, when their envoys demanded that he pay them tribute, he so overawed them that they considered themselves lucky to have escaped with their lives. Aurelian visited Rome but soon marched out again, to Pannonia, to fight and defeat the Vandals; he whipped them so badly that they made peace and gave him 2,000 cavalry to use as he wished. Aurelian marched back to Italy to face an invading force of Jugunthi: he fell into an ambush. His army broke, but he reconstituted his force, while the Jugunthi scattered to plunder, and he consulted the Sibylline books and offered sacrifices to establish a point beyond which the barbarians could not pass. The cities of northern Italy built walls, while Aurelian fought the enemy in three battles, won three victories, and saved Rome.

In 271 Aurelian authorized the construction of new walls around Rome (12 miles in length, 20 feet high), he decided that he could no longer spare the resources to defend Dacia, he crushed three rebellions (one in Dalmatia), and in the spring he collected his army, marched along the line of the Danube where he slew 5,000 Goths, marched through Asia Minor, and met the Palmyrenes on the banks of the Orontes near Antioch. Aurelian knew that he could only defeat Palmyra if he could defeat their heavy cavalry, the cataphracts, and he created a new unit, the "club men," to fight them. His first assault was driven back, but he ordered a counterattack, and his club men carried the day. After he had accepted the surrender of Antioch, he advanced on the Palmyrenes at Emesa, and once again his club men defeated the heavily armored Palmyrene cavalry. (Aurelian proclaimed that the battle was won only because the sun god had helped him.) Aurelian advanced on Palmyra and offered terms to Zenobia; she refused them and he pressed the siege of Palmyra, even after he was wounded, and he defeated her, took her prisoner, and accepted the city's surrender. Aurelian left Zenobia her title *queen*, now vassal to the emperor, and he placed a Roman garrison in her city.

In 272 Aurelian was back on the Danube, where the Carpi were trying to cross; no sooner had the Romans beaten them back when Aurelian heard the news that Zenobia had massacred the Roman garrison. Zenobia was one more of many rulers who misestimated Rome. Aurelian marched back, took Palmyra, and set his troops loose to loot and burn, raze the walls, and turn the flourishing city back into a desert village. Aurelian put down yet one more revolt, this one in Egypt, and then he turned to the last region that did not acknowledge him as emperor, the Gallo-Roman empire. Its new emperor, Tetricus, sent him a message: "Save me, invincible one, from the evils around me!" In 274 Aurelian responded; he scattered the troops of the Gallo-Roman Empire, welcomed the person of the Gallo-Roman emperor as a deserter, and celebrated a triumph with the emperor and Zenobia marching before him. (After the triumph Zenobia was married off to a senator, and the emperor was appointed corrector of Lucania.) At last, once again, one man, Aurelian, was acknowledged to be emperor by the whole of the Roman Empire.

Aurelian tried to gain an ascendancy over the armies by asserting that the sun god, not the troops and not the Senate, had given him the empire—his very success proved that he had a divine patron. He had restored the defense line of the Rhine–Danube even if he had not addressed the causes behind the German invasions, and his last project was to restore Mesopotamia as part of the Roman Empire. He considered Persia to be the greater risk to the Romans because one king directed the vast resources of that empire. On his way east he defeated the Jugunthi and Alemanni in Rhaetia (in 274), but in 275 he was brought down by the smallest incident. He had told his secretary that he intended to punish him for some act of malfeasance, and the secretary defended himself by forging a document falsely implicating Aurelian's generals in a plot to assassinate the emperor. The generals believed that they would be executed, and they defended themselves by murdering Aurelian. When they discovered the deception, they executed the secretary, but the deed was done.

The generals, conscious of their own naiveté and credulity, lost confidence in themselves and appealed to the Senate to choose an emperor. The Senate labored for six months before producing a 75-year-old senator named Tacitus. Tacitus, who was supposed to be another Nerva, was not enthusiastic about his role. He was less enthusiastic when he had to set out to meet a Gothic invasion of Asia Minor; already he was unpopular, he was not in good health, he was under a considerable strain, and he collapsed and died on the way. His half-brother Florian appointed himself emperor, but the eastern army chose to bestow the purple on its commander, the Illyrian Probus. When Probus accepted, Florian's army melted away, and Florian was executed in 276.

The new emperor, Probus, rejected any immediate campaign against the Persians and, after he had gained control of the armies, he marched back towards Rome along the banks of the Danube, fought the Goths there, and defeated them. After a visit to Rome, he went to Gaul to meet a massive invasion, north and south, by the Franks, the Lugii, the Alemanni, the Burgundians, and the Vandals. In 276–277 in a series of battles, Probus fought the Lugii, captured their chief, and freed sixty cities, while his lieutenants fought the other Germans. Together they killed tens of thousands of Germans. Probus invaded their territory and forced nine chiefs to kneel at his feet and swear obedience: the German chiefs sent him 16,000 Germans to fight in his army, they paid a tribute of grain and cattle, and they agreed to disarm. Probus declared the Gallic campaign officially concluded.

Between 278 and 280 he cleared Rhaetia, fought the Vandals in Illyricum, faced down a rebellion in the east, pacified Asia Minor, put down disturbances in Egypt, and repopulated the Roman side of the Danube by settling 100,000 Bastarnae in Thrace. Probus, on the one hand, secured the limes of the empire with military force, and, on the other, addressed the causes of the invasion by finding land for the land-hungry Germans. Neither the predecessors of Probus nor Probus himself had any doubts that a Roman army would defeat a German army. Therefore he could expect that Germans settled within the empire could be contained and would eventually become romanized. Roman officers were becoming more comfortable with Germans, and Germans were rising in importance within the Roman army. The commander of the Roman fleet had a Gothic wife; he used to ply his wife's relatives with drink until they became indiscrete. When Britain rebelled, the rebellion was put down with German mercenaries. All in all it seemed that the Germans were becoming romanized and the Romans were becoming germanized.

Probus celebrated his victories with a huge triumph in Rome (in 281–282), he prepared for a campaign against Persia, and in the flush of his success he speculated that Rome so dominated the world that soon it would no longer need the army. In the autumn of 282, at Sirmium, the army rioted and murdered him. Carus, the praetorian prefect in Rhaetia, became emperor.

Probus and his predecessors, who together restored the empire, justly have been given the title the Courage of Illyria (*virtus Illyrica*). In justice, however, the Roman army must receive its due. For forty years the army was rushed from one crisis to another, with no end in sight. Its ascendancy over the enemy saved the empire, but its role, all too often, as the instrument of its generals' personal ambition was a threat to the empire, and if it had not so often refused to be used and expressed its refusal in the only way it had, by murdering the candidates it would not support, the empire might have fallen in the third century. Naturally the emperors did not view assassination the same way the army did.

Carus owed his elevation entirely to the army; the Senate, previously excluded from command, now did not wish any part of it. Carus had two sons, both of whom he named caesar: Carinus was left behind as emperor of the west to defend Gaul and Numerian accompanied his father to the east for the long-awaited campaign against the Persians. (Numerian was a poet and a good-intentioned soul, not the best qualifications for an emperor.) Carus issued coins that expressed optimism and hope. Along the Danube on his way east (in 282–283) Carus defeated an invasion of the Quadi and Sarmatians and then continued to his area of operations in Persia; he crossed the Euphrates, reoccupied Mesopotamia, crossed the Tigris, and took the capital, but in July he died under mysterious circumstances.

The Praetorian prefect, Aper, claimed that Carus had been "struck by lightning." His explanation convinced no one, and Aper was an object of suspicion, which was not alleviated by the discovery in a closed litter of the dead and decomposing body of Numerian (one of Carus's two sons). Aper tried to convince the army in assembly to support him against Carus's remaining son in the west, Carinus, but, as he spoke, Diocles, one of his generals, sitting behind him, remembered a prophecy that he would become emperor when he had slain a boar (in Latin, *aper*). He rose, struck Aper down with his dagger, and the army proclaimed him emperor.

Diocles came from Dalmatia; of humble birth, he had risen through the ranks to command an army, he had been a governor and consul, he was subtle and a severe disciplinarian, he understood the problems of the empire, and he thought he had the answers. Diocles also believed that he needed a more imposing name; he lengthened Diocles to Diocletian.

# 33

# Reform and Revolution
## *Every Soldier, Every Civilian in the Chain of Command*

When (in 285) the last son of Carus lost his life, Diocletian became the undisputed ruler of a reunited Roman Empire, reunited but racked with problems: foreign invaders, internal rivals, shattered economy, and a disloyal army that, while it had fought magnificently against its foreign enemies, had shown itself all too willing to proclaim a commander emperor and then, if confronted by another Roman army with its own "emperor," to lynch one or the other, or both, while turning to a third "emperor." Where the historian might see in the armies a commendable instinct to avoid civil war, Diocletian saw a threat to his own security and, hence (in his mind), to the security of the empire.

Diocletian soon acknowledged that foreign and internal enemies made his task too great for one man: he appointed his friend and most trusted general, Maximian, first to be his *caesar* (an assistant emperor) and then in 286 to be *augustus*, emperor of the west, while Diocletian was emperor of the east. Diocletian created two imperial courts, theoretically equal in every way, with their own commanders, Praetorian prefects, and armies, but Maximian, although theoretically equal to Diocletian in every way—title, court, and army— nonetheless was "Hercules" to Diocletian's "Jupiter," and "Jupiter" formulated policy.

Diocletian intended to make the whole of the empire, civilian and military, completely and totally subordinate to the imperial staff and the emperor. He would leave no place for the Senate—the new emperors had not even sought the Senate's formal, and empty, consent—nor for any rival to the imperial authority. Diocletian created a career track so that a man in the ranks, a man of humble birth (like Diocletian himself), could be promoted from centurion to civil servant in the imperial bureaucracy, and from civil servant to a member of the equestrian order. Eventually, if Diocletian had his way, the empire would be staffed and run exclusively by ex-centurions.

Diocletian divided the empire into dioceses, the dioceses into provinces, the provinces into districts; he divided the resources, land, humans, and animals, into taxable units; and he appointed a commander for every level so that the authority of the emperor would reach down through an imperial chain of command, not only to every soldier, but to the lowliest subject in the farthest removed district of the empire. His system would compel economic stability—sons were to follow the professions of their fathers (unless a son wanted to join the army), good coins would replace debased coins, citizens would buy and sell commodities at prices set by an imperial price guide (and both buyer and seller were liable to execution, if they violated the price guide); his system would compel citizens to give the requisite amount of public service, to pay taxes, and, finally, to be available to serve in the army so that the emperors could rebuild and reinforce the limes. Diocletian had personal command of a large, mobile central army, Maximian would command a second; each emperor had in his army a sizeable component of cavalry, and lancers, shock troops, and a personal bodyguard. Diocletian scattered the rest of the army in small units along the limes. These small units—too small to be a threat to the emperor—would form the first line of defense, which, breached, would summon the emperor and his army.

Soldier and subject were to look up the chain of command, layer after layer, to the remote figure of the emperor, the symbol of the empire, the "Rome" of this age, a man marked by his divine character and destiny and selected by an all-powerful divinity. When Diocletian visited Rome, he was borne on a litter (and he had to duck slightly under the gate—the emperor was too large to easily fit through a gate meant for mere mortals), the Senate came out of the city to meet him and escort him, his bodyguard wore silver armor, he had silk banners inflated in the shape of dragons, the people along the parade route clapped in time, priests burned incense before him, and Diocletian looked as enormous as his forty-foot statue. He was above the throng, and he gave no response to its applause.

Nevertheless, these newly elevated figures did not overawe their enemies, and the two emperors continued to fight against foreign invaders and internal rivals. The man whom Maximian appointed in 286 to command the Roman fleet and fight the Frank and Saxon pirates proved to be less interested in defeating the Franks and Saxons than in stealing their booty; when word reached him that he was to be relieved of his command, he declared himself king of an independent Britain (and a small strip of Gaul). Maximian ignored the "king" of Britain for the moment to repel (286–287) an incursion of Alemanni and Burgundians across the upper Rhine; in 288 Maximian sent his Praetorian prefect, Constantius the Green, to defeat the Franks, in 289–290 he had to suppress a rebellion by Moors in Africa. Diocletian was no less busy. In 286 he was operating in Pannonia and Moesia against the Germans, and in 288 he forced the Parthian king to cede Mesopotamia, he put his own candidate on the Armenian throne, and he and Maximian, working together, defeated the Chaibones and Heruli in Rhaetia, and in 289 he defeated the Sarmatians. In 290 he had to deal with an incursion of Saracens in Syria, in 291 a rebellion in Egypt, and in 292 the Sarmatians again.

In the face of the constant threats, and as his vision of the empire continued to evolve, Diocletian took the next step he deemed necessary to ensure the stability of the empire. He chose the men (the "caesars") who would succeed himself and his colleague. For Maximian, who had a son, he chose Maximian's Praetorian prefect, Constantius the Green, a Dardanian and a proven general. For himself he chose Galerius, an able, if blunt, general. The two caesars were required to divorce their wives and marry the daughters of their augusti. Thus Diocletian transformed the empire into a tetrarchy.

The tetrarchs divided the empire into four areas of operation. Diocletian Augustus held the east (in particular, Egypt, Libya, Arabia, Bithynia), his caesar Galerius had Illyricum and western Asia, Maximian Augustus held the west (in particular, Rome, Italy, Sicily, Africa, Spain), and his caesar Constantius the Green held Gaul and Britain. The caesars were to do the heavy fighting. If they won, so much the better. If they lost, their loss could be retrieved by their augustus wth his army; if they were judged incompetent, they could be cashiered; and, in dire emergency, the two augusti could cooperate and support each other against enemies within or without.

Along the borders of the empire and within, the tetrarchy reestablished imperial authority. In 293 Constantius the Green returned all of Gaul to the empire, and three years later he, in command of one army, and his Praetorian prefect, in command of another, crossed the English Channel. His Praetorian prefect slipped across in the fog, burned his boats, forced the rebels into battle, defeated and killed their leader, and pursued the survivors to London. The sack of London was prevented only when Constantius himself sailed up the Tiber with a second army.

The tetrarchy worked well. Maximian defeated a coalition of rebel Moors (in 297–298), Constantius the Green, though defeated once and forced to run for his life, nonetheless recovered and defeated the Alemanni in Gaul (in 298), Diocletian ordered Galerius to clear and resettle the Roman bank of the Danube (in 294–297) and then, in 297, he summoned Galerius to drive Narses, the king of Persia, out of Syria. When Galerius fell into an ambush and was forced to retreat, Diocletian received him with scorn, ordered him to walk on foot behind the augustus's chariot and then told him to go and redeem himself. Galerius forced the Persians to sue for peace and to cede Mesopotamia and Armenia.

The tetrarchy had succeeded in gaining control of the armies, securing the Roman borders, establishing a clear succession, and further protecting the person of the emperor by setting him apart from the rest of humanity—as a man whose imperial destiny had been established in heaven. But whose heaven, pagan or Christian? As Diocletian had opened imperial service to new classes of Romans, so Christians had risen to the highest levels of the army and the imperial staff. They were present when Diocletian presided over the sacrifices and the interpretation of the signs, and on one crucial occasion, when his soothsayers told him that they could not read the omens because the Christians were making the sign of the cross, Diocletian dismissed Christians, first from his personal staff, then from the imperial staff, and from the officer corps. He needed little persuading by Galerius that the well-being of the whole empire depended upon the preservation of the worship of the old gods and the elimination of Christianity from the empire. In 303 he ordered that all inhabitants of the empire prove their loyalty to Rome by performing a sacrifice in front of an official. The imperial bureaucracy was put to the test: to reach every inhabitant of the empire, force compliance, and issue a certificate of compliance (or identify and punish recalcitrance). In the east churches were destroyed and scripture burned, but in the west Constantius refused to authorize any persecution in his domain.

In 305, after an illness, Diocletian decided that the time had come for himself and Maximian to abdicate: Galerius became Augustus in the east, Constantius the Green became Augustus of the west, and Galerius appointed his adopted son, Maximin Daia, as his own caesar and his relative Severus as the caesar of Constantius. The succession was fraught with tension. Maximian had not wanted to abdicate, and he had a son with imperial ambitions. Constantius had an adult son of his own, Constantine, who was living at the court of Galerius, almost as a hostage. He had been schooled to believe that one day he would rule; he was an imposing figure, a leader, and sympathetic to Christianity. Constantius asked Galerius to release Constantine. Galerius could hardly refuse, but Constantine suspected that Galerius might have him murdered and, the moment he was given his release, he fled from Constantinople, galloping from way station to way station, commandeering fresh horses, and leaving the others dead. He reached his father in June 306.

Constantius introduced his son to his army and Constantine, as his father had done already, won their loyalty. When Constantius died (July 306), Constantine was acclaimed emperor by the army. He sent his portrait to Galerius with the message to either send him the purple or burn the portrait. Galerius found a brilliant compromise—he promoted Constantius's caesar, Severus, to augustus and appointed Constantine Severus's caesar—but the compromise enraged Maxentius, the son of Maximian, and he bribed the Praetorian Guard in Italy to hail him as Augustus. The turmoil attracted a German invasion of Gaul, but Constantine was quite capable of dealing with the Germans—Constantine's coins show him dragging a German by the hair, kicking Germans, trampling Germans—and after he had defeated them, he enlisted a large number of Germans in his bodyguard and in the legions, both as common soldiers and as officers, thus *romanizing the Germans and germanizing the Romans.*

The tetrarchy was in disarray, a council summoned by Diocletian failed, six men were calling themselves *augustus*, and the augusti formed alliances with each other, betrayed each other, and fought each other; by October of 312 Constantine was on the march against his last rival in the west, Maxentius in Rome; and Constantine's ally in the east, Licinius, was about to open his successful campaign against his last remaining rival in the east. On 27–28

October 312, the eve of the expected battle with Maxentius, Constantine had a vision of the Chi-Rho and heard a voice declare, "In this sign you will conquer." Constantine had the symbol painted on his soldiers' shields and in the morning, at the battle of the Milvian Bridge, Constantine routed Maxentius. (Maxentius was trampled to death in the rout.) Constantine needed no further proof; when, on the next day, he entered Rome, he entered Rome as the first Christian emperor. Constantine's ally in the east, Licinius, issued a prayer (which came to him in a vision). "Supreme God, hear our prayers. we stretch our arms to You, listen, holy and supreme God." He defeated his rival who had vowed to Jupiter that he would extirpate the Christian faith if he won.

For ten years Constantine and Licinius ruled the empire in uneasy cooperation, sometimes testing each other's strength, sometimes cooperating against the Goths along the Danube. In 324 the cooperation broke down, Constantine proclaimed a crusade to liberate Christians from the persecution of Licinius, "a hideous serpent uncoiling," and the two emperors fought each other for the whole of the empire at the battle of Adrianople in 324. Constantine had 130,000 infantry; Licinius had 165,000. Constantine forced Licinius to retreat into Asia Minor and in September 324 at the battle of Chrysopolis Constantine defeated him again. Licinius surrendered and was executed several months later.

Constantine was sole emperor of a reunited Roman Empire. He was forced by his experience of the recent past to react to two facts, first, that a divided army divides its loyalty and, second, that a static defense could not stop barbarian attacks. He formalized the arrangement of his predecessors, a large central reserve under his direct command and a system of forts along the limes, built to survive an attack, to stop minor raids, to impede the advance of an invading army, and to serve as rallying points and as supply depots for the central reserve. The weakness of this system is more apparent under Constantine than under the tetrarchy because the tetrarchs controlled four central armies and Constantine only one. Consequently Constantine had to increase the reaction time of the central army. He reduced the legion to about 1,000 men, incorporated mailed cavalry (the cataphracts), disbanded the Praetorian Guard (made obsolete by the new army), and replaced the Guard with small bands (500 men) of German mercenary cavalry.

The real weakness of the empire, the deteriorating economic base and the inability to find the way to economic recovery, was a result, to be sure, of the turmoil of the last century, but it was also the result of a new point of view in the empire. Diocletian had attempted to give the emperor total control of the empire and everyone in it (and thereby made the empire totally dependent upon the ability of the emperor). To meet the immediate problem of the empire Diocletian could hardly have devised a better system; on the other hand, to devise a system to ensure future economic resources and a source of manpower and the ability to meet new, unexpected challenges, he could hardly have done worse. The army had grown in size, and it and the imperial bureaucracy consumed more of the empire's resources than the empire could afford.

A comparison of the empire of the early fourth century A.D. with the republic of the second century B.C. provides a startling contrast. The republic, faced with a number of threats, appointed republican magistrates to command the armies reacting to the threats. The republic in an emergency could field upwards of a quarter of a million men and more than twenty armies without those men or their commanders (if they were competent) being a threat to the republic. The republic could afford to field such numbers because it did not need to support the men after the campaign was over. The empire had a larger population base to draw upon but could not draw upon it because the emperors feared (rightly) that trained soldiers, returned to their homes, would be a potential army for an usurper. When the empire recruited a soldier, it was financially committed to that soldier for a minimum of twenty years. Constantine's temporary solution was to hire cheap barbarian units instead of recruiting expensive citizen units.

Constantine's conversion to Christianity infused the empire with new vigor and new purpose. He recognized the jurisdiction of episcopal courts, and he put the authority of the state behind the Christian church. On 11 May 330 he celebrated the birthday of Constantinople (formerly Byzantium), the capital of the new empire; Constantinople had a senate and artwork scavenged from the whole empire, but no temples. Christians quickly rose in both the civil service and in the army. Christians went on evangelical missions. One missionary, Ulfilas, the son of a Christian family carried off by the Goths, was appointed bishop to the Goths. He translated the Bible into Gothic, and he convinced many Goths to embrace Christianity.

In the east, Sapor II, the king of Persia, was put on notice that all the Christians in the Persian's domain were under the protection of the new emperor, Constantine. Sapor decided to forestall Constantine by eliminating the threat of Christian Armenia, now a natural ally of the Romans. Sapor replaced the Armenian king in 334 with a candidate of his own choice. Constantine reacted (in 335) by sending his son Constantius II to campaign against Persia; Constantius forced Sapor to sue for peace.

Constantine died on 22 May 337. He had felt that his time was near, and he had himself baptized, discarded his purple robes, and clothed himself in white. He had already directed that the empire should be divided among his three sons and all his male relatives, but after the heirs had bickered for weeks without reaching any agreement, the army assumed control and murdered all the members of the royal court except the direct descendants of Constantine (and two cousins, one in hiding and one just a child). The three sons did agree upon a threefold division of the empire, but by 350 Constantius was the only brother left. The other two brothers had fought each other, the victor had been overthrown by a pagan officer of German descent, and the pagan's request to Constantius to recognize him as emperor of the west was rejected. Instead, Constantius nominated one of the two surviving cousins as caesar, marched west and defeated the usurper, first at a particularly bloody battle at Mursa (28 September 351), and then, finally, (in the summer of 353) at the battle of Mons Seleucus in Gaul.

Constantius, perhaps because the usurper had been a pagan and had appealed to pagans to support him, ordered the death penalty for anyone caught sacrificing or worshipping idols, and he removed from Rome the altar of Victory, where senators had offered incense since the time of Augustus. Constantius was conscientious and far from incompetent, but he accepted uncritically what his secret agents reported to him. When in 354 he heard from them that his cousin, commanding the eastern army, intended to rebel, he had him executed. Yet the empire remained too large for a single man to rule. He needed an associate, and he turned to Julian, the last male relative of Constantine.

Julian had survived because he was so young (only six when Constantine died), and he appeared unambitious and insignificant; he professed Christianity, but he had fallen in love with the culture of Athens and was a pagan at heart. In 355, as Constantius himself was preparing for war against Sapor, Julian was sent to Gaul as caesar to fight the Franks. (Julian's chief of staff was picked personally by Constantius.) Julian quickly assumed command and won some victories, but the raids continued. The Alamanni—after a succession of successful raids and skirmishes, after driving even Julian behind walls, after seeing Roman cooperation break down in a futile attempt to coordinate a converging movement on the Alamanni—decided on a major campaign in Gaul under their king, Chnodomarius. Julian was ready to fight, and the two sides met at the battle of Strasbourg (A.D. 357).

The Roman army had to march about twenty miles. It set out at dawn, the foot soldiers in the middle, their flanks guarded by cavalry squadrons including cataphracts and archers ("a formidable kind of armed men"). After eight hours marching, they reached the vicinity of the enemy camp and Julian suggested to the troops that they prepare a fortified camp wherein they could rest, refresh themselves, and prepare to attack the next dawn. The soldiers "gnashed their teeth, clashed their spears on their shields," and demanded that Julian lead them immediately against the enemy. Julian's Praetorian prefect also urged him to attack while they had all the Alamanni fixed in one location and reminded him of "the hot tempers of the soldiers which could turn them so easily to riot." A standard bearer cried out, "Advance, Caesar, luckiest of all men!"

The Romans advanced slowly, and when they came in sight of the Alamanni, they formed up in a close-packed wedge formation, and the Alamanni also formed up in wedges. The Alamanni put all their cavalry opposite the Roman cavalry on the Roman right. As the cataphracts had the advantage over the Alamanni cavalry because they wore mail armor and their hands were free while the Alamanni had to hold reins and shield in one hand and spear in the other, the Alamanni reinforced their cavalry with skirmishers and light infantry. The Alamanni had dug trenches on their right from which to spring ambushes, but the Romans expected trickery and halted on the edge of the trenches and waited to see what would happen.

Julian, protected by a bodyguard of 200 men and identified by a dragon banner, rode back and forth calling upon his men to restore Rome's majesty; the

Alamanni called upon their leaders to dismount and share the fortunes of the common soldier. King Chnodomarius, a gigantic, muscular man, was the first to dismount, and the other princes followed his example. Then the trumpets blared, the two sides hurled their spears at each other, and the Alamanni charged. "The Alamanni, their long hair streaming, their eyes blazing with madness, made a terrifying sight."

The two sides, densely packed, pushed each other back and forth, and clouds of dust obscured the field. Then the Roman cavalry commander was wounded and the Roman cavalry withdrew; Julian rushed to the spot to stop the retreat, but the cavalry and Julian were out of the battle long enough for the Alamanni to force their way into the Roman formation. There they were checked momentarily by Julian's German troops before they broke through to the center of the army, where the Roman master of troops commanded a special unit. The two sides hacked at each other, the Romans sheltered behind their phalanx of shields, the Alamanni gone beserk, trying to break the formation and shouting war cries above the shrieks and moans of the wounded and dying. The Romans stabbed at the unprotected sides of the Alamanni, until they broke the impetus of their charge and forced them to turn and run.

The Romans pursued them to the banks of the Rhine and struck them until their swords were dulled, their spears broken, and then they stood on the banks of the river and threw javelins at them. The Alamanni who had preserved their shields in their flight used them as miniature rafts to take them to the other side. Chnodomarius surrendered and was sent to Rome where he died of old age. The Romans estimated that the Alamanni had numbered about 35,000 and that they themselves had been outnumbered three to one. They acknowledged 243 dead.

Julian's Germans were so valuable to him that he learned their language. One of the commanders in his subsequent campaign against the Persians was Vadomarius, who had been king of an Alamannic canton. As king, Vadomarius led raids into Roman territory (in 352–353), his own territory had been raided in retaliation, and he had concluded a peace treaty with the Romans. Under the cover of the peace treaty, even as he accepted the local Roman commander's invitations to banquets, he continued to raid Roman territory. Roman patience ran out, Vadomarius was arrested while he was attending a banquet, and he was sent to Spain. (His son succeeded him as king.) During Julian's campaign in the east, Vadomarius was the "leader of the Phoenicians," and under Julian's successor, Valens, he conducted the siege of Nicaea and successfully commanded troops against the Persian king Sapor II in 371. This German king was at home in the Roman world, at least as that world was represented by the army, and he was a trusted commander, although his loyalty was pledged to the emperor and the army, not to the abstract entity Rome.

Julian tried to ameliorate the radical division between government and governed in Gaul with a total reorganization of the administration and a remission of taxes. His reforms were opposed by his own chief of staff (Constantius's man), who ordered a larger tax. When Julian refused, the chief of staff reported to Constantius, and Constantius ordered Julian to collect the tax. Julian made a personal appeal to the people of Gaul and collected more money than the chief of staff had demanded. Julian's success aroused the suspicions of Constantius, and Julian was ordered to send several large contingents of troops east to Constantius for the Persian War of the winter 359–360. Julian agreed, but his troops refused to serve so far away from their homes. They convinced Julian to let them proclaim him emperor (February 360), and they raised Julian on a shield, a custom followed by the German tribes. Julian asked Constantius to recognize him as co-emperor. Instead, Constantius gathered an army, and Julian and Constantius marched to a confrontation averted only by the death of Constantius in 361.

Thus Julian became sole emperor of the Roman Empire. Julian hated Christianity as the enemy of the Hellenic past he loved. He withdrew the privileges Christians had enjoyed and reintroduced sacrifice and the emperor cult. He forbade Christians to teach in the schools and refused them public careers. He looked the other way as old scores were settled.

Julian was young, intelligent, and attractive, but his lack of experience, or of judgment, doomed his campaign against Persia. He led half of his army of about 65,000 men down the Euphrates and directed the other half to take the northern route and support him by a separate operation. Julian's fundamental error was to predicate his own strategy on his expectations of what Sapor would do, that is, that Julian would be able to fight a decisive battle against Sapor at the very beginning of the campaign and then have things all his own way. Instead, Julian did not get his battle, he was harried by the Persian king all the way to Ctesiphon, and there—the Roman army no longer having the engineering capabilities of Julius Caesar or Trajan's army—he dared not risk a siege with the enemy army so close; nor could he retreat up the Euphrates (which he had stripped of supplies on the march down), and so he chose to retire up the Tigris towards a juncture with his northern army.

Julian faced continual harassment by the Persian cavalry, all the supplies he needed were destroyed by Sapor's army, and on 22 June 363 Julian was compelled to fight the Persians near Maranga. Julian forced the Persians to break off the battle, but he had not knocked them out, his army continued to suffer under constant attack, and, three days after the battle, Julian rushed from his tent without his armor to rally his rear guard, then under attack; he was shot with an arrow, and he died of his wound.

### 59. A Roman Soldier, c. 214 A.D. (from a tombstone)

### 60. Constantine's Troops (312 A.D.)

Note the round shields and spears (which seem to have replaced the sword as the principal weapon).

# 34

# The Fall of Rome

## *External Enemies, Internal Weaknesses, Lack of Resources, Incompetent Emperors . . .*

A council of army officers in Mesopotamia selected the next emperor, Jovian. Jovian was a genial man, about thirty years of age, a Christian, and no great strategist: he accepted a disadvantageous treaty with the Persians to free himself to return to Constantinople. He reigned for only eight months; at his death in February of 364 an imperial council convened at Nicaea and chose as their next emperor a Pannonian tribune named Valentinian. Valentinian (in the opinion of the senatorial class) was a violent, brutal man, hot tempered, a poor judge of character, uncultured and suspicious of those who were, but he was also hardworking, a capable administrator, and a Christian. The council required Valentinian to choose a colleague and he chose his 36-year-old brother Valens. Valens was loyal, a hard worker, conscientious, and a Christian, but he was suspicious by nature and an untested general. Once again, two emperors divided the Roman Empire. Valentinian took charge of Illyricum, Italy, Africa, and Gaul; Valens was left to rule the east. As the emperors before them, they had problems raising money and men—Valentinian ordered the height requirement for recruits to be reduced to 5' 7''.

In the east Valens faced a rebellion (in 365) by a distant relative of Julian; the rebellion had the support of Athanaric, king of the Visigoths, and, perhaps for that reason, two German generals appointed by Valens betrayed him and joined the rebellion. Valens defeated the rebels, had the German generals executed, cut off the subsidy he had been paying Athanaric (to keep the peace and to furnish the Romans with troops), and invaded Visigothic territory (367–369).

No sooner had he forced the Visigoth to come to terms than he learned that the Persian king, Sapor, had invaded Armenia and put his own candidate on the throne. Valens was forced into a war against Persia, a war that dragged on for years, sometimes under the personal direction of Valens and sometimes through subordinates, a war which cost men and money and was ultimately unsuccessful. In the west Valentinian remained on the Rhine to fight the Alemanni, while he sent his count of military affairs, Theodosius, to fight the Saxons and the Picts in Britain in 367. Theodosius defeated them and Valentinian promoted him master of horse and count of the Saxon shore to replace the former occupant of the office who had been killed in action.

The emperors and their subordinate commanders enjoyed such a string of successes that they no longer feared a massive barbarian attack, but they were still unable to prevent the small bands raiding Roman territory, gathering loot, and running for cover. Trajan, Marcus Aurelius, or Septimius Severus would have invaded and occupied the territory where the raids originated. Valentinian just did not have the resources; he and his brother were forced into a reactive, though still capable, defense. Moreover, Valentinian, partly because of his own character but also because of the nature of the empire of his time, could not rest easy while a subordinate was winning victories in the field. When Valentinian learned of a rebellion of Moors in Africa (in 372—several Roman regiments had joined the rebels), he sent Theodosius to put it down, but when Theodosius overcame the rebellion, Valentinian, suspicious of Theodosius's success, his ability, and his possible ambition, ordered him executed.

In 375, while Valentinian was in Illyricum to address the problems of the limes there, he gave an audience to some Quadi and Sarmatian envoys; the envoys' insolence so enraged him that he had a stroke and dropped dead. His son Gratian, 16 years old, already designated as his successor, became emperor and, under pressure from the army, promoted his younger brother, Valentinian (II)—four years old—to be co-ruler. Gratian secured the loyalty of the important Pannonian segment of the army by promoting Pannonians to all ranks. Gratian commanded the army and the army, now a mixture of German and Roman, pagan and Christian, dominated the government.

The succession was smooth, the new emperor was firmly in control, and the Roman army, east and west, protected Rome's borders; at this moment, when the empire seemed to be stable and secure, catastrophe struck. A people unknown to the Romans, a terrifying people, the Huns, advanced from the borders of China across South Russia to the Black Sea; they were horse archers and they used stirrups, which gave the Romans the impression that they were *glued to the backs of their horses.*

"The Huns slash the cheeks of their newborn sons with a knife, so that the whiskers will grow in patches around the scars. They are short and muscular and monstrously ugly. They eat the uncooked roots of wild plants and the raw flesh of beasts; the meat they put between their thighs and the backs of their horses to warm it a little. They dress in linen cloth or in the skins of field mice sewn together; they wear the same clothing indoors and out until it falls off them. They have no fixed abode. Their families live entirely in wagons; in wagons they have intercourse with their wives, and their wives bear their children and rear them to the age of puberty in their wagons. By night and day they buy and sell, eat and drink, and even sleep on the backs of their horses. They are faithless and unreliable and totally without a sense of right and wrong. They lust for gold.

"When they fight, they form in wedge-shaped masses, they divide into small bands and attack from all directions. They shoot arrows tipped with sharpened bone, they close and fight hand to hand with swords; and then, when they have concentrated their enemy's attention on the swords, they lasso them, entangle them, and immobilize them. The Huns seem not to care whether they live or die."

This savage race plundered and slaughtered their way to the borders of the kingdom of the Ostrogoths. The Ostrogoths tried in vain to defend themselves— their army was crushed, their king committed suicide, and the survivors fled west with stories of such horror that the Visigoths refused to obey their king, Athanaric, and fight the Huns. Instead they appealed to Valens; they swore that they would serve in the Roman army if he would only grant them refuge inside the empire. Valens received the offer at a time when the Roman army was no longer attracting volunteers (to a lifetime of hard service little better than slavery) and the ranks had to be filled by conscription; some potential recruits rendered themselves unfit for service by chopping off their right thumb (an act punishable by immolation), and new recruits were branded to identify them should they desert.

Valens granted the Visigoths' appeal, sent many of them to serve in the east, some to serve in the west, and he instructed the imperial bureaucracy to feed and administer the bulk of the Visigoths, who remained where they had crossed the Danube. The Roman bureaucrats, who with the best will in the world would have found their bureaucracy overwhelmed by the sheer number of Goths, turned the situation to their own personal profit, sold the Goths the food which was supposed to have been supplied gratis, sold some of the Goths into slavery, and generally treated the Goths like scum. The Goths rallied behind the leadership of the Gothic king Fritigern and began to march towards Adrianople.

Valens sent a unit of foot archers and cavalry to check the advance of Fritigern and the Goths—he thought he was putting down a mutiny of about 10,000 men—while he advanced to Adrianople; there he received Richimer, the chief of staff of his nephew, Gratian, the emperor of the west. Richimer advised Valens to await the arrival of his nephew. Valens also received an envoy (a Christian elder) from the Gothic king Fritigern, who demanded that the emperor cede to the Goths the whole of Thrace. Valens rejected both advice and demand, and on 9 August 378 he led his army, stripped for rapid marching, forward under a blazing sun to meet Fritigern and the Goths; in the early afternoon, after an eight hour march, the Romans came within sight of the laagered wagons of the Goths.

Valens was surprised that he had encountered the Goths so soon, and he was taken aback by the size of the Gothic army, but he drew up his army (as it arrived on the battlefield), with his advance guard of cavalry on the right, then the infantry in formation, and finally on the left the rest of the cavalry as it straggled from different roads onto the battlefield. Although Valens was surprised, he had also taken the Goths by surprise—Fritigern did not have all his cavalry in camp—but Valens frittered away the surprise, accepted the Goths' request for a parley, and allowed Fritigern to spin the parley out until the Gothic cavalry had all returned. Valens did not look to the security or well-being of his own force—to fortify a camp in which his troops could rest, eat, and drink (but no more had Julian before the battle of Strasbourg). His troops were hungry and thirsty, tired from the long, rapid march, and further discomfited by smoke from huge bonfires lighted by the Goths.

When Fritigern learned that his cavalry had returned, he ordered the attack. The Gothic cavalry drove the Roman cavalry back on the right. The Roman cavalry on the left advanced to the ring of wagons, but Valens had allowed it to advance unsupported, and it was surrounded and destroyed. The infantry, now bereft of cavalry, was hidden in clouds of dust and smoke. The Goths fired arrows from all directions, and their infantry advanced on the Romans, but the Romans fought with courage and tenacity. Hand to hand with sword and axe, the two sides hacked at each other, split breastplate and helmet, until the Gothic cavalry overpowered the Roman infantry, and the Roman line broke and fled. Without a fortified camp the Romans had no place of refuge. Two-thirds of the Roman army was killed. The emperor was killed, and his body was never found.

The Goths stormed the gates of Adrianople, but the gates had been blocked from within by huge boulders, and the Goths squandered their lives to learn that the city was impregnable. At last they were willing to listen to Fritigern, who advised them—and with them some Alans and Huns—to advance on Constantinople. Meanwhile, as the Goths pillaged their way towards the city, word of the catastrophe reached the Romans farther to the east, and they murdered all the Goths in the army and sought help from the Saracens. The Goths reached Constantinople and there they sat, making futile attacks upon the walls, until a Saracen, naked except for a loincloth, slit a Goth's throat and drank his blood. The Goths, already depressed by the size of the city, were horrified by the sight, and they broke off the attempt to take Constantinole and turned to pillaging and looting the countryside.

Gratian called on Theodosius, the son of the executed general, to restore the situation. On 19 January 379 Theodosius was declared augustus. He was to be the last emperor of a united empire. Theodosius immediately instituted a rigorous conscription: the sons of soldiers all were enlisted, in every district an official was placed in charge of recruitment, those who had sought to avoid service by amputating their thumbs now were enlisted in labor battalions at a rate of 2 to 1, and barbarians were recruited directly into the legions. Still, the Roman army, undersized and demoralized, had to limit its operations to pursuing and hunting down small bands of looters that had broken off from the main Gothic force, until the Goths themselves fought what amounted to a minor civil war over the spoils. Theodosius gave refuge to the Visigothic king, Athanaric, whose leadership had been rejected by his own people, treated him as a king, and, when Athanaric died, gave him a magnificent funeral—an act that won over many Goths.

In 382 Theodosius negotiated a treaty with the Goths already inside the empire; he allowed them to settle along the Danube as a federated people, that is, an independent entity allied to, and theoretically subservient to, the emperor, who would use them to defend the line of the Danube and, thereby, to retrieve a disaster brought on by the bad judgment of his predecessor. Theodosius did succeed in stabilizing the border—in 386 he prevented bands of Ostrogoths from crossing the Danube into Roman territory—but he left a disastrous legacy for his successors (within fifteen years of his death the Goths under their king, Alaric, would sack Rome). Theodosius stabilized the eastern border by agreeing with Persia to a partition of Armenia, but in the west in 383, the emperor Gratian (who had appointed Theodosius), a well-educated, moral, and good-looking young man, but an incompetent emperor, was overthrown by Magnus Maximus, the commander of troops in Britain.

Theodosius tried to avert civil war. He recognized Maximus as the emperor of the west with but one condition, that Maximus recognize Gratian's heir, Valentinian II (13 years old), as emperor of Italy, Illyricum, and Africa. Foolishly Maximus rejected the offer and invaded Italy in 387; Valentinian fled, Theodosius brought his army west, and, in two battles, he defeated and killed Maximus. Theodosius remained in the west (he left the east under the regency of his son, Arcadius) until he had restored order and could, he thought, entrust the west to Valentinian and his master of troops, Arbogast. In 391 Theodosius returned to Constantinople. Theodosius had restored the empire, but he had had to rely on German troops, troops who, in the end, followed him because of their respect for him as an individual.

Theodosius divided up the army commands in the east by region and appointed a master of troops to each region so that no single master of troops was powerful enough to dominate his rivals or become a rival to the emperor, but in the west one master of troops commanded all the imperial armies. In 392 Valentinian quarreled with his master of troops, Arbogast, and Arbogast murdered him, appointed a Roman professor of rhetoric as a figurehead emperor, and fortified the entrance into Italy against the expected attack of Theodosius, who arrived in 394. Theodosius ordered the 20,000 federated Goths in his army to assault the position along a narrow front (the battle of the Frigid River, A.D. 394). The first day the Goths were unable to break through (10,000 Goths were killed in the fighting), and Arbogast and his puppet celebrated a victory that night, but the next day Theodosius ordered a new assault. The new assault was at the point of failure when a fierce wind rose at the backs of Theodosius's men, the wind drove dust into the eyes of the enemy and blinded them, and the Goths broke through their defenses, burned the wall and towers, and captured the puppet emperor, who was beheaded. Arbogast committed suicide.

Early in 395 Theodosius died. (Since he was the last emperor to control the whole empire, some historians place the end of the Roman Empire in 395.) Honorius, his son, (10 years old) became emperor of the west. Arcadius, his other son (17 or 18 years old) became emperor of the east. The descendants of

Theodosius ruled until the middle of the fifth century. The Theodosian emperors were decent human beings, but they were too young and they were overborne by their advisers, who counselled them on what was best for the advisers first and the emperors and the empire second and third.

In the west the master of troops was Stilicho, a Vandal who had been picked by Theodosius. Stilicho has been used as a symbol of the barbarization of the Roman Empire, but he is a symbol that cuts both ways—his father, a Vandal, had been an officer in a Roman cavalry unit, his mother was Roman, he grew up among the imperial family, and he married a niece of the emperor Theodosius I. Stilicho, as a favorite of Theodosius, as a member of the imperial family, and as a German, rose to command the western army.

At this time the army of the west comprised probably—in toto—a quarter of a million men, as did the army of the east. Of that quarter million about 35,000 were specialized troops—riverine engineers, mounted and unmounted archers, pikemen, artillery. The rest of the Roman army was divided into field and border troops. The field troops were divided into *comitatenses* and *palatini*. The palatini were an elite within the comitatenses (probably originating from the emperor's palace guard). The comitatenses were divided further into vexillationes (cavalry), units of about 600 men, auxilia in units of 1,200 men, and the legions of 1,200 men (commanded by a tribune). A unit of cavalry and a unit of infantry might act together as a combined command. The cavalry mixed light and heavy. An imperial supply system ensured that horses were examined and purchased, fed, exercised, and ready for the cavalry or supply train. The supply service also bred horses. Non-Roman units were incorporated in the army; allied forces, like the Goths at the Frigid River, were used for one campaign and then released. The border (*limitanei*) troops were divided into cohorts and legions, and the cavalry into *alae*. Their primary occupation was rebuilding and repairing the line of defensive fortifications. Their commanders, tribunes and prefects, began their careers in the imperial "police force" and there learned their duties and gained experience before being sent to a unit as commander.

Infantry outnumbered cavalry about two to one, and perhaps a quarter to a third of the infantry were trained to use the bow. In a battle the ratio of infantry to cavalry might be ten to three in numbers, two to one in units. The Roman infantry of this period carried an oval shield and still wore helmets and chest armor—linked rings or scale (bronze plates sewn on leather—Romans who shipped armor out of Roman territory were liable to criminal prosecution). Soldiers may have increased their speed of movement by marching without armor and, therefore, may occasionally have had to fight without it, but soldiers generally were expected to carry their arms and armor, twenty days' rations, blanket, water jug, identification, pickaxe, tent quarter, stake, boots, woolen blouse, cloak, trousers, and any personal items (altogether a load in the range of sixty pounds). The soldiers were not paid a regular salary, but they did receive their equipment and supplies, a five-year bonus, bonuses on the accession of an emperor, and (if the soldier survived) a discharge bonus. At the beginning of the fourth century the military budget consumed about 50–60 percent of the annual income of the empire; as territory, and income, was lost, the military consumed more and more of the income.

The barbarians who joined the Roman army as individual recruits were treated the same as everyone else, they probably joined for the same reasons (security, action, escape), and they were probably as loyal to their unit as everyone else. Individual Germans could rise through the ranks to a position one rank below the highest position in the Roman state and army. In the period from the mid-fourth to mid-fifth century the army, officer and enlisted, appears to have maintained a ratio of about 70 percent Roman citizen to 30 percent non–Roman.

Such was the army that Stilicho commanded. Stilicho was a first-rate commander laboring under a great disadvantage—he could not recruit nor operate in Roman territory beyond the divide of east and west, and the divide at that time denied him the recruiting ground of Illyria, which Stilicho believed was crucial to the survival of the west. Stilicho argued that Illyria had been assigned to the east as a temporary measure by Theodosius. Moreover, Stilicho was frustrated strategically.

Stilicho's greatest enemy was Alaric, the king of the federated Goths. Alaric's objectives are not clear and perhaps were not clear to himself. He had to satisfy the Goths and his own personal ambition. He may have wanted recognition through a high imperial position, he may have wanted to have a large portion of the Roman Empire ceded to him, but his actions rather suggest that he had no clear objective beyond the ravaging of the empire for Gothic benefit. At first Stilicho was able to maneuver both the eastern and western armies to pursue Alaric and corner him in Thrace, but Stilicho seemed to the eastern government to be more of a threat than Alaric was, and at the point of success Stilicho was ordered to release the eastern army and to cease operations in the east. When he obeyed, Alaric looted Greece and sacked and destroyed Sparta, thus ending the history of that ancient city. If both emperors had gone into the field and cooperated against Alaric, they might have eliminated him and broken the Goths, but the emperors were content to live a dream-life at court and rule through intermediaries.

In 401 Alaric entered Italy and attacked Milan. In two battles in the next year (402) Stilicho defeated him and forced him to quit Italy, but in 405 Stilicho had to concentrate on a new German invasion; he crushed the Germans, but the constant warfare was draining his manpower and he was unable to replace the citizens he lost from the recruiting ground to which he had access; he was convinced that the western empire had to control Dalmatia and Macedonia, he made this goal policy, and the policy made the eastern emperor his enemy. In 405–406 Stilicho crushed an invasion of Italy by a band of Goths under their leader Radagaisus. Stilicho surrounded them, defeated them, killed Radagaisus, and accepted the surrender of the surviving Goths. In 407 Stilicho had to give Alaric, who was in Epirus, a huge bribe not to support a massive invasion of Gaul by the Vandals and Alans. Such payments were a part of Roman policy;

they were cheaper than a large-scale military operation, and, in this case, the payment gave Stilicho a free hand to defeat the invasion, but all was not well within the Roman world. A rival emperor rose in Britain and invaded and conquered Spain.

In 408 Arcadius, the emperor of the east, died, and his infant son Theodosius II was made emperor. Honorius was dissuaded from going east—which he probably should have done—but he decided to send Stilicho. With Stilicho away from the court and separated from the army, the court flatterers finally convinced the emperor that Stilicho was disloyal. Without going into the field themselves, or ever risking themselves, they still had determined that Stilicho had fallen short of total victory because he did not want to defeat fellow Germans. The whisperers had their way, Stilicho was arrested, brought back in chains, and executed without a hearing. At the news of his death 30,000 Germans left the ranks of the Roman army and joined Alaric.

Whatever Stilicho's intentions and ambitions might have been, the emperor recognized one partial truth—that the master of troops, as the sole commander of the army, was a threat to the emperor so long as the emperor remained detached from the army. Augustus, Vespasian, Trajan, Severus, the soldier emperors, Diocletian, all had recognized (in different circumstances) that their power lay with the army and that the army constituted the greatest threat to their power. The emperors after Theodosius grasped that one fact and no other. Stilicho and his army dominated the situation until Stilicho's execution, the emperor had no plan past ridding himself of the suspected Stilicho, and from then on the enemies of Rome held the balance of power in the west.

Honorius refused Alaric's demand for cash. Alaric laid siege to Rome (no longer the residence of the emperor), and the city bought him off with 5,000 pounds of gold, 30,000 pounds of silver, and 3,000 pounds of pepper. The next year, 409, Alaric again came to Rome and again extorted a payment; in an attempt to enhance his own position he created a shadow emperor, but when he found that this shadow emperor brought him no advantage, he murdered him. In 410—another date for the "fall of the Roman Empire"—Alaric came back to Rome and sacked it. Alaric's capture of Rome crushed morale throughout the Roman world. Pagans blamed Christians. Christians were silent.

Alaric died soon after he sacked Rome, but the German advance continued: various German tribes divided Gaul, the Vandals occupied Spain, the Saxons invaded Britain, and the Romans did not have the resources to prevent the loss of the western empire. In 415 the emperor sent the king of the Visigoths to drive the Vandals from Spain. The Visigoths were successful, but then they became involved in a series of wars to determine which Germans would be the masters of Gaul, and in 429 Romans in Africa invited the Vandals under their king, Gaiseric, to come to Africa and settle an internal dispute; once there the Vandals occupied Numidia, in 439 Gaiseric seized Carthage, and in a peace of 442 the Romans recognized him as the ruler of Africa. In 446 Britain was officially abandoned.

As the Germans divided up the western empire, in the east in 434 the Huns received a new king, Attila. Attila terrified the Romans; he was a pagan, the commander of the finest horsemen in the world, and a relentless enemy. He transformed his kingdom into a powerful empire, and he demanded that the Romans of the eastern empire pay him a subsidy not to invade Roman territory. In 443 he was paid 6,000 pounds of gold by the Romans, and he was promised an annual payment of 2,100 pounds, but four years later Attila drove the Romans from the south bank of the Danube and forced them to agree to abandon a strip of land five days' journey wide. After this triumph Attila turned his attention to the west in response to a plea by an imperial princess to save her from an unhappy marriage; Attila demanded her hand in marriage and half of the western empire as her dowry. In response to this demand the Roman master of troops convinced the Germans that they had as much to lose as the Romans, and in 451 a huge army composed of Romans, Visigoths, Franks, Burgundians, and Alans fought a battle against Attila in Gaul and defeated him. Attila himself escaped, but he died in 453 and the empire he had created dissolved.

Both west and east had been ravaged by these wars; the eastern empire could raise troops but could not help the west, and the western empire was at the end of its resources. The emperors ruled in name only; the power belonged to the Germans. In 476 Romulus Augustulus, a self-proclaimed emperor who himself had scant legal claim to the throne, was deposed by the German king, Odoacer. Odoacer asked the eastern emperor for formal recognition, the emperor refused, and Odoacer ruled in his own name as king. The western empire was no more. The eastern empire survived until 1453.

Various reasons have been advanced for the fall of the west: the loss of moral fiber (through Christianity, the loss of faith in the gods, personal decadence), the folly of the emperors isolated in the court, the exclusion of the Senate, the heavy taxation, the large bureaucracy, the destruction of the bureaucracy (which supplied the army), the loss of Roman fighting ability, the change from legion to cavalry, from heavy armor to light or *no* armor, the fortress mentality of the empire, the increased organization, numbers, and fighting ability of Rome's enemies . . . . No single explanation is satisfactory, but throughout this study of the history of ancient warfare we have found the relationship between the citizen and the military to be crucial, and by the fifth century the ordinary inhabitants of the Roman Empire had little at stake in the success of the empire. In the end, the Roman Empire of the west did not have the resources to rebound from a string of disasters brought about by incompetent emperors.

## Map 24: The Fall of the Roman Empire

Southern Gaul (Visigoths 412-507)
Spain (Visigoths 415-711)
Africa (Vandals 429-548)
Britain (Anglo-Saxons 450- )
Northern Gaul (Franks 486- )
Italy (Ostrogoths 489-554)
  Rome sacked by Alaric 410
  Last emperor of the West deposed 476

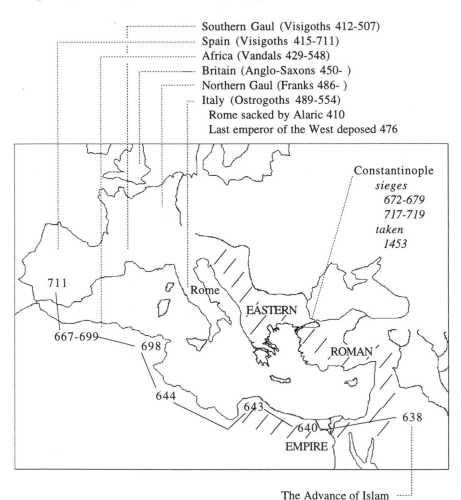

Constantinople
*sieges*
  *672-679*
  *717-719*
*taken*
  *1453*

711

Rome

EASTERN

ROMAN

667-699

698

644

643

640

638

EMPIRE

The Advance of Islam

# Afterword
## The Lessons of Ancient Warfare

To study war is to study the violent means by which societies attempt to gain their objectives against other societies.

If we consider that battles are no more than a matter of maneuvering men so that they can drive chunks of metal into the flesh of their enemies, not much has changed from the ancient world to the present except the types of metal chunks—copper, bronze, iron, lead, steel, depleted uranium—and the delivery systems. Ancient armies at the dawn of history fought in formation, modern armies fight in formation and, while formations are influenced by the weapons used—so the Romans opened the phalanx to give swords swinging distance—and the instruments of delivery have changed—from arrow, sword, and spear, and axes and slings, to crossbow, musket, rifle, and machine gun—the concept of a mass of men, organized and acting in concert, has not changed. The armies, ancient or modern, which define their objective clearly, which seize the initiative, which surprise the enemy while securing themselves from surprise, which outmaneuver the enemy, mass at the critical point, and obey a single authority win the battle.

Philip, Alexander's father, said that it is better to have an army of deer commanded by a lion than an army of lions commanded by a deer; Alexander himself told his men that their greatest advantage was that their leader was Alexander. Alexander lived and practiced what modern (Western) military theorists teach to their pupils as the principles of war. The principles were developed out of an analysis of Napoleon's campaigns and today are supposed to guide military officers in the practice of their profession and to guide historians in their analysis of campaigns and leadership. The principles are (in order of importance): the objective, the offensive, surprise, mass and economy of force, security, unity of command, maneuver, and simplicity.

Alexander was a military genius. No other ancient commander was so quick to understand and defeat his enemies' plans, so quick to analyze a problem and grasp the solution—and, not coincidentally, no other ancient commander was as well educated as Alexander, by the greatest soldier and diplomat of his age,

Philip, and by the greatest philosopher, humanist, and scientist of any age, Aristotle. In every aspect of warfare Alexander outthought and outfought his enemies. He enunciated his military objective in the simplest and most forceful terms: he would meet Darius on the battlefield, fight him, and kill him. He forced Darius to react to him, and although Darius and the Persians chose where to fight, Alexander seized the initiative by doing the unexpected—by attacking in the evening instead of the morning at the Granicus or by maneuvering off the prepared battlefield at Gaugamela. He brought together a large enough force to defeat the Persians but kept it small enough to be supplied and to be mobile. As bold as he was in the attack, just so cautious was he in securing his troops against attack. He was the complete commander.

Other men were great battle leaders, but not necessarily great strategists; their victorious battles did not always determine the outcome of the war. Pyrrhus of Epirus, who approached Alexander in tactical ability, defeated the Romans in two battles, drew a third, and was driven from Italy. Hannibal crossed the Alps, invaded Italy, defeated the Romans in three massive battles in which the Romans may have lost as many as 100,000 men, and could not win the war. Hannibal has been criticized, in the ancient world and the modern, for not marching on Rome after the battle of Cannae, but his objective—to break apart the Roman "confederation" and reduce Rome in status—was unattainable because it was based on a misunderstanding of the Italian situation. Hannibal could not win without destroying Rome, and he did not have the resources, nor could he acquire the resources, to accomplish that objective; thus his campaign, though spectacular, was futile—no offensive, no matter how brilliant, can overcome an ill-conceived objective. Similarly Li Kuang led more than seventy successful campaigns against the Huns, and yet upon his death China was hardly more secure from the Huns than it had been before him.

Objective is the first principle of war and rightly so. Hannibal's objective was misconceived and unattainable, whereas the objective as conceived by Alexander was so brilliant, so logical, and so simple that it has received too little attention from modern historians; he did not just define his objective as the Persian king nor state his objective in the most simple terms—Alexander would meet Darius in battle, kill him, and thus become king in his stead—but he defined the war for the enemy as well—the Persians were fighting to protect the right of their king to rule; they were not fighting for their independence or to avoid subjugation or to preserve their personal power. They were not the enemy of Alexander. When they accepted him as their king, they became his subjects no less than the Macedonians were his subjects. Alexander's defined objective echoes the spirit of Sun-Tzu's precept never to corner your enemy and drive him to desperation.

Societies—be they a radical democracy or the monarchy of a god-king—lose wars when they have no clear objectives or their objectives are beyond their resources. Stated so baldly, it might seem that no society would ever enter a war without a clear understanding of what it wanted and how it meant to gain what it wanted, but many did. The Athenian democracy, for one, fought—and lost—just such a war against the Spartans. By contrast, the early republic of Rome fought always for a defined objective. Neither success nor failure diverted the Romans from their stated objective, and so the enemies of Rome who, at the beginning of a war rejected Roman terms, by the end considered them generous. Moreover, the Romans saw objectives beyond the immediate war (as did Alexander)—the enemies of the moment would be the allies, associates, and citizens of the future. The Roman republic integrated the defeated Italians into the Roman system and eventually granted Roman citizenship to all free Italians. The Roman policy of inclusion made them the most powerful state of the Mediterranean world. No other ancient state, with the partial exception of China, so assimilated its defeated enemies. The Roman system made Rome powerful despite some mediocre leaders, and it put few restraints on the abilities of its brilliant leaders.

Caesar was a great strategist. In eight years he so pacified Gaul that it never rebelled; he isolated the Gauls, divided them and used tribe against tribe, exterminated those who resisted, and rewarded those who helped, even to admit some to the Senate. On the other hand, at the personal level, while his victories in the civil wars put him in a position to dictate his own terms as first man in Rome, he failed to define his position in a way that was acceptable to senatorial Romans.

By contrast, the most powerful state of the Greek world was Sparta, but when the Spartans determined to conquer the little town of Tegea and turn the population there into state slaves, the Spartan army was soundly defeated because Sparta did not have the resources to overcome a people who were willing to fight to the death. The Spartans were forced to recognize that they did not have the manpower to conquer and subjugate even a relatively weak neighbor, let alone Arcadia or the rest of the Peloponnesus. They had to redefine their objective, not to conquer, but to secure and control the Peloponnesus. Just so long as they held to that objective, they preserved their power, but when the Spartans of the fourth century grew ambitious and defined the Spartan objective as a Spartan-ruled empire encompassing the whole of Greece, Sparta lost everything.

When societies do not work with one purpose within the limits of their own resources, they fail. Various reasons have been advanced for the fall of the western Roman Empire: the loss of moral fiber (through Christianity, the loss of faith in the gods, or loyalty to "Rome" as an ideal, personal decadence), the folly of the emperors isolated in the court, the exclusion of the Senate, the heavy taxation, the large bureaucracy, the destruction of the bureaucracy (which supplied the army), the loss of Roman fighting ability, the change from legion to cavalry, from heavy armor to light (or to *no*) armor, the fortress mentality of the empire, the increased organization, numbers, and fighting ability of Rome's enemies. . . . No single explanation is satisfactory.

If we analyze the military aspect of the Roman Empire—or any society—and ask the question How did the objectives of its various leaders change over time? we find an interesting answer. In the first two centuries of the empire, while the primary objective of the Roman emperor was security, both the security of the person and position of the emperor and the security of the borders of the empire, the security of the empire was ensured as often by aggressive campaigns as by passive defense. Augustus solved the immediate personal problem of how to maintain control of the army and the Senate or, generally, how to eliminate the adventurers who used the Roman army for personal advancement, by assuming absolute control of the army. The result was that the foreign policy of the empire was directed by one will that ended the two-century-long, ill-disciplined expansion of the republic's borders. Nonetheless the means at the disposal of the emperors enabled them to secure the empire and invade, punish, and, if necessary, subjugate their enemies.

Augustus created (and lost) the province of Germany, subsequently initiated the conquest of Germany (and abandoned it when the Illyrians rebelled), Claudius added Britain, Trajan responded to Dacian aggression by the conquest and conversion of Dacia to a Roman province, and Marcus Aurelius attempted (and failed) to subjugate Germany. Free Germany remained a threat that drained the empire's resources while, by contrast, the conquered and assimilated provinces of Spain, Gaul, and Illyria were prosperous economic units in the empire and a source of manpower for the Roman army. The crisis of the third century forced the emperor to narrow the objectives of the empire to defense; no emperor ever again set as an objective the subjugation and integration of Germany as a province. The later imperial army overbore the empire and consumed its resources, so that it was far less able to cope with emergencies than the late republic—and every attempt to solve the immediate problems weakened the base from which the resources came. Both Rome and China incorporated alien nations within their own borders with equally disastrous results, even though the Chinese were successful in expelling the majority of the Huns from their borders. If the Romans could have integrated the Germans as they had the Illyrians, perhaps the fifth-century empire would have been saved by the *virtus Germanica* as the third century empire was saved by the *virtus Illyrica*. The Roman army to the end was superior to any single foe, but it was an army without a strong economic base and without adequate sources of manpower.

The Roman emperors could have solved their manpower problems with a short-term draft, but they believed that the population they ruled would become dangerous to themselves if they trained it generally for war. Thus they kept only a small proportion of the empire's population under arms and preferred to hire foreigners for specific campaigns. Han China divorced the emperor himself from the army, so that simple command of the armies did not mean that an individual had ultimate power, and the Chinese did levy men from their whole domain for short-term enlistments; consequently the emperors had enormous resources of manpower, but so did local pretenders.

No society can accomplish its objectives without the organization and marshalling of the society's resources, and in the organization and application of resources, in communications and logistics (the least-studied field), we find the greatest changes between the ancient and the modern world. We can clothe, feed, resupply, and medicate an army of a million, and we can send and receive messages from the highest command to the lowest. In any war most of the time and energy is consumed in supporting and advancing the military forces to the point of action. All ancient armies depended to some extent on local supply and labor, but even so the best had an efficient comissariat to organize that supply. The masters of organization in the ancient world were the Assyrians, Chinese, and Romans.

In Trajan's column most of the scenes depict the Roman army on the march. For instance, between the formal beginning of the campaign (the lustration of the army and the sacrifices and the formal address by the emperor) and the forming of the army before battle, there are sixteen scenes: construction of a fort, the auxiliaries on guard, inspection by Trajan, more construction, the advance of scouts and a watering party, construction of a road, another fort, legionnaires on parade, the first prisoner, construction of two camps, a river crossing, another camp, auxillaries crossing a bridge, a deserted fort, and road construction. The column depicts also the supply column and the artillery.

Ancient armies mostly fought with the same kind of equipment, but the introduction of the bow and arrow, bronze in place of copper, the composite bow, iron in place of bronze, the short Roman sword, and other innovations all gave one side a temporary advantage unless, like the Roman short sword, it was part of a greater organizational reform. Yet one change had profound and revolutionary effects, perhaps the greatest effects of any change until the nuclear age or even including the nuclear age—the creation of the weapons system of the horse, chariot, and composite bow.

The chariot gave such an advantage that it conquered wherever it went, and the people armed with the chariot spread from the steppes west to Britain and east to India and China. Unlike a single invention, the weapon system required acquisition of scarce items (like horses), extensive training of horses and men, and the skill of craftsmanship in building the chariots. The chariot weapons system made relatively primitive people the masters of the Eurasian continent. (Compare gunpowder or nuclear weapons—the great powers before the invention were the very powers that adopted the new technology.) So long as the chariot people kept exclusive control of the chariot, they were the masters of the lands they occupied and even the lands neighboring on their own, but soon enough the great civilizations of the Near East and China adopted the chariot and achieved parity with the original chariot people. Just so the Athenians maintained their superiority at sea, not because their ships were technically superior to others, but because they had developed a system to construct, support, repair, and man a fleet. Their democracy furnished and organized the manpower. So long as they operated within the limits of their resources, their superior numbers, training, morale, and organization gave them supremacy at sea.

Of the greatest area of ignorance in ancient military authorties, as perhaps in the modern, is the importance of economics. Augustus was one of the few who understood the importance of balancing the size of the military with the economic output of the empire. Pericles, too, seemed to understand the economic underpinnings of the Athenian fleet and the war against Sparta, but even he underestimated how much war cost. Wealthy societies have an enormous advantage if their leaders understand how to employ the wealth and understand the limits of their wealth. One strategy, used by Philip, the Roman emperors, and the Chinese, was to pay a potential enemy enough to avoid war, but less than the war would cost. Philip used the payments to delay war until he was ready; the Romans and Chinese hoped to avoid war altogether. "Subsidies" or "foreign aid" are as valid as a battle but, like fortifications, they must be backed by a force adequate to defend them.

The societies that were the most successful in war were the societies that could afford war. We find the Chinese debating the costs of war after Wu-ti had been emperor, and we find a tacit acknowledgment of this issue in the policy of Augustus, whereas the Athenians never grasped this point. The masters of war, however, were the Romans of the republic. They developed a system that did not depend upon the tactical brilliance of any single individual—and, indeed, they were not particularly distinguished in tactics—but they had a strategic reach unlike any other people. They truly did understand that the victor has won only the ability to shape the peace; victory by victory, they shaped the world around them the way they wanted it. Moreover, they could afford mistakes in the field because they had organized their resources better than any other society in their world.

Historians used to connect war with agriculture. Once human beings turned to agriculture, they had fixed abodes, and they had to defend their homes, their fields, and their crops. Moreover, they had a stockpile of supplies from which they could draw rations (once they had an organized and stable society), and they could carry the rations and support themselves in a raid on their neighbors. If preagricultural tribes came into conflict, the conflict revolved around the territory through which each gathered food. There were no settlements to attack, nothing permanent to destroy, nothing permanent to defend. Ancient armies were drawn from the farm.

Ancient explanations of the reasons for war vary. If the Standard of Ur truly reflects Sumerian values—battle followed by a presentation of booty to the ruler (who is seated at a feast)—then the Sumerian justification for war was the booty. The ruler may be the human ensi or he may be the patron god; the humans may be represented as enjoying the fruits of their victory directly as they feast or indirectly as they please their god, but the basic principle is the same—the object of war is the material acquired. Acquiring the material pleases the god. War, then, is acquisition, justified because the acquisition is prescribed or ordained by a god. Acquisition was most apparent with the Assyrians' yearly hunts to round up booty, which profited the kings and the patron god of Assyria, Ashur. The Egyptians needed no middleman to interpret the will of the gods—their king was a god.

To the Greeks of the *Iliad* war was a normal condition of human existence; the Trojan War was a duel between Greeks and Trojans and between the gods supporting each side. When Herodotus came to explain the causes of the Persian wars, he recalled the Trojan War and other incidents between east and west in the mythical past, a kind of feud extending over generations. The wars were composed of raid and counterraid, and the purpose was domination of neighbors more than conquest (though conquest did occur). Until the historian Thucydides wrote, wars were considered to be caused by concatenations of incidents, a multi-city (or multi-nation) feud that draws its neighbors into the feud and continues until one side admits defeat and agrees to the other's terms.

Thucydides, when he came to explain the causes of the Peloponnesian War, did list such incidents, but he saw greater underlying causes. That is, the incidents caused the war to break out at a particular moment, the underlying causes made war inevitable—the Athenians' power had grown, and the Spartans were afraid of it. Thucydides found the causes of war in human psychology. Although the Spartans justified the war as a war "to free the Greeks" and the Athenians as a war to establish their freedom of action, each side (according to Thucydides) acted as they did to maintain or extend their power.

When the Greek historian Polybius came to explain how Rome had become master of the world, he stated that he did not have to explain why: they saw that they could and so they did. The Romans themselves rather believed that each war they fought was a just war, brought about by a hostile action taken against them that required redress. War was justified only after the Romans had followed a set religious procedure to give the hostile party a chance to provide redress and, failing that, to follow a ritual that compelled divine powers to support the Roman cause.

China, as the central kingdom with a mandate from heaven, did not have to justify war on its borders in moral terms; it had a right to defend itself and to defend itself by annexing the borderlands. In contrast to the imperial powers, invaders seemed to share a common attitude and purpose often justified in their religion, to come as the instruments of a violent and vengeful god—to burn the enemy, to slay him, in the name of Indira or Jehovah; they believed that as they fought human enemies, their gods fought the enemy gods. Their objective was not the conquest and assimilation, but the extirpation or expulsion or enslavement of the indigenous population. Often the invaders settled down and separated into states, each choosing to worship a patron god, and ready to turn their aggressive spirit against each other, as in Sumer and Greece.

As we consider the Romans, we conclude that the wars following the Gallic sack of Rome were designed to unite Italy under the Romans and to provide security, at first from another Gallic attack and then from any hostile power in Italy. When the Roman Senate was approached by the Mamertines in Sicily, it could not decide whether to help them, to become involved outside Italy in what might be a long and complicated war; and so it put the question before the Roman people (who would pay the price), and the Roman assembly voted to accept the alliance and to fight the Carthaginians. In the same way the Spartans developed the best army in Greece, an army that enabled them to dominate the Peloponnesus, but the Spartans hesitated to extend their reach across the Aegean to the island of Samos or to support the Ionians against Persia. Thucydides praises them for never moving beyond the limits of their power, and another Athenian of that time analyzes the inherent weakness of their alliance, that they had to muster their allies, march through potentially hostile territory, carry all provisions with them, and possibly face a coalition of their former allies. They could not afford to lose a battle, or their alliance might fall apart. Successful societies recognize their limits.

Societies produce military systems that reflect their own values; these military systems are not always, or even mostly, the best that could be produced, but that is beside the point, until one society meets another in war. Most of the ancient societies were monarchies, almost all of the imperialistic powers were monarchies, but the Roman republic and the Athenian democracy were also successful. The Athenian democracy gave the Athenians the full use of their whole manpower and in turn was shaped by the necessities of maintaining a navy. The Roman republic challenged ambitious men to outdo each other in foreign conquest and so rise to the top of the state in wealth and power.

Alexander fought, and his men fought because men prove their courage by fighting and because they also profit by victory. Individual soldiers can become wealthy. A man who has not been born into a great family can nonetheless reach the heights of his society by his prowess in war, in China as in Rome. War creates an aristocracy and levels class distinctions. As Sarpedon says in the *Iliad*, "Glaucus, why are we two honored above all the others in the feasts in Lycia with all we want to eat and drink, and why do all look upon us almost as gods, and why do we possess rich orchards and fertile fields along the river? Do we not stand first among the Lycians, when they go into battle, so that someone of the heavy-armored Lycians might say, 'Not unjust is it that our kings hold Lycia, eat the fat hams, and drink honey-sweet wine; they prove their right when they fight in the front ranks of the Lycians.'

"Nonetheless, my friend, if we could avoid this battle and so live forever, I would advise us to withdraw, but no man can escape death, and so I say, let us go forward and win glory for ourselves or give it to another."

Individuals, such as Alexander or Chandragupta, were successful because of personal characteristics of leadership, strategic understanding, bravery, and tactical mastery, but systems, such as the Egyptians, the Romans, or the Chinese, were successful because of their unity (even in the republican Senate), stability, and organization. The most stable society of the ancient world was the Old Kingdom of Egypt. The king held absolute power, as only a ruler considered a god on earth could have, but the god-king's realm had no powerful foreign rivals, had easily defined and defended borders and enough native resources to satisfy his own and his subjects' needs. In similar fashion Assyria first closed off the passes into its heartland and then attacked from a secure base; Ch'in was described as a mountain fastness out of which soldiers poured like water from a pitcher; Philip secured his borders first.

In war the god-king of Egypt enjoyed a matchless unity of command. Rulers of other societies attempted to present themselves as gods, the Third Dynasty of Ur, Alexander, the Roman emperors, but they found limited success, and none of the three enjoyed enough time or stability to establish the tradition fully. Ur collapsed from discord within and invasion from without, Alexander died at the age of thirty-three, and the heir to the Roman imperial emperor cult converted to Christianity.

Successful societies balance their resources with their military needs. The most successful societies in the ancient world maintained that balance either by isolation, like the Old Kingdom of Egypt, or by assimilation and integration, like Rome and China. The successful societies offered its members a form of rule they accepted, whether they accepted an absolute rule because they believed their king was a god, as the Egyptians did, or whether they accepted a consensus of those who bore arms, as the Greeks did. As the examples of the Egyptians, Assyrians, Romans, and Chinese also show, societies that lose their internal cohesion become vulnerable to external attack.

History tells us that unity behind a mediocre plan is better than disunity behind a brilliant plan, that it is better to defer to another than to fight, that our individual ego and ambition needs to be subordinate to a common good, that those societies are the strongest in which individuals in the pursuit of their own personal objectives accomplish their society's objectives. The lessons of history are hard, not because they are difficult to understand, but because they tell us to be realistic about ourselves, about our abilities, our violent and fallible nature, about our resources, and about our ability to understand situations and formulate attainable objectives. Nonetheless, one simple precept was acknowledged throughout the ancient world—from the Chinese military philosopher Sun Tzu to the sacred precinct of Apollo at Delphi—a simple precept acknowledged to be the path to success in life and in war:

Know yourself.

**61. Hadrian's Wall (near Haltwhistle)**

# SOURCES

## INTRODUCTION

The literary sources for ancient warfare are sparse until we reach the Greeks. The Greeks are the first people to take us into the minds of the combatants and the first to analyze why battles were fought as they were, why the victors won and the defeated lost, and how the battle fit into the greater strategy of the war. Sources for the ancient Near East are mostly pictorial representations of the victor, sometimes with a bare account of the event. (The exception—The Old Testament—tells us incidentally of warfare in a small compass by a people militarily insignificant.) Today, when we read some statement like "Patton drove through France," we know that the author meant "the unit Patton commanded," and we know that behind the word "drove" is a complex operation of which Patton was but one element. In ancient Egypt, and the rest of the ancient Near East, such an expression was meant to convey the literal truth. The king was the principal warrior, all others were peripheral, and what was written, by virtue of its being written, was made true. So King Thutmose III could relate an accomplishment while hunting:

The sun-god Ra vouchsafed me another notable victory when he gave me a triumph in the Niyan slough where I bagged several herds of elephants. My Exalted Self fought herds of 120 elephants each. No king had done anything like this since the days when the gods ruled on earth, not even by those who in olden times first were given the white crown. I speak without exaggerating any part of it.

We are not expected to analyze this account—nor his accounts of battles.

Any account of ancient warfare will reflect a Western bias because the sources reflect a Western bias. The only substantial eyewitness accounts, the only account written by the commanding general, and the only account giving us the warrior's experience, all come from Western sources (Homer, Herodotus, Thucydides, Xenophon, Polybius, Caesar, Livy, Arrian). These authors, and other Western authors, described strategy and tactics and analyzed battles in an historical context. No such accounts exist for the ancient Near East. The Old Testament describes wars in the context of God's will, not human strategy, and shows little interest in the details of battles. The only comparable accounts are

Chinese. The shih–chi, Han–shu, and the Art of War of Sun Tzu do show an appreciation of strategy and tactics, but the first two are not principally about war and they are retrospective. Sun Tzu is rather more theoretical and less detailed than Greek and Roman sources.

Nonetheless, the great leaders of ancient societies would have been able to recognize, analyze, and understand the abilities of each other.

## General Works

Andreski, Stanislav. *Military Organization and Society.* Berkeley, 1968.

Barash, David. *Sociobiology and Behavior.* London, 1977.

*The Cambridge Ancient History.* 1st–3rd eds. Cambridge, 1925–present.

Coblentz, S. A. *From Arrow to Atom Bomb: The Psychological History of War.* New York, 1953.

Davies, J. G. "Violence and Aggression: Innate or Not?" *Western Political Quarterly* 23 (1970), 611–623.

Delbruck, Hans. *History of the Art of War Within the Framework of Political History.* 4 vols. Westport, CT, 1975.

Dupuy, T. N. *The Evolution of Weapons and Warfare.* New York, 1980.

Dyer, Gwynne. *War.* New York, 1985.

Feest, Christian. *The Art of War.* London, 1980.

Ferrill, Arther. *The Origins of War,* London, 1985.

Finley, M. I. *The Ancient Enemy.* Berkeley, 1973.

Gabriel, Richard A. *The Culture of War.* Westport, CT, 1990.

Gabriel, Richard A., and Karen Metz. *From Sumer to Rome.* Westport, CT, 1991.

Goren, Geoffrey. "Man Has No Killer Instinct." In Ashley Montagu, *Man and Aggression.* New York, 1973.

Heath, E. G. *Archery: A Military History.* London, 1980.

Hogg, O. F. G. *Clubs to Cannon.* London, 1968.

Jones, Archer. *The Art of War in the Western World.* Chicago, 1987.

Keegan, John. *A History of Warfare.* New York, 1993.

Laffoot, Robert. *The Ancient Art of Warfare.* 2 vols. New York, 1966.

Leakey, Richard, and Roger Lewin. "It Is Our Culture, Not Our Genes That Makes Us Killers." *Smithsonian* 8 (1977), 56–58.

Lorenz, Konrad. *On Aggression.* New York, 1963.

McRandle, James H. *The Antique Drums of War.* College Station, TX, 1995.

Newman, James L. *The People of Africa.* New Haven, CT, 1995.

Oakeshott, Ewart R. *The Archaeology of Weapons.* New York, 1963.

Otterbein, Keith F. *The Evolution of War, A Cross-Cultural Study.* New Haven, CT, 1970.

Rapoport, Anatol. "Is Warfare a Characteristic of Human Beings or of Culture?" *Scientific American* 213 (1965), 115–118.

Riches, David. *The Anthropology of Violence.* Oxford, 1986.

Schneider, Joseph. "On The Beginnings of Warfare." *Social Forces* 31 (1952), 68–74.

Sho, James. *Religious Mythology and the Art of War.* Westport, CT, 1981.

Wright, Quincy. *A Study of War.* Chicago, 1965.

# INTRODUCTION

## Notes to the Chapter

xv · Homer's war could have ended—*Iliad* XXII 111–125.
xvi · Hector and Ajax—*Iliad* VII 70ff, 233–243 (*Iliad* XVII 175ff).
xvi · Glaucus and Diomedes—*Iliad* VI 119–236.
xvi · Menelaus and Paris—*Iliad* III 314ff, IV 112ff.
xvii · Diomedes—*Iliad* V.
xvii · Sarpedon and Glaucus—*Iliad* XII 310–328

## General Works

Childe, Gordon V. "War in Prehistoric Societies," *Sociological Review* 23 (1942), 126–138.
Fried, Morton. "Warfare, Military Organization, and the Evolution of Society," *Anthropologica* 3 (1961), 134–147.
Turney-High, H. H. *The Military: The Theory of Land Warfare as Behavioral Science.* West Hanover, MA, 1981.
———. *Primitive War: Its Practice and Its Concepts.* Columbia, SC, 1971.

# PART I. THE ANCIENT EAST

Arnett, William. "Only the Bad Died Young in the Ancient Middle East." *International Journal of Aging and Human Development* 21, no. 3 (1985), 155.
Burres, Alice. "The Spearman and the Archer: An Essay on Selection in Body Build." *American Anthropologist* 61 (1959), 457–469.
Casson, L. *Ships and Seamanship in the Ancient World.* Princeton, NJ, 1971.
Childe, Gordon V. "Horses, Chariots and Battle-Axes." *Antiquity 15* (1941), 196–199.
Clay, A. T. *The Empire of the Amorites.* New Haven, CT, 1919.
Conteneau, Georges. *Everyday Life in Babylon and Assyria.* London, 1954.
Cook, J. M. *The Persian Empire.* London, 1983.
Cottrell, Leonard. *The Warrior Pharaohs.* New York, 1969.
Coughlan, H. "The Evolution of the Axe from Prehistoric to Roman Times." *Journal of the Royal Anthropological Society* 73 (1943), 27–56.
Crouwel, J. H. *Chariots and Other Means of Land Transport in Bronze Age Greece.* Amsterdam, 1981.
Davidson, Marshall B. *Lost Worlds.* New York, 1962.
Stillman, Nigel, and Nigel Tallis, *Armies of the Ancient Near East, 3000 BC to 539 BC.* Worthing, England, 1984.
Wilson, Thomas. "Arrow Wounds." *American Anthropologist* 3 (1901), 513–531.
Yadin, Yigael. *The Art of Warfare in Biblical Lands in Light of Archaeological Discovery.* New York, 1963.

## 1. CIVILIZED WAR

### Notes to the Chapter

3 · "kingship down from heaven"—William W. Hallo and William Kelly Simpson, *The Ancient Near East, A History*, 2nd ed., New York, 1998, p. 34.
4 · arms of Gilgamesh—John Gardner, John Maier, Richard A. Henshaw, *Gilgamesh*, New York, 1984, p. 110.
5 · Sargon's story—ANET 119 (= James B. Pritchard, *The Ancient Near East: An Anthology of Texts and Pictures*, Princeton, 1973.)
6 · "I washed my spears"—C. J. Gadd, "The Dynasty of Agade and the Gutian Invasion." *Cambridge Ancient History*, chapter 19, vol. 1.1, 3rd ed., Cambridge, 1971, p. 422.

### General Works

Diakonoff, M. I. "On the Area and Population of the Sumerian City-State." *Journal of Ancient History* 2 (1950), 77–93.
Kramer, Samuel N. *The Sumerians*. Chicago, 1963.
Kramer, Samuel N. *The Cradle of Civilization*. New York, 1969.
Oppenheim, A. Leo. *Ancient Mesopotamia*. Chicago, 1977.
Weeks, A. "The Old Babylonian Amorites: Nomads or Mercenaries." *Orientalia Librariensia Periodica* 16 (1985), 49–57.

## 2. THE EGYPTIANS

### Notes to the Chapter

9 · the Delta—Herodotus II 14.
10 · hand to hand with bearded foreigners—*Annales du Service des Antiquitates de l'Egypt* 38 (1938) 520, pl XCV.
10 · using Nubian mercenaries—tomb in Inti (V Dynasty), Petrie, Fl., *Deshasheh* pl iv.

### General Works

Erman, A. *The Literature of the Ancient Egyptians*. New York, 1966.
Hoffman, Michael A. *Egypt Before the Pharaohs*. New York, 1979.
Lawrence, A. W. "Ancient Fortifications." *Journal of Egyptian Arcbaeology* 51 (1965), 69–94.
Schulman, Alan R. "Chariots, Chariotry, and Hyksos." *Journal for the Study of Egyptian Antiquities* 10 (1980), 105–153.
Spalinger, Anthony. *Aspects of the Military Documents of the Ancient Egyptians*. New Haven, CT, 1982.
Spencer, A. J. *Early Egypt: The Rise of Civilization in the Nile Valley*. Norman, OK, 1995.

# 3. THE CHARIOT PEOPLE

## Notes to the Chapter

13 · "No king"—C. J. Gadd, "Northern Mesopotamia and Syria." *Cambridge Ancient History*, chapter 1, vol. 2.1, 3rd ed., Cambridge, 1973, p. 10.

14 · "withdrew from the battle"—*Iliad* 17. 426–428, 436–440.

14 · "The bow"—Rig-Veda VI 75.2–6 = Geldner, Karl Friedrich, *Der Rig-Veda*. 3 vols. *Harvard Oriental Series* 33–35, Cambridge, MA, 1951; Griffith, Ralph T. H., *The Hymns of the Rigveda, Chowkhamba Sanskrit Studies*, vols. 35–36, Varanasi, India, 1963.

15 · "When Murshilish was king"—Trevor Bryce, *The Kingdom of the Hittites*, Oxford, 1998, pp. 102–103.

15 · "A prince"—Warrior Code of the Bhagavad-Gita 2.31–38; R. C. Zaehner, *The Bhagavad-Gita with a Commentary*, Oxford, 1969.

16 · "burn up the enemy"—RV VI 45.18, 47.26.

17 · the "Battle of the Ten Kings"—RV VII 18, 33, 83.

17 · The Battle Between the Kurus and the Pandavas—Pratap Chandra Roy (trans.) and Hiralal Halder (ed.), *The Mahabharata (Bhisma Parva)*, 2nd ed., vol. 5, Calcutta, 1955–1962(?), Sections 44–49. I have paraphrased the passage and given intelligible names to the participants, either translations of their names or their chief epithet.

19 · Mycenaean records  Sterling Dow, "The Linear Scripts and the Tablets as Historical Documents." *Cambridge Ancient History*, 3rd ed., vol. 2, part 1, Cambridge, 1973, Chapter 9, pp. 624–626.

## General Works

Drews, Robert. *The End of the Bronze Age: Changes in Warfare and the Catastrophe, ca. 1200 BC*. Princeton, 1993.

Eberhard, Wolfram. *A History of China*. Berkeley, 1977.

Griffith, Ralph T. H., and J. L. Shastri. *Hymns of the Rig-Veda*, Delhi, 1973.

Littauer, M. A., and J. Crouwel. *Wheeled Vehicles and Ridden Animals in the Ancient Near East*. Leiden, Netherlands, 1979.

Majumdar, R. C., and A. D. Pusalker. *The History and Culture of the Indian People*, vol. I: *The Vedic Age*. London, 1951.

Maspero, Henri (trans. Frank A. Kierman, Jr). *China in Antiquity*. Cambridge, MA, 1978.

Moorey, P.R.S. "The Emergence of the Light, Horse-Drawn Chariot in the Near East, 2000–1500 B.C." *World Archaeology* 18 (1986), 196–215.

Mylonas, George E. *Mycenae and the Mycenaean Age*. Princeton, 1966.

Piggot, S. *The Earliest Wheeled Transport from the Atlantic Coast to the Caspian Sea*. London, 1983.

Piotrovsky, R. *The Ancient Civilization of the Urartu*. London, 1969.

Singh, Sarva Daman. *Ancient Indian Warfare with Special Reference to the Vedic Period*, Leiden, Netherlands, 1965.

Speiser, E. A. "The Hurrian Participation in the Civilization of Mesopotamia, Syria and Palestine." *Journal of World History* 1 (1953), 311–326.

Vermeule, Emily. *Greece in the Bronze Age*. Chicago, 1964.

## 4. THE EGYPTIAN EMPIRE

### Notes to the Chapter

21 · Seqenenre—ANET 231–232.
22 · Kamose—ANET 233.
22 · Ahmose—ANET 233–234.
22 · Thutmose I, "the dirty ones . . . the water that runs upside down"—*Papyrus and Tablet*, pp. 25, 26.
24 · "You think the soldiers"—Miriam Lichtheim, *Ancient Egyptian Literature*, vol. 2, Berkeley, 1976, p. 172.
24 · Joppa—ANET 22–23.
25 · Megiddo—ANET 235–238.
26 · Mitanni—ANET 239–240.
26 · "Take care of the horses"—Erman, p. 211.
26 · "I followed my master"—*Papyrus and Tablet*, p. 28.

### General Works

Faulkner, R. D. "The Battle of Megiddo." *Journal of Egyptian Archaeology* 28 (1942), 43–49.
Faulkner, R. D. "Egyptian Military Organization." *Journal of Egyptian Archaeology* 39 (1953), 30–43, 32–47.
Schulman, Alan Richard. *Military Rank, Title, and Organization in the Egyptian New Kingdom.* 1964.
Yadin, Yigael. "Hyksos Fortifications and the Battering Ram." *Bulletin of the American School of Oriental Research* 137 (1955), 23–32.

## 5. BALANCE OF POWER

### Notes to the Chapter

30 · Hittite oath—ANET 353–354.
30 · "When a people under my control"—O. R. Gurney, *The Hittites,* Baltimore, 1962, p. 78.
31 · Qadesh—ANET 255–256.
32 · Sea Peoples—ANET 262–263.

### General Works

Burn, Alfred. *The Battle of Kadesh.* Harrisburg, Pa., 1947.
Goedicke, Hans. "Considerations of the Battle of Kadesh." *Journal of Egyptian Archaeology* 52 (1966), 71–80.
Hawkins, J. D. "Assyrians and Hittites." *Iraq* 36 (1974), 67–83.
Sandars, N. K. *The Sea Peoples: Warriors of the Ancient Mediterranean.* London, 1978.

# 6. THE HEBREWS

## Notes to the Chapter

33 · Joshua—*Joshua* 8.10–25.
35 · Gideon—*Judges* 7.16–22.
37 · David—I *Samuel* 13.4–7, 17.

## General Works

Herzog, Chaim, and Mordechai Gichon. *Battles of the Bible.* Jerusalem, 1997.

# 7. THE ASSYRIANS

## Notes to the Chapter

41 · Ashurnasirpal—Georges Roux, *Ancient Iraq*, 3rd. ed., London, 1992, p. 286.
42 · "Ashur spread terror"—Roux, p. 289.
42 · "I took the city"—Roux, p. 291; *Papyrus and Tablet*, p. 99–100.
42 · Shalmaneser III—Roux, p. 297.
43 · Tiglath-pileser—Roux, p. 305.
44 · Samaria—II *Kings* 17 1–6.
44 · Sargon II—ANET 284–285.
44 · "pharaoh, king of Egypt, is to those who trust him."—II *Kings* 18: 19–21.
44 · Sennacherib's annals—ANET 287–288.
44 · "departed, and went to dwell at Nineveh"—II *Kings* 19: 35–36.
45 · Arabs—ANET 297–299.
45 · Ashurbanipal—ANET 275–276.

## General Works

Luckenbill, D. D. *Ancient Records of Assyria and Babylon.* 2 vols. Chicago, 1926.
Maoitius, W. "The Army and Military Organization of the Assyrian Kings." *Zeitschrift fur Assyriologie* 24 (1910), 90–107.
Olmstead, A. T. *The History of Assyria.* Chicago, 1951.
Postgate, J. N. *Taxation and Conscription in the Assyrian Empire.* Rome, 1974.
Reades, J. "The Neo-Assyrian Court and the Army: Evidence from the Sculptures." *Iraq* 34 (1972), 87–112.
Saggs, W. F. "Assyrian Warfare in the Sargonid Period." *Iraq* 25 (1963), 141–149.
Tadmor, H. "The Campaigns of Sargon II of Assur." *Journal of Cuneiform Studies* 12 (1958), 22–46.

# 8. THE MEDES AND CHALDAEANS

## Notes to the Chapter

47 · "I spend my days crying out, 'Oh!' and 'Alas!'"—*Cambridge Ancient History* 3.2.168.
48 · Ashur-Nineveh—ANET 303–305.
49 · "Woe to the city"—*Nahum* 3.

49 · "man but three inches short of a hundred."—Alcaeus *Oxford Book of Greek Verse* 134.
50 · "So they took the king"—II *Kings* 25:1; *Jeremiah* 39:1–9.
50 · Nebuchadrezzar's personal aqccounts—Roux, p. 380; *Papyrus and Tablet*, p. 104.
51 · "enemy of Marduk"—Roux, p. 382; *Papyrus and Tablet*, p. 124.
51 · "three days that the city had changed masters."—Herodotus I 190–191.

## 9. THE PERSIANS

### Notes to the Chapter

53 · Cyrus—Herodotus I 107–130.
53 · "Marduk said to him"—Olmstead, p. 36.
54 · "Teucer, having strung"—*Iliad* VIII 266–272.
56 · "Cyrus king of Persia says"— *Ezra* 1.2–4.
56 · Epitaph of Cyrus—Arrian *Anabasis* 6. 29.
58 · "To me Ahura-Mazdah"—Olmstead, p. 116.
58 · "When Ahura-Mazdah saw"—Roland G. Kent, *Old Persian, Grammar, Texts, Lexicon*, New Haven, CT, 1950, pp. 138–139.
58 · Darius wrote a letter to one of his satraps—Russell Meiggs and David Lewis, *A Selection of Greek Historical Inscriptions*, Oxford, 1969, #12.
58 · Xerxes with the satrapies—Olmstead, p. 232; Kent, pp. 151–152.

### General Works

Frye, Richard N. *The Heritage of Persia.* Cleveland, Ohio, 1963.
Jackson, A. V. *Persia: Past and Present.* New York, 1966.
Olmstead, A. T. *History of the Persian Empire.* Chicago, 1948.
Sykes, General Sir Percy. *A History of Persia.* 2 vols. London, 1958.
Zoka, Yaha. *The Imperial Iranian Army from Cyrus to Pahlavi.* Teheran, 1970

## PART II. THE GREEKS

### General Works

Connolly, Peter. *Greece and Rome at War.* Englewood Cliffs, NJ, 1981.
Connolly, Peter. *The Greek Armies.* Morristown, NJ, 1985.
Hanson, Victor Davis. *Warfare and Agriculture in Classical Greece*, rev. ed. Berkeley, 1998.
Hanson, Victor Davis. *The Western Way of War: Infantry Battle in Classical Greece*. New York, 1989.
Hanson, Victor Davis (ed.). *Hoplites: The Classical Greek Battle Experience*. New York, 1994.
Pritchett, W. K. *The Greek State at War.* Berkeley, continuing series.
Warry, John G. *Warfare in the Classical World.* New York, 1980.

## 10. THE GREEK WAY OF WAR

### Notes to the Chapter

63 · "make shrines for the gods, and divide up the farm land into lots."—*Odyssey* VI 9–10.

64 · "an island, wooded, with so many wild goats we could not"—*Odyssey* IX 106–115.

64 · The Phocaean colony at Alalia—Herodotus I 166.

65 · "The Spartans swore an oath"—Pausanias IV v 8.

65 · The Messenians left the rich land—Pausanias IV xiii 6 (Tyrtaeus).

65 · "men who stand their ground"—Thucydides IV 126.5.

66 · "Spartans, show no fear"—Tyrtaeus XI.1.

66 · "I don't care"—Tyrtaeus XII.1.

67 · Archilochus— *Oxford Book of Greek Verse* 103, 104.

### General Works

Cartledge, P. "Hoplites and Heroes." Journal of Hellenic Studies 97 (1977), 18–24.

Greenhalgh, P. *Early Greek Warfare: Horsemen and Chariots in the Homeric and Archaic Ages.* Cambridge, 1973.

Holladay, A. J. "Hoplites and Heresies." *Journal of Hellenic Studies* 102 (1982), 97–103.

Lawrence, A. W. *Greek Aims in Fortification.* Oxford, 1979.

Salmon, J. "Political Hoplites." *Journal of Hellenic Studies* 97 (1977), 84–101.

Snodgrass, A. *Arms and Armor of the Greeks.* Ithaca, NY, 1967.

Snodgrass, A. *Early Greek Armor and Weapons.* Edinburgh, 1964.

Snodgrass, A. "The Hoplite Reform and History." *Journal of Hellenic Studies* 85 (1965), 110–122.

## 11. "GO TELL THE SPARTANS"

### Notes to the Chapter

69 · "Who are these Spartans?"—Herodotus I 153.

71 · "Spartans, the Athenians need you"—Herodotus VI 106.

73 · Oracles—Herodotus VII 140–141.

74 · Damaratus—Herodotus VII 209.

75 · Epitaph—Herodotus VII 228.

75 · Aeschylus *Persians* 353–432.

### General Works

Burn, A. R. *Persia and the Greeks.* London, 1962.

Ferrill, Arther. "Herodotus and the Strategy and Tactics of the Invasion of Xerxes." *American Historical Review* 72 (1966), 102–115.

Griffith, G. T. *The Mercenaries of the Hellenic World.* Groningen, Netherlands, 1968.

Grundy, G. B. *The Great Persian War.* London, 1901.

Hignett, C. *Xerxes' Invasion of Greece.* New York, 1963.

Pritchett, W. K. "Platea Revisited." *University of California Publications in Classical Studies* 1 (1965), 103–121.
Shrimpton, Gordon. "The Persian Cavalry at Marathon." *Phoenix* 34 (1980), 20.

## 12. THE PELOPONNESIAN (ARCHIDAMIAN) WAR

### Notes to the Chapter

79 · "murdered Greece"—Pausanias VIII 52.3.
80 · Democracy, one Athenian—[Xenophon] *Athenaion Politeia* 4–6.
83 · "Sail! Sail!"—Thucydides IV 2.8.
83 · "Do what you think best."—Thucydides IV 38.
83 · Arrows—Thucydides IV 40.

### General Works

Jordan, Borimir. *The Athenian Navy in the Classical Period.* Berkeley, 1975.
Kagan, Donald. *The Archidamian War.* Ithaca, NY, 1974.
———. *The Fall of the Athenian Empire.* Ithaca, NY, 1987.
———. *The Outbreak of the Peloponnesian War.* Ithaca, NY, 1969.
———. *The Peace of Nicias and the Sicilian Expedition.* Ithaca, NY, 1981.
Kelly, Thomas. "Thucydides and the Spartan Strategy in the Archidamian War." *American Historical Review* 87 (1982), 399–427.

## 13. THE PELOPONNESIAN (DECELEAN) WAR

### Notes to the Chapter

87 · Battle of Mantinea—Thucydides V 63–73.
90 · Nicias sent a letter to Athens and asked to be relieved.—Thucydides VII 12–14.
93 · Battle of Arginusae—Xenophon *Hellenica* I vi 16–34; Diodorus Siculus XIII 98.3–4.
93 · Battle of Aegospotami—Xenophon *Hellenica* II i 20–29.

## 14. THE DEMISE OF HOPLITE WARFARE

### Notes to the Chapter

95 · Battle of Cunaxa—Xenophon *Anabasis* I 8; we learn of the expedition from Xenophon who out of a spirit of adventure accompanied Cyrus. The account he wrote—the *Anabasis*—is one of the great adventure stories of all time.
96 · Agesilaus in Asia Minor— *Hellenica Oxyrhychia* XI–XII.
96 · Battle of Nemea—Xenophon *Hellenica* IV ii 18.
97 · Battle of Coronea—Xenophon *Hellenica* IV iii 10ff.
97 · Wounds—Naphthali Lewis, *The Interpretation of Dreams and Portents*, Sarasota, 1976, pp. 40–41.
98 · The Battle of Leuctra—Plutarch *Pelopidas,* Xenophon VI iv 8–15, Diodorus Siculus XV lv 7–lxi.1.

98 · The Battle of Mantinea—Xenophon VII v 21–24, Diodorus Siculus XV lxxxv 3–lxxxvii 6.

### General Works

Anderson, J. K. *Ancient Greek Horsemanship*. Berkeley, 1961.
Anderson, J. K. *Military Theory and Practice In the Age of Xenophon*. Berkeley, 1970.
Anderson, J. K. "Wars and Military Science: Greece," in Michael Grant and Rachael Kitzinger, eds., *Civilization of the Ancient Mediterranean*, vol. 1, 675–689, New York, 1988.
Best, J.G.P. *Thracian Peltasts and Their Influence on Greek Warfare*. Groninger, Netherlands, 1969.
Lazenby, J. F. *The Spartan Army*. Wiltshire, England, 1985

## 15. PHILIP AND THE MACEDONIANS

### Notes to the Chapter

102 · "Stop being king"—Bradford, Alfred S. *Philip II of Macedon: A Life from the Ancient Sources*, Westport, CT, 1992, p. 50.
104–105 · donkey laden with gold,—Bradford, p. 95.
105 · Philip once said—Bradford, p. 64.
106 · "Philip is our general"—Bradford, p. 147.

### General Works

Adcock, F. E. *The Greek and Macedonian Art of War*. Berkeley, 1957.
Cawkwell, G. L. *Philip of Macedon*. London, 1978.
Chadwick, John. *The Macedonian World*. Cambridge, 1976.
Hammond, N. "Training in the Use of the Sarissa and Its Effect in Battle." *Antichthon* 14 (1980), 53–63.
Hammond, N., and G. T. Griffith. *A History of Macedonia*, vol. 2. Oxford, 1979.
———. "Peltasts and the Origins of the Macedonian Phalanx," in *Ancient Macedonian Studies in Honor of Charles F. Edson*, pp. 161–179, Thessaloniki, 1981.
Marsden, E. W. *Greek and Roman Artillery*. Oxford, 1971.
Soedel, Werner, and Vernard Foley. "Ancient Catapults." *Scientific American* 240 (1979), 150–160.
Whitehead, David. *Aeneias the Tactician: How to Survive under Siege*. Oxford, 1990.
Winter, F. E. *Greek Fortifications*. Toronto, 1971.

## 16. ALEXANDER THE GREAT

### Notes to the Chapter

109 · The Battle of the Granicus—Arrian I 13–16.4.
111 · The Battle of Issus—Arrian II 7–11.
112 · The Siege of Tyre—Diodorus XVII 40.2–46.4.

113 · The Battle of Gaugamela—Arrian III 9.5–15.7.
115 · "So I go away, poorer"—Plutarch *Alexander* 54.

## General Works

Borza, Eugene N. "Fire from Heaven: Alexander at Persepolis." *Classical Philology* 67 (1972), 233–245.
Bosworth, A. B. *A Historical Commentary on Arrian's History of Alexander.* 2 vols. Oxford, 1995.
Brunt, P. A. "Alexander's Macedonian Cavalry." *Journal of Hellenic Studies* 83 (1963), 27–46.
Engels, Donald. *Alexander the Great and the Logistics of the Macedonian Army.* Berkeley, 1978.
―――. "Alexander's Intelligence System." *Classical Quarterly* 30 (1980), 127–136.
Gruen, Peter. *Alexander of Macedon.* Garden City, NY, 1950.
Hamilton, J. R. "The Cavalry Battle at Hydaspes." *Journal of Hellenic Studies* 76 (1956), 26–31.
Manti, Peter A. "The Cavalry Sarissa." *Ancient World* 8 (1983), 75–83
Markle, M. "The Macedonian Sarissa, Spear, and Related Arms." *American Journal of Archaeology* 82 (1978), 483–497.
Milius, R. D. "Alexander's Pursuit of Darius Through Iran." *Historia* 15 (1966), 249–257.
Neumann, C. "A Note on Alexander's March Rates." *Historia* 20 (1971), 196–198.

## 17. INTO INDIA AND BEYOND

### Notes to the Chapter

118 · Battle of the Hydaspes—Arrian V 14–19.
119 · "The whole world will be filled"—Arrian VII 26.3.
120 · The Battle of Raphia—Polybius V 82–86.
120 · "The Gauls captured"— Pausanias X 22.3–7.

## PART III. THE EAST

### General Works

Huang, Ray. *China: A Macro History.* New York, 1990.

## 18. INDIA: CHANDRAGUPTA

### Notes to the Chapter

126 · Robbers, etc.—E. J. Rapson, ed., *Cambridge History of India*, vol 1: *Ancient India.* New York, 1922, p. 489.
126 · Arthasatra—Percival Spear, ed., *The Oxford History of India*, 4th ed., Delhi, 1981, pp. 100–115; Kautilya (trans. L. N. Rangarajan), *The Arthashastra*, New Delhi, 1992.

127 · "I conquered Kalinga"—Spear, pp. 118–119; Radhakumud Mookerji, *Asoka*, Delhi, 1962 (1995), pp. 162–170.
128 · The Elephant Battle—Roy, *Mahabharata (Bhisma Parva)*, 44–50.

### General Works

Dayal, Raghubir. *An Outline of Indian History and Culture*. 2nd ed., New Delhi, 1984.
Dikshitar, V. R. Ramachandra. *War in Ancient India*. Delhi, 1948 (1987).
Jha, D. N. *Ancient India in Historical Outline*. New Delhi, 1998.
Kar, H. C., Lt. Col. *Military History of India*. Calcutta, 1980.
Kern, Fritz. *Asoka, Kaiser und Missonar*. Bern, 1956.
Majumdar, R. C. *Ancient India*. Delhi, 1977.
Majumdar. R. C., and A. D. Pusalker. *The History and Culture of the Indian People*. Vol II: *The Age of Imperial Unity*. Bombay, 1968.
Mookerji, Radha Kumud, *Chandragupta Maurya and his Times*. Delhi, 1966.
Narain, A. K. *The Indo–Greeks*. Oxford, 1957.
Sharma, L. P. *History of Ancient India*. Delhi, 1987.
Tripathi, Ramashankar. *History of Ancient India*. Delhi, 1999.
Woodcock, George. *The Greeks in India*. London, 1966.

## 19. CHINA: SPRING AND AUTUMN

### Notes to the Chapter

130 · The thousand chariots charge; Chariot wheel stuck; the period is divided into the Spring and Autumn (722–481)— Tso-chuan, political history of Eastern Chou (770–403 B.C.) complied 4th–2nd B.C., commentary on the Ch'un-Ch'iu ("Spring and Autumn Annals"); James Legge, *The Chinese Classics*, Hong Kong, 1972.
131 · Battle of Ch'ang P'u—Wen replies that he will be ready at the crack of dawn.— Frank A. Kierman, Jr., "Phases and Modes of Combat in Early China," pp. 27–66 from *Chinese Ways in Warfare*, ed. Frank A. Kierman, Jr., and John K. Fairbank, Cambridge, MA, 1974.
132 · Two Typical Careers—Wu Tzu-hsü—Shih-chi "Historical Records" Ssu-ma Ch'ien (or "Records of an Astrologer") 1st century B.C.

### General Works

Sun Tzu, *The Art of War*. Trans. Samuel B. Griffith. Oxford, 1971.

## 20. CHINA: THE WARRING STATES

### Notes to the Chapter

138 · The Lord of Shang—Ssu-Ma, Ch'ien. *Grand Scribe's Records, The Memoirs of Pre-Han China*, (ed. William H. Nienhauser, Jr.), Vol. 7, Bloomington, IN, 1994, pp. 87–96.
139 · "More than 400,000 were decapitated."—"To cut off a head" was then an expression which meant "to kill in battle." Here we have the term *wan*, which,

like Herodotus' *myriad*, is an expression that just means an indefinite but large number.

139 · As the Chinese historian put it: "When it poured out its soldiers"—Ssu-Ma, Ch'ien, *Grand Scribe's Records, The Memoirs of Pre-Han China*, (ed. William H. Nienhauser, Jr.), Vol. 7, Bloomington, IN, 1994.

### General Works

Chang Ch'i-yün. Trans. Orient Lee. *China's Cultural Achievements During the Warring States Period.* Yangmingshan, Taiwan, 1983.

Cotterell, Arthur. *The First Emperor of China.* London, 1981.

Dawson, Raymond, ed. and trans. *Sima Qin, Historical Records.* Oxford, 1994.

Eberhard, Wolfram. *A History of China.* Berkeley, 1977.

Maspero, Henri. Trans. Frank A. Kierman, Jr. *China in Antiquity.* Cambridge, MA, 1978.

Nienhauser, William H. Jr. (ed.). *The Grand Scribe's Records,* vol. I: *The Basic Annals of Pre-Han China.* Bloomington, IN, 1994.

Zhang Wenli. *The Qin Terracotta Army.* London, 1996.

## 21. CHINA: THE FORMER HAN

### General Works

Watson, Burton (trans.). *Sima Qin, Records of the Grand Historian: Han Dynasty I–II.* New York, 1993.

## 22. CHINA: THE LATER HAN

### General Works

Young, Gregory. *Three Generals of Later Han.* Canberra, 1984.

## 23. THE PARTHIANS

### Notes to the Chapter

161 · Carrhae—Plutarch *Crassus* 25–33.

### General Works

*Cambridge History of Iran*, vol. III (1): *The Seleucid, Parthian and Sasanian Periods.* Cambridge, 1983.

Humphreys, Eileen. *The Royal Road: A Popular Hisoty of Iran.* London, 1991.

## PART IV. THE ROMAN REPUBLIC

### General Works

Brunt, P. A. *Italian Manpower, 225 B.C.–A.D. 14.* Oxford, 1971.

Connolly, Peter. *The Roman Army.* London, 1975.

## 24. THE DEVELOPMENT OF THE ROMAN SYSTEM

### Notes to the Chapter

168 · "naked except for his shield"—A. Gellius IX xiii 19
170 · "You will wash my garment"—Appian *Samnite Wars* 2.
170 · "They are not barbarians"—Plutarch *Pyrrhus* 16.
170 · "Yes, one more like it"—Ibid. 21.
172 · "sit and sweat"—Naevius frg. 36 (Baehr); Ennius (Vahlen) 227–231.
174 · "let them drink then"—Cicero *de natura deourm* II 7.

### General Works

Adcock, F. E. *The Roman Art of War Under the Republic.* Cambridge, MA, 1940.
Breeze, D. V. "The Organization of the Legion: The First Cohort and the Equites Legionis." *Journal of Roman Studies 59* (1969), 50–55.
Fabricus, E. "Some Notes on Polybius' Description of *Roman Camps.*" *Journal of Roman Studies* 22 (1932), 78–87. (Polybius is the primary source for the history of the First Punic War.)
Keppie, L. *The Making of the Roman Army.* London, 1984.
Lazenby, I. F. *The First Punic War.* Stanford, CA, 1996.
O'Connell, Robert L. "The Roman Killing Machine." *Quarterly Journal of Military History* I (Autumn 1988), 35–41.

## 25. HANNIBAL

### Notes to the Chapter

180 · "For four days and three nights"—Polybius III 79.
180 · "Flaminius was completely"—III 84.
180 · "The Romans are most to be feared"—III 79.
184 · "The Roman formation and ranks"— Polybius XV 15.7.
185 · Battle of the Metaurus—Livy XXVII 48.
185 · as the Roman historian Livy wrote—XXVIII 12.
186 · The Battle of Ilipa—Polybius XI 20ff; Livy XXVIII 15.
187 · Battle of the Great Plains—Livy XXX 8ff.
187 · Battle of Zama—Livy XXX 33ff, Polybius XV 13.
188 · Scipio rejected the offer—Polybius XV 8.14.

### General Works

H. H. Scullard. *Scipio Africanus, Soldier and Politician.* Bristol, 1970.

## 26. THE CONQUEST OF THE MEDITERRANEAN

### Notes to the Chapter

192 · Battle of Cynoscephalae—Polybius XVIII 22.8.

194 · Battle of Pydna—Plutarch *Aemilius* 21. Neither the account of Livy or of Polybius survives for this crucial battle, but Plutarch seems to have followed Polybius's account.

195 · Carthage must be destroyed—Appian *Punic Wars (Libyke)* 69.

195 · "Spurius Ligustinus, spoke to an assembly of the people"—Livy XLII 34.

197 · "Italy rather than a province"—Pliny *Natural History* III 31.

## 27. THE BREAKDOWN OF THE ROMAN SYSTEM

### Notes to the Chapter

199 · "All of Rome could be purchased"—Sallust *Jugurtha* 36.

201 · "Do you have any messages"—Plutarch *Marius* 18.

202 · The armies met at Campi Raudii—Ibid. 18–27.

203 · "to at last quench his thirst for gold"—Appian *The Mithridatic Wars* 21.

204 · Sulla lost thirteen men—Ibid. 41–50; Plutarch *Sulla* 21.

206 · Spartacus—Plutarch *Crassus* 8–11.

207 · "Too large for an embassy"—Appian *The Mithridatic Wars* 85.

### General Works

Blois, L. de. *The Roman Army and Politics in the First Century before Christ*. Amsterdam, 1987.

Smith, R. E. *Service in the Post-Marian Roman Army*. Manchester, England, 1958.

## 28. JULIUS CAESAR

### Notes to the Chapter

210 · "The soldiers in their higher position"—Caesar *bellum Gallicum* I 25.

210 · "On the next day Caesar"—Ibid. I 51ff.

212 · "men of tremendous courage"—Ibid. II 27.

212 · "a standard bearer of the tenth legion"—*Bellum Gallicum* IV 24–26.

213 · only 800 escaped—*BG* VII 22–28.

214 · "Vercingetorix selected the best"—Plutarch *Caesar* 27.9–10.

214 · "Of the 3,000,000 inhabitants"—Ibid. 15.

216 · "It is the duty of a general"—Caesar *Bellum Civile* I 72.

218 · dead men do not bite—Plutarch *Pompey* 77.

219 · "a trumpeter to give"—[Caesar] *Bellum Africum* 82.

### General Works

Caesar, *Civil Wars, Bellum Africum, B. Alexandrinum, Hispaniense*.

Fuller, J.F.C. *Julius Caesar*. New Brunswick, NJ, 1965.

Grant, Michael. *Julius Caesar*. London, 1972.

## PART V. THE ROMAN EMPIRE

## 29. THE CREATION OF THE EMPIRE

### Notes to the Chapter

224 · "the whole of Italy" (and subsequent quotations)—Augustus *Res Gestae (Operum Fragmenta),* Torino, 1969.
From the notebooks of Charles Edson, found in the vicinity of Philippi, Latin graffiti which seem to refer to the Laconians—a facsimile (62):

227 · "Varus, give me back"—Suetonius *Augustus* 23.
227 · "Get Another"—Tacitus *Annales* I 23.
228 · "Gather seashells"—Suetonius *Gaius* 46.
229 · "The infantry have a"—Josephus Jewish Wars III 95.
230 · "No one will believe"—Suetonius *Domitian* 21.

### General Works

Birley, E. *Roman Britain and the Roman Army.* Kendal, Scotland, 1953.
Campbell, J. B. *The Roman Army, 31 BC–AD 337 : A sourcebook.* New York, 1994.
Goldsworthy, Adrian Keith. *The Roman Army at War: 100 BC–AD 200.* Oxford, 1996.
Grant, Michael. *The Army of the Caesars.* New York, 1974.
Hardy, E. G. "Augustus and His Legionnaires." *Classical Quarterly* 14 (1921), 187–194
Junkelmann, Marcus. *Die Legionen des Augustus, Der römische Soldat im archäologischen Experiment.* Mainz am Rhein, 1986.
Luttwak, Edward N. *The Grand Strategy of the Roman Empire.* Baltimore, MD, 1976.
Parker, H.M.D. *The Roman Legions.* Cambridge, England, 1958.
Ramsay, A. M. "The Speed of the Roman Imperial Post." *Journal of Roman Studies* 15 (1925), 60–74.
———. "The Roman Siege of Masada." *Journal of Roman Studies* 52 ( 1962), 142–155.
Robinson, H. Russell. *The Armour of Imperial Rome.* London, 1975.
Schonberger, H. "The Roman Frontier Army in Germany." *Journal of Roman Studies* 59 (1969), 144–197.
———. *The Roman Imperial Navy.* Cambridge, England, 1960.
Syme, R. "Some Notes on the Legions Under Augustus." *Journal of Roman Studies* 23 (1933), 14–33.
Thiel, J. H. *Studies on the History of Roman Sea Power in Republican Times.* Amsterdam, 1946.
Watson, G. R. "The Pay of the Roman Army: The Republic." *Historia* 7 (1958), 113–120.
———. "The Pay of the Roman Army: The Auxiliary Forces." *Historia* 8 (1959),
———. *The Roman Soldier.* Ithaca, NY, 1969.

Webster, Graham. *The Roman Army.* Chester, England, 1956.
———. *The Roman Imperial Army of the First and Second Centuries A.D.* New York, 1979.

## 30. THE ARMY OF TRAJAN

### Notes to the Chapter

232 · "We proceeded to Berzobim"—Priscian *Inst. Gramm.* 6.13.
232 · "Go back"—Cassius Dio LXVIII 8.1.

### General Works

Cichorius, C. *Die Relief des Trajanssäule.* Berlin, 1886–1900.
Florescu, Florea Bobu. *Die Trajanssäule.* Bonn, 1969.
Lehmann-Hartleben, K. *Die Trajanssäule: Ein römisches Kunstwerk zu Beginn der Spätantike.* Berlin-Leipzig, 1926.
Frank Lepper and Sheppard Frere, eds. *Trajan's Column, a New Edition of the Cichorius Plates.* Dover, NH, 1988.
Richmond, Sir Ian. *Trajan's Army in Trajan's Column, British School at Rome.* London, 1982.

## 31. THE ASCENDANCY OF THE ARMY

### Notes to the Chapter

243 · "Satisfy the army"—Cassius Dio LXXVII 15.2.

### General Works

Becatti, G. *La Colonna di Marco Aurelio,* Milan, 1957.
Campbell, B. "The Marriage of Soldiers Under the Empire." *Journal of Roman Studies* 68 (1978), 153–166.
Caprino, C., et al. *La Colonna di Marco Aurelio.* Rome, 1955.
Johnson, Anne. *Roman Forts of the 1st and 2nd Centuries AD in Britain and the German Provinces.* New York, 1983.
Kennedy, David, and Derrick Riley. *Rome's Desert Frontier from the Air.* London, 1990.
Petersen, E., et al. *Die Marcus–Säule auf Piazza Colonna in Rom.* Munich, 1896.
Smith, R. E. "The Army Reforms of Septimius Severus." *Historia* 12 (1972), 481–500.

## 32. THE AWFUL THIRD CENTURY

### Notes to the Chapter

245 · let the "mama's boy"—Herodian VI 9.
250 · "Save me, invincible one"—*Scriptores Historiae Augustae, Thirty Tyrants* XXIV 3.

252 · "struck by lightning"—SHA, Carus, Carinus, Numerian VIII 2, XIII

## General Works

Eadie, J. V. "The Development of Roman Mailed Cavalry." *Journal of Roman Studies* 57 (1967), 161–173.
Speidel, M. "Exploratores, Mobile Elite Units of the Roman Army." *Epigraphical Studies* 13 (1983), 63–78.

## 33. REFORM AND REVOLUTION

### Notes to the Chapter

257 · "In this sign you will conquer"—Lactantius *de mort. pers.* 44.5., Eusebius *vita Constantini*.
257 · "Supreme God, hear our prayers"—CAH XII, 689.
259 · The Battle of Strasbourg—Ammianus Marcellinus XVI 12.27–57.
   Ammianus Marcellinus, who came from Antioch and whose first language was Greek, was the last great historian of Rome. He served in the army and rose to a high position in the years 353–360. He was intelligent, fair (though he expressed the views of a member of the upper classes), and a pagan. Ammianus's description of battles tends to be more rhetorical than detailed. He admired Julian and ignored or excused his errors and belittled the actions and motives of others.

### General Works

Barnes, T. D. *The New Empire of Diocletian and Constantine.* Cambridge, MA, 1982.
Burckhardt, J. *The Age of Constantine the Great.* New York, 1949.
Johnson, Stephen. *Late Roman Fortifications.* London, 1983.
Jones, A.H.M. *Constantine and the Conversion of Europe*, 2nd ed. New York, 1962.
Williams, S. *Diocletian and the Roman Recovery.* New York, 1985.

## 34. THE FALL OF ROME

### Notes to the Chapter

264 · "The Huns slash the cheeks"—Ammianus Marcellinus XXXI 2.1–12.

### General Works

Boak, Arthur. *Manpower Shortage and the Fall of the Roman Empire in the West.* Ann Arbor, 1955.
Elton, Hugh. *Warfare in Roman Europe, AD 350–425.* Oxford, 1996.
   Despite the statement of Vegetius that the Roman infantry abandoned body armor and helmets, neither contemporary illustration nor subsequent history bear this out.
Maenchen-Helfen, O. J. *The World of the Huns.* Berkeley, 1973.
Matthews, J. F. *Western Aristocracies and Imperial Court, 364–425.* Oxford, 1975.
Salmon, E. T. "The Roman Army and the Disintegration of the Roman Empire." *Proceedings of the Royal Society of Canada* 52 (1958), 43–60.

Thompson, E. A. *A History of Attila and the Huns.* Westport, CT, 1948.

## SOURCES

283 · A. Kirk Grayson and Donald B. Redford, *Papyrus and Tablet*, Englewood Cliffs, NJ, 1970, p. 27.

# INDEX

Achaea 98
Achilles 14
Actium 224, 227
Adad-nirari 43
Adrianople 123, 257, 265-266
Aedui 209-210
Aegates Islands 174
Aegina 72
Aegospotami 93-94
Aeneas 104, 171-172
Aeschylus 72, 75, 291
Aetolians 120-121, 192, 196
Afghanistan 125
Agade 6-7, 286
Agesilaus 96-98, 292
Agis 87-88, 90
Agricola 230
Agrigentum 172
Ahmose 22
Ai 33-35
Ajax 54
Akhnaten 29-31
Akkad 4, 6-7, 45, 55
Akki 5
Alalia 64
Alans 230, 266, 269, 271
Alaric 267, 269-270
Albinus 242-243
Alcibiades 87-92
Alemanni 247-251, 254-255, 263
Aleppo 15

Alesia 213-214
Alexander 103, 106-107, 109-115, 117-119, 125, 141, 163, 170, 219, 240, 273-275, 280-281
Alexandria 113, 218, 226
Allia 167
Alps 178, 184, 201, 228, 274
Amalekites 35
Amarna revolution 29
Ambrones 201
Ammonites 39
Amorites 4, 6-7, 11, 21, 33, 285-286
Ampheia 65
Amphipolis 84, 90, 102-103
Amunhotep 29
Amurru 32
Anatolia 6, 13, 15, 18, 31, 50
Annam 151
Antigonus 120-121
Antiochus 120-121, 159-160, 193-194, 196
Antipater 102, 107, 109
Antoninus Pius 239
Antonius 218, 223
Apennines 180
Aper 252
Apopi 21
Apulia 169, 180-182
Aquae Sextiae 201
Aquileia 201, 240, 246
Aquitania 209, 212

Arabs  45, 238
Arachosia  125
Aramaeans  39, 42-43
Aramaic  56
Arausio  201
Arbogast  267
Arcadia  87-88
Arcadius  267, 270
Archelaus  203-205
Archidamus  81
Archilochus  67
Aretes  110
Argeads  101
Arginusae  93-94
Argos, Argives    18,  63,  65-66,  71,
     79-80, 87-88, 97, 101, 171
Ariminum  180
Ariovistus  209-210
Aristotle  107, 115, 274
Armenia      161-162,  205,  207,  228,
     238-240, 245, 255, 258, 263, 267
Arminius  226-227
Arrapcha  48
Arretium  180
Arsaces  159
Artaphernes  71
Artaxerxes  95-96
Artemisium  73-74
Arthasatra  126-127
Arverni  213
Aryans  13, 15-17
Arzawa  32
Asculum  170, 203
Asher  36
Ashur  1, 41, 43, 47-49, 278, 289
Ashurbanipal  45, 47-48
Asia Minor    50, 58, 69, 92, 96, 106,
     109-110, 121, 127, 194, 203, 228,
     240, 242, 248-251, 257
Asoka  125, 127, 294
Asopus River  76
Aspis  173
Assyrians  1, 26, 41-45, 47-50, 57, 59,
     277, 281, 289
Astyages  53
Aten  29
Athanaric  263, 265-266
Athens, Athenians      70-73,  75-77,

79-85,   87-94,   96-98,   101-103,
     105-106, 204, 277-280, 291
Athos  71, 73
Atrebates  211
Attalus  121
Attila  271, 300
Atuatuci  201
Aufidus  170
Augustulus  271
Augustus (emperor)  121, 225-227, 259,
     270, 276-278
Augustus (title)    243, 248, 253, 255-
     256, 266
Aurelian  249-251
Aurelius  155, 239-241, 264, 276
Avaricum  213
Avidius Cassius  240–241
Babylon  15, 42, 44-45, 47-51, 53-57,
     114, 119, 160, 243
Bactria  55, 147, 150-151, 159-160
Baecula  184
Baetis Valley  219
Balbinus  246
Balikh  48
Balissus  161
Baltic  18
Bardiya  58
Bastarnae  251
Benjamin  44
Beneventum  171
Berzobim  232
Bessus  114
Bethaven  37
Bethbarah  36
Bethel  35
Bethshittah  36
Bithynia  207, 255
Bocchus  200
Boeotia  18, 97-98, 101, 105, 204
Bologna  179
Bosporos  69
Brasidas  84-85, 87
Brennus  120-121
Britain  228, 230, 239, 242-243, 246,
     251, 254-255, 264, 267, 270, 276
Bruttium  182, 186
Brutus  223-224
Buddha  125, 134

Burgundians 251, 254, 271
Byzantium 105, 242, 249, 258
Caesar (the person) 201-224 passim, 275
Caesar (the title) 242-259 passim
Caligula 227-228
Calah 48-49
Callicratidas 93
Callisthenes 115
Callium 120
Cambyses 56-57, 69
Camillus 167-168
Campania 169, 181
Campi Raudii 202
Canaanites 33
Cannae 181-182, 274
Cappadocia 239
Capua 169, 181-182, 206
Caracalla 243-244
Carchemish 26, 32
Carians 70
Carinus 252
Carmel 25
Carnuntum 241
Carpi 247-248, 250
Carrhae 162
Carthage, Carthaginians 64, 103, 171-173, 175, 182-183, 185-187, 195, 270
Carus 251-253
Carystus 71
Cassius 223-224, 240-241
Cato 191, 195, 219
Catulus 174, 202
Celtiberians 191-192
centurion 195-196, 212, 217, 225, 227, 253
century (unit) 167-168, 196, 232
Ceylon 127
Chaeronea 106-107, 204
Chalcidians 64, 84, 103, 105
Chalcis 64
Chaldaeans 45, 47, 49-50
Chandragupta 123, 125-127, 280
Ching 137, 147-148
Ching-ti 147
Chios 70, 77
Chosroes 238

Chou 129-130, 132, 137, 140
Christianity 127, 256, 258-259, 261, 271, 275, 281
Chrysopolis 257
Chuang 132
Cilicia 32, 110, 206-207
Cimbri 200-202
Cimmerians 44
Cithaeron 77
Claudius (Appius) 172
Claudius (the Proud) 174
Claudius (Nero) 182, 184
Claudius (the princeps) 227-228, 276
Claudius (Gothicus) 249
Clearchus 95
Cleitus 110, 114-115
Cleombrotus 98
Cleomenes 70-71
Cleon 81, 83-85
Cleopatra 121, 218, 224
cohorts 161-162, 185, 204, 214, 216-219, 231-232, 268
comitatenses 268
Commodus 241-242
Confucianism 157
Confucius 134, 141
Conon 93
Constantine 256-259
Constantinople 256, 258, 263, 266-267
Constantius the Green 254-256
Constantius the emperor 258-261
consul 167, 169-172, 174, 178, 180-181, 184, 186, 191-192, 194-195, 199-203, 205, 207, 228, 252
Coracesium 207
Corbulo 228
Corcyra 81-82
Corinthians 74
Cornelia 187
Coronea 97
Corsica 172-175
Costoboci 241
Cotta 207
Crassus 161-162, 205-207, 211, 224-225, 240
Craterus 117-118
Cremona 229

Crete  10, 18-19
Crocus Fields  105
Croesus  54-55, 69
Ctesiphon  238, 240, 243, 261
Cunaxa  95
Cyaxares  47-48, 50
Cyrene  127
Cyrus the Great  51-57, 69
Cyrus the Younger  92-96
Cythera  83
Dacians  230-231, 235-238
Dalmatia  250, 252, 269
Damaratus the Spartan  74
Danes  246
Dardanian  255
Darius the Great  57-58, 69-75
Darius (opponent of Alexander)  106,
    109-114, 119, 274
Dasyus  17
Datis  71
David  32-33, 37-39, 59
Decebalus  230-231, 237-238
Decelea  90, 92-93
Decius (consul)  169
Decius (emperor)  247
Delian League  79, 98, 103
Delium  84
Delphi  54, 63, 73, 80, 87, 103, 105,
    121, 204
Demaratus the Corinthian  110
Demetrius Poliorcetes  120
Demetrius of Pharos  178
Demosthenes the general  82-83, 90-91
Demosthenes the orator  105-106
Dendra  18-19
Denyen  32
Der  48
Diocletian  252-257, 270
Diodotus  159
Domitia  197
Domitian  229-231
Doura  240
Drepana  174
Duillius  172-173
Dyrrhachium  217
Eannatum  5
Ebro River  178, 182, 214
Ecnomus  173

Edomites  39
Egnatia  195, 224
Egypt, Egyptians  1, 8-11, 18–27, 29,
    31-32, 44-45, 48-50, 54, 57, 69,
    80, 113, 121, 127, 129, 171, 218,
    224-226, 229, 242, 249-251, 255,
    278-281
Ekron  39
Elagabalus  244-245
Elah  37
Elamites  4, 7, 45, 55
Elbe River  225
Elephantine  10, 57
Eleusis  18, 92, 241
Elis  87, 95, 98
Emesa  250
Emporium  182
Epaminondas  97-99, 101
Ephraim  36
Epidaurus  204
Epirus  170-171, 195, 269, 274
Erech  55
Eretria  64, 70-71
Esarhaddon  44
Ethiopia  57
Etruscans  64, 168-169
Euboea  64, 71, 101
Eumenes  194
Euphrates River  22, 48, 95, 238
Eurymedon  90
Euthedemus  160
Fabius  180-181
Farina  186
Ferghana  150-151
Fertile Crescent  50
Flaccus  196
Flamininus  192-193, 195
Flaminius  178-180
Flavians  229–230
Fulvius  196
Gablini  48
Gad  37
Gadatas  58
Gades  178
Gaiseric  270
Galatians  194
Galba  228
Galerius  255-256

Gallienus 248-249
Gallus 226, 247-248
Gandhara 147
gastraphetes 103
Gath 37, 39
Gaugamela 113, 274
Gauls 120-121, 167-170, 177-182, 184-185, 191, 197, 200-201, 209-214, 275
Gedrosian Desert 119
Germanicus 227-228
Germans, Germany 200-202, 209-211, 213, 225-228, 230–231, 240-241, 245-248, 251, 254, 256, 260, 269-271, 276
Geta 243
Gideon 33, 35-37
Gilead 37
Gilgal 37
Gilgamesh 3-4
Goliath 37
Gordian 246
Goths 246-251, 257-258, 265-269
Gracchi, Gaius and Tiberius 192, 196-197
Granicus 109, 114, 274
Gratian 264-267
Gutians 4, 6-7
Gylippus 89-91
Hadrian 238-239
Hadrumentum 219
Halys River 15, 50, 54
Hammurabi 13
Han River 133
Han (land) 137, 140
Han (dynasty) 141, 143-156, 276
Han Hsin 145
Hannibal 175, 177-182, 184-189, 193, 219, 274
Hanno 172
Harpagus 53
Hasdrubal (the brother-in-law) 175, 178
Hasdrubal (the brother) 184-185
hastati 168, 183, 187-188, 195-196, 200
Hatshepsut 24
Hellespont 73, 76-77, 93
Helvetia 200, 202

Helvetians 209-211
Heraclea 170
Heracles 101
Herodotus 279
Heruli 254
Hezekiah 44
Hiero 171-172
Himalayas 17
Hippias 71-72
Hittites 14-15, 18, 26, 29-32, 41
Ho-lu 133
Honorius 267, 270
hoplites 65-67, 71, 73, 76, 82-84, 89-90, 96-97
Hsiang Yü 144
Hsiao 138-139
Hsiung-nu 138, 141, 153, 160
Huan 130
Hunan 156
Huns 138, 141, 146-156, 160, 264-265, 270, 274, 276
Hurrians 13, 15
Hydaspes 58, 117
Hyksos 21-22
Hyrcania 159
Hysiae 66
Iberians 181, 185
Ilerda 214-216
Iliad 3, 54, 63, 107, 278, 280
Ilipa 186
Illyrians 101-103, 177, 225-226, 276
Immortals 74
India 13, 17, 117-118, 120, 123, 125, 127, 155, 159, 240, 277
Indo-Iranians 13
Indus River 17, 69, 160
Insubres 178
Ionians 54, 70, 92, 96, 280
Ipsus 120
Iranians, Iranian plateau 13, 16, 43, 45, 48, 51, 56, 114, 119, 163
Ireland 230
Ishtar 5
Israelites 33-37, 39, 42, 44
Jains 125
Janus 225
Jaxartes 55, 151-152
Jericho 33-34

Jerusalem  39, 44, 50, 56, 207, 229
Jesse  37
Joash  35-36
Jogbehah  36
Joppa  24-25
Jordan River  33
Joshua  33-35
Juba  218
Judah  22, 39, 44, 47, 50
Jugunthi  249-250
Jugurtha  199-201
Julian  259-261, 263, 266
Jung  139
Kalingas  127
Kansu  147-148, 151
Kao Tsu  143
Karkar  42
Karkemish  49
Karkor  36
Kassites  18, 29-30, 41
Kautilya  126
Kedemites  35
Kish  4-5
Kniva  247
Korea  151
Kuang-wu-ti  154-156
Kurus  17, 127
Kush  155
Kushan  155
Laconia  63, 69, 76, 90, 98
Lade  70
Laelius  184, 186-188
Lagash  4-6
Lamachus  89-90
Lampsacus  93
Langobardi  240
Larsa  13
Latins  168-169, 197, 203
Laurium  72
Lebanon  50, 110
legions  161, 170, 173, 177, 179-182,
    184, 191, 193-196, 204-206, 209,
    211-216, 218-219, 224-229, 231,
    239-240, 242-243, 246-249, 256,
    266, 268
Lelantine War  64-65
Leptis  219
Lesbos  70, 77, 81, 93

Leuctra  98
Li Kuang  148-149, 274
Li Kuang Li  151
Li Ling  149-150
Liang  157
Libya  10, 31, 255
Ligurians  185, 201
Lilybaeum  174
limitanei  268
Lingones  213
Liu Pang  141, 143-147
Liu Yüan  156
Livius  184-185
London  255
Lü  146
Lü Pu-wei  139-140
Lucanians  170
Lucullus  206-207
Lugalzaggisi  5-6
Lugii  251
Lusitania  191
Lydians  45, 54, 57
Lyons  242
Lysander  92-93
Macrinus  244
Magnesia  194
Magnus Maximus  267
Mago  179
Mamers, Mamertines  171-172, 279
Manasseh  36
Manchuria  151
maniples  168, 170, 183-184, 188,
    193, 200, 232
Manlius  168
Mantinea  87-88, 98
Maranga  261
Marathon  18, 71-73
Marcellus  178
Marcomanni  240-241, 248
Mardonius  70-71, 73, 76-77
Marduk  51, 53, 55
Margiana  162
Marius  200-205, 219
Maroboduus  226
Masada  229
Masinissa  186-188
Massilia  178, 191, 197, 201, 216
Mauretania  200, 232

Mauryan 125 127
Maxentius 256–257
Maximian 253-256
Maximin Daia 256
Maximinus 245-246
Maximus 246
Medes, Media 42-47, 47-51, 53-54, 74,
    160, 240, 245
Megalopolis 98
Megara 83, 87
Megiddo 25-26
Melos 88
Memnon 109
Memphis 22, 57
Mende 84
Meng T'ien 141
Mesopotamia 3-8, 10-11, 13, 18, 21-
    22, 50, 55, 70, 161, 228, 238, 240,
    244-255 passim, 263
Messana 171-173
Messenia 64-66, 69, 98
Metellus 199
Michmash 37
Midian 35-37
Milan 248-249, 269
Miletus 50, 54, 70, 110
Miltiades 70-72
Milvian Bridge 257
Minos 19
Mitanni 13, 24, 26, 29-31, 41
Mithradates the Parthian 160
Mithridates the Persian 110
Mithridates the Pontic king 203-207
Moabites 39
Moesia 232, 247-248, 254
Mongols, Mongolia 138, 147, 155,
    157
Moors 254-255, 264
Motya 103
Munda 219
Mursa 258
Mursilish 15
Muwatallish 31
Mycenaeans 19
Mykale 77
Mylae 173
Mytilene 81, 93
Nabonidus 51, 53, 55

Nabopolassar 47-49
Nahum 49
Nanking 156
Naphtali 36
Naram-Sin 6-7
Narmer 9-10
Narses 255
Naupactus 80
Nebuchadrezzar 48-50
Nefertiti 29
Nemea 96-97
Neptune 183
Nero 227-228
Nerva 230-231, 251
Nervii 211-212
Nicaea 260, 263
Nicanor 193
Nicator 125
Nicias 83, 85, 87, 89-91
Niger 242
Nimrud 42
Nineveh 44, 48
Nippur 6, 48
Nisibis 243
Nobah 36
Norsemen 246
Nubia 9-10, 18, 23, 26, 31
Numantia 192, 196
Numerian 252
Numidians 181, 187-188
Octavian 223-225
Odoacer 271
Olbia 247
Olympias 103
Orchomenus 204
Ordos 155
Orontes River 42
Osroes 239
Ostrogoths 247, 265, 267
Otho 228
Oxus Valley 16
oxybeles 104
Paeonians 102-103
Palestine 10-11, 42, 44, 56
Palmyra 18, 248-250
Pandavas 17, 127
Pannonia 242, 248-249, 254
Parmenion 102-103, 107–111, 114

Parni 159
Paros 67
Parthians   147, 155, 159-162, 225,
    228, 231, 240, 243-244
Parushni 17
Patna 125
Paullus (Cannae) 181
Paullus (Pydna) 194-195
Pausanias the Spartan 76-79
Pausanias the Macedonian 106
Peloponnesians 81-82, 93
peltasts 83, 97
Penuel 36-37
Pepy 10
Pergamum 121
Pericles 31, 79-81, 87, 278
Perinthus 105
Persepolis 114
Perseus 194-195
Persia   53-57, 70-71, 80, 92, 97,
    106-107, 114, 203, 244-246, 248,
    250-252, 255, 258, 261, 263, 267,
    280
Pertinax 242
phalanx   4, 11, 61, 65-67, 72, 77, 88,
    95, 97-99, 102, 105-106, 109, 111,
    113-114, 119, 159-160, 167, 170,
    192-195, 211, 260, 273
Pharos 218
Pharsalus 218
Pheidon 65-66
Pherae 192
Philip II   101-107, 170, 273, 278, 281
Philip V   182, 192-193, 195
Philip the Arab 246-247
Philippi 224
Philippopolis 247
Philistines 32, 37-39, 45
Philotas 114
Phocaeans 64
Phocians 105
Phoenicians 32, 42-43, 45, 56-57, 260
Phraates 160
Phraortes 47
Picenum 180
pilum 168-169, 200, 202, 229
Pinarus 110-111
Piraeus 79, 93-94, 204

Placentia 179
Plataea 76, 81
Pleistoanax 85
Plemmyrium 90
*Poliorketike* 104
Polybius 279
Pompeians 214-219
Pompey the Great   205-207, 214, 216-
    218
Pompey the Younger 219
Porus 117-118, 125
Postumus 248
Potidaea 80-81, 103
praetor   177, 185, 196, 203, 205-206
Praetorian Guard   224-225, 228-229,
    231, 242-246, 256–257
Praetorian prefect   228, 240, 244-246,
    251-252, 254-255, 259
primus pilus 196, 225
principate 227-228
principes 168, 183, 187-188, 196, 200
Probus 251-252
Psammetichus 45, 57
Ptah 31
Ptolemies 120, 171, 218
Pydna 103, 194
Pyrenees 178, 184, 192
Pyrrhus 170-171, 274
Qadesh 24-26, 31
Quadi 240-241, 248, 252, 264
quinqueremes 172, 174
Radagaisus 269
Ramses 31-32
Raphia 119
Ravenna 241
Red Eyebrows 153-154
Regulus 173
Remi 211
Rhaetia 230, 248-251, 254
Rhodes 109, 195
Rhone River 178, 201
Rhosaces 110
Richimer 265
Rimush 6
Romulus 271
rorarii 168
Roxane 119
Roxolani 230

Sacae 160
Salamis 73, 75-76
Salinator 184
Samaria 42, 44
Sammuramat 43
Samnium 169-170, 181-182
Samos 70, 75, 92-93, 280
Samothrace 103
Sapor 246, 258-261, 263
Saracens 255, 266
Sardinia 172-175
Sardis 70, 96
Sargon 5-7, 44, 53, 55, 59
Sarmatians 241, 248, 252, 254-255
Sarmizegethusa 236-237
Sarpedon 280
Sassanian 243, 245
Saul 37-38
Saxons 247, 254, 264, 270
Scandinavia 246
Scione 84
Scipio (pater) 178-182
Scipio Africanus 184–194 passim, 219
Scipio Aemilianus 192, 195
Scorpion 10
Scotland 230
Scythians 44, 47-48, 56, 64, 69, 147
Sea Peoples 32
Segesta 89
Seleucia 160, 243
Seleucids 121, 127, 159-160
Selinus 89
Semites 5-6
Sempronius 178-179
Sennacherib 44
Senones 170
Sentinum 169
Sepeia 71
Seqenenre 21-22
Sequani 209
Servilius 179-180
Sestos 93
Severus (Septimius) 242-243, 264, 270
Severus Alexander 244-245
Severus the Tetrarch 256
Shaaraim 39
Shalmaneser 42
Shang (dynasty) 16, 129

Shang (Lord of) 138-139
Shantung 153
Sharuhen 22
Sheklesh 32
Shuppiluliumash 30-31, 59
Siang (Duke) 130
Sibylline books 249
Sicily, Sicilians 82, 89–90, 103, 170-175, 182, 196, 206, 255, 279
Sicoris 214-215
Sicyon 96
Sippar 48
Sirmium 249, 251
Sogdiana 150-151, 162
Solomon 32, 39
Sophonisba 186
Spain 64, 175, 177-179, 182-184, 186, 191-192, 195-197, 201, 206, 214, 225, 248, 255, 260, 270, 276
Spartacus 206
Spartans 54, 64-67, 69, 71-77, 79-85, 87-90, 92-99, 101, 224, 244, 275, 279-280
Sphacteria 82-83
Spithridates 110
Spurius Ligustinus 195
Stilicho 268-270
Subarians 3, 7
Succoth 36, 39
Sudas 17
Suebi 230
Sui 157
Sulla 200-201, 203-205, 219
Sumerians 3-11, 59
Sura 240
Susa 114, 118-119, 160
Sutekh 31
Syphax 186-187
Syracuse 89-94, 103, 171-172, 182
Syria 11, 18, 24, 26, 30-32, 42-44, 49, 51, 54, 56, 110, 162, 228-229, 239-240, 246-248, 255
Szechwan 156
Tabbath 36
Tabor 37
Tacitus 251
Taoism 156
Tapae 234

Tarbisu  48
Tarentum  170-171, 181
Tegea  275
Tempe  73
Terracina  169
tetrarchy  255-257
Tetricus  250
Teucer  54
Teuta  177
Teutones  200-202
Theodosius  264, 266-270
Themistocles  72-73, 75-76
Thermopylae  73-74, 97, 105, 107,
   120-121
Thessaly  18, 73, 97, 101, 105, 107,
   192, 204
Thrace  71, 73, 97, 103, 205, 246, 248,
   251, 265, 269
Thucydides  84, 279-280
Thuti  24-25
Thutmose  22-26, 59
Tiberius  225-228
Ticinus  178-179
Tien Shan Mountains  155
Tigris River  3, 43, 48, 55, 238, 243,
   252, 261
Tigurini  200-202
Tikrit  48
Titus  229-230
Tjekker  32
Tochari  160
Tonkin  151
tortoise  162, 183, 205, 236
Trajan  219, 231-232, 234-238, 264,
   270, 276-277
Transalpine Gaul  208
Trebia River  179
triarii  168, 178, 183, 188, 193, 200
triremes  72, 75-76, 79, 89-90, 112,
   172
Troezen  73
Troy, Trojans  171-172, 279
Tung Cho  156
Tunis  173, 187
Turkestan  152, 155
Tutankhamen  29, 31
Tyre  112
Ulfilas  258

Umma  4-6
Ur  4, 6-7, 11, 278, 281
Ur-Nammu  7
Uruk  3-7, 48
Utica  186-187, 195
Uvarkhshatra  47
Vadomarius  260
Valens  260, 263, 265-266
Valentinian  263-264, 267
Valerian  247-248
Vandals  240, 247, 249, 251, 269-270
Varro  181
Varus  226-227
Vercingetorix  213
Verus (Lucius)  31, 239-241
Vesontio  211
Vespasian  229-230, 270
Victorinus  249
Viriathus  191
Visigoths  247, 263, 265, 270-271
Vitellius  228-229
Vologases  239
Wei (place)  133-134, 137-140
Wei (dynasty)  156
Wei Ch'ing  148
Wei Yang  138
Weshesh  32
Wey  133, 138
Wu Ch'i  133–134
Wu-ti  147-148, 151-152, 278
Wu Tzu-hsü  132–133
Xanthippus  173-174
Xenophon  96
Xerxes  58, 73-76
Yahu  57
Yamkhad  13
Yellow Turbans  156
Yen-ling  132
Ying  133
Yüeh-chieh  147, 150, 152
Zagros  43, 54
Zalmunna  36-37
Zama  187
Zebah  36-37
Zedekiah  50
Zenobia  249-250
Zerah  34
Zererah  36

**About the Author**

ALFRED S. BRADFORD is the John Saxon Professor of Ancient History at the University of Oklahoma. He served with the 1/27th Infantry in Vietnam. He has been a research assistant and a member at the Institute for Advanced Study in Princeton, New Jersey.